MW00339383

Studies in Rhetoric/Communication

Thomas W. Benson, Series Editor

THE GENUINE TEACHERS
OF THIS ART

THE GENUINE TEACHERS OF THIS ART | *Rhetorical Education in Antiquity*

Jeffrey Walker

The University of South Carolina Press

© 2011 University of South Carolina

Published by the University of South Carolina Press
Columbia, South Carolina 29208

www.sc.edu/uscpress

Manufactured in the United States of America

20 19 18 17 16 15 14 13 12 11   10 9 8 7 6 5 4 3 2 1

Library of Congress Cataloging-in-Publication Data

Walker, Jeffrey, 1949–
   The genuine teachers of this art : rhetorical education in antiquity /
Jeffrey Walker.
      p. cm. — (Studies in rhetoric/communication)
   Includes bibliographical references (p.   ) and index.
   ISBN 978-1-61117-016-0 (cloth : alk. paper)
   1. Rhetoric—Study and teaching. 2. Rhetoric, Ancient—Study and
teaching. 3. Persuasion (Rhetoric)—Study and teaching. I. Title.
   P53.27.W35 2011
   808.00938—dc22

                                                    2011015296

This book was printed on Glatfelter Natures, a recycled paper with 30 percent
postconsumer waste content.

I dedicate this book to the memory of Leonard Nathan,
my old mentor, excellent teacher, *didaskalos mou,* who passed
away while it was being written.

CONTENTS

SERIES EDITOR'S PREFACE

In Greek and Roman antiquity, intensive and prolonged study of rhetoric was the key preparation for active civic life. In *The Genuine Teachers of This Art,* Jeffrey Walker explores, in four extended essays, the practice of rhetorical education from Isocrates to late antiquity, with intensive treatments of Isocrates, Cicero, and Dionysius of Halicarnassus, and the practice of declamation.

In his opening essay on Cicero's dialogue *De oratore,* Walker argues that whereas the usual interpretation regards Crassus as speaking for Cicero in the dialogue, with Antonius as a mere foil, Cicero instead prompts us to read the dialogue as a genuine argument, thus rebalancing the scale between philosophical, Aristotelian rhetoric (represented by Crassus) and the rhetoric of Isocrates, often represented as the sophistic and handbook traditions (defended by Antonius).

The works of Isocrates that have come down to us represent his teaching as in contrast to the technical or handbook tradition of later rhetorical pedagogy. Walker speculates that Isocrates probably did write a *technê,* now lost, but known among his successors, and that it is possible to make useful conjectures about it and its influence on later teaching of rhetoric. And so, instead of seeing Isocrates as hostile to the handbook tradition, Walker suggests that Isocrates may very well have been its founder, thus providing a link between the philosophical and handbook traditions and in the process redeeming the handbook tradition as at least potentially legitimate mode of rhetorical pedagogy.

In Dionysius of Halicarnassus, Walker finds a teacher and scholar who employs a rhetorical perspective on literary criticism not as the application of prescriptive formulae and not simply to offer good examples for students, but as a means of extending the insights, understandings, sensibilities, and abilities of his students as practicing rhetors.

Professor Walker offers fresh and challenging perspectives on the continuity and variation of the pedagogy of ancient rhetoric, and of its coherence and contemporary relevance as an "art of producing rhetors."

THOMAS W. BENSON

ACKNOWLEDGMENTS

I thank the National Endowment for the Humanities and the College of Liberal Arts at the University of Texas at Austin for the fellowships that enabled me to get this book seriously underway during the 2007–2008 academic year. I also thank Jim Denton at the University of South Carolina Press for being extraordinarily patient while I slowly brought the manuscript to completion.

I thank, too, the colleagues and students who have encouraged and stimulated this project, including prominently the late and sorely missed Michael Leff, who invited me to speak on this subject at the Alliance of Rhetoric Societies meeting in 2003, as well as to conduct the seminar on ancient rhetorical pedagogy at the 2005 Rhetoric Society of America summer institute at Kent State University and to lecture on the same subject at the University of Memphis in 2008. Those were invaluable opportunities, without which this book might not have been written. Debra Hawhee, likewise, invited me to participate in the University of Pittsburgh symposium on "Revisionist Classical Rhetorics" in 2005, another invaluable opportunity. Marjorie Curry Woods generously read drafts of most chapters and made judicious comments and suggestions, as did Vessela Valiavitcharska. Patricia Roberts-Miller and her seminar students provided useful responses to chapter 1, and Thomas Blank very thoroughly and thoughtfully commented on the Isocrates chapters. Antonio Raul de Velasco has given this project a responsive and encouraging ear from the beginning. I also thank the readers for the University of South Carolina Press, whose comments on the original manuscript of this book were judicious, fair, and helpful.

Finally, I thank my patient and loving wife, Yoko Walker, who has had to put up for years with a husband who spends his weekends hunched in front of a keyboard; and my son, Eliot Walker, who now is a lawyer and thus a genuine practicing *rhêtôr,* and a good one too, and gave me the examples from torts textbooks I discussed in this book.

Prologue

Rhetoric and / as Rhetorical Pedagogy

Different people have defined the art of rhetoric differently. Let
this be added to the ancient definitions: Rhetoric is a discipline
of speech that exercises the *rhêtôr* in evenly balanced cases.

*Anonymous Byzantine scholar (c. tenth century),
as quoted in Christian Walz, ed.,* Rhetores Graeci *7.1:49*

Overviews

One can, of course, define rhetoric in different ways. "Rhetoric" may mean (1)
persuasive discourse, as opposed to nonpersuasive, which is a standard popular
conception, or *practical oratory,* discourse delivered in deliberative, judicial, and
ceremonial forums, which is a traditional (if outmoded) scholarly conception.
One can say, for example, that an issue "generated a lot of rhetoric." Or "rhetoric" may mean (2) the *persuasive practices* or "devices" of persuasive discourse, as
when one says, "The rhetoric of the President's speech was effective" or talks
about "the rhetoric *of*" something, such as national security policy or Christian
conservatism. "Rhetoric" may also mean (3) the *critical analysis or description* of
those practices, or a *theory* of the general principles that underlie the practices
that have been described—an account of what makes "rhetorical" discourse
persuasive or unpersuasive, as Aristotle suggests (in *Rhetoric* 1.1.2). Or finally,
"rhetoric" can be defined as (4) the *teaching* of persuasive discourse or *the cultivation of rhetorical capacity* (speaking/ writing ability), the "prescriptive" counterpart to the "descriptive" activities of criticism and theory. No doubt other
definitions are possible, but these, I think, are the basic modalities.

All of these modes of definition are valid, insofar as they are in widespread
use. However, the first two are not particularly helpful for rhetoric as an academic discipline, aside from naming the object of study in a general way. One
problem is that, if "everything is rhetorical," as is often said, definitions 1 and 2
do not define anything in particular and thus make "rhetorical studies" the study
of all signification and human behavior, a task performed already by a range of

other disciplines, such as the social sciences, linguistics, cultural studies, or psychoanalysis, which never have felt the need to identify themselves as rhetoric or to pay much serious attention to rhetorical theory.[1] A further problem of defining rhetoric as persuasive discourse or persuasive practices is that it can open rhetoric to the traditional charge of being something added to communication—empty talk, spin, manipulation, or equivocation, of which there cannot be a respectable study, unless the study is merely defensive ("how to see through rhetoric and get to the facts").[2] Even if that charge can be avoided, a comprehensive study of all persuasive practices across histories, cultures, classes, places, and times (and so on) would be impossible and would dissolve rhetorical studies into an incoherent miscellaneousness. (What would be the principle of selection?) Moreover, definitions 1 and 2 make a category mistake. The term *rhêtorikê,* after all, names "the art of" the *rhêtôr,* the "speaker," not the speaker's speech or its devices. (Literally it means the "speakerly art.") Even Aristotle's definition focuses on the *capacity* of the *rhêtôr,* his or her *dunamis,* for intelligent thought and speech in practical decision making.

The third definition of "rhetoric," an "art" concerned with critical analysis and theory, seems more useful as the basis for a credible academic enterprise. Indeed, it is hard to imagine any teaching of rhetorical skill divorced from the critical/theoretical enterprise that would not be vapid. But without the teaching enterprise of the fourth definition, the critical/theoretical enterprise has little point. What is the critical/theoretical study of persuasive practices *for,* if not the production of a *rhêtôr?* Without that point of application, as I have argued elsewhere,[3] rhetoric ceases to be a distinct disciplinary practice and becomes simply a kind or counterpart of literary studies, a critical hermeneutic or philosophical theory of "rhetoricality,"[4] detached from the training of actual speakers or writers. The student will be an appreciator, interpreter, analyst, judge, or theorist of discourse, but not an excellent producer of it. Further, even if rhetoric as criticism/theory is taken as propaideutic to rhetorical production, there is no direct link between being able to articulate the theory and being able to actually perform what the theory describes, or to perform it well. As Augustine points out, surely on the basis of his own experience as a teacher (and the accumulated lore of generations of teachers before him), no one can *be* eloquent and think of the "rules of eloquence" at the same time; moreover, knowing the "rules" has no necessary connection to the acquisition of rhetorical skill (*De doctrina Christiana* 4.4). In short, it is possible for critical-theoretical studies to produce a great deal of sophisticated theory that simply has no use or consequence in guiding the process of acquisition, or in performance.

So the fourth definition is primary. By defining "the art of the *rhêtôr*" as an *art of producing a rhêtôr,* one puts the other definitions into relation. The pedagogical project sets the agenda for the critical-theoretic one and determines the appropriate objects of study. Criticism and theory are distinctly "rhetorical" insofar as they observe "rhetorical objects" and critique practices and articulate general principles that are relevant to the process of training a *rhêtôr*. Its pedagogical enterprise is what ultimately makes rhetoric rhetoric and not just a version of something else.[5] I offer this book, then, as a contribution to the study of rhetoric as a pedagogical tradition.

Foundations

Any study of rhetorical education in antiquity owes much to the foundational work of Henri Marrou's monumental *Education in Antiquity,* first published in 1948, and Donald Lehman Clark's 1957 *Rhetoric in Greco-Roman Education,* both of which remain indispensable and still provide the basic outline.[6] That outline has been amplified by the many works of George Kennedy from 1963 to the present,[7] and more recently Raffaella Cribiore, Yun Lee Too, Malcolm Heath, Debra Hawhee, and others have furnished new perspectives and new data to which I am indebted, particularly regarding identity formation, habituation, performance, pedagogical methods, and the contents of the curriculum.[8] Likewise there has been new work (since 1965) on the reinterpretation and recovery of classical rhetoric for the modern classroom.[9]

The basic outline goes somewhat as follows. Elementary education, for those who could afford it, extended from roughly age seven to fourteen or fifteen and was focused on *grammatikê,* "grammar" (literally the "art of letters"), meaning basic literacy training and the study of literature, Homer and the poets first, then prose writers and orators. In addition to learning to write and speak in the literate dialect, the student learned to properly read aloud or recite the canonic authors, or parts of them; parse and explain their language; and interpret the meaning of their texts, both overt and "hidden." Instruction in interpretation (*hermêneia*) entailed instruction in logic (the rules of inference) as well.[10] Alongside grammar and logic, the elementary student might also learn arithmetic, geometry, music, and astronomy.

Rhetorical training, for those who had the desire and the wherewithal to continue their education, which often meant traveling from home to a larger city or metropolis where teachers could be found, extended from age fifteen or sixteen to perhaps twenty, though the timing and length of study could vary considerably from individual to individual. Some might stay with the rhetorician for just a year or two, and others might stay for four years or longer, depending on the student's purposes and circumstances. Dio Chrysostom's *Discourse* 18, for example, is addressed to a wealthy middle-aged businessman who wants a short course in rhetoric that won't take too much of his time.

With the rhetorician the beginning student might read, recite, listen to, and discuss exemplary prose texts (*logoi,* "speeches" in particular) and do "preliminary exercises," or progymnasmata, in the basic elements of discourse, including sententious and useful sayings, fable and narrative, refutation and confirmation, and comparison. At the intermediate to advanced levels, the student might continue the study of exemplary texts but mainly composed and sometimes delivered complete speeches for imaginary cases ("hypotheses") in declamation exercises (*meletê,* "practice, rehearsal"). Alongside rhetoric, or after it or instead of it, a few might also study the various branches of moral and natural philosophy, medicine, or, in later antiquity, law. Finally, after leaving the rhetorician, some students might go on to careers as orators and politicians, while others, probably the larger part, remained in private life. In the Hellenistic kingdoms established by Alexander's successors, later, in the Roman Empire, and later still, in the Byzantine Empire, students also might pursue careers in the imperial bureaucracy or find a position on some magnate's staff.

Differences

Although there certainly were differences from rhetorician to rhetorician, place to place, and century to century, and developments in what was taught, the basic pattern remained remarkably stable from its emergence sometime between the fourth and second centuries B.C.E. (and I think in the fourth) to the end of antiquity and beyond. It is important to remember that in all that time there was virtually nothing resembling modern public education. In the Hellenistic and Roman periods there were limited and competitively sought municipal and imperial subsidies for some grammarians and rhetoricians, and perhaps other teachers, at least in the larger centers. But most teachers were not subsidized, and even the holders of prestigious municipal "professorships" charged and depended on tuition fees, as the subsidies generally were modest and often inadequate. Libanius, for example, complains that he can't pay his teaching assistants a living wage with the stipend granted him by the city council of Antioch. The rhetorician's school in essence was a private enterprise, a small, and in many cases precarious, business. With no official institutional structure to hold it in place, the general pattern of rhetorical training simply persisted as a tradition—passed on from teacher to teacher and from generation to generation, or, as Cicero writes, from Isocrates to "all" subsequent rhetoricians.

But the tradition also admitted change, variation, and evolution in the specific contents of the teaching. One might think of the propagation, evolution, and general stability of the classical system of rhetorical education as "viral": like a virus it passed from generation to generation, was instantiated differently in each rhetorician's schoolroom, and underwent mutations in its particulars, while yet remaining recognizably "the same" in general outline. The most probable explanation for that remarkable, homeostatic stability-in-variation over such a long period of time is that the traditional rhetorical *paideia* was effective, met the needs and aspirations of its student clientele, and performed important social functions. In short, it worked.

What follows is not a synoptic history but a series of topically linked, overlapping, and extended essays—on Cicero's *De oratore*, Isocrates, declamation, and Dionysius of Halicarnassus—that reflect on and reexamine various aspects of ancient rhetorical education roughly from Isocrates to late antiquity, with a few forays into Byzantine (medieval Greek) sources for whom the classical secular *paideia* still was a live tradition. These four pieces are not exactly a "syllogistic" progression, as Kenneth Burke would say,[11] and can be read in a different order, or independently, but they are meant to be read in the order given. The later essays presuppose the earlier, but each can also stand on its own

First is a reinterpretation of Cicero's *De oratore*, reading against the grain of the received interpretation. That interpretation holds (1) that Crassus is the dialogue's central speaker and Cicero's mouthpiece while Antonius is a foil, and (2) that the dialogue argues for a synthesis of the "Aristotelian" (meaning "philosophical"), "Isocratean" (sophistic), and "technical" (handbook) traditions— though Cicero in fact recognizes just *two* traditions, or what he calls the two "streams" of rhetorical teaching, the sources of which he labels "Aristotle" and "Isocrates." I argue that Antonius *also* speaks for Cicero, and, reading the dialogue from Antonius' point of view, that Cicero's intent is not so much an Aristotle-plus-Isocrates synthesis as an Isocrates-versus-Aristotle agon that ends in essence with an embrace of "Isocrates" as the embodiment of an ideal rhetorical education before the philosophical schools "usurped" what originally and properly belonged to rhetoric. (But with the proviso that the well-educated orator should "eavesdrop" on the philosophers occasionally, at least as a matter of humane general culture; no one thinks an orator should be an anti-intellectual ignoramus.) Notably, Antonius calls Isocrates "the teacher of all rhetoricians" and calls the rhetoricians "the genuine teachers of this art" *in contradistinction to* Aristotle and the rhetorical teaching of the philosophical schools in the Hellenistic age. From Cicero's Antonius, then, I derive the title of this book.

Next I address the now-conventional distinction between Isocrates and the "technical" (handbook) tradition. Contrary to the entrenched assumption (since 1963) that Isocrates disdained the *technai* and did not write a *technê*, and taking Antonius' remarks as my cue, I maintain that Isocrates very probably *did* write a *technê*, as several ancient sources suggest, that it was superceded by the *technai* of later generations and went out of circulation, and that it was the ancestor of the classical *technê* tradition that is visible to us now in the surviving handbooks.

Of course, neither this argument nor the conventional view can be proved to a certainty, given the state of the evidence available, but I do think the argument for an Isocratean *technê* sufficiently probable to warrant at least tentative belief.

Following that is a frankly speculative effort to conjecture, not "reconstruct," what the *Technê of Isocrates* probably would have contained. Arguing from the traces of *technê* in Isocrates' extant writings and from correspondences in the fourth-century *Rhetoric to Alexander,* I suggest that it very possibly would have contained virtually all of the components of the classical *technê,* from an introductory prolegomenon to treatments of an early form of the progymnasmata and declamation—the latter divided into preliminary inquiry (an embryonic form of "stasis" analysis), the parts of the oration ("invention"), and style (composition, diction, and figuration). In short I take as credible not only Quintilian's remark that he has seen a copy of the *Technê of Isocrates,* which he also seems to have read, but also Dionysius of Halicarnassus' remark that rhetorical teaching was in a "confused" state before Isocrates and that Isocrates gave it a new form and set it on what was to be its future course. Thus Isocrates launched the basic rhetorical *paideia* that worked so well and was so remarkably stable for so long.

The argument that there is no opposition between Isocrates and the *technê* tradition, and that he actually could be the "father" of it, raises the question of how Isocrates' notion of rhetoric as "philosophical" can be squared with the handbooks and the regimen of exercise they supported. This question is partially addressed with respect to the progymnasmata, but it is addressed at length in chapter 4. This considers the student's experience of rhetorical education and focuses especially on declamation as "civic theater"—both in the sheltered "garden" of the school and in the public "concert" performances of the Second Sophistic (literally in theaters or concert halls, *theatra* and *ôdeia*). Declamation was, and is, an extraordinarily effective mode of both rhetorical pedagogy and practical "philosophy," as declaimers and audiences explored and performed the argumentational, political, and moral possibilities of specified situations. This chapter also returns to the topic of the use of the *technai* in rhetorical education and especially in the guidance of students doing declamation exercises.

I then consider the definition of "rhetoric" as an "art of producing rhetors" and examine Dionysius of Halicarnassus as a possible and viable model for what might be considered "rhetorical criticism" or "rhetorical scholarship" today. While a large book could be written on Dionysius, this chapter presents a fairly thorough and, I think, the only recent analysis of the whole corpus of Dionysius' extant writings, from his "critical essays" to his letters and his twenty-volume history of early Rome (of which the first half survives mostly intact). I consider his writings, in short, as the scholarship of a rhetorician and as part of the project of rhetorical education.[12]

Finally, the epilogue reflects on the classical tradition's implications for modern rhetoric, the differences between writerly and readerly orientations to discourse, the surprising correspondences between classical rhetoric and modern "creative writing" instruction, connections between ancient and modern writing instruction, and Aristotle's critique of sophistic pedagogy.

One might ask why there is no chapter on Quintilian, whose *Institutio oratoria* (*The Education of an Orator*) arguably is the largest, most comprehensive example of what all the other rhetorical *technai* in antiquity were up to. My defense is that Quintilian is a constant presence throughout this book and figures large in places and that a chapter or two on Quintilian would be insufficient; it is time for someone to write a comprehensive new study. I have been more focused here on revising the reputation of figures in the rhetorical tradition, particularly the writers of handbooks, who commonly have been dismissed as "dumb schoolmasters" or relegated to minor status in a pantheon of theorists dominated by philosophers. There is a lot of research available on Quintilian, but little on Dionysius, despite his real significance in the rhetorical tradition.

One might also take my arguments to task; one might catch me in contradiction. Is what I have written here truly a "rhetorical" study according to my own definition or what I see as the classical definition? Perhaps, perhaps not. The reader will decide. Perhaps like Whitman I should say, "Do I contradict myself? / Very well then, I contradict myself. / (I am large, I contain multitudes.)"[13] But perhaps, after all, I do not contradict myself. Perhaps I should say that, like Dionysius of Halicarnassus, I have written a panegyric history, a sort of encomium, of the genuine teachers of this art in the ancient world, and I have reflected on them as a paradigm that still is relevant in ours.

The use of the term "sophist" is sometimes a touchy point: who in antiquity can and cannot be called a sophist? I use the term loosely, but generally with the meaning of a professional performer and "professor" of rhetoric: a master performer who teaches others to be performers.[14] Libanius was the head of the municipally subsidized school of rhetoric at Antioch and bore the title "sophist"; his teaching assistants bore the title "rhetor."

About Translations and Transliterations

All the translations in this book are mine, unless otherwise indicated. Likewise, unless otherwise indicated in citation, I have used the readily available Loeb editions of Greek or Latin texts. In the transliteration of Greek or Latin terms I have not been totally consistent—sometimes presenting a word in the inflected

form used in the passage being quoted, at other times presenting the "diction-
ary" form, or the infinitive form (of verbs), or the singular or plural nominative
form (of nouns or adjectives), for example, *technê/technai,* "handbook/hand-
books." The decision in each case was based on what seemed most appropriate and accessible in the context. In the English rendering of Greek proper
names I generally have followed convention rather than strict transliteration,
especially for well-known names, for example, Dionysius instead of Dionysios
(Διονύσι), Isocrates instead of Isokratês (Ἰσοκράτης), and so forth. As for the
transliteration itself, I have followed the standard practice of representing η (eta,
"long e") as *ê* and ω (omega, "long o") as *ô* and not rendering the classical Greek
diacritics for tone accent and "breathings," while representing "rough" breathings with an *h*. Thus ῥητορική = *rhêtorikê*. All errors of translation and transliteration—as well as, of course, fact and interpretation—are mine alone.

ONE | Cicero's Antonius

Neither the bland prolixity of the Academics,
Nor yet the painful pointlessness of Aristotle.

Timon of Phlius, Silloi fr. 35–36, in Diogenes Laertius 4.67, 5.11

Listening to Antonius

Roughly midway into the second book of Cicero's great and complex dialogue, *De oratore*, as the orator Marcus Antonius begins his discussion of the role of "commonplaces" (*loci*) in rhetorical invention, Quintus Lutatius Catulus—an enthusiast of Greek high culture—remarks with approval that Antonius seems to be following the theories of Aristotle's *Topics* and is less indifferent to Greek philosophy than he pretends (2.152). Antonius replies that an orator should show no trace of artifice, or of "things Greek." He does, however, see no harm in "eavesdropping" (*subauscultando*) on the discussions of Greek philosophers, since it would be "brutish and inhuman" to take no interest in such themes as how to rightly live, think, and speak; and he admits that he has "briefly tasted" what the schools of philosophy have to say (2.153). In sum, he sees no reason not to listen to the philosophers a little, now and then, but he also sees no reason to study them in depth or even to pay them much serious attention. (He would rather read historians and orators; 2.60–61.) In effect he denies that his account of *loci* is really "Aristotelian," even if it looks that way. And even, one might add, if many readers of *De oratore* have thought it looked that way as well.[1]

Catulus then objects that the Romans have always had a wonderful love of philosophical pursuits, and he invokes as "witnesses" against Antonius' "declaration of war against philosophy" the three philosophers who famously came to Rome on embassy from Athens in 155 B.C.E.—Carneades the Academic, Diogenes the Stoic, and Critolaus the Peripatetic (2.154–156). In their free time these three delivered lectures that greatly impressed the Romans, attracted crowds, and filled the young nobility with enthusiasm for Greek learning. In reply Antonius reiterates his stance: "I myself do not disapprove of those pursuits" (*ego ista studia non improbo*) if they are "kept within limits" (*moderata modo sint*); but he repeats that having a reputation for such interests or showing a tincture of them hurts the orator's effectiveness. And then he makes the following crucial statement:

> Among those three most illustrious philosophers whose visit to Rome you mentioned, do you see that it was Diogenes who claimed to teach an art of speaking well [*artem bene disserendi*] and of distinguishing the true from the false, which he called by its Greek name, dialectic [διαλεκτική]? In this art, if it is indeed an art, there is no instruction [*praeceptum*] about how truth should be discovered [*inveniatur*], but only about how it should be judged [*iudicetur*]. For with respect to every statement we might make that something is or is not, if it is said without qualification, the dialecticians undertake to judge whether it is true or false; and if it is brought forth conjointly and other propositions are added to it, they judge whether these have been properly added and whether the conclusion of each and every argument [*rationis*] is true. In the end they pierce themselves with their own sharp subtleties, and in their investigations they encounter not only many problems that even they themselves cannot solve, but also previously woven webs of argument, and strong ones, by which they nearly are undone. This Stoic, then, is no help to us at all, since he does not teach how I shall discover what to say; and he actually hinders me, since he also finds many problems that he denies can be solved at all, and he teaches a kind of speaking [*genus sermonis*] that is neither limpid, nor copious, nor fluent, but meager, dry, abrupt [*concisum*], and hairsplitting [*minutum*]—which, if anyone approves of it, he nevertheless must admit is not suitable for an orator. For this speaking of ours is adapted to the ears of the multitude, to charm and move souls, and in proving, to weigh things not in a goldsmith's balance but, so to speak, in the scales of popular opinion. Therefore let us dismiss that entire art which is too mute when it comes to devising arguments, and too loquacious when it comes to judging them.

I suppose that Critolaus, whom as you recall accompanied Diogenes on that visit, may have been more useful for this pursuit of ours. For he was a follower of this Aristotle from whose discoveries I seem to you to deviate but little. And between this Aristotle and *the genuine teachers of this art* [*hos germanos huius artis magistros*]—and I too have read that book of his in which he sets forth the arts of speaking of all his predecessors [*superiorum*], and those in which he said a few things of his own [*sua quaedam*] about it—there seems to me to be this difference: that with the same acuity of mind with which he had observed [*viderat*] the essential nature of all things, he likewise discerned [*aspexit*] what pertained to the art of speaking, *which he despised;* while those who considered it the one thing worth cultivating have dwelt on the treatment of this single art, not with the same sensibility [*prudentia*] as he, but with greater application in this particular kind of endeavor. (2.157–160; emphasis added)[2]

Antonius, of course, is responding not only to Catulus's suggestion that his approach to rhetoric is "Aristotelian" but also to a deep and fundamental thread in the discussion, which in turn is a deep and fundamental thread in the discourse of rhetoric from antiquity to the present day: the question of the relationship between philosophy, or "theory" in the sense of a philosophical account of principles, and the art and practice of rhetoric.

Lucius Licinius Crassus, the host and principal speaker of the dialogue, has started the debate with a more or less Isocratean encomium of rhetoric (1.29–34), which can be paraphrased as follows: Rhetoric is the discursive art through which civil communities and their institutions are created and sustained; the ideal orator ranges over the whole realm of human culture, must speak about all things, and therefore must have knowledge of all things. These expansive claims are countered immediately by Quintus Mucius Scaevola the Augur (and jurisconsult), who denies that rhetoric is what sustains the possibility of civil community—indeed, it may be corrosive, especially when used irresponsibly (1.35–40). Crassus' Isocratean claims to knowledge, moreover, lie open to objections from the philosophical schools, who will show that it is they, not rhetoric, that speak about politics, ethics, and every other branch of learning (1.41–43). To this point Antonius later adds the retort of Charmadas the Academic, in a conversation at Athens, to the notion that rhetorical study cultivates civic wisdom. Every aspect of political theory, huffed Charmadas, is treated by the philosophers, and one can find no treatment of it in the rhetoricians' "little books" (*libellis;* 1.85–86). More damning still, however, is Scaevola's crowning point: "The Peripatetics will prove triumphantly that even those very things that you consider the special equipment of orators and the ornaments of speaking are to be sought from themselves, and they would show that on these subjects Aristotle and Theophrastus have written not only better but also much more than all the teachers of speaking [*dicendi magistros*]" (1.43). It seems that the philosophers not only were better political theorists, but even were better rhetorical theorists than the rhetoricians themselves. Or so, at least, the philosophers claimed.

What is Cicero's position on these matters? First of all, it is fair to suppose that all the speakers in this dialogue are Cicero, or versions of him, and speak for different aspects of his thought. All, especially Crassus and Antonius, are figures from his youth, people he has known and loved. The setting is the eve of the outbreak of the "Social War" between Rome and its Italian "allies" (*socii*), which will in turn precipitate the wars and proscriptions of Marius and Sulla and the unraveling of the Roman republic. All but one of the dialogue's speakers (Cotta) will die in this civil strife. Crassus will die within a week. The speakers are on holiday, at Crassus' country estate at Tusculum, during the Roman games in September of 91 B.C.E., and they have taken up their two-day discussion of rhetoric as a diversion from the previous day's more serious discussion of the political situation. One can ask to what extent each speaker's arguments are gambits for the sake of the game. This is even true for the statements of "Cicero himself" to his brother Quintus in the prefaces to each of the three books, especially the first, where once again an ideal of philosophic rhetoric (Crassus' position) is opposed to Quintus' apparently more practical view (Antonius' position). The point is that the dialogue plays out a friendly, even brotherly agon between the two positions.

Antonius is more central to the dialogue's agon than usually is supposed. He is no mere foil for Crassus. Notably in Cicero's *Orator* (69–74 ff.) it is *Antonius,* not Crassus, who is invoked as the source of the oratorical ideal that Cicero champions to Brutus. This ideal is framed almost entirely in technical terms: Antonius' ideal orator is not a Crassian orator-philosopher but a master of style, a master of technique, with a flawless sense of the opportune and the appropriate in any situation and the ability to speak accordingly. So let us turn to Antonius—or rather Cicero speaking through Antonius, wearing the practical orator hat—in that longish passage that I have quoted.

The first thing one might note is a certain ironic tone, as in "*this Aristotle [isto Aristotele]* from whose discoveries *I seem to you [tibi ego videor]* to deviate but little," which underscores that it is Catulus who thinks Antonius is following Aristotelian precepts while Antonius has made no such avowal. Antonius may well be "deviating," perhaps a lot. While he admits that he has read at least some of Aristotle's works on rhetoric—apparently the *Compendium of Arts (Sunagôgê Technôn),* a synoptic collection of sophistic rhetorical teachings, plus what appears to be the books we now know as the *Rhetoric*—Antonius also implies that Aristotle's work on rhetoric is mostly a synthesis of things collected from his sophistic predecessors. Aristotle's original contribution, Antonius suggests, amounts to *sua quaedam,* "a few things of his own" (literally "his somethings").[3] The tone of this remark resembles that of Cicero's youthful attitude toward Hermagoras in *De inventione* (1.8). After faulting Hermagoras for including "theses" on general questions within the concerns of rhetoric, and for lacking eloquence, he mitigates the criticism with faint praise: "Not that I think the handbook [*ars*] published by him is written very badly, for he seems to have satisfactorily arranged the material he selected with ingenuity and industry from earlier handbooks [*ex antiquis artibus*], and to have added not nothing (*nonnihil*) himself." This sort of damningly faint praise is now applied, in *De oratore,* to Aristotle.

How much did Aristotle crib from his sophistic predecessors? It is impossible to say, but we do have Aristotle's well-known remark (*Rhetoric* 1.1.4) that what distinguishes the sophistical from the philosophical *rhêtôr* is not his "faculty" or art but his moral purpose; that is, both use the same tools, the same techniques, but with different intentions.[4] This looks like a defense of the fact that Aristotle is including in the *Rhetoric* what his contemporaries would recognize as precepts from sophistic handbooks—the parts of the oration, for example, or the types of proof—plus *sua quaedam*.

Antonius' suggestion of derivativeness sheds some doubt on the notion that Aristotle "discerned" the principles of rhetoric "with the same acuity of mind with which he had observed the essential nature of all things." Did Aristotle look at rhetoric itself (the actual practices of orators) at all, or, as seems likely, a collection of published *technai* (rhetorical handbooks)? One can argue that "discerning," observing, or theoretically grasping is not the same as knowing when it comes to rhetoric. The knowing that rhetoric requires is a *sophia*, in the double Greek sense of "wisdom" and "skill," or "know-how," savoir-faire. Further, those earlier sophists whose precepts Aristotle gathered in the *Compendium* and recycled in (parts of) the *Rhetoric* are named as his *superiores*, which can mean "predecessors" in time, but can also mean "superiors" in the sense of "betters." Finally and most important, it is they who are named the "genuine teachers of this art" (*hos germanos huius artis magistros*). Where does this leave Aristotle, or Antonius' seeming Aristotelianism?

More significant still is Antonius' discussion of Diogenes' claim to teach "an art of speaking well [*artem bene disserendi*] and of distinguishing the true from the false," which he names as dialectic (2.157). Antonius argues forcefully that dialectic is useless to the orator. Aristotle's opening premise in the *Rhetoric*, of course, is that "rhetoric is a counterpart [*antistrophos*] of dialectic" (1.1.1 1354a) and largely a matter of enthymematic reasoning, with the enthymeme defined as the "rhetorical syllogism"—that is, quasi-syllogistic argumentation on practical issues used in continuous speech before crowds of nonphilosophers who cannot follow a complex line of reasoning (for example, 1.1.11, 1.2.8).[5] One must wonder, then, what Antonius' demolition of dialectic as a basis or model for "an art of speaking well" does to an Aristotelian approach to rhetoric.

It is possible, of course, that Diogenes' failure to recognize a distinction between rhetoric and dialectic is what makes the Stoic approach to rhetoric so useless. Cicero seems to suggest this in his *Topica* (2.6–8). The Aristotelian recognition of some sort of difference-in-similarity, as expressed in the notion of dialectic and rhetoric as "counterparts,"[6] may save Peripatetic rhetoric from those problems. But Antonius' remark that "I suppose [*puto*] that Critolaus [the Peripatetic] . . . may have been more useful" suggests only a weak commitment to that idea.

Even if rhetoric is understood as an *antistrophos* of dialectic (and not simply identical with it), the problem of dialectic as a model for rhetoric is fairly serious. The central problem, as Antonius sees it, is that dialectic is an art of testing, examining, and judging arguments rather than inventing them. Its inherent motives lead it away from ever coming to resolution on the argument originally proposed and toward an endless critique of the logical problematics of its terms, propositions, and assumptions (and the assumptions behind the assumptions behind the assumptions, and so on), so that the dialecticians eventually "pierce themselves with their own sharp subtleties" (*se compungunt suis acuminibus;* 2.158) and end up trapped in logical aporias from which they cannot extricate themselves. Since the purpose of rhetoric is to inform or affect decision making, as Aristotle recognizes (for example, *Rhetoric* 1.2.12–13, 1.3, 1.4.1–3), dialectic's tendency to render all questions undecidable, and thus to paralyze both orator and audience, seems distinctly counterproductive.

A modern if approximate illustration of what Antonius has in mind may be seen in Jacques Derrida's somewhat notorious response to a question about the events of September 11, 2001. Derrida, being interviewed in New York by philosopher Giovanna Borradori about five weeks after the attack, was asked if he considered it "a major event, one of the most important historical events we will witness in our lifetime, especially for those who never lived through a world war." Derrida's reply was a 549-word excursus on the problematics of the *name* "September 11," which ended as follows:

> For the index pointing toward this date, the bare act, the minimal deictic, the minimalist aim of this dating, also marks something else. Namely, the fact that we perhaps have no concept and no meaning available to us to name in any other way this "thing" that has just happened, this supposed "event." . . . This very thing, the place and meaning of this "event," remains ineffable, like an intuition without concept, like a unicity with no generality on the horizon or with no horizon at all, out of range for a language that admits its powerlessness and so is reduced to pronouncing mechanically a date, repeating it endlessly, as a kind of ritual incantation, a conjuring poem, a journalistic litany or rhetorical refrain that admits to not knowing what it's talking about. We do not in fact know what we are saying or naming in this way: September 11, *le 11 septembre,* September 11. The brevity of the appellation (September 11, 9/11) stems not only from an economic or rhetorical necessity. The telegram of this metonymy—a name, a number—points out the unqualifiable by recognizing that we do not recognize or even cognize that we do not yet know how to qualify, that we do not know what we are talking about.[7]

Derrida's answer—only the beginning of a wide-ranging discussion that runs for fifty-one pages in print—occasioned a flurry of negative and probably unfair commentary, mainly in university hallways and on blogs, when it was published in 2003. I remember a colleague bringing me a copy of it, with a triumphant gleam in his eye, as if it were the final proof of the pointlessness of Derrida's whole enterprise. (There were, of course, defenders too.) But the justifiability of Derrida's remarks, or the validity of his methods, is not at issue here. Let us say, with Antonius, that it would be brutish and inhuman to take no interest in a thoughtful, philosophical exploration of the meaning of September 11 and the problem of global terrorism; any intelligent, liberally educated person who wishes to speak, write, or simply think about such things may profit from lending Derrida an ear. The "Antonian" problem, instead, is that Derrida's ways are not the orator's, and they could be disabling for him.

While Derrida's excursus on the name "September 11" is not exactly an exercise in Stoic dialectic, it does exemplify the dialectical probing and problematizing of presuppositions that Antonius has in mind. Derrida's basic argument—that "September 11" functions as a shorthand name for a collection of still-recent events whose nature and implications had not yet been fully understood—is probably correct. But it is also a deferral, which turns out to be an infinite deferral, of the question that has been posed. Derrida's position is that we don't yet know what the terms of the question mean and that we must examine the conceptual structure and presuppositions of those terms before we can even begin to speak. The interview never does get back to Borradori's initial question but goes on to interrogate the notions of "international terrorism," the nation-state, sovereignty, the possibly illusory distinction between terrorism and war, and what the proper response to "international terrorism" (if it can ever be sufficiently defined) might be. In essence Derrida converts the practical issue posed by the events of September 11 into a series of abstractions and calls for a complete deconstruction and reformulation of the entire apparatus of thought by which those abstractions are formulated and deployed, which in turn will require a "mutation" of the international order, or the emergence of what he portrays as a presently unthinkable "democracy to come,"[8] all before there can be any "solution" to "the problem of terrorism" in general. Meanwhile, the questions of *how* this change would come about and at what pace are left in the realm of the "incalculable": perhaps it will take generations, perhaps centuries.[9]

Everything Derrida says may be true; I think much of it is. But it does indeed end, just as Antonius says of Stoic dialectic, in a realm of imponderables, insolubles, and aporias. There is little that can be used in a civic discourse confronted with the practical question, What should we do now? Or what should be the policy of the United States and its allies in the immediate present or the next few months and years, and why? It would be difficult to wait, in October 2001, for the reformation of Western thought (which will happen how?) and a "mutation" of the international order through many generations (which will happen how?) while the leaders of Al Qaeda sit in their training camps and plot their next attack. The civic orator who needs to speak to questions of practical decision and action in a given set of circumstances will find little in either Derrida's remarks or the general Derridean procedure that will help him discover what he should say, or could say, or do, with any practical and desirable effect.

There is no reason, of course, why philosophy, or "dialectic," should have to provide that sort of help. Antonius' point, simply, is that it doesn't. One certainly can argue that a philosophical interrogation of the conceptual structure of an argument provides a useful service by slowing down the movement to judgment and action—that is, by providing a critical check on the productions of rhetorical invention and their potential to elicit a too-quick, too-enthusiastic, unreflective assent. But that, again, is Antonius' point: Dialectic as a technique of interrogating arguments provides resistance to, or hinders, what rhetorical invention otherwise generates and enables. For that reason dialectic cannot itself, alone, play the role of rhetorical invention.[10]

Antonius, in sum, casts serious doubt on whether dialectic, especially the dialectic of the philosophic schools, and Stoic dialectic most of all, can serve as a model or basis for rhetorical invention, or for rhetoric per se. But there is still, perhaps, the possibility that the Aristotelian notion of rhetoric and dialectic as "counterparts" may render Peripatetic theory more useful for the orator. Antonius does, as Catulus remarks, *seem* to be drawing his discussion of *loci* from Peripatetic sources, though Antonius resists admitting that and casts ironic light on Aristotle's relation to his sophistic *superiores*—the writers of all those rhetoric manuals (*technai*) that he surveyed in the *Sunagôgê Technôn* and that he both disparaged and borrowed from in the *Rhetoric*.[11] And connected to that disparagement there is this further problem to consider: Antonius' remark that Aristotle "despised" rhetoric.

"Despising" Rhetoric

Here is perhaps the most famous line in Aristotle's *Rhetoric:* "Estô de rhêtorikê dunamis peri hekaston tou theôrêsai to endechomenon pithanon." That, of course, is the opening sentence of *Rhetoric* 1.2. The usual translation is "Rhetoric is a faculty of observing the available means of persuasion in any given case," or something to that effect. Every living rhetorician has learned that line in school. It is, for many, the fundamental definition of rhetoric, and it has been the keynote to a great deal of rhetorical theorizing in modern and postmodern times, though it had surprisingly little impact in antiquity. Its main apparent advantage for modern thought is its concept of the rhetorical *dunamis* as an ability to survey all possible arguments in a particular situation, which in turn implies a measure of intellectual responsibility. It offers an alternative to the practice of merely working up a mostly unexamined idea or striving to "win" an argument or debate without troubling to consider what might really be the course of wisdom. Is this what Aristotle added to the teachings of the sophists before him? Perhaps, but it could also be derived from them, or some of them, such as Protagoras, Antiphon, or Isocrates, who clearly seem interested in canvassing the range of what might be said in order to find the best available opinion.[12] Either way, the notion of rhetoric as a "faculty" of surveying the possibilities of an issue clearly has great appeal.

However, if one puts aside the familiar translation and looks again at Aristotle's Greek, it becomes apparent that the line can be read in different ways. First of all, the phrase "rhetoric is"—the usual way the definition gets invoked— elides the fact that Aristotle's *estô de rhêtorikê* employs a third-person imperative, *estô,* meaning something like "let rhetoric be." Aristotle is invoking a stipulative definition, as in a speculative argument or mathematical hypothesis, where one says "let the value of X be Y." He is using this language to invoke an opening position, a starting point, for a particular theoretical account of rhetoric.

More important is the phrase *to endechomenon pithanon,* which is generally known as "the available means of persuasion." Actually, nothing explicit is said about *means of* persuasion. *To pithanon,* a neuter form of the adjective *pithanos* ("persuasive, credible") rendered as a noun phrase by adding the definite article, *to,* literally means "the persuasive." Rhetoric is a faculty of observing what is persuasive in a given case. And what about "available"? The word *endechomenon,* a participle of the verb *endechomai* employed as a neuter adjective, can variously be rendered as "admissible," "acceptable," "allowable," "approvable," or "possible." So now, instead of "the available means of persuasion," we have "what is admissible, acceptable, or allowable as persuasive."[13]

In this view, Aristotle is defining rhetoric not so much as a faculty of invention whose job is to find the available means of persuasion in any given case in order to build an argument, but as a faculty of critical judgment whose job is to evaluate arguments already presented. As such it is closer to the dialectic of Diogenes. This reading seems to be borne out too by the verb *theôrêsai,* an aorist infinitive form of *theôrein,* which can be rendered as "observe, consider, judge, speculate, make inferences about," or even simply "to be a spectator, to gaze." Why does Aristotle not use the verb *heuriskein,* "to discover or invent"? He seems to be thinking of rhetoric as a faculty of critical judgment or contemplation, to be employed *by the audience* of an oratorical performance. It is, in short, a faculty of being able to resist the suasive force of the speaker's sophistic wiles and theatrical gestures while making up one's mind about the merits of the case. This looks like an art for a magistrate or judge, or, possibly, a "gazing" philosophical observer.

At the outset of the *Rhetoric,* Aristotle says, "It is possible to observe [*theôrein* again] the reason why some speakers succeed by chance and others through practiced habit" and "all would agree that such an examination is the work of a *technê*" (1.1.2). Here, again, rhetoric is an art or *technê* not of speaking but of observing or indeed *theorizing* how or why speakers succeed or fail, or of theorizing what constitutes speaking "well," as when Aristotle remarks that one can speak as well as possible, according to the principles of the art, and still fail to persuade because of the defects of the audience (1.1.14). Aristotle makes rhetoric a kind of critical theory, a hermeneutic of the rhetorical, an effort to account for what makes the persuasive thing persuasive, an enthymeme enthymematic, or a speech well formed. This seems to imply such scholarly activities as giving detailed interpretive accounts of particular rhetorical transactions, or the perhaps more philosophical activity of attempting to abstract the general principles that underlie a collection of observations, in order to construct a theory of rhetoric's nature and constituent components. Aristotle, of course, does only the latter of these two things.[14]

The *Rhetoric,* then, seems to embody at least three ways of understanding "rhetoric":

Rhetoric as a philosophical hermeneutic of the rhetorical, as theory

Rhetoric as an art of critical judgment to be applied in deciding what is
    legitimately persuasive or whether a speaker has spoken well, regardless
    of actual success or failure

Rhetoric as a system of "rules" or precepts to be applied by the would-be
    orator who must perceive *to endechomeon pithanon* (in the sense of "the
    available means of persuasion" or "the possibly persuasive") in order to
    construct an artistically well-formed speech

I think it is fair to say that all three motives are present in the text that has come down to us. Aristotle does appear to shift between philosophical *theôria,* precepts useful for exercising critical judgment, and practical advice for the would-be orator. One easily can argue that these three motives are necessarily interdependent and say that "advice for speakers" that is uninformed by philosophical-theoretical reflection has limited value, or that a capacity for rhetorical production without a capacity for rhetorical analysis and critical judgment will be dangerously vapid. As the teenaged Cicero of *De inventione* says, fresh from his lessons with his rhetoric teachers, "Wisdom without eloquence does too little good for civil communities, but truly eloquence without wisdom is generally very harmful and does no good at all" (1.1).

But one also can account for the *Rhetoric's* mixed motives by viewing it as a compilation that is inconsistent, incoherent, or confused. And one can do this in two ways. On one hand, one can invoke the widely held view that the *Rhetoric* is a collection of lecture notes composed at different times, with changing motives and opinions—a bundle of disparate materials, or at most the rough drafts of two separate treatises (books 1–2 and book 3 of the text we have) that were never put in finished form by Aristotle but were thrown together and edited at some point, reputedly in the first century B.C.E. (by Tyrannio and Andronicus, at Rome), so that the text is necessarily inconsistent with itself.[15] On the other hand, with or without that story, one can argue that the *Rhetoric* is an effort to systematize a collection of "how-to" precepts derived from earlier sophistic *technai,* such as Aristotle gathered in the *Sunagôgê Technôn,* combined with his "added" gestures toward philosophical *theôria* and critical judgment, while bringing in bits and pieces from logic, psychology, politics, and so forth, so that, again, the resultant text is incoherent.[16] But whichever line of argument one chooses, I think it is fair to say that in the *Rhetoric* the motives toward judgment and *theôria* are predominant.

One way to argue this last point is to look at Aristotle's treatment of theoretical, practical, and productive arts and sciences (*theôrêtikê, praktikê, poiêtikê*) in the *Metaphysics* (1.1, 6.1). Theoretical knowledge, he says, is superior to knowledge based on mere experience, and the theoretical arts or sciences in general are superior to the practical and productive ones, because they give an account of "the principles and causes of existing things" (6.1.1). Such accounts possess the highest form of wisdom (*sophia*). Theology, moreover, is the highest form of theoretical inquiry (*Metaphysics* 6.1.11).[17] Thus, one can infer, the highest form of rhetorical *technê* or of rhetorical *sophia* would be embodied in neither practical ability nor the giving of particular bits of practical advice, but in theoretical, contemplative knowledge and the ability to give a rationally coherent account of the general principles governing the observable phenomena of rhetoric—a "metaphysics" or "theology" of rhetoric, if you will.[18] This is what Antonius describes as Aristotle's "observation" of "the essential nature of all things," including rhetoric.

But one might consider the matter another way. In the last book of the *Politics,* Aristotle ponders the education suitable for the "citizens" (*politai*) of his ideal city-state, the ruling class who will do military service when young, participate in councils and governance when mature, and serve in priesthoods when old, while supported by the slave labor of farmers, merchants, artisans, menials (*geôrgoi, agoraioi, banausoi, thêtes*), and all others who practice "vulgar" occupations (*Politics* 7.8–9). In Aristotle's discussion the adjective *phortikos,* "vulgar, coarse, burdensome, onerous," typically alternates with *banausos,* "mechanical, lowly, related to manual crafts, suitable to an artisan," or *thêtikos,* "menial, servile, suitable to a laborer." Aristotle's view is that all property should be owned in common by the "citizen" class, while those in the noncitizen classes, meaning those who work with their hands, should be slaves (*douloi*) or serfs (*perioikoi*) and should be the common property of the state, that is, of the citizens. He does suggest that "it is better for all the slaves to have their freedom set before them as a prize [*athlon*]," in order to make them more cooperative (7.9.9). But *athlon*, a prize awarded to the victor of a contest, clearly implies that only a few will win their freedom while all compete for it.

Aristotle recognizes that the "citizen" class, or what he also calls the "deliberative" or "bouleutic" part of the polity (*to bouleutikon; Politics* 7.8.6), must be trained in those "useful" arts that are "necessary" to their role (*ta anankaia tôn chrêsimôn*, the necessary part of the useful). He also says, however, that the young citizen must not be trained in arts that will make him "vulgar," but only those that are suitable to the *eleutheros*, the freeborn male (8.2.1). What this means is clarified when Aristotle turns to education in music, in the last chapters before the text breaks off (8.4–7). The student, he says, should not be trained to become a professional musician, partly because the work of a paid performer is "too menial" (*thêtikôteran*), and especially because the performer must play to mixed or varied audiences, including the vulgar, and therefore must perform the "distorted" kinds of music (*parakechrôsmena*) that mimic and move the emotions of their "perverted souls" (*hai psuchai parestrammenai;* 8.7.7). To do so is, in Aristotle's view, ethically degrading. Through miming and arousing the characteristic moods and emotions of his vulgar listeners, and through repetition of this mimesis, the performer will himself become habituated to those moods and emotions—they will become part of his own *êthos*—and in consequence he will be vulgarized and rendered morally corrupt. Thus, as Aristotle reasons, the young *eleutheros* should play music only to the point of learning how to appreciate it properly, or, perhaps, to sing a decorous tune or two at a dinner party. And he should not be trained on the instruments of professional musicians, but only on the simplest instruments sufficient for learning the principles of music. Moreover, he should play only the "ethical" kinds of music that are conducive to good morals, such as the Dorian mode, which is "very steady" (*stasimôtatês*) and "has a manly character" (*êthos echousês andreion;* 8.7.10). Other kinds, especially the "active" and "passionate" types of music (*praktikê, enthousiastikê*) that arouse *pathos* in the soul and make low-class people dance about (8.7.5–6), should only be listened to, for the purpose of learning critical discrimination.

What does the *Politics'* account of musical education imply for rhetoric? A few things might be said. First, one must admit that in the *Rhetoric*, Aristotle does not seem to be describing an ideal rhetoric in the way that he describes an ideal constitution in the *Politics*. Nevertheless there are traces of an ideal. Just as the *Politics* describes the "best constitution" (*politeia aristê*) as something to be legislated by the "statesman" (*politikos*), so the *Rhetoric* shows an interest, especially in its opening chapters, in the requirements for "well-regulated" courts and assemblies, and the more well regulated they are, the less there is for rhetoric to do. As he says, "If all trials were handled as they now are in some cities, and especially the well-regulated ones, [the writers of rhetorical handbooks] would have nothing to say" (1.1.4).

Aristotle's chief example of a well-regulated court is the Areopagus at Athens, which did not permit emotional appeals, as opposed to the popular jury courts, which did. The Areopagus was a senior council consisting of former magistrates whose main function in Aristotle's day was to judge murder trials, though it had once been the city's ruling council. It probably numbered no more than two hundred members. Popular juries, by contrast, were large, heterogeneous groups chosen by lot from all segments of the male citizenry and could number from 201 to 1,001 or more. (Socrates was tried before a jury of 501.) Further, Aristotle, like Isocrates before him, considers "deliberative" discourse the noblest form of rhetoric and prefers the term *symbouleutikon,* the "advisory" discourse of a *symboulos* or "councilor" in a council meeting (*boulê*), rather than *dêmêgorikon,* "public speaking" in a popular assembly (the preferred term in the *Rhetoric to Alexander*). The Athenian *Boulê* consisted of five hundred elected representatives from the city tribes; the Assembly (*Ekklêsia*) was open to all male citizens who wished to attend and required six thousand for a quorum.[19]

In the discussion of character types that follows Aristotle's discussion of emotions (2.12–17), the golden mean that emerges—the best type of audience for practical civic discourse, with the best emotional, ethical, and prudential predispositions—is mature men in positions of power, *hoi dunamenoi* in the "prime of life." These are the very sorts of persons qualified to be Areopagites. In contrast stands the "depravity" (*mochthêria*) of large popular audiences in poorly regulated assemblies, the undisciplined, uneducated crowds that respond to such "vulgarities" as theatrical gesture and emotional delivery (3.4–5).

Aristotle's ideal realm of rhetoric, in sum, is the restricted and regulated deliberative world of the "bouleutic" citizen class of his ideal polity: relatively small group discussions among mature, powerful men in council, or the practical judgment of a magistrate or ruler who must survey the arguments in a dispute (both actual and possible) and judge what ought to be persuasive. The nearest models, besides the Areopagus at Athens, would seem to be the Spartan oligarchy or the Macedonian royal court—Alexander with his "synod" (*sunedrion*) of generals, councilors, and high officials—though Aristotle does not say so explicitly (which would be dangerous for him in Athens).[20] Beyond this realm, the Aristotelian *politikos* may sometimes have to speak before assemblies of common people and engage in rhetorical vulgarities, especially at Athens. But like the musician, he should avoid it as much as possible, lest he corrupt himself. Clearly the young student should not be doing it. He should only be *observing* it and learning to pass critical judgment.

Perhaps, then, this is what Antonius means when he says that Aristotle "despised" rhetoric. From Aristotle's point of view, civic oratory is a necessary if "vulgar" art that a *politikos* must understand—and thus an appropriate object of *theôria*.[21] Such knowledge is useful for the statesman. But beyond a certain limit, or beyond a certain restricted kind of rational, dignified civic discourse suitable to the councils of the powerful, the actual practice of rhetoric is beneath his dignity. And it becomes increasingly distasteful as the audience becomes wider, more heterogeneous, and more popular.

There is a further tension in Antonius' comment that Aristotle "discerned what pertained to rhetoric" with the same "acuity" with which he "observed the essential nature of all things." Note that these are verbs of seeing (*aspexit; viderat*), as if rhetoric were chiefly something to be looked at, like a biological specimen or a phenomenon of nature, rather than something to be done. There is a reason, beyond its reader-unfriendly style and its inconsistencies, why Aristotle's *Rhetoric* had little impact in antiquity, even when it was available (and it may well have been available, if little read, throughout the Hellenistic period).[22] The cultivation of an actual, functional capacity for rhetorical action requires something other than, or in addition to, contemplation of the rhetorical, and more than theories or "theologies" of good deliberation. Moreover, as Antonius suggests, Aristotle's supposed act of looking-at-rhetoric consists of collecting what the sophistic *technai* have said already, adding "some things of his own" (*sua quaedam*) and re-presenting the synthesis *as if it were a theory*, a philosophical account of the principles of civic speech.[23]

In sum, then, Aristotelian rhetoric appears to be oriented more to the distanced, philosophical, or "dialectical" activities of theorizing rhetorical phenomena and judging arguments than to the actual production and performance of public discourse—or to the training of an actual, practical orator. As such it seems very much open to Antonius' critique, and to his remark that Aristotle at bottom "despised" rhetoric.

Antonius on Topics: Sophistic, Progymnasmatic Precedents

When Antonius provides his supposedly Aristotelian account of topics for invention (*De oratore* 2.162–172), as is well known, the list is nearly identical with what one finds in Cicero's *Topica*, down to verbatim repetition of some examples and explanations. At the outset of his *Topica*, moreover, Cicero suggests that its account is Aristotelian. But the suggestion is equivocal. Cicero presents himself as responding to a jurisconsult named Trebatius, who once *incidisti in Aristotelis Topica quaedam* while browsing the bookshelves at Cicero's Tusculan villa (*Topica* 1.1). *Quaedam* could be rendered here as "a certain, some sort of," so that Cicero's phrase could be taken to mean that Trebatius "happened upon" (*incidisti*) "some sort of *Topics* of Aristotle" or "some sort of Aristotelian *Topics*"—

if *Topica* is the title of a work and not simply *topica,* "an art of topics" that is in some way "Aristotelian." In sum, the phrase may mean only that Trebatius found a multivolume work (several scrolls) on topics that made some reference to Aristotle's *Topics* or included those words in its title. Perhaps it was a rhetorical handbook on invention, which claimed to be derived from Aristotle? Jonathan Barnes has argued forcefully that, whatever Trebatius "happened upon," it was not a copy of Aristotle's *Topics,* which Cicero probably had never read.[24]

But whatever Trebatius was looking at, he was excited at this *inscriptione* and asked about it, prompting Cicero to explain that "these books contained a system for finding arguments, so that we may come upon them rationally and methodically without any wandering, discovered by Aristotle" (*ab Aristotele inventam;* 1.2). This remark fairly strongly suggests a work on topics invoking Aristotle as the original discoverer of the art, not a work actually by Aristotle. It also clearly echoes not Aristotle but Isocrates, in his early (and pre-Aristotelian) manifesto, *Against the Sophists:* "Training has made such men [who have talent and experience] more artful and more resourceful in discovering the possibilities of the matter in question, for it has taught them to take from a readier source what they otherwise hit upon haphazardly" (15).[25] Isocrates' "more artful" (*technikôteros*) also can be read as "more methodical": Cicero's Latin comes near to being a gloss or paraphrase of Isocrates' Greek. But Isocrates nowhere uses the word "topics" (*topoi*) to describe the "readier source." Perhaps what Aristotle "discovered," then, is the *description* of this artful, methodical approach already taught by Isocrates as a *technê topikê,* an "art of topics."

But again, whatever Trebatius was looking at, on being asked to explain the books' contents, Cicero urged him to read them himself, or to consult "a certain very learned rhetorician" (*doctissimo quodam rhetore;* 1.2) who could explain the method. Trebatius tried both, but the books were too repellingly obscure, and "that great *rhetor,* as I believe, replied that he was unfamiliar with *Aristotelia*" (1.3). *Aristotelia* might be rendered as "Aristotle's works" or "Aristotelian doctrines." Either way, it seems that Cicero directed Trebatius to a great and learned *rhetor* who was unfamiliar with *Aristotelia* for an explanation of the art of topics expounded in the books Trebatius had been looking at. Cicero further remarks that he is not surprised that the great *rhetor* was unfamiliar with Aristotle, since Aristotle "is unknown to the philosophers themselves, apart from a very few" (1.3). Almost nobody reads Aristotle.[26] Thus Cicero sent Trebatius to the *rhetor* without an expectation that the *rhetor* would know anything about Aristotle's *Topics,* or any other Aristotelian work, but with an expectation that he would give Trebatius an explanation of what the treatise on topics contained. Trebatius apparently bungled the transaction by framing it as a request for instruction in *Aristotelia.*

I think Cicero is having fun with these coy maneuvers. And there is more: Cicero says that he has written his *Topica* while on a ship, without his books, far from his library, in southern Italy, en route from Velia to Rhegium (*Topica* 1.5; *Ad familiares* 7.19), a voyage of about 150 miles or perhaps three or four days in good sailing weather. Cicero's *Topica* consists of twenty-six chapters occupying about thirty-nine pages, in Latin, in Harry Hubbell's Loeb Cassical Library edition.[27] If the journey took three days, that's a little more than eight chapters a day, or thirteen Loeb pages a day. (Were they written while sitting on the windy deck? Or in a dark cabin below deck?) Thus we are to imagine that Cicero wrote the book fairly rapidly, from memory and without access to the treatise whose contents he supposedly was relating and which he probably had not read in some years.

Moreover, as virtually every commentator on the *Topica* has remarked, the book bears no resemblance to Aristotle's *Topics*. Cicero begins by dividing the "methodical treatment of argumentation" (*ratio diligens disserendi*) into two parts, defined by the Greeks as dialectic (*dialektikê*) and topics (*topikê*; 2.6), one concerned with judgment and the other with invention—a distinction that Aristotle does not make. Cicero then dismisses dialectic as not useful and focuses on topics, which he first divides into those that are intrinsic and extrinsic to the subject under discussion, that is, topics for entechnic ("artistic") and atechnic ("inartistic") proofs (2.8). The intrinsic topics consist of a relatively short list, running from arguments from definition, division, and etymology to arguments "from things connected in some way to the subject under discussion" (3.11): conjugate terms, genus and species, similarity, difference, contraries, adjuncts, antecedents, consequents, contradictions, cause and effect, and comparisons with greater, lesser, and equal things. These are discussed first briefly (2.8–4.23), followed by a short discussion of extrinsic proof (4.24), and then both kinds of proof are discussed again in detail, with examples mainly drawn from judicial discourse (4.25–20.78). This discussion occupies the bulk of *Topica*. It is followed by a division of questions for disputation into "theses" (general propositions) and "hypotheses" (specific cases), with "theses" divided into "theoretical" issues (matters of knowledge, such as whether law is natural or conventional) and "practical" issues (matters of action, such as whether a philosopher should enter politics; 21.79–82). Next comes a short discussion of the stases for both theoretical and practical theses, after which Cicero discusses which topics are suitable for which stasis (23.87–90). He then turns to hypotheses, divides them into judicial, deliberative, and encomiastic, sketchily reviews the standard stases for hypotheses (24.90–25.96), and notes that "the proper arguments for these cases, chosen from these topics that we have set forth, are explained in the rules for oratory" (25.92). So again each stasis divides into some selection from the overall list of topics. The final chapter (26.96–100) discusses the parts of an oration and addresses some parting remarks to Trebatius, with a confession that "I have included more than you requested."

The *Topica* looks more than anything like a Greek rhetorical handbook. In its division of each stasis into a selection of topics drawn from a common list, it prefigures what we see two centuries later, worked out in elaborate detail, in Hermogenes' *On Stases*.[28] At the same time it gestures toward an extant (Hellenistic) tradition in "the rules for oratory," namely, the influential treatment of stasis developed by Hermagoras of Temnos, who taught at Rhodes in the mid-second century B.C.E. But Cicero's treatment also seems unusual, to us, in its inclusion of a stasis system for the arguing of theses. Where has it come from? There have been various speculations: the New Academy, especially under Philo of Larissa, who embraced epistemological skepticism and apparently taught both rhetoric and the practice of antilogy, and was one of Cicero's many teachers; or Philo's successor, Antiochus of Ascalon, with whom Cicero had studied also, though Antiochus rejected Philo's skepticism and supposedly set the course for Neoplatonism. Or perhaps the source was some form of Peripatetic teaching on rhetoric and disputation that Cicero had encountered somewhere. Or, perhaps, it was a sophist such as Apollonius Molon, who taught rhetoric at Rhodes and thus could be seen as a successor to Hermagoras and was also one of Cicero's instructors; or Demetrius the Syrian, with whom Cicero studied at Athens; or Menippus of Stratonicea, Diogenes of Magnesia, Aeschylus of Cnidus, or Xenocles of Adramyttium, with all of whom Cicero studied while in Asia.[29] It is possible, too, that the provision of a stasis system for both theses and hypotheses derives originally from Hermagoras, who, as the young Cicero says in *De inventione* (1.6.8), included the arguing of theses within the concerns of rhetoric. Or then again, perhaps it was all of them, philosophers and sophists alike, and Cicero has come up with his own approach as a synthesis of their teachings, which seems fairly likely. But nothing can be proven conclusively.[30]

It is instructive, however, to compare Antonius' list of topics—or, for that matter, the nearly identical list in *Topica*—with those given for the "thesis" exercise in Aelius Theon's *Progymnasmata*.[31] This is the earliest surviving treatise on progymnasmata, dating probably to the first century C.E. The author may be the "Aelius Theon of Alexandria," mentioned in the *Suda* as a writer of treatises on progymnasmata and rhetoric as well as a *Commentary on Xenophon, Isocrates, and Demosthenes;* and he may be the Theon cited by Quintilian in connection with stasis theory (*Institutio oratoria* 3.6.48), which would put him earlier than 90 C.E.[32] Within the *Progymnasmata* itself, Theon mentions Theodorus of Gadara and "the great Dionysius of Halicarnassus," both of whom are figures of the middle to late first century B.C.E., and no one later.[33] The honorific mention of Dionysius would seem to place Theon in the Isocratean or "philosophical" rhetorical tradition with which Dionysius identifies himself; and Theon cites Isocrates repeatedly. He also mentions Apollonius of Rhodes, who is probably Apollonius Molon—Cicero's teacher—as "one of the older authorities" (*tôn presbuterôn tis*) on the pedagogical methods he discusses for use with progymnasmata.[34]

But whoever he may have been, and though he wrote in the century after Cicero's death, it seems reasonable to see Theon as a representative of a well-established teaching tradition that already would have been in place, at least among Greek rhetoricians, in Cicero's day. In his opening chapter Theon presents himself, much as Dionysius of Halicarnassus does,[35] as a representative of the tradition of "the ancient rhetoricians" (*hoi palaioi tôn rhêtorôn*) who thought that students of rhetoric should have an acquaintance with "philosophy"; he then notes that he is not the first to have "written about these things" (the progymnasmata),[36] says that he has made some additions to "the exercises already transmitted" and given them definitions,[37] and remarks that "it is not unclear that [these exercises] are very useful to those acquiring rhetorical ability."[38] When Theon discusses the thesis exercise, he mentions Hermagoras' treatment of it, and of the "comonplace" exercise as well,[39] which suggests that the "transmitted" exercises were in place at least by the middle of the second century B.C.E. Theon's "additions" are probably his discussions of such classroom activities as listening to readings, reading aloud, paraphrase, elaboration, and counterassertion (*antirrhêsis*), which are not discussed in other surviving progymnasmata texts, though it seems likely that they were normal parts of classroom practice. In any case it is clear that he regards the exercises themselves as already well known.

Quintilian, likewise, at the end of his discussion of what he calls "preliminary exercises" (*primas exercitationes,* 2.4.36)—his list is similar to Theon's[40]—says, "With these [exercises] the ancients mainly exercised their faculty of speech, though adopting their method of arguing from the dialecticians" (2.4.41), which would seem to suggest the practice of arguing general questions, that is, "theses." He then cites a tradition (which he cannot substantiate) that the practice of declamation was first instituted around the time of Demetrius of Phaleron and makes it a point to say that he is not yet discussing declamation (2.4.41–43). In other words, Quintilian thinks that the progymnasmata were in use in the fourth century B.C.E., before declamation became a standard practice in rhetorical training. He probably is wrong about declamation (we see the arguing of fictitious cases as early as Gorgias of Leontini),[41] but the point is that, like Theon, Quintilian sees the progymnasmata as "ancient" and connected to a philosophical version of the sophistic tradition, which is to say a tradition that probably should be traced to Isocrates. Isocrates, of course, describes the philosophical training in discourse that he imparts as a "gymnastics" (*gumnastikê*) for the mind (*Antidosis* 181–185), which seems to imply *gumnasmata*, "exercises," which is Theon's term for progymnasmata. In the next generation after Isocrates, we find the earliest known explicit reference to "the progymnasmata," which appears in the *Rhetoric to Alexander*, a sophistic text of the mid–fourth century B.C.E.[42]

If we compare the topics discussed by Antonius to those included in Theon's discussion of the thesis exercise, they line up as follows (I present Antonius' in order, while arranging Theon's to correspond):

Antonius (*De oratore* 2.164–173)	Theon on thesis[43]
Definition and partition (*Definitione, partitione*)	From the implicit (*ek tês periochês*)
Word meaning (*ex vocabulo*)	[The implicit?]
Connected terms (*coniuncta*)	[The implicit?]
Genus (*genera*)	From the whole (*ek tou holou*)
Species (*partes generibus*)	From the part (*ek tou merous*)
Resemblances (*similitudines*)	From the similar (*ek tou homiou*)
Differences (*dissimilitudines*)	[The unsimilar?]
Opposites (*contraria*)	From the opposite (*ek tou enantiou*)
Attendant circumstances (*consequentia*)	From consequents (*ek tôn meta to pragma*)
Consistencies (*consentanea*)	From concomitants (*ek tôn para to pragma*)
Antecedents (*praecurrentia*)	From antecedents (*ek tôn pro tou pragmatos*)
Contradictories (*repugnantia*)	[The opposite?]
Causes and results	From the end [for which something is done]
(*Causas rerum, quae ex causis orta sunt*)	(*Ek tou telous*)
Comparisons with greater things (*maiora*)	From the greater (*ek tou meizonos*)
Equals (*paria*)	[The similar?]
Lessers (*minora*)	The lesser (*ek tou elattonos*)

Theon's list includes many other topics not mentioned by Antonius (though some appear in the *Topica*). This difference may be accounted for by the fact that Theon considers the thesis to deal with either "theoretical" or "practical" questions and to be spoken "in assembly and lecture-hall" (*en ekklêsia kai akroasei*), that is, as a kind of deliberative discourse.[44] Antonius, on the other hand, like Cicero (or Trebatius) in the *Topica*, seems interested in topical invention chiefly as a resource for judicial argument—though the *Topica* does distinguish "theses" from "hypotheses" and, like Theon, divides "theses" into "theoretical" and "practical."

When one looks at the parts of Theon's list that correspond to Antonius' (and the *Topica*'s) list of inventional topics, it is clear that Antonius' list, while slightly different, does not extend beyond what the rhetoric student of the first century B.C.E. would have encountered in the thesis exercise. The same is true for the "commonplace" exercise, which has a similar though shorter list.[45] And where Antonius and Theon appear to differ, their treatments suggest that the difference is more a matter of terminology than functionality. Thus we see, for example, that Theon seems to have nothing directly corresponding to Antonius' topics of definition, partition, word meaning, and connected terms, all of which have to do with categorical reasoning based on the semantic content of a term; yet it is apparent that Theon's topic "from the implicit" (*ek tês periochês*, "from what is included") gathers these functions under a single head.

It is of course possible that Antonius' (and the *Topica*'s) "Aristotelian" account of inventional topics is from the Academic, Peripatetic, or Stoic sources that have at one time or another been proposed. Such things were discussed and taught in those schools in the Hellenistic era, and Cicero certainly was acquainted with them, especially the Academy. Likewise the Hellenistic schools of philosophy that included rhetoric in their concerns undoubtedly borrowed from, as well as criticized, the teachings of the sophists, just as Aristotle did. However, Antonius' account could just as well derive from a Greek sophistic tradition that descends from Isocrates and passes through such rhetoric teachers as Hermagoras, Apollonius Molon, Dionysius of Halicarnassus, and Theon and portrays itself as philosophical.

In this Greek tradition, the philosophical dimension of rhetoric is first cultivated in the progymnasmata, especially in the thesis exercise, which itself is the culmination of earlier, simpler exercises that also prescribe the handling of certain topics, such as the commonplace exercise (called *topos* by Theon and *koinos topos* by later authorities). The commonplace, which contains many of the same topics as the thesis, involves amplification of the already-given badness (or, sometimes, the goodness) of an action or character; for example, so-and-so is a proven "tyrant," and there are things to be said about the wickedness of tyrants on the way to drumming up emotion and exhorting the judge to show no mercy. The commonplace is thus an excursion into popular ethics and political philosophy, with an affective dimension. While progymnasmata manuals typically associate it with the functions of epilogues, Theon adds that "some have defined" it "as a starting-point for epicheiremes," thereby inserting it into the structure of argumentation.[46] This use of the commonplace resembles Chaim Perelman's notion of developing "presence" for the beliefs and values one wants to use as the starting points or bases of an argument.[47] One resorts to the topics of the commonplace for the purposes of amplification and emotion. The thesis, on the other hand, expands the commonplace by introducing strategies of argument (and additional topics) by which one might, for example, argue about what "tyranny" is, what its definition includes and implies, whether it is bad, or whether it should be opposed. (These are the stases of fact, definition, judgment, and action.) Both thesis and commonplace, when inserted into a practical oration, have a similar function, namely, to establish and intensify general premises grounded in the deep communal beliefs and emotions of the audience.

One might, at least speculatively, trace a history of the thesis exercise and other progymnasmata, keeping in mind Quintilian's remark about the preliminary exercises as the means through which "the ancients" exercised their powers of speech while adopting the reasoning methods of "dialectic" (that is, philosophy). We see the beginnings of the thesis in the early sophists, for example, in the practice of antilogy first associated with Protagoras (which Diogenes Laertius regards as the beginning of dialectical disputation)[48] or in any sophistic discourse that might be considered philosophical, such as Antiphon's arguments about natural and conventional law.[49] In Isocrates it appears we already have a method of topical invention without the name, insofar as he speaks of acquiring "knowledge of the elements [*ideai*] out of which we speak and compose all our discourses" and of teaching students "to select from these elements those which should be used for each subject-matter" (*Against the Sophists* 15–16).[50] Though the terminology is different and less precise, this statement prefigures Cicero's discussion, in the *Topica,* of which topics are appropriate for which stases (23.87–90)—or indeed the entire tradition of handling topics in stasis theory. In his letter *To the Children of Jason,* Isocrates speaks of this proto-topical (and perhaps proto-stasiotic) approach to the teaching of rhetorical invention as original with himself, and as something that others have imitated (*Letters* 7.7–8).[51] Notably Quintilian attributes the coining of "stasis" as a rhetorical term to Isocrates' student Naucrates (*Institutio* 3.6.3.)

Aristotle, of course, traditionally has been credited with developing the first systematic, theoretical account of logic—and, in the *Topics,* of developing a topical method of arguing "dialectical problems," which, as he says, "are nowadays called theses" (*Topics* 1.9.35 104b). In *Sophistical Refutations* he claims explicitly to be the first. The art of rhetoric has made great strides, he says, since the early sophists, but before himself nothing was done concerning logic or the methods of disputation (34, 183b–184a). This resembles, of course, what he says in the *Rhetoric* about his predecessors' supposed inattention to logical demonstration and the enthymeme.[52] Such claims seem ungenerous to Plato, as well as the early sophists and Isocrates, all of whom at least provided starting points. Isocrates, for example, identifies the ability to "fashion the whole speech fittingly with enthymemes" as an essential component of rhetorical skill and makes it dependent on the ability to select and combine *ideai* suitable to the subject matter (*Against the Sophists* 16–17), which, again, sounds very much like an approach to topical invention without the name.[53] If Isocrates wrote those words around 390 B.C.E., as is generally supposed, Aristotle had not yet been born. Similarly, the *Rhetoric to Alexander,* composed perhaps around 340 B.C.E., proceeds from a non-Aristotelian tradition yet has a fairly well-developed sense of common inventional topics, including both general premises and modes of proof and amplification, which it refers to as *tas koinas ideas,* "the common forms." This language echoes Isocrates.[54]

Why Aristotle?

Antonius'"Aristotelian" account of topical invention, or for that matter Cicero's account in *Topica,* seems likely to derive from the sophistic handling of progymnasmata—especially the commonplace and thesis—in a Greek tradition going back at least to Hermagoras and possibly to Isocrates, while the notion and terminology of "topics" (*topikê*) may be an Aristotelian addition, absorbed and adapted in the sophistic schools of the Hellenistic era. Those schools, after all, especially in an Isocratean tradition, would have considered it brutish and inhuman to take no interest in such things. It is even possible that the *Topica*'s stasis system for the argument of theses is Hermagorean in origin. But even if Antonius' or the *Topica*'s account derives from, say, a New Academic source such as Philo of Larissa, the probability is that Philo's rhetorical teaching has been adapted from sophistic teachings in the Hellenistic tradition—especially the Hermagorean sorting of inventional topics into a system of stases. (Crassus makes this point explicitly, at 1.55.)

Antonius' point in this discussion of invention is to reverse young Cicero's criticism of Hermagoras for including theses in his art of rhetoric. It is notable that, in *De inventione,* he grounds this criticism in the authority of Aristotle: "I think everyone easily perceives that such questions are far removed from the duty of an orator . . . therefore the material of the art of rhetoric seems to me to be what I have said Aristotle approved" (1.6.8, 1.7.9), that is, the subject matters of the judicial, deliberative, and epideictic genres of practical civic discourse, and especially for Cicero, the judicial. The mature Cicero knows better, and in *De oratore* that mistaken view from his youth is repeatedly attributed to "these teachers [*istorum magistorum*] to whom we send our sons . . . who think themselves learned [but are] dull and unrefined" because they separate "theses" from "hypotheses" and concentrate almost exclusively on the latter (2.133). It is noteworthy that Antonius does not say *rhetorum,* "rhetoricians," but *magistorum,* "schoolmasters." Meanwhile, the corrected view that Antonius now espouses and that Crassus will agree with—that every case, every hypothesis, turns on a question of general principle, a thesis (2.134, 3.104–107, 3.111–121)—is *also* associated, through Catulus' observations, with the authority of Aristotle. There are three main points to be noted here.

First, the association with Aristotle or the hint that Antonius' account of invention is (like the *Topica*) somehow "Aristotelian" may simply be a strategy for endowing views attributable to Hellenistic rhetoricians with the status of "philosophy," or with the dignity of an erudition that suggests a gentlemanly education and provides some snob appeal for Cicero's upper-class Roman reader.[55] As William Fortenbaugh has argued, Cicero regularly invokes Peripatetic (and other philosophic) sources in "self-serving," sometimes contradictory, and often erroneous ways to dignify material that mostly looks like "handbook stuff," or as a way to puff his own authority as a thinker.[56]

But one might put that point another way. Cicero's re-presentation of ideas from the Greek rhetorical tradition as the ideas of "Aristotle" or the Academy or other philosophical schools is consistent with an already well-established strategy in the criticism and teaching of poetry and other literature, namely, that a poet's work is "good" if it presents ideas that can be identified with, or shown to anticipate, the doctrines of famous philosophers or schools. The clearest (if later) articulation of this approach is found in Plutarch's *How the Young Man Should Study Poetry* (in the *Moralia*), but it dates back as far as the fifth century B.C.E.[57] It would have been a familiar critical strategy to anyone with an education like, or merely approaching, that of Cicero. (And, of course, we still do it today: Don DeLillo's *White Noise* is "good" because one can read it as a meditation on a number of poststructuralist ideas about language, identity, postmodern culture, and so forth; Dan Brown's *Da Vinci Code* is not "good," or is not "serious" literature, insofar as one cannot do so.)

In sum, invoking Aristotle or the Academy—acquaintance with whose views requires a degree of leisured erudition—sounds better, when addressing a gentleman reader, than attributing one's views to some Rhodian rhetorician who spends his days making boys sweat through speaking exercises. But it also works to justify the rhetoricians' views by suggesting that they are consistent with the views of esteemed philosophers. Thus we find young Cicero (in *De inventione*) ostentatiously invoking Aristotle as support for his exclusion of theses from the business of an orator, and likewise the grownup Cicero (in *De oratore*) invoking Aristotle, again, for his rejection of that view—although, let us remind ourselves, the invoking is done through Catulus and treated with seeming irony by Antonius.

Further, Cicero sometimes uses the term "Aristotelian" simply as a general synonym or metonymy for "philosophical." We see this in an oft-cited letter of October 54 B.C.E.: "I have written in the Aristotelian manner, or so I intended, three books in the form of disputation and dialogue *On the Orator* [*De oratore*] ... They differ from the common precepts, and encompass all the rhetorical doctrine of the ancients, both Aristotelian and Isocratean" (*Ad Familiares* 1.9.23).

Similarly, much earlier, in Cicero's *De inventione,* we find Aristotle and Isocrates identified as the two "fountains" from which all rhetorical teaching has flowed (2.2.7–8). Thus *all* rhetorical teaching is divided into just two streams: on one hand, a sophistic (and Greek) tradition from the rhetorical schools of the Hellenistic age, which is summed up under the title "Isocrates," and on the other hand, a tradition of philosophical (and Greek) theorizing, which is summed up under the title "Aristotle." These are the fountainheads, it seems, of all rhetorical teaching. In *De oratore* itself, Crassus identifies the philosophical tradition broadly with the followers of Socrates, but especially the Peripatetics and Academics (3.59–68, 122), while asserting that the successors of Plato (the Old Academy) held essentially the same views as Aristotle (3.67). In his later *Academica,* Cicero repeats that assertion and further cites Philo of Larissa's opinion that the Old and New Academies were actually unified in their basic doctrine (of epistemological skepticism; *Academica* 1.4.13, 17). The Old and New Academies and the Peripatos, this argument says, are essentially the same.[58]

From this point of view, "Aristotelian" simply means "philosophical" or any treatment of rhetoric in the philosophical tradition that springs from the matrix of the early Peripatos and Academy. Further, the idea that *De oratore* is "in the Aristotelian manner" (*Aristotelio more*) probably means no more than that it is dialectical in the sense of featuring an interchange of contrasting arguments— theses—on the nature and requirements of an ideal art of rhetoric.[59] Indeed this is Crassus' explicit view at *De oratore* 3.80: The perfect orator is he "who can, in the Aristotelian manner [*Aristotelio more*], speak on either side on any subject" or can otherwise engage in philosophical disputation.

Second, although the "dull and unrefined" teachers and the "common precepts" from which *De oratore* differs are sometimes identified as Greek—in line with both the Roman custom of bashing Greekishness and the upper-class custom of regarding anyone whose job is teaching boys as socially inferior[60]—it seems likely that Cicero is mainly criticizing the Roman reception and adaptation of Hellenistic rhetorical training. In another letter of October 54 B.C.E., to his brother Quintus, he says: "Your boy Cicero (and mine) is exceptionally devoted to his rhetoric teacher Paeonius, a man, I think, who is thoroughly trained and of good character. But as you know, the kind of education I prefer is somewhat more learned [*eruditis*] and philosophical [*thetikôteron*]. In any case, I for my part have no wish to impede the boy's course of instruction, and he himself seems more attracted to declamation and to enjoy it more. Since I myself was trained that way, I am willing to let him follow the same itinerary, for I am confident that he will arrive at the same place."[61] Both Cicero (when a boy) and his nephew now have gotten their basic training in rhetoric almost exclusively through declamation exercises. Cicero would like the boy's training to be *thetikôteron,* "more philosophical"—literally "more thesis-y"—though he is confident that his namesake will come around.

The basic training of Cicero and his nephew seems typical for the Roman world. Early in the first century B.C.E., not long after the dramatic date of *De oratore,* both the young Cicero of *De inventione* and the author of the *Rhetoric to Herennius* make gestures toward "philosophy"—and the *Rhetoric to Herennius* makes occasional references to what look like progymnasmata (but are not identified as such). Yet both treatises are designed almost exclusively for practice with declamations on judicial and deliberative hypotheses.[62] And, of course, young Cicero excludes the arguing of theses from the concerns of rhetoric. At the end of the first century C.E., we find Quintilian introducing his discussion of "preliminary exercises" with a remark that he will "put off for a while that which alone is called the 'art of rhetoric' in popular opinion" (2.4.1), by which he means training in declamation. Quintilian sees himself as introducing a Greek approach that is typically not part of Roman rhetorical instruction, though he, like Cicero, thinks it should be. Later, when he begins his discussion of declamation, he says, "I am now at the point where I must discuss that part of the art from which those who have passed over the foregoing [preliminary exercises] generally begin" (2.11.1). To relegate the progymnasmata to the grammarian or skip them entirely is common practice.

Suetonius, in his brief history of the Roman grammarians and rhetoricians from the late second century B.C.E. up to about 100 C.E. remarks that the grammarians taught preliminary rhetorical exercises, such as "set themes [*problêmata*], paraphrases, addresses, [and] statements of cause," so that "their pupils' speech would not be altogether unadorned and dry when they were handed over to the teachers of rhetoric" (*De grammaticis et rhetoribus* 5.5). Later he notes that the earliest Latin rhetoricians did teach "the kind of thing the Greeks call theses [*theseis*], refutations [*anaskeuas*] and confirmations [*kataskeuas*]," all of which are progymnasmata, but the practice faded out quickly and was replaced by *controversiae* (judicial declamations; 25.4).[63] If Suetonius is correct, that fading out would mark the transition from a direct copying of Greek rhetorical instruction to the Roman adaptation of it. Antonius, then, and Cicero, may be faulting those "dull and unrefined" teachers who work within this Romanized tradition rather than the Greek one descended from "Isocrates" and "Aristotle." Crassus, likewise, voices criticism of the (for him) new phenomenon of "Latin rhetoricians," whom he faults for completely lacking the "learning and knowledge worthy of humane culture" that the Greek rhetoricians still possess (3.93–94).

Third, this pairing of "Isocrates" and "Aristotle" in a philosophical and Greek rhetorical tradition brings us back, again, to the relation between the two, and to Antonius' seeming Aristotelianism. For after his discussion of inventional topics, styled as Aristotelian by Catulus but closer to what we find in the pro-gymnasmatic thesis exercise, he progresses to an Aristotelian discussion of ethos (brief) and pathos (at greater length; 2.182–216), which Caesar extends with a long digression on humor (2.216–290). All this may or may not have Peripatetic sources. As Elaine Fantham argues, Antonius' treatment of ethos and pathos differs significantly from Aristotle's in ways that reflect the differences between fourth-century Athenian and first-century Roman sociopolitical contexts and cultures;[64] and one might argue for the Stoic sources supposedly behind the treatment of emotions in Cicero's *Tusculan Disputations*, though *De oratore*'s repeated references to the uselessness of Stoicism would undercut that. But whatever the source, Antonius cannot be seen as "correcting" a deficiency of Hellenistic rhetorical instruction. Although we find no explicit, separate treatment of emotional psychology comparable to Aristotle's in the extant Hellenistic handbooks, it is hardly credible that the sophists who taught rhetoric had overlooked the rhetorical role of emotion. As Aristotle says, his sophistic predecessors were concerned with almost nothing else (*Rhetoric* 1.1.3–4). As James May and Jakob Wisse observe, the Hellenistic manuals included affect in their treatment of different parts of the oration: ethos in the prologue, pathos in the epilogue, arousal of prejudice or sympathy in a narration, and so on.[65] The *Rhetoric to Herennius,* for example, discusses the moving of "pity" (*misericordia*) in its treatment of the use of commonplaces to amplify a proof (2.31.50). As Chaim Perelman has argued, all facets of rhetoric have an affective dimension, from the general premises that provide the "starting points" of argument to the valuative and emotive resonance of all natural language.[66] If affect is present in every facet of rhetoric, and one is necessarily dealing with it all the time, there is no need to provide a separate, theoretical treatment of it; and Perelman offers none. Neither do the ancient rhetoricians. They focus on structuring what the speaker does, and discuss emotive techniques wherever they might be relevant.

Yet however Aristotelian Antonius' (and Caesar's) discussion of emotion may be, it too is ironically undercut. In book 1, as he is arguing against the notion that the orator should be learned in all branches of philosophy, Antonius says, "What great and impressive orator, when he wished to make the judge angry with his adversary, ever was at a loss because he didn't know whether anger is a feverish disturbance of the mind, or a desire to avenge pain? Or who, when he wished his speech to stir up the other emotions in a jury or assembly, said the things that philosophers usually say?" (1.220). This argument is followed by an evocation of both Stoic and Peripatetic theories of emotion as not only useless to an orator but actually counterproductive, because they are remote from the ways that people actually think and feel in everyday life. The philosopher's theories are suitable for whiling away some leisure hours, discussing what the wise man's emotions *ought* to be or what "anger" *really* is but not much more; an orator who tried to apply those theories systematically would be ridiculous (1.220–224). Antonius, of course, later downplays his refutation of Crassus in book 1 as deliberate oppositionality, and not necessarily his real opinion, but that statement may itself be another piece of gamesmanship. The fact, however, is that no speaker in *De oratore* refutes Antonius' argument about the irrelevance of philosophic theories of emotion to actual oratorical practice. The point is repeatedly made that, to stir emotion effectively, the orator must be in tune with the values and attitudes of his audience, and must actually feel what he wishes them to feel (1.222–224, 2.189–190). More than a theory of emotional psychology, one needs a direct, intuitive, felt knowledge of what is outrageous, pitiable, admirable, ridiculous, and so forth for the community that one addresses. And one knows (and feels) these things by being steeped in the traditions, institutions, lifeways, and experiences of one's culture, or otherwise having a deep experiential knowledge of human nature.

Further, in book 2, as Caesar develops his long digression on humor—a theoretical excursus he wittily calls a detour into the "Pomptine Marshes" (2.90)—he repeatedly makes the point that no theory of humor can ever make one funny (2.218, 2.227). Crassus responds: "In my opinion, the virtue and utility of these precepts is not that we shall be guided by rules of art to discover what to say, but that, *when we have learned what they refer to,* we shall be sure of what is right, and shall understand what is defective, in what we attain by means of talent, application, and exercise" (2.232; emphasis added). Once again, theory, rhetoric *in modo Aristotele,* provides an art of *judgment,* or a theoretical hermeneutic of emotional phenomena such as laughter or derision, but does not facilitate the invention of things to say that will provoke those emotions. If a speaker needs to run mentally through the definitions and rules of humor ("the premises of the laughable are . . ."), or tries to crank out jokes according to those rules ("to turn a witticism, one should start with . . ."), and does not know these things intuitively, he probably will never raise a laugh. He certainly will never tell a good joke ex tempore, or possibly any joke at all. The moment will have passed, perhaps the audience will have left the building, by the time he finally formulates his wooden joke. The rhetoric of humor is a paradigm case of the rhetoric of emotion. Perhaps it is a paradigm case of rhetoric in general.

But there is more. Crassus' point seems to validate theory as a resource for critical reflection, as by means of it the speaker can identify what is "right" (*recta*) or "defective" (*prava*) in what he has done, or others have done, and say why, and thus he presumably would be able to improve or help others improve. But this critical study is not propaideutic to the acquisition of rhetorical skill. Rather, it follows from it. One can apply the precepts of theory to critical reflection only when he has learned what they refer to. How does one do that? Evidently not through learning the precepts themselves.

Crassus' remark here verges on an observation arrived at in modern studies of the teaching of grammar in writing instruction: explicit enunciation of the rules of grammar has little to no effect on the grammaticality, much less the elegance, of student writing, and it makes no difference whether one enunciates the rules of traditional grammar, structuralist grammar, transformational-generative grammar, or some other grammar. Moreover, explicitly stated grammatical rules are, on one hand, always inadequate to linguistic realities and, on the other hand, and crucially, usually incomprehensible to anyone who has not grasped already, by experience, an intuitive knowledge of the rule in question.[67] This is one reason why a person who speaks a second language according to textbook rules is likely to speak it oddly, even incorrectly according to the intuitions of a person with "native" fluency, and why true fluency usually emerges from instruction coupled with intensive and extended immersion experiences. Or consider—to stick with examples from linguistics—Noam Chomsky and Morris Halle's famous 1968 study, *The Sound Pattern of English*, a rigorous, theoretical account of the rules of English pronunciation so complex that it scarcely can be understood without an advanced degree in linguistics and, for that reason as well as others, cannot possibly be used to teach anyone correct, much less impressive, pronunciation.[68] Yet all competent speakers of the language have an intuitive knowledge of everything the rules describe, with little need to consciously reflect on it. And indeed the speakers know more, since Chomsky and Halle declared their theory incomplete. So how would one teach a person English pronunciation, or *impressive* pronunciation?

A sports analogy may be helpful. Try explaining the rules and principles of, say, baseball to someone who has never played the game, or try explaining what is going on at any given moment in a game. Even if your inexperienced interlocutor could achieve some understanding of your explanation, or could develop a critical appreciation of the game, or could manage to construct an ingenious theory of it—"baseball is a counterpart of cricket," "baseball is an allegory of timelessness punctuated by momentary crises"—that person still would be unable to compentently play the game. Or again, to shift the metaphor, consider what complexities might be involved in a complete theoretical account of a tennis player hitting a ball over a net: the physics of the ball's trajectory, the complexities of weather and atmospheric conditions, the physiological processes involved in the player's ability to see and anticipate the ball's movement, the player's hand-eye coordination as she brings the racquet to the ball, the working of nerves and muscles, the physics again of the force exerted by the racquet, and so on. And yet, if one were to teach someone to play tennis well, what would one need to say?

In other words, enunciations of the rules or principles of rhetoric are mostly meaningless unless and until one knows already, through an intuition grounded in experience and practice, what they refer to—though they may produce interesting "observations" and theoretical speculations that are irrelevant to the cultivation of actual ability or to actual performance. This line of thought runs through the rhetorical tradition. We hear it early, for example, in Isocrates' famous denial that there can be a rigidly "ordered art" (*tetagmenê technê*) that can tell a speaker how to speak effectively in any given situation. At the same time he asserts that the right kind of training process (*paideusis*), an "art of exercise" (*gumnastikê*) for the mind, can make students with sufficient talent, experience, and discipline "more artful" or more skilled (*technikôteros*) in thought and speech, provided that the teacher sets appropriate examples for imitation and provides explanations that "leave out nothing that can be taught" (*mêden tôn didaktôn paraleipein; Against the Sophists* 12–13, 15, 17–18; *Antidosis* 180–185). Likewise we hear it late, in Augustine's *De doctrina Christiana* (4.4), when he says that no one can *be* eloquent and think of the rules of eloquence at the same time, and moreover that conscious knowledge of those rules will be no help to someone who lacks an internal feel for it.

The importance of that observation cannot be overemphasized. The person who "knows" (that is, can recite) the rules of eloquence but lacks an internal feel for it has not yet learned, as Crassus says, to what the rules refer, and consciously thinking of the rules can actually be an impediment to performance. They operate successfully only when they have been so internalized, so habituated, so subtilized within a complex repertoire of behaviors that there is no longer a need to think of them, though they might later be used as touchstones for after-the-fact reflection. Moreover, at that point any explicitly stated schoolbook rule will be inadequate to what the knower has come to know. Thus Cicero's speakers, who are seasoned orators, both assert the value of the rules and (occasionally) declare their silliness. The purpose of rhetorical training, in essence, is to develop an internalized knowledge, a habitude, a crafted intuition, a trained capacity for improvisational invention, a feel for the performance of eloquence, through the convergence of what Crassus and the whole Isocratean tradition calls "talent, application, and exercise." The materials of the rhetoricians' "little books," when viewed from this perspective, are best understood not as an attempt at "theory," at least not in the Aristotelian sense of a systematic account of principles, or a "metaphysics" of the rhetorical, or an "ordered art" that provides clear rules (a recipe) for producing effective speech in any situation, but as a pedagogical apparatus—things that teachers can say to students, explaining what can be explained, to guide and illuminate their practicing.

Why, then, invoke Aristotle at all, or the philosophical tradition of rhetorical theorizing for which "Aristotle" serves as a metonymy? Perhaps to dignify a *thetikôteros* (more thesis-based) Greek approach to rhetorical training that really is sophistic, or Isocratean, through an identification with philosophy as practiced in the famous schools. Or perhaps because, as Crassus suggests, theory provides a critical perspective or a set of touchstones by which the trained, experienced *rhetor*—who has "learned what the rules refer to"—can reflect on his own and others' performances. Or perhaps, as Antonius suggests, because it provides a cultured intellectual recreation by which liberally educated men can decorously while away some leisure time, which is what the speakers in this dialogue are doing. (Crassus' point about freedom as the ability to sometimes do nothing, and his anecdote about the statesmen Laelius and Scipio reverting to boyhood pastimes in the countryside and collecting seashells on the beach, seem relevant here; 2.22–24.)[69]

One might argue, too, that the Hellenistic rhetorical tradition in its Isocratean strain regards it as brutish and inhuman to take no interest in the philosophers' ideas and appropriates whatever seems useful. As the young Cicero of *De inventione* either observes or repeats from his teacher's lessons, the streams from the two "fountains" of Isocratean and Aristotelian rhetorical teaching already had merged, as the Hellenistic rhetoricians absorbed the philosophers' contributions (2.6–9) and, we can presume, as the philosophers who took up teaching rhetoric also borrowed from the rhetoricians. Or, yet again, if Cicero has constructed *De oratore* as an elaborate, entertaining literary game of *argumentum in utramque partem,* "argument on both sides" delivered by different versions of himself wearing the masks of his boyhood mentors, perhaps he has invoked both "Aristotle" and "Isocrates" not only to dignify one by means of the other but also to place them in an agonistic relation and to echo and play out the rivalry between philosophy and rhetoric in the Hellenistic world. If, as Cicero says in his letter of 54 B.C.E., he has written the dialogue to "encompass" (*complectuntur*) both Isocratean and Aristotelian approaches to rhetoric, that encompassing may be not so much a matter of "Isocrates plus Aristotle," as is sometimes assumed, but of "Isocrates *versus* Aristotle" in a more or less friendly wrestling match.

The Crassian Position

When Scaevola makes his opening objection to Crassus' Isocratean encomium of rhetoric, he is arguing, as Crassus explicitly points out (1.45–46), the position of the philosophic schools, or what Cicero in his letter of 54 B.C.E. sums up under the title "Aristotle": The orator qua orator has no knowledge, except perhaps for what the rhetoricians' "little books" may say about prologues, narratives, and the like; his only proper domain is practical civic discourse in law courts, political assemblies, and ceremonial gatherings; he must turn to the philosophic schools for knowledge of political, ethical, and legal theory, and everything else that he may need to know, including even rhetorical theory. Crassus' response to this argument (1.45–73) prefigures his ultimate position in book 3. After objecting that the philosophers have excluded the orator "from all learning and knowledge of greater things" and have confined him to "law-courts and petty public meetings, as if in some pounding-mill" (1.46), Crassus develops an argument that, even if so confined, the orator still must speak about nearly all matters treated by philosophers, especially politics, ethics, and justice, and for this reason he will need to have wide-ranging knowledge. This includes a "deep insight into the characters of men and the whole range of human nature" (1.53), without which it is impossible to move an audience's emotions, as well as knowledge of the subject matter in question and of rhetorical art itself. Thus endowed, as Crassus argues, the orator will not only speak about everything the philosophers may discuss but will speak about it better.[70]

There is an ambiguity in this position. On one hand, particularly with reference to matters of rhetorical art, Crassus argues that what "Aristotle and Theophrastus," and presumably later philosophers, have written in their treatises on rhetoric has mostly been borrowed from what belongs to rhetoric already—that is, the teachings of their sophistic and Hellenistic *superiores*—so that "what the orator has in common with them, I do not borrow from them" (1.55). This implies, on one hand, that the orator does not need or cannot use what the philosophers may have added, and that, on the other hand, beyond rhetoric itself there may be further things that orators and philosophers have in common, and that the orator need not borrow either, namely, knowledge of politics, ethics, justice, human nature, and the characters and mores of his fellow citizens. In fact, Crassus makes this point explicitly: One might entrust the natural sciences and other specialized subjects to the philosophers and other experts, but questions of "human life and conduct . . . have always been the orator's" (1.68). While both orators and philosophers may discuss these things, the orators have a knowledge that is not dependent on the philosophers, though they may listen to them. It is inherent to their art, since it is part of the culture of the public sphere and part of the rhetorical *paideia,* as when, for example, one argues theses or develops commonplaces, or incorporates them in declamations or in actual orations. There are things to say about "justice," for example, that are grounded in common understandings, the flux of communal opinion, rather than the philosophers' hair-splitting and frequently counterintuitive theories of what justice really is or ought to be. Like the knowledges needed to move emotions or raise a laugh, rhetorical philosophies of politics, ethics, justice, and so forth, are rooted in the thought and experience of the civil community the orator addresses, and not (only) the abstruse, detached, and often-impractical speculations of the philosophic schools. The philosophers may insist the subject matters comprising civil wisdom belong to them alone, but as Crassus says, "While I grant that they may discuss all these things in a secluded corner to while away their leisure, nevertheless I will entrust and deliver this to the orator:

that he will develop with all gravity and attractiveness what they dispute in a thin and bloodless kind of speech" (1.56). That is, the orator will independently treat all these matters in his own more accessible, engaging, and pragmatic way. The philosophers may certainly talk about them too, in their obscurer way, and as a man of broad culture the orator probably should take some interest in their ideas, or "eavesdrop" as Antonius says, but he need not borrow from them.

On the other hand, in arguing that the "complete and perfect orator" is "he who on all subjects can speak with variety and fullness" (1.59), Crassus suggests that even in the business of the forum, "often there is something from some obscure branch of knowledge that must be taken up and employed" (1.59–60). For these matters, one can become informed by consulting the relevant experts. Crassus reasserts his claim that the orator, once he has consulted, will speak about these matters better than the experts do themselves, but he has entered a slippery slope. For in arguing that the orator will get from the philosophers and experts the requisite knowledges for obscurer, more specialized matters, Crassus goes further and begins to require that he be learned, as well, in even those things the philosophers "share" with orators. Hence he asserts that the orator who wishes to move the passions of his audience will be unable to do so "without a most diligent and searching examination of all those theories expounded by the philosophers" (1.60). Really? Later, similarly, he will insist that the orator should also be a thorough scholar of the law, reducing it to a systematic art and knowing all of it inside out (1.166–203)—a discipline that does not yet exist in Cicero's day and a requirement that, in our own time, even the most competent and best-educated lawyers cannot meet. Thus in proposing a "perfect orator" who will range over the totality of human thought and knowledge, Crassus seems to require him to be deeply schooled in all the doctrines of the philosophic schools, as well as the institutions, lifeways, literature, and experience of the civil community in which he lives and speaks.

The heart of Antonius' retort (1.209–262) is his remark, which we have seen already, that no capable orator was ever "at a loss" about how to move his audience for lack of the correct philosophical theory of emotional psychology (1.220). More broadly, the orator's duty is not to be an all-purpose philosopher but to speak to questions in civic discourse, public issues, and for this "he has no need for the philosophers' definitions" (1.222). Indeed, the philosophers' theories of politics, ethics, and justice are often "completely at odds with the everyday ways of life and customs of civil communities" (1.224–225) and thus are likely to provide an exceedingly strange foundation for actual, practical civic discourse. Moreover, even if it were desirable for the perfect orator to master all the doctrines of the philosophic schools, and all of the civil law too, that would take a ridiculous amount of erudition and a ridiculous amount of time. As

Antonius maintains, "We see that men of the very greatest intellect and the most abundant leisure have used up their entire lives" in philosophic studies, even on a single subject (1.219). Just the project of mastering the totality of the civil law requires more time than any one person could possibly have and is unnecessary anyway (1.234–255). Such endeavors would leave the would-be orator no time to actually develop his rhetorical abilities, an arduous and lengthy process in itself (1.256–257). The practical result of Crassus' ideal, then, would not be the perfect orator he desires, but a pale, withered, haggard, squinting scholar, with a wheezy voice and a "bloodless," hairsplitting speaking style.

But Antonius' ultimate position—his compromise position—is not so far from Crassus either. As Antonius says, "Since his faculty of speech should not be destitute and naked, but sprinkled with a pleasing variety drawn from many things, let it suffice for the good orator to have heard much, seen much, and to have gone over much in thought and reflection, and much too in his reading, not having acquired it as his own, but having sampled it as something foreign [*aliena*]" (1.218).

It is enough to be a person of broad culture and wide-ranging thought, to be acquainted with many things through both experience and conversation, to be well read, and to have "sampled" the philosophers' discussions, very much in the manner of someone visiting a foreign culture and learning about its ways. It would be unsuitable for a person of liberal education to do otherwise. And when the orator is working up a case and needs a particular bit of specialized knowledge, he can look it up or talk to the relevant experts (1.248–250). This is in fact Crassus' core position too, before he gets carried away into arguing that the perfect orator must master all fields of knowledge—which he admits is an ideal, not a description of any actual orator. In essence, both Antonius and Crassus line up on the side of "Isocrates," in opposition to Scaevola's statement of the claims of the philosophic schools (or "Aristotle"), while Antonius offers a pragmatic, and Isocratean, corrective to Crassus' overextended idealism.

It is noteworthy that, when the younger orators Sulpicius and Cotta ask Crassus to give his views on the art of rhetoric, including the question whether it is an "art" (*ars*) at all, he objects that they are treating him like "some idle and talkative little Greek," expresses scorn for "the impudence of those people who sit on their chair in the school [*schola*] and ask whether anyone in the large crowd of men would like to propose a question," and adds that he should have borrowed a Greek philosopher from a neighboring estate, one Staseas the Peripatetic, for the young men's amusement (1.102–105).[71] It is only when Scaevola retorts that "they are not asking for the typical useless prattle of some Greek, nor an old song from the schools, but something from the wisest and most eloquent man of all" that Crassus agrees to give his views (1.105). Thus Crassus' treatment of rhetoric is set up explicitly in contradistinction to the "useless" (*sine usu*) theoretical discourse of the philosophic schools, and of the Peripatetics in particular.

Crassus begins with a clear Isocratean frame. He denies that there is any "art of rhetoric" in the philosophers' rigid sense of "art"—a systematic, theoretical account offering exact and certain knowledge of the principles of speaking—though he allows that an organized collection of some useful observations made by "skilled and experienced men" may be called an art in the looser, more popular sense of the term (*vulgari opinione;* 1.107–112). Then he waxes for several pages on the crucial importance of natural ability (113–133) while noting that training can improve both modest and great endowments (1.114–115). All this is Isocratean. When he returns to "art," Crassus promises to disclose "my customary method" (*rationem*) of training and then declares, "To begin with what befits a well-born, well-educated man, I will not deny that I learned all those common and well-worn precepts" of the rhetoric schools (1.135, 138). The standard contents of the Hellenistic course in rhetoric are then reeled off in rapid summary (1.138–146) and capped as follows: "With these things almost the entire teaching of these artifexes [*artificum*] is concerned; and were I to say it was no use, I would be lying. . . . Truly in my opinion the significance in all these rules is not that orators, by following them, have won a reputation for eloquence, but that certain people have observed and collected what eloquent men did spontaneously; so eloquence is not born from art [*artificio*], but art from eloquence. Nevertheless, as I said before, I do not reject it; for even if it is scarcely necessary for speaking well, still it is not unworthy of a gentleman to be acquainted with it" (1.145, 146).

On one hand this tricky passage rehearses the notions that rhetorical precepts have little value unless and until one knows by experience what they refer to, that the art is founded on observations of what the eloquent do spontaneously, and that knowledge of the art's precepts—the ability to state them—may amount to little more than a mark of gentlemanly (*liberalis*) education. These are things that nearly all male members of the Roman upper classes have in common from their school days; it is part of their identity as members of an elite.[72] On the other hand, Crassus allows that the rhetoricians' precepts are in fact useful, and he clearly has not forgotten them, even if they are merely an "old song" to him now; they are, it seems, pretty much what teachers can say to students to guide their exercises and explain what is explainable. They embody, and serve to help recall, the process of instruction that has cultivated the capacity of all the speakers in this dialogue for effective thought and speech, and that has made them what they are. Notably, the rhetoricians are named as "artifexes," master artists or fashioners of something—namely, rhetorical ability—or orators. One might say, in other words, that the art embodied in the rhetoricians' familiar precepts is not so much an art of speaking per se as an art of producing persons skilled in speech. Thus it is "scarcely necessary for speaking well" *in the act of speaking itself,* since no one can be eloquent and think of the rules of eloquence at the same time and since speaking merely by the rules that are taught to schoolboys can only produce a mechanical, juvenile banality at best or a vapid froth of thoughtless words at worst; yet the rhetorician's schoolroom art, his "art of exercise," is essential to the preparation of an orator.

Crassus' brief litany of precepts is followed by an equally brief litany of training practices (1.147–159). These include, in order of mention: declamation on realistic cases, "writing as much as possible" in declamation exercises, paraphrase of Latin models and translation of Greek, exercises in delivery and memory, and experience with real cases. To these practices he adds another set, introduced with a "furthermore" (*etiam*): wide reading in poetry, history, and "the writers and teachers of all the noble arts," who should not only be read but also "praised, interpreted, corrected, criticized, and refuted," with all questions "argued on both sides" (1.158); thorough learning of the civil law and the institutions and policies of the state (1.159); and finally, cultivation of an urbane wit with which to "salt" one's discourse (1.159). The first group more or less reflects the basic Roman training—declamation exercises leading to practice with real cases, presumably with some sort of apprenticeship in the transition—with the addition of the more literary activities of writing out declamations and doing paraphrases and translations, which Crassus says will cultivate greater deliberateness and thoroughness in invention, and greater elegance and impressiveness in speech. It is noteworthy that these writing exercises, especially paraphrase and translation, can be seen as an "advanced" extension of grammatical training,[73] and that they resemble progymnasmata from the Greek rhetorical tradition as discussed, for example, by Theon.

Likewise the next group, which Crassus seems to present as supplemental but necessary—the reading, critical study, and disputation of the arguments of famous authors, followed or accompanied by advanced studies in civil law and institutions and the acquisition of urbane wit—also constitutes an extension of grammatical training and resembles such philosophical progymnasmatic activities as refutation and confirmation, encomium and invective, and, especially, the arguing of theses. Moreover, if the study of law and civic institutions is to include the critical and disputative activities prescribed for Crassus' wide-reading program, which seems likely, that too would produce a progymnasma, namely, the evaluation of a law or proposed law and, in the long run, with greater development and maturity, a political-philosophical excursus such as Cicero's *De re publica.* (The critique or defense of a law was the final stage in the sequence of progymnasmata and the bridge to declamation.) Only the subject of witticisms, which is thrown in last, seems not to obviously fit this "progymnasmatic" pattern, although what Caesar calls "stinging" wit seems relevant to invective. Crassus does not clearly treat these practices as preliminary or foundational to rhetorical training; rather, he seems to regard them as a "graduate-level" continuing education appended to the otherwise usual Roman training.

It is possible, however, that Crassus' account of his "customary method" simply reflects the order in which he, like Cicero, has come to things in the course of his own development. As Crassus says in book 3, "I cannot say that I learned the things I am now dealing with in just the way I say they should be learned. ... The forum was my school, and my teacher the customs, laws, and institutions of the Roman people, and the traditions of our ancestors" (3.74, 75). Both Crassus and Cicero first came to rhetoric in just the way that Cicero's nephew now is coming to it—through declamation and practical experience—and came to its more philosophical (and Greek) dimensions later. In the Greek (and Isocratean) tradition, however, that dimension both precedes rhetorical training proper in the progymnasmata and continues to constitute its core.

I already have examined Antonius' objections to Crassus' overextension of his Isocratean ideal into philosophy per se, and Antonius' (or Cicero's) ironized presentation of what Catulus thinks is an "Aristotelian" account of invention. But before I turn to Crassus' ultimate positions in book 3, let us also consider Antonius' general remarks on rhetoric, early in book 2, as he announces what he says are his real opinions. For his basic position, like that of Crassus, is mostly Isocratean: He begins by denying that there could ever be an art of rhetoric in the philosophers' sense of art, as *tetagmenê technê,* an ordered or systematic art with clear and certain rules, and he affirms that a nonsystematic but organized collection of useful precepts can be called an art in some looser sense, and that these precepts and the training that goes with them exclusively belong to rhetoric and no other discipline (2.32–38, 83–84). This is the same point that Crassus has argued in book 1. Antonius then argues the equally Isocratean point that rhetoric cannot and need not give rules for every kind of discourse and points out that even the Greeks, for whom history writing is a major rhetorical genre, do not give rules for historiography; all that is required, he says, is training in the most difficult kinds, mastery of which implies, and makes easy, mastery of all the others (2.41–70). These most difficult kinds appear to be two: "theses" on general questions concerning "all that pertains to the practices of citizens and human conduct, and that involves everyday life, the business of the state, our civil society, how people commonly think, and human nature and character" (2.68); and "hypotheses," primarily on judicial themes, or real cases, which Antonius in typical Roman fashion regards as the most difficult and crowning kind (2.72). This last point is half-Isocratean. Isocrates too thought that mastery of the highest and most distinguished kind of discourse implies and makes easy the mastery of all other kinds, but for him the highest and most difficult kind is panegyric (*Antidosis* 46–50)—such political-philosophical or "deliberative" discourse as *On the Peace, Areopagiticus,* or *Panathenaicus,* as well as the *Panegyricus.*[74]

Antonius' discussion is punctuated by Caesar's and Catulus' exclamation (2.59) that he is better acquainted with Greek literature than people think—he has been citing Greek historians—which prompts his remarks (2.60–61) that he reads the Greeks only for entertainment and for a certain stylistic "coloration," picked up like a tan from walking in the sun; that he finds the philosophers and poets mostly unintelligible; and that he prefers historians and orators, who write "as if wanting to be friends with those of us who are not learned" (2.61). This orientation toward audience-friendly civic discourse and history writing, and his impatience with philosophers, is basically Isocratean. (The problem with poetry seems to be sheerly a matter of language: the archaisms and dialects of Greek poetic diction make it a "foreign language" to him; 2.61.)

When Antonius turns to rhetorical training, he emphasizes the importance of natural ability (2.84), experience, and *preparation.* As he says, a person at the threshhold of declamation should be "neither dull-witted, nor unpracticed, nor unacquainted with general literature and humane culture" (2.72). Or again, the candidate for training should be "imbued with literature" (*tinctus litteris*), should have done "some listening and some reading," and should have learned "even these precepts" of rhetoric while also possessing the requisite voice, physique, energy, and fluency (2.85). This implies an ample grammatical (that is, literary) education, resembling, if less extensive than, what Crassus has suggested (1.158), while the notion of being "not unpracticed" (*non inexercitato*) invokes the necessity of "exercises" prior to training in declamation, or in other words, progymnasmata. This is, in fact, nearly the same position that Crassus will arrive at in book 3, having admitted (3.74–80) that the more extreme version of his ideal orator is unattainable in reality:

> Since the orator may wander freely in this wide and measureless field [of all subjects that apply to the life of a civil community], and is on his own ground wherever he takes a stand, all the resources and ornaments of speaking are abundantly available to him. For a fullness of matter begets a fullness of language, and if the matter of which one speaks is honorable in itself, this begets a certain natural splendor in the words—provided only that the would-be writer or speaker has been prepared with a liberal training and instruction *when a boy,* that he burns with enthusiasm, that he brings natural ability and has been exercised in abstract disputations on general questions, and that he has chosen the most distinguished writers and orators for study and imitation. (3.124–125; emphasis added)

In the end, Crassus' ideal project of being learned in all fields, and of reading, critiquing, and disputing "the writers and teachers of all the noble arts," boils down to the more realistic goal of being broadly and well educated in boyhood (*puerili*). Here is reflected the Greek and Isocratean notion of an extensive literary education, imitation, and the progymnasmata, including especially the thesis exercise, as the philosophical foundation and continuing core of the rhetorical *paideia* (rather than an "advanced" extension of it, as Crassus and Antonius elsewhere suggest). Beyond this, the orator who "wanders freely" over all subjects relevant to civil life can do research or consult an expert when necessary: it is easy, says Crassus, for a person with a quick and well-trained mind to quickly master all that he needs to know for any practical purpose (3.86–89). Indeed, "all the arts are treated in one way by those who put them to practical use, and in another by those who so delight in the treatment of the art itself that they are moved to do nothing else in life"; thus the orator, as a free-range practical public intellectual—as philosophical in an Isocratean mode—need not consume himself in endless study or the endless theoretical speculations of the philosophic schools (3.86). Once again, it is enough to "eavesdrop" or "sample" their discussions and to take whatever may be useful. On this point, then, Crassus and Antonius converge.

Antonius' discussion of training is interrupted, somewhat oddly, by Catulus' remark that he doesn't need "some Greek teacher [*doctore*] who will reel off for me the precepts everybody knows, when he has never laid eyes on the forum or a court of law" (2.75). This may reflect impatience with, or snobbishness toward, the run-of-the-mill rhetorician at Rome, or a tradition, even among the Greeks, of teaching rhetoric mechanically as a set of recipes, such as Isocrates criticizes in *Against the Sophists* and likewise associates with classroom hacks with no experience or skill in actual public discourse (9–13). On the other hand, the impatience may not be with the "reeling off" of precepts per se, since that is what Crassus and Antonius themselves are doing. The impatience, rather, may be with the teacher's inexperience and nonpractice of the art he supposedly is teaching, with a reeling off of rules disconnected from the activities the rules refer to. A clarification lies in what comes next. Catulus illustrates his point with an anecdote about "that Peripatetic called Phormio," who attempted to lecture Hannibal on the art of generalship though he had never seen a battlefield, and whom Hannibal pronounced a "crazy old man" (2.75–76). Thus the Greek teacher who "reels off" rhetorical precepts for court and forum but is innocent of actual practice there is associated with an "Aristotelian" philosophical tradition. Recall Crassus' quip that he should borrow "Staseas the Peripatetic" from a neighboring estate to entertain the young men with chatter on the art of rhetoric.

This line of argument goes further. Antonius responds by saying that he has encountered "many Phormios" teaching rhetoric and introduces for the first time in *De oratore* what will be his oft-repeated opinion that "their teaching is ridiculous" (*perridicula*) because they separate "theses" from "hypotheses" and restrict rhetorical instruction to the latter (2.77–78). It is hard to escape the inference that "they," as "Phormios," are Peripatetics or other philosophers who teach rhetoric by lecturing on its principles and, like Aristotle, restrict the orator's domain to practical civic discourse—and thus to hypotheses, while theses are the philosopher's business—although they have little real experience and seem ridiculous, even naïve, to a practiced orator. But whoever "they" are, Antonius casts himself as "Hannibal" to their "Phormio." Next Antonius describes them as dividing rhetoric into five parts (invention, arrangement, style, memory, delivery), which James May and Jakob Wisse contend is a Peripatetic approach to the organization of rhetorical theory, as distinct from the sophistic approach which organized its teaching of invention according to the analysis of the case (stasis) and the parts of the oration (for there are characteristic topics of invention and modes of development for each part), such as we see in the *Rhetoric to Alexander*, the *Rhetoric to Herennius*, Quintilian, the Hermogenic corpus, and elsewhere.[75] Antonius views the five-part division and the rules given in each part with less severity than Catulus, and even finds the classification tidy, but thinks that it is mostly obvious and shows "a lack of experience" (2.79–82). Finally, he faults the "Phormios" of rhetoric for imagining that it is an art like others, that is, a systematic theoretical account of a field of knowledge (2.83–84). In sum, Antonius' criticism of these people both implicitly associates them with Peripatetics and more explicitly echoes Isocrates' critiques of those who treat rhetoric as if it were an "ordered art" and classroom hacks who reel off rules without experience of what they refer to.

From this Antonius turns to the familiar Isocratean position that not art but "a mind that is keen and vigorous as well as subtle and resourceful" makes for excellence in rhetoric (2.84), and he then invokes the primacy of natural ability enhanced by liberal education and broad experience plus instruction, imitation, and intensive practice in both speech and writing (2.85–97).[76] In the midst of his discussion of imitation, he invokes Isocrates as *magister rhetorum omnium, cuius e ludo, tanquam ex equo Troiano, meri principes exierunt,* the "teacher of all rhetoricians, from whose school, as if from a Trojan horse, nothing but eminent men came forth" (2.94), and thus seems to identify Isocrates as the fountainhead of the Hellenistic tradition of teaching rhetoric.[77] Meanwhile the "eminent men" who came forth from his "school"—the Latin here is *ludus,* a place for gaming, exercise, and practice, as distinct perhaps from *schola,* a place for leisure and learned discussion—are identified as writers, orators, and rhetoricians, including Naucrates, whom Quintilian thinks the first to use "stasis" as a rhetorical term (2.94–95). Likewise Cicero himself, in the prologue to book 2, refers to Isocrates as "the father of eloquence" (*pater eloquentiae;* 2.10). These statements constitute a fairly strong endorsement. "Isocrates," then, with his "ludic" pedagogy of instruction, imitation, and practice resting on a broadly philosophico-literary foundation, appears to be the tradition with which Antonius and Cicero align themselves, in contrast to the "Phormios" from the philosophic *scholae.*

When Antonius turns to precepts for the arguing of real-world cases (2.99), he begins by discussing the analysis of the case, with a very interesting description of his own, and probably Cicero's, actual practice. He interviews the client, informs himself about the case as fully as possible, and then plays out an imaginary dialogue among the advocate, opponent, and judge, after which the crucial point at issue, the stasis, "immediately comes to mind" (2.91–104). Antonius says the point at issue must be a question of fact, quality, or definition—these are standard stasis headings; compare the *Rhetoric to Herennius*—but he goes no further and omits the usual discussion of how each stasis breaks down into substases, each with its own selection or "division" of topics.[78] He does not actually reject that analysis but observes, twice (2.117–120, 2.162–163), that it is performed by "those who teach" (*qui docent*) and is "more suited to the training of young men" (*adolescentulos;* 2.117) because it guides the beginner through the process of discovery by providing a ready-made procedure. For the more practiced speaker with developed habits, however, such supports are no longer necessary (just as, one might say, training wheels are no longer necessary to someone who has learned to ride a bicycle).[79] Moreover, when one has recognized that theses and hypotheses cannot be separated, and that all particular cases resolve into the general issues that are at stake (2.133–134), the whole system of stases and topics that the rhetoricians teach to boys can be reduced to the relatively small master set of topics by which theses can be argued and from which the speaker will select for any given case (as Cicero points out in the *Topica*). This is close to the Isocratean notion of a limited set of *ideai* that can be variably recombined depending on the specific needs of any particular subject matter at hand. And from here begins Antonius' supposedly "Aristotelian" account of invention—the point at which this chapter started.

When Crassus takes his turn, in the afternoon of the second day (book 3), it is ostensibly to treat the part of rhetoric that Antonius has left to him. According to the division of labor he says they had established in their morning conversation (in book 2), Antonius was to treat "what things the orator must say," leaving to Crassus "how they must be furnished with distinguished style" (*ornari,* "fitted out, adorned, equipped, made splendid"; 3.19, 2.120–128). This is notably not the Peripatetic division of rhetorical lore that Antonius has mentioned (invention, arrangement, style, memory, delivery; 2.79). Rather, it is a division that can be found recurrently in the critical essays of Dionysius of

Halicarnassus, who explicitly identifies himself as a philosophical rhetorician in the tradition of Isocrates (*On the Ancient Orators* 1, *Lysias* 16, *First Letter to Ammaeus* 2).[80]

Dionysius divides "speaking well" (*to legein eu*) into the "domains" of subject matter (*ho pragmatikos topos*) and style (*ho lektikos topos*), or what might broadly be called "thought" and "expression," or in Cicero's terms *ratio* and *oratio* or *sapientia* and *eloquentia*.[81] Further, Dionysius' *pragmatikos topos* includes what he calls "preparation" or "discovery" (*paraskeuê, heuresis*) and the "employment of the things prepared" or "arrangement" (*chrêsis tôn paraskeuasmenôn, oikonomia*).[82] "Employment," in turn, is treated in terms of the parts of the oration but is still under the general category of "thought" or the treatment of subject matter. The *lektikos topos* includes diction (*eklogê tôn onomatôn*, literally "word choice") and the "composition" (*sunthesis*) of words in rhythmically structured phrases, clauses, and periods. Diction, in turn, includes "proper (nonfigural) expression" (*kuria phrasis*) and "figural construction" (*tropikê kataskeuê*). The conceptual framework, then, looks something like this:[83]

Pragmatikos topos (domain of subject matter; thought)
    Paraskeuê/heuresis (preparation/discovery)
        Krisis (judgment)
    Chrêsis/oikonomia (employment/arrangement; the parts of the oration)

Lektikos topos (domain of expression; style)
    eklogê tôn onomatôn (word choice; diction)
        Kuria phrasis (proper expression)
        Tropikê kataskeuê (figural construction)
    Sunthesis tôn onomatôn (composition of words)

Dionysius applies these concepts variably and flexibly, sometimes changes the terms (for example, *taxis* for "arrangement"), and eclectically appropriates ideas from grammarians and philosophers, including Theophrastus (for the "virtues of style"), when they are useful to him. But the terms *pragmatikos topos* and *lektikos topos* occur consistently and seem to be the chief organizing ideas of his "Isocratean" approach.

Antonius' approach has fallen very much into this pattern. Taking up the *pragmatikos topos,* he has discussed the analysis or "preparation" of the case—substituting his own process of investigation, the inventional topics of the thesis, and a discussion of emotion for the usual account of stasis, followed by the "employment of things prepared" in the parts of the oration (and in different genres), supplemented by a short account of memory. Even his incorporation of seemingly Aristotelian elements, coupled with a certain irony and resistance to the philosophers' claims on rhetoric, is similar to Dionysius' adaptation of Theophrastus and others while resisting Peripatetic claims that their philosophy "encompasses" all of rhetoric. Crassus, too, in his discussion of style, will invoke the Theophrastian "virtues of style"—correctness, clarity, ornamentation, appropriateness—only to dismiss the first two as obvious and elementary. He focuses on ornamentation, which he subdivides into diction (proper and figural) and composition, followed by short discussions of appropriateness and delivery. That is, he invokes the Theophrastian account of style but also converts it into something like a Dionysian account of the *lektikos topos*.

Dionysius of Halicarnassus, of course, belongs to the generation after Cicero. His *floruit* was between 30 and 8 B.C.E., and he probably was born about the year 55, when Cicero was writing *De oratore*; he would have been a young boy or adolescent when Cicero was murdered in 43. Thus while Cicero's speakers cannot be using an approach derived from Dionysius, they do seem pretty clearly to be reflecting an Isocratean, late Hellenistic rhetorical tradition of which Dionysius is the "great" next-generation representative. Similarly, Cicero's detailed treatment of prose rhythm in the *Orator*, which he claims is the first of its kind in Latin, is strongly reminiscent of, though earlier than, the kind of analysis found in Dionysius' *On the Composition of Words*. Both Dionysius and Cicero appear to be working from a shared Isocratean-Hellenistic background. Nothing is known about Dionysius' teachers, or what relation they could have had to Cicero's preceptors, especially his later ones—the Greek sophists he studied with in the East. But sheerly as a matter of unprovable if tantalizing speculation, someone such as Apollonius Molon at Rhodes comes to mind.

The relevant point for what will be the conclusion of this chapter, however, is that Crassus begins his account of the *lektikos topos* by critiquing the very division that he and Antonius have adopted: expression cannot really be separated from thought, words from ideas, or rhetoric from knowledge, except as a convenient fiction for discussion (3.19–24). This argument opens a long, proleptic digression on "speaking as a whole" (3.25) in which he revisits the relationship between rhetoric, philosophy, and knowledge, and arrives at his final position (3.25–147). We have seen already that he makes concessions to Antonius' pragmatist objections to his ideal, impossible "perfect orator," and settles on the realistic notion that the would-be orator, in addition to having the requisite natural endowments of mind and physique, should have received a broad liberal education "when a boy," should be practiced in the arguing of "theses," and should have adopted good models to study and imitate (3.125). Likewise we have seen that Crassus' learned and philosophic orator need not be universally learned, nor a philosopher per se, but endowed with sufficient intelligence and discipline to quickly learn what he needs to know and to handle it in his own pragmatic, accessible, and "full-blooded" way (3.86–89). All we need note, at this point, is the following.

On the grounds that thought and expression are inseparable, Crassus argues that distinguished style arises from distinguished thought and agrees with Antonius that the way to achieve the most potent speech is to connect the particular matter in dispute (the hypothesis) to the underlying, general principle at stake (the thesis; 3.104–125). The best orator will always be the one who can wax philosophical, perceptively develop resonant big ideas, and apply them forcefully to the case at hand with captivating, distinctive, emotively compelling style. For this one needs a wide-ranging education, a developed capacity for thought and inquiry, indeed, the ability to argue everything on both sides, and a cultivated, virtually poetic power of expression. One could argue that this approach to "distinguished" style anticipates or reflects an earlier Greek version of what we see in the Second Sophistic treatise of "Longinus," *On the Sublime.*

Crassus' general line of argument is set up with a double evocation of the near-infinite variety through which great eloquence presents itself, and of "Isocrates, the incomparable teacher" (*doctor singularis*), who famously could develop the individual capacities of his students through literary study, intensive exercise and practice, and a limited core of recombinable, widely applicable precepts (3.25–36). As Isocrates himself puts it, "Do not suppose you may be ignorant of even one of the celebrated poets or the sophists, but of the former become a hearer and of the latter a student, and prepare yourself to be a judge of the lesser and a competitor of the greater; for through these exercises [*gumnasión*] shall you most quickly become the sort of man required, as I have shown, to rightly rule and properly govern the state" (*To Nicocles* 13).

Being a "judge of the lesser and a competitor of the greater"—evaluating and disputing the arguments made by famous authors—implies the philosophical activities of the thesis (and presumably other exercises, such as refutation and confirmation, up through declamations on imaginary cases, or hypotheses). This, clearly, is the kind of educational program that Crassus has in mind for the orator he seeks, or that Cicero wishes for his nephew. Isocrates, moreover, stands as the great and culminating figure for an old sophistic tradition that, as Crassus argues, embraced both "eloquence" and "wisdom" in a single *paideia* before the followers of Socrates accomplished "that undoubtedly absurd, unprofitable, and reprehensible separation of tongue and mind [*cordis*], so that one set of people teaches us to think [*sapere*] and another to speak" (3.61).[84] That separation, he argues, was brought about by the withdrawal of philosophy from active civic engagement, in favor of a turn toward abstract metaphysical speculation, theory building, and research into specialized subjects which, when one was freed from the daily demands of civic life, could be pursued at almost endless leisure (3.56–61).

The results have been, on one hand, the kind of philosophy Antonius complains about and that Crassus says the orator need not pursue—obscure, overspecialized, abstracted, theoretical, metaphysical, impractical, disconnected from the real life of the community and even from normal human nature as well as useless to the orator—and, on the other hand, the gradual encroachment of this philosophy on domains of thought and speech that most properly belong to rhetoric, such as politics, ethics, and justice. The philosophers have so fully claimed the arguing of theses that rhetorical instruction, while gesturing toward it, does virtually nothing with it. This could be rhetoric as taught by the hacks that Isocrates critiques and Dionysius too excoriates (3.107–110; for Dionysius, see *On the Ancient Orators* 1–2), but it could also be rhetoric as taught in the philosophic schools. The philosophers have encroached on even what was left to rhetoric when Aristotle restricted it to speeches in courts of law, political councils, and public assemblies. As Crassus says, "At the present time, with Philo, whom I hear is greatly thriving at the Academy, even the study and practice of these cases [hypotheses] is now customary" (3.110). This represents not an improvement of rhetorical instruction but an absorption and diminishment of it at the "Phormio"-like hands of the philosophic schools. For as Crassus puts it a little later, "It is ours, I say, this whole estate of practical wisdom [*prudentiae*] and learning [*doctrinae*], which, as if it were neglected and abandoned, men with too much leisure have invaded while we were preoccupied with business; and they have gone so far as to laugh at the orator and mock him, as Socrates does in *Gorgias,* or to give some precepts for the orator's art [*oratoris arte*] in little books that they entitle 'rhetorics' [*rhetoricos*]—as if the things they say about justice, duty, the foundation and government of civil communities, the whole conduct of life, and even, finally, the explanation of nature, were not the property of rhetoricians" (*rhetorum;* 3.122).

The mention of "little books" titled *Rhetoric* seems, on one hand, to be a dig at Aristotle, and after him a philosophical tradition of writing "rhetorics." On the other hand, "little books" (*libellis*) is also an obvious and surely deliberate echo of the Academic Charmadas' sneering remark, mentioned at the beginning of the dialogue (1.85–86), that the rhetoricians' "little books" (*libellis*) contain no knowledge worth mentioning. Charmadas is sneering at a conception of rhetoric that is itself a philosophical invention. Thus Crassus here, in his final statement on the issue, loops back to the arguments that Scaevola raised at the beginning of the dialogue. He argues that the philosophic schools have "invaded" rhetoric's true domain—the art or faculty of speaking with intelligence, grace and power on any and every subject, but especially the subjects relevant to civil life—and that rhetoric must reclaim its "stolen" patrimony, namely, the philosophical-rhetorical tradition of the early sophists and Isocrates, even if that means reappropriating the necessary knowledge "from those who have plundered us" (3.123; see also 3.137 and 3.125–143). That is, rhetoric must when necessary "sample" the philosophers' often abstruse, impractical, and sometimes useless theoretical discussions for what it may find interesting and usable, though this is in truth a reappropriation of what always has belonged to it.

In sum, Crassus' overly idealistic picture of the perfect orator, under the pressure of Antonius' pragmatism and his skeptical resistance to philosophic theorizing, is modified. Crassus' ultimate position, the point at which he and Antonius converge, is an embrace of the "ancient" sophistic tradition that culminates in Isocrates, and that, with Isocrates as the "father of eloquence" and the "teacher of all rhetoricians," descends from him down through the Hellenistic era. Though the preserved evidence for the third to first centuries B.C.E. is extremely spotty, one might guess that this tradition continues through such figures as Hermagoras of Temnos, Apollonius Molon, and others who now are little more than names. Dionysius' placement of himself in the tradition of the "followers of Isocrates"—and Aelius Theon's identification with a philosophic rhetoric and his citations of Hermagoras, Apollonius, the "great Dionysius of Halicarnassus," and other authorities whose teaching he is "transmitting"— implies a tradition persisting through generations of teachers, over centuries, that we now can barely see.[85] This Isocratean-sophistic rhetorical tradition is, of course, the tradition of those people Antonius identifies as Aristotle's *superiores,* and as "the genuine teachers of this art."

One more observation is needed. It is striking that Crassus' final discussion of the relationship between philosophy and rhetoric is capped by two remarks from Caesar and Sulpicius—forming a built-in audience-reception index that gives the whole argument its final note. Caesar declares, in a witty rejoinder to Crassus' closing arguments, that he need not bother much with the philosophers and "still can be content with what is ours" (3.146), meaning the rhetorical *paideia.* Sulpicius is more emphatic: "To tell the truth, Crassus, I have no need for your Aristotle or Carneades, or for any of the philosophers. . . . For me our common [*vulgaris*] knowledge of what concerns the forum and community is quite sufficient for the sort of eloquence I have in view" (3.147). And here the matter ends. Crassus devotes the rest of book 3 to a technical discussion of the *lektikos topos.*

Cicero's Position(s)

In book 1 of *De oratore,* after Crassus responds to Scaevola's critique of his encomium of rhetoric, Scaevola laughs and says, "I will not wrestle with you, Crassus, any more. For in this very speech you made against me, you have resorted to some artifice, so that you both conceded to me what I said was not the orator's, and at the same time—I don't know how—you wrenched these things away and handed them back to the orator as his property!" (1.74). Crassus somehow manages to grant and occupy both sides of the issue in a single speech; he has his cake and eats it too. This is in itself a comic manifestation of a deeply ingrained penchant in rhetorical culture for *argumentum in utramque partem,* "argument on both sides."[86] And it is Cicero's penchant as much as, or even more than, Crassus'. In *De oratore,* Cicero surely is having fun. It is a carnival of *argumentum in utramque partem,* and it sometimes feels like a hall of mirrors, as the speakers maintain a genial harmony and cheerfully ironize and undercut each other's arguments, and even their own, with gusto, as well as form agreements. As I suggested earlier, all the characters are Cicero. He occupies all positions, and sometimes more than one at once, though perhaps some characters and some positions are more Cicero than others.

But I do not think that Cicero means only to celebrate a *charivari* of double or multiple perspective, in a great and fundamentally comic *ludus* of rhetoricality for its own sake, playing endlessly with positions and coyly never coming to resolution. That irresolution, after all, is the problem with "dialectic," as Antonius sees it—as good as it may be to unsettle too-much settled judgments now and then, especially when they really need unsettling. The ultimate purpose of *argumentum in utramque partem,* and of rhetoric in general, is to arrive at a thoroughly deliberated judgment, having passed through the welter of differing possibilities and having given them all their due, and remaining aware of the provisionality of all conclusions. Crassus does defend his Isocratean ideal, by both granting Sacevola's strongest points and then reusing them as grounds for his own position.[87]

So what is Cicero's position? I have, of course, deliberately been reading *De oratore* against the grain of the usual interpretations, by viewing it from the perspective of Antonius—or, rather, the perspective of Cicero the practicing orator—and I have argued that this perspective, despite Antonius' seeming but undercut Aristotelianism, pulls the argument in the direction of an Isocratean approach to rhetorical *paideia* (the formation of an orator). But the argument has two fronts. On one side Cicero, like Isocrates, critiques the classroom hacks who teach rhetoric purely as a collection of verbal techniques divorced from a wider, philosophico-literary education, including the progymnasmata and the arguing of theses. On the other side, this argument for a philosophical rhetoric grounded in the tradition of Isocrates inescapably raises the already centuries-old question of the "dispute between philosophy and rhetoric" in Hellenistic as well as Roman intellectual circles, and this requires Cicero to fend off the claims of the philosophic schools to be the true owners and teachers of everything that Crassus' "perfect orator" must know. This is done mainly on the grounds that what they teach is a "theoretical" set of precepts, both for rhetoric and for civic life, that separates rhetoric from wider philosophical concerns and is largely disconnected from actual practice and experience, and even from the life, thought, and language of the civil community the orator must address.[88]

Cicero was, of course, himself very much devoted to philosophical pursuits, and to the study and critique of philosophic doctrines—with a preference, it seems, for the New Academy of Philo and its skeptical, probabilistic philosophy, its practice of argument on both sides in theses and hypotheses, and its supposed continuities with the earlier Academy and Peripatos—not to mention the early sophists, with their own epistemological skepticism and "pragmatist" embrace of probabilistic knowledge.[89] Cicero's attraction to philosophizing is made clear by the extant corpus of his literary dialogues and by reports, such as Augustine's, of his "exhortation to philosophy" in the lost *Hortensius*.[90] Cicero in 55 B.C.E. was very much the retired orator turned gentleman philosopher. And Crassus is very much Cicero. It is significant that, in the opening of *De oratore*, the speakers compare the setting (under a plane tree in the garden of Crassus' suburban villa) to Plato's *Phaedrus* (under a plane tree by the banks of the Ilissus, outside the city wall). It is perhaps significant, as well, that Cicero closes his *Partitiones oratoriae*, a rhetorical review book for his son, putting in Latin what the boy has been learning in Greek, with a remark that he has presented "all the parts of oratory, which indeed have flourished within this Academy of ours" (*illa nostra Academia;* 139). This could be taken to mean that Cicero has presented the "parts of oratory" as taught by the Academy in his day.[91] On the other hand, "this Academy of ours" could be a playful reference to Cicero's "philosophizing" with his son, just as the speakers in *De oratore* compare the portico in Crassus' "palaestra" to the gymnasia at Athens, where the philosophers hold their schools (2.20). They are holding an "academy," in a little interlude of peace before the bloodbath soon to come. And, of course, Crassus declares that Plato in his dialogues, specifically the *Gorgias*, is a "consummate orator" (1.47). So what kind of philosophizing is it? One could argue that Cicero, in all his philosophic writings, is carrying out the injunction of Isocrates and Crassus that an orator worthy of the government of the state must read, engage with, critique, and argue *in utramque partem* the ideas of "all the poets and the sophists," that is, "all" the great writers of the past who make significant claims to civil (and other kinds of) wisdom. So perhaps Cicero, as an author of dialogues, is still the orator in full Isocratean mode, "eavesdropping" on and engaging with the doctrines of the philosophic schools—arguing theses—and reappropriating for rhetoric, on its own terms, what always has in fact belonged to it.

In this activity lies the reply to Charmadas' huffy and mistaken charge that the rhetoricians have nothing to say about civic wisdom or any other kind of wisdom in their "little books." For if one takes into account not only the political-philosophical "panegyrics" of Isocrates and other sophistic writings of that kind (including histories, among Isocrates' followers) but also the production, over centuries, in the daily business of the rhetoric schools thousands upon thousands of progymnasmata and declamations, all devoted to questions of civic, ethical and other kinds of wisdom—in which, as Antonius and Crassus recognize, a general "philosophical" principle is always at stake—it would seem that, in fact, they had quite a lot to say. Or that instead of prescribing a particular doctrine that specified in advance what one should say or do, they provided a set of resources, embodied as a trained capacity, for the copious invention of things to say.

So I will say that, being both Antonius and Crassus, and all the other speakers (in lesser degrees), Cicero lays out a web of arguments that check and qualify each other and that, in the end, suggest an argument that "the genuine teachers of this art" are not the philosophers, as interesting as they may be, but the rhetoricians, the descendants of Isocrates, in the Hellenistic age.

TWO | On the *Technê* of Isocrates (I)

Then behold! Isocrates appeared, the teacher of all rhetoricians, from whose school, as if from a Trojan horse, nothing but eminent men came forth.

Cicero, De oratore *2.94 (Antonius speaking)*

From here, as it were, the road divides into separate ways. For when the students of Isocrates were pre-eminent in every kind of study, and he was already old (he lived, in fact, to be ninety-eight), Aristotle began to teach rhetoric in his afternoon lectures, often quoting in modified form that famous line from *Philoctetes,* "It would be shameful to keep silent and permit Isocrates to speak." There is an *ars* from each of them, but that of Aristotle contains more books.

Quintilian, Institutio oratoria *3.14–15*

It is said that [Isocrates] also wrote an art of rhetoric, but in the course of time it was lost. Someone will ask, How is that known? We say that Aristotle the philosopher mentioned it when he was surveying rhetorical handbooks.

Zosimus, Life of Isocrates *(fifth century)*

They say that [Isocrates] also wrote an art of rhetoric, which we indeed have seen, inscribed with the man's name; but some say that he relied more on training than on art.

Photius, Bibliotheca *260.486b (ninth century)*

Was There a *Technê* of Isocrates?

This chapter's epigraphs represent a longstanding tradition, or pair of traditions, in rhetorical scholarship. The first, represented here by Cicero and Quintilian, divides the rhetorical tradition into two main streams: a sophistic stream of rhetorical teaching that flows from Isocrates through "all" subsequent rhetoricians, or those whom Antonius calls "the genuine teachers of this art," and a philosophical stream of rhetorical theorizing that flows from Aristotle, or from an Academic/Peripatetic nexus that begins with Plato's dialogues on rhetoric and Aristotle's afternoon lectures on the subject.[1]

The second scholarly tradition—the main subject of this discussion—is a persisting question whether Isocrates wrote a *technê,* meaning a "handbook" or an "art" in the sense of the kinds of material one finds in the ancient rhetorical handbooks that have survived. That question is not trivial, since the two traditions are related and they suggest a closer relation between Isocrates and the handbook tradition than is generally supposed.

The second tradition is in part an explanation for the first, as an Isocratean *technê* would be the instrument of transmission of an Isocratean rhetoric, or an Isocratean approach to teaching rhetoric, to all subsequent rhetoricians in antiquity. Such an argument need not claim that there were copies of a *Rhetoric of Isocrates* in circulation throughout antiquity or that all generations of rhetoricians actually had access to it—though Quintilian speaks as if he has seen it and is able to say that it has fewer books than Aristotle's *Rhetoric.* Likewise, the Byzantine scholar and Orthodox patriarch Photius, writing as late as the ninth century, emphatically declares that he has "seen" (*ismen*) an "art of rhetoric" (*technên rhêtorikên*) inscribed or titled (*epigraphomenên*) "with the man's name" (*tou andros tôi onomati*) somewhere in the libraries of Constantinople—probably the Patriarchal library, the imperial palace library, or his personal library, which seems to have been extensive.[2] Zosimus, in his fifth-century *Life of Isocrates,* believes that Isocrates' *technê* has disappeared but reports the information (from what source it is impossible to say) that Aristotle mentioned it in his *Sunagôgê Technôn* (*Compendium of Arts*), which also has disappeared but which we know was a survey of the contents of the *technai* produced by his sophistic predecessors.[3]

There are other references to Isocrates' *technê* besides those included in the epigraphs. The young Cicero of *De inventione,* writing early in the first century B.C.E., recites the notion of "two streams" of rhetoric flowing from Isocrates and Aristotle, a story that he probably has gotten from his teachers; roughly three and a half centuries after Isocrates' death, it is a well-established idea. He also mentions Aristotle's *Sunagôgê,* opining that it effectively replaced all the early sophistic *technai* it summarized—thereby causing them to go out of circulation—and says that "from [Isocrates] himself an *ars* is known to exist, which I have not found [*non invenimus*]. From his students [*discipulorum*], however, and from those who continually have set out from that teaching [*ab hac disciplina*], I have gotten [*reperimus*] many precepts of the *ars* [*multa de arte praecepta*]" (2.2.6–8). Elsewhere and later in his career (*Brutus* 12.45–48), he briefly describes some of the contents of Aristotle's *Sunagôgê,* and he very sketchily mentions its discussion of Isocrates.[4]

The implication is that, if Isocrates did indeed write a *technê,* by the early first century B.C.E. it had mostly gone out of circulation but had been absorbed, expanded, revised, superseded, and continued by the *technai* composed or taught by his own students and by successive later generations of teachers who "continually set out" from and continued to propagate and develop the Isocratean *technê* as it variously came to them. One must imagine, perhaps, a "viral" form of propagation, as opposed to a tradition founded on interpretation of a fixed, canonic master text. The Isocratean *technê* "mutated" or was modified as it moved from rhetorician to rhetorician. Thus young Cicero, two and a half centuries after Isocrates' death, cannot find the original *technê,* for it is everywhere and nowhere, and Zosimus, six centuries later, considers that it has disappeared, though it seems Quintilian and Photius, each probably with access to better libraries, found a copy. A few copies of the original Isocratean *technê* may have bounced around, or rested in cobwebbed book bins, for centuries—an antique curio—while the Isocratean *disciplina* itself stood embodied, in updated and proliferated forms, in the many *technai* that remained in regular use and, therefore, in the small number that still survive today.[5]

That line of argument, however, creates new problems of its own. Chief among them is that it flies in the face of the fairly settled modern opinion that Isocrates did not write a *technê* and, indeed, that writing a *technê* would have been antithetical to his philosophy. The keynote for that line of opinion is Karl Barwick's 1963 article "Das Problem der isokrateischen Techne," which reviews the history of the question, examines the ancient fragments and *testimonia,* and concludes that none of the evidence clearly supports the existence of an Isocratean *technê.* Instead, suggests Barwick, testimonies such as Quintilian's and Photius's are misidentifications of a treatise written by another, "younger" Isocrates who was active in the first half of the first century C.E.[6] This is possible. Just as the rhetorical treatise attributed to Aelius Aristides in Byzantine manuscripts is not by him, just as most of the Hermogenean corpus is not by Hermogenes, and the treatise *On the Sublime* attributed to Longinus is probably not his either,[7] we have no certainty that the *Rhetoric of Isocrates* that Photius saw was really by Isocrates.

However, if Barwick's younger Isocrates was really active and wrote a *technê* in the first half of the first century, it seems unlikely that Quintilian, writing near the end of that same century, clearly in full command of the available rhetorical lore and the relevant contemporary sources, would have been unaware of him. He certainly is aware of the difference between the second century B.C.E. Hermagoras, famed for inventing stasis theory, and whose *Rhetoric* has also disappeared, and the more recent "Hermagoras, the student of Theodorus," who was active as a rhetorician in the late first century B.C.E. (Quintilian 3.1.15–19). Moreover, it seems likely that a first-century copy of a *Rhetoric* written by a first-century Isocrates would need to distinguish him from the older, more famous one and would do so with some sort of epithet (for example, "Isocrates of Smyrna"), as is the case with Quintilian's Hermagorases.[8] Just such a distinction is applied to the fourth-century B.C.E. "younger Isocrates" from Apollonia in Pontus, who was a student of Isocrates and had a successful career as a *rhêtôr:* Zosimus, in his listing of Isocrates' distinguished students, mentions him as "Isocrates (he of the same name)"; and the Byzantine encyclopedia known as the *Suda* firmly identifies him as "Isocrates of Apollonia" and describes him as a "student and successor of the great Isocrates" (*megalou Isokratous*).[9] My conclusion is that while Photius may have seen a faux Isocrates, or an *Art of Rhetoric* by some other Isocrates, Quintilian probably did not. But even if what Quintilian saw was not a genuine Isocratean *technê,* there is still the problem of the *technê* that young Cicero declares is "known to exist" (though he has not seen it) nearly two centuries before Quintilian and a century before the *floruit* of Barwick's "younger Isocrates."

There is the problem, too, of the Isocratean *technê* reportedly discussed in Aristotle's *Sunagôgê Technôn.* What did Aristotle say about it? Cicero, in his very brief overview in the *Brutus* (12.46–48), reports that Aristotle began his survey with the Sicilians Corax and Tisias, who "put together" in writing (*conscripsisse*) an "art and precepts" (*artem et praecepta*) for "precise and orderly" (*accurate et discripte*) speaking in the courts; then he discussed Protagoras's and Gorgias's teaching of disputation on "notable subjects" (*rerum illustrium*), "which we now call commonplaces" (*communes loci*), as well as "praise and blame" of things (*laudes vituperationesque*); then the "similar" writings (*similia*) of Antiphon; then the teachings of Lysias, who gave up teaching rhetoric early on to become a logographer; and then Isocrates. The suggestion is that Corax and Tisias "put together" a general method (*ars*) and particular precepts (*praecepta*) for handling the parts of a judicial oration (*discripte,* "orderly," implies a division into parts) while Protagoras and Gorgias developed what would later be recognized as philosophical types of progymnasmata (encomium/invective, commonplace, and thesis), and Antiphon did likewise. As for Isocrates, according to Cicero's report, he "at first denied that there was an art of speaking [*artem dicendi*]" when he was still a logographer, but later he "ceased to write speeches for others" (*orationes aliis destitisse scribere*) and "wholly devoted himself to composing *artes*" (*totumque se ad artes componendas transtulisse;* 2.12.48). And that is all.

Barwick argues[10] that Cicero's plural, *artes,* signifies not "handbooks" but "works of art," that is, speeches artfully composed and used as examples or demonstration texts for teaching. The Greek word *technê* can function in the same way, and as Barwick points out, the Pseudo-Plutarchan *Life of Isocrates* and the so-called *Letter of Speusippus* (Plato's successor) to Philip of Macedon both employ the plural in references to Isocrates' *technai.*[11] The suggestion, then, is that Isocrates wrote not a *technê* in the sense of a preceptive handbook but a collection of *technai,* in the sense of exemplar texts. Indeed, Robert Cole has argued that the sophistic *technai* of the late fifth century B.C.E., or the pre-Aristotelian *technai* in general, were simply collections of model speeches or extracts that illustrated methods for handling whole orations; particular parts of orations, such as introductions; or particular techniques, such as forms of proof, amplification, and rhythmic composition.[12] Isocrates' *technê* would, in this light, be understood as a collection of *technai* in the late-fifth-century manner—presumably the existing corpus of his speeches (*logoi*) and letters.

There are certain problems with that argument. First of all, in *De inventione* Cicero clearly writes of an Isocratean *ars,* meaning an "art" or "handbook." Moreover, he attributes to it "many precepts" he has gathered from Isocrates' successors and does not speak of it as a collection of examples. Similarly, in Cicero's discussion of Aristotle's *Sunagôgê* in the *Brutus, ars,* when applied to Corax and Tisias, seems initially to mean not a collection of exemplar texts but an art in the sense of a method of "precise and orderly" speaking, constituted by the collection of *praecepta* that they "put together" in writing, that is, in a handbook. Further, in the discussion of Isocrates, the point is that Isocrates at first denied the existence of an *ars* of speaking but later reversed himself and set to "composing *artes,*" meaning the very thing that he had formerly dismissed.

Now consider that the meanings of *ars,* besides art as craft or method, a handbook, or a work of art, also include the notion of "device," technique, or principle—an "artifice." Indeed, the use of *ars* to mean a "work of art" is a metonymic extension of that meaning: one points to a statue and says, "Behold the art of Phidias," meaning the statue as an embodiment of the art by which it was produced. In fifth- to fourth-century B.C.E. Greek, *technê* had the same potential, as in Sophocles' line "mixing-bowls there are, the skillful art of man" (*andros eucheiros technê; Oedipus at Colonus* 472). Xenophon speaks of the "arts [*technai*] of war" (*Cyropaedia* 1.6.13, 14, 26, 41, and 8.1.37; and *Memorabilia* 2.1.26); here the arts of war are the particular techniques and principles comprised by the general art of war, not examples of the art. There is a rough parallel in the modern English phrase "verbal arts": one can speak of an "art of speech" or discourse that comprises various verbal arts (devices of logic, style, delivery, textual interpretation, and so forth). Consider, too, that in Cicero's phrase *componendas artes,* the verb *compono,* "compose," more specifically means (among other things) "put together, arrange, form." This echoes the description of Corax and Tisias as "putting together" in writing (*conscripsisse*) an "art and precepts." By *componendas artes,* then, cannot Cicero, and before him Aristotle, mean Isocrates' putting together or compiling of the various *technai* that constituted his *technê*?

In *Against the Sophists* (12–17), Isocrates famously argues against the notion of a *tetagmenê technê,* meaning an "ordered art" or "science" consisting of fixed prescriptive rules, and stresses instead the notion of discourse production as a "creative act" (*poiêtikon pragma*).[13] The "most artful" (*technikôtatos*) speaker, he asserts, is the one who can discover in a methodical, nonrandom way the possibilities of a subject, take account of the circumstances (*kairôn*), select appropriately from the various elements or "forms" (*ideôn*) from which all discourses are composed, and effectively "mix them together" (*mixai pros allêlas*) in an original invention. If, as Cole suggests, by *tetagmenê technê* Isocrates means, and rejects, the use of "fixed," fill-in-the-blank model texts as boilerplate for particular types of speech, it is unlikely that his own *technê* would consist of precisely what he rejects. It is much more likely that a main emphasis of his *technê*—and its original contribution—was the "creative," fluid synthesis of *technai* in the sense of "artistic elements" or "devices," though Isocrates refers to these as "forms" (*ideai*). Thus Cicero's highly elliptical report of Aristotle's discussion of Isocrates may, perhaps, be taken to mean that Aristotle described Isocrates as "composing *artes,*" either in the sense of "putting together" a collection of rhetorical techniques and precepts or in the sense of combining "artistic elements," artifices, in an original, flexible approach to invention.

As for the Pseudo-Plutarchan *Life of Isocrates* and the *Letter of Speusippus* that Barwick cites, neither provides especially strong evidence for his case. What Pseudo-Plutarch says is this: "Some say that [Isocrates] composed *technai* [*technas sungegraphenai*], but others that he employed not method but exercise" (*Isocrates* 838f). *Technai* here cannot mean "works of art" or "demonstration texts," since it is the implied object of the denial that Isocrates "employed method" (*methodôi chrêsasthai*): the employment of "method" is a defining characteristic of a *technê,* according, at least, to Aristotle (*Rhetoric* 1.1.1). So *technai* seems here most likely to mean "principles" of rhetorical art or "artistic devices." To say that Isocrates composed (*sun-graphô,* "put together in writing") a collection of *technai* is to say that he wrote a *technê,* a handbook. Notably, Zosimus—whose *Life of Isocrates* is based largely (though not entirely) on Pseudo-Plutarch—seems to read Pseudo-Plutarch in exactly this way, rendering "some say that he composed *technai*" as "it is said that he wrote an art of rhetoric" (*technên rhêtorikên egrapse*). *Technai* seems simply to be a synonym or metonym for *technê,* an art consisting of a collection of precepts. Pseudo-Plutarch employs *technai* at two other points, in his *Life of Lysias* (836b) and *Life of Isaeus* (839f), with more or less the same meaning. The early sophistic *technai,* of course, very probably contained examples that illustrated rhetorical techniques and principles, as do all existing rhetoric manuals from antiquity and from all other times. But their essential matter would have been the techniques and principles.

Plato's *Phaedrus,* which is closer in time to Isocrates, portrays the typical sophistic *technê* as offering specific techniques or principles, even carrying the technical-terminological urge to silly extremes (for example, 266c–267d). It has long been argued, persuasively I think, that the *Phaedrus,* like the *Gorgias,* is a thinly veiled critique of Isocrates.[14] That Isocrates is the target in the *Phaedrus*'s representation of the typical contents of sophistic *technai* is pointedly made clear by the reference to "Tisias and Gorgias," who "make small things seem great, and great things small, by the power of speech, and new things old, and old things the reverse, and who discovered speaking briefly and at endless length on all subjects" (267a–b). Gorgias reputedly taught Isocrates (and Tisias Gorgias), though modern scholarship doubts the connection;[15] the story may mean little more than that Isocrates studied Gorgias's writings, or was the recipient of a teaching descended from Gorgias. But there is a stronger link than filiation. The passage clearly is a deliberate echo (though not an exact quote) of an Isocratean precept that finds its fullest extant statement in the *Panegyricus:* "Speech has such a nature that it is possible to discuss the same subjects in many ways, and to make great things humble, and bestow grandeur on little things; and to describe old things in new ways, and speak of recent events in an ancient manner" (8).[16] The same idea crops up elsewhere in Isocrates' writings (*Helen* 13; *Busiris* 4; *Panathenaicus* 36), and it is cited by Pseudo-Plutarch as Isocrates' view of the function of rhetoric (*Life of Isocrates* 838f) and recited later by Syrianus and much later by the Byzantine scholar John Siceliotes.[17] Likewise Speusippus, who is Isocrates' contemporary, declares in his *Letter* that Isocrates "professes to teach how to say old things in a new way, and new things in an old way" (9).[18] This notion appears to have been widely recognized, even in Isocrates' lifetime, as a central or important component of his teaching. Thus it, and the various technicalities of prologues, narratives, proofs, style, and so on, are invoked as the typical contents not only of sophistic *technai* in general but of the Isocratean *technê* in particular, so that Socrates and Phaedrus can dismiss it as dealing merely in "preliminaries." The important point here, in short, is that the Isocratean *technê* and/or the typical sophistic *technai* are represented as collections of technical precepts, not as collections of sample speeches.

Speusippus was an exact contemporary of Isocrates—the two men died in the same year (339/8 B.C.E.)—and he was head of the Academy when he wrote his letter to Philip of Macedon (c. 340).[19] These facts make him a good witness for the nature of the Isocratean *technai/technê,* although he is hostile. The letter is meant to discredit Isocrates and his students (especially Theopompus, who was then at Philip's court) and to gain some favor for the Academy, which Philip never much liked. Amid Speusippus' arguments we find the following two statements: "Isocrates declares in his *technai* that one must make the listeners well-disposed by the praise of [their] ancestors" (4) and "Isocrates says in his *technai* that it is fitting to present familiar, well-known examples, but taking no heed of his *technê,* he employs alien, shameful examples that are contrary to his argument" (10).[20]

These remarks are part of a criticism of the treatment of Philip's ancestors and deeds in Isocrates' *To Philip.* In essence, according to Speusippus, Isocrates has failed to properly celebrate Philip's ancestry, and in attempting to praise his deeds, has failed to draw comparisons from "familiar and well-known" examples (that is, from within the Macedonian royal house), focusing instead on "alien" (barbarian) and "shameful" examples that are more suitable to blame than praise. While Speusippus' uses of the word *technai* in these statements could possibly be taken as references to Isocrates' speeches, they more probably refer to *principles of art,* which Isocrates overtly teaches but supposedly violates in practice. Moreover, in the second statement, *technai* and *technê* seem clearly to be alternative expressions for the same idea: Isocrates says one thing in his *technai* but in practice ignores his *technê.* Here *technai* seems to mean the rhetorical teachings contained in the *technê.*[21]

Even Aristotle is spoken of as the author of rhetorical *technai.* In an anonymous scholium on Hermogenes' discussion of *kôla* and *kommata,* we find this: "Aristotle among the philosophers, in his so-called arts of rhetoric [*en tais rhêtorikais legomenais technais*], and Isocrates among the sophists, seem to have arrived first at the meaning of these words in the analysis of discourses not presented in verse."[22]

It is not possible that *rhêtorikai technai* here can mean "rhetorical works of art" or demonstration texts composed by Aristotle, since it is fairly certain that he never produced any. It is clear too that what is meant must be "rhetorical arts" in the sense of "rhetorical teachings" or "rhetorical handbooks," since what is referred to is the use of the technical terms *kôlon* and *komma* "in" his *technai.* It is vaguely possible that by Aristotle's *rhêtorikai technai* the scholiast means the three books of Aristotle's *Rhetoric*—his "rhetorical manuals"—though *kôlon* and *komma* are discussed only in the third. It is possible as well that *en tais rhêtorikais technais,* positioned between the parallel phrases "Aristotle among the philosophers" and "Isocrates among the sophists," is meant to signify the "rhetorical arts" of both: "Aristotle the philosopher, and Isocrates the sophist, *in their so-called rhetorical arts,*" were the first to use the terms *kôlon* and *komma* in the analysis of prose style. But however one sorts these possibilities, it is certain that *rhêtorikai technai* means either Aristotle's *Rhetoric,* or its three books, or the rhetorical precepts it contains; and it may also mean Isocrates' *Rhetoric,* or its (two?) books, or its precepts. In none of these cases can *technai* mean "works of art" or demonstration texts. This scholion, moreover, is not the only reference to Aristotle's *technai.* In his *First Letter to Ammaeus,* Dionysius of Halicarnassus, in the late first century B.C.E., refers repeatedly to Aristotle's *Rhetoric* as his "*technai*" or "*rhêtorikai technai"* (for example, 2, 7, 8, 10, 11, 12); in fact, he *never* refers to the *Rhetoric* in the singular, as a *technê.* That the *Rhetoric* specifically is meant (as opposed to other Aristotelian writings on rhetoric) is very clear, as Dionysius is arguing that the *Rhetoric* was written after Demosthenes had made most of his important speeches, and he quotes from it at length.

Finally, there is not a single example (as far as I know) of a clear reference by any ancient writer to Isocrates' speeches or letters that refers to them as *technai.* The word invariably used is *logoi,* "speeches" or "discourses," or some reference to genre, such as *sumbouleutikon* (deliberative/advisory), *dikanikon* (judicial), *panêgurikon* (panegyric), *enkômion* (encomium), *epistolê* (letter), and so forth. And every use of the word *technai* in reference to Isocrates can be understood as arts, or as artistic devices, methods, principles, or precepts. Isocrates' *technê,* or his *technai,* was something other than his *logoi.*

Perhaps the notion that the pre-Aristotelian *technai* were simply collections of model speeches and excerpts should be revisited.[23] In the first place, as I have suggested, even if those *technai* consisted largely of such materials, they all would have been presented as examples of particular principles, techniques, or devices, such as the division of a speech into prologue, narration, proofs, and epilogue, or the use of argument from probabilities, and so forth, and there necessarily would have been at least a brief explanation of what the examples exemplified. That explanation would have been the essential substance of the *technê.*[24] It is possible that the explanation would have been supplied orally by the sophist, but that would have rendered the sophist's handbook, if he wrote one, a mostly inscrutable object, useless by itself as a means of transmitting or memorializing the substance of the art. One might argue that the sophist would have had a proprietary interest in keeping his explanations out of print, thus forcing would-be students to come to him for instruction in the mysteries of rhetoric.[25] That argument, however, is weak, since, as rhetoricians from Isocrates to Augustine have asserted, book knowledge of rhetorical principles and techniques is in itself ineffective without an extended period of guided practice and correction by an expert teacher. Circulation of the sophist's teachings in book form would have worked as an advertisement for his training program, just as the performance and circulation of "display" speeches (*epideixeis*) would have been advertisements for his practical mastery of the art. There certainly is no sense in later antiquity that publishing a rhetoric manual is bad for the sophist's business; on the contrary, it establishes him as an authority.

In Plato's *Phaedrus,* just after Socrates and Phaedrus review the supposedly trivial technicalities with which the sophistic *technai* are concerned, Phaedrus concedes that "the substance of the art (*to tês technês*) that those men teach and write about as 'rhetoric' [*hôs rhêtorikên*] does seem to be that sort of thing" (269c). The discussion then turns to the notion of proof from probability. The sophistic *technai* maintain that the rhetor need not know the truth, but only what seems probable to his audience (272d)—note that this is a principle. This observation leads Socrates to invoke "Tisias himself," whom "you have studied carefully" (*pepatêkas akribôs;* 273a). The verb *pepatêkas* literally means "have tread upon, walked in, dwelt in, frequented"; when used in relation to a written text, it can be rendered by "have studied" or "have thumbed the pages of." *Akribôs,* "carefully," can also be rendered as "exactly, thoroughly." The suggestion is that Phaedrus has read the rhetoric of Tisias with minute attention. Whether the actual Tisias is meant, or whether "Tisias" is a cover for Isocrates or for sophistic rhetoric generally, does not matter here. The point is that Phaedrus is represented as gleaning statements of rhetorical principle from a published sophistic *technê.*

Socrates goes further: "Now, let Tisias tell us if he does not say that probability (*eikos*) is anything other than what most people believe" (273a–b). This statement echoes Isocrates' assertions that wisdom, and the goal of the training he offers, is the ability to deliberate and speak about the best course of action in particular situations, based on conjecture or opinion (*doxa*) about probabilities (see, for example, *Against the Sophists* 2, 7–8; and *Antidosis* 271). The principle is echoed, of course, in Aristotle's understanding of the nature of rhetorical argument (*Rhetoric* 1.1.11). But the statement attributed to Tisias has a nearer echo in the *Rhetoric to Alexander's* definition of probability as a form of proof: "A probability [*eikos*] is a statement supported by examples in the minds of the audience" (1428a). The unknown author, usually identified in modern scholarship as Anaximenes of Lampsacus, goes on to briefly explain the probable as what people generally feel to be consistent with their personal knowledge and experience.[26] The *Rhetoric to Alexander* seems to have been written sometime shortly after 341 B.C.E. (Isocrates, again, died in 339/8), and it postdates the *Phaedrus*, but it probably reflects the contents of the typical fourth-century sophistic handbook, or at least the type of sophistic handbook produced in the wake of Isocrates' extremely influential teaching.[27]

In the *Phaedrus,* however, Socrates and Phaedrus are portrayed as discussing verbatim statements in the handbook of "Tisias himself": Does Tisias say this about probability? Phaedrus grants that he does. Socrates then remarks that Tisias, "having discovered this clever and artful thing" (*touto sophon kai technikon heurôn*), "wrote" (*egrapsen*) the most famous (or infamous) item in his *technê,* that in a case of assault involving a weak man and a strong man, neither should tell the truth but should appeal to probability. Each should accuse the other of starting the fight. The weak man should argue that a weakling like himself would never attack a hulk like his opponent, and the strong man should argue that it is unlikely that he would have attacked the weak man, since he would have known that everyone would suspect him, and so on (273b–c).[28]

There are two points to make here. First, surely Tisias (or whoever it was) intended this strong man / weak man example as an illustration of how probability might be deployed "antilogistically," on opposing sides of the same case, especially when there are no witnesses, and Plato has misrepresented it, along the lines of popular misperception, as an egregious example of sophistic indifference to the truth. Surely, if Tisias successfully taught methods of judicial argument that were felt to be of practical value and worth the price of instruction, it is unlikely that his strong man / weak man example could have illustrated a principle as silly as Plato suggests.

The second and more important point is that this passage in the *Phaedrus* shows us, in effect, the contents of a typical "page" from a sophistic *technê* as Plato's audience would have understood it, circa 370 B.C.E., when Isocrates already had been teaching for twenty years and indeed was the most prominent sophist in Athens. It is possible that Plato and his audience would have in mind the fifth-century *technai* that Aristotle would later survey, which therefore must have been available in Plato's day, as well as early-fourth-century *technai*, including that of Isocrates, but it is enough for my point if the reference is only to the latter. On the typical sophistic "page" that Socrates and Phaedrus are "reading," we find the articulation of a principle or technique—proof from probabilities, with "probability" defined much as the *Rhetoric to Alexander* defines it—followed by an illustrative example in the form of the strong man / weak man case.

Finally, there is Oxyrhynchus Papyrus 3.410, which the *Oxyrhynchus Papyri* editors describe as a largish fragment (four columns) from a second-century C.E. copy of a rhetorical *technê* in literary Doric which is probably datable to the beginning of the fourth century B.C.E. (The copy seems to have been made hastily and somewhat carelessly, probably by a scholar for his own use.) As the editors argue, the treatise's Doric dialect "is the same as that found in the fragments of Archytas of Tarentum and other Pythagoreans, and in the anonymous *Dialexeis Éthikai.*" Thus it is likely to have come from the same milieu, that is, the intellectual circles of Doric-speaking southern Italy at the turn of the fourth century.[29] If that is correct, Oxyrhynchus Papyrus 3.410 is the earliest surviving example of a rhetorical *technê* and probably reflects the character of written *technai* in the late fifth century, such as the followers of Tisias and Corax might have produced. Notably, it consists not of sample texts, but of precepts for the presentation of "high-mindedness" (*megaloprepeia*) in the different parts of a judicial oration. (The preserved fragments discuss the proemium and narrative.) Indeed, no examples at all are given in the parts that still can be read.

In sum, statements that Isocrates wrote *artes* or *technai* probably do not mean his *logoi,* and it is unlikely, too, that the sophistic *technai* of the late fifth and early fourth centuries, including Isocrates' *technê,* consisted simply of sample speeches and excerpts. That part of Barwick's argument may be dismissed, along with his proposal of a first-century "younger Isocrates" as the author of the *Rhetoric of Isocrates* that Quintilian or Photius saw.

Isocrates' Attitude toward *Technê*

There remains, however, the fairly settled current assumption that writing a *technê,* especially a preceptive *technê,* such as the "Rhetoric of Tisias" that Phaedrus and Socrates discuss, or such as the *Rhetoric to Alexander,* would have been antithetical to Isocrates' philosophy.[30] How much should that idea be credited? Its *locus classicus* is the oft-remarked passage in *Against the Sophists,* in which Isocrates rejects the notion of an "ordered art" or "science" (*tetagmenê technê*) that can prescribe fixed rules for the production of one or another kind of discourse, or an exact calculus for the correct handling of any situation (9–18; see also 21, and *Antidosis* 271, 274). There is also the fact that, as David Roochnik has pointed out, Isocrates at no point in any of his extant writings uses the explicit phrase *technê logôn*—"art of words, speeches, discourse"—to name what he teaches and practices, preferring instead such locutions as *philosophia* (meaning the pursuit of practical wisdom and the cultivation of practical ability in deliberation and counsel), *logôn paideia* (training in discourse), *epimeleia* (study, exercise), or *askêsis* (training, discipline); nor does he use the word *rhêtorikê,* which, as Edward Schiappa has pointed out, makes its first and almost only recorded fourth-century appearances in the writings of Plato and Aristotle.[31]

Isocrates' nonuse of the word *rhêtorikê* in his extant writings does not signify much and may be quickly dispensed with. *Rhêtorikê* simply is not in circulation, for Isocrates, as an available term for what his contemporaries would call *technê logôn,* or what the later Latin of Cicero and Quintilian calls *ars dicendi* or *ratio dicendi,* the art or method of speaking. By later antiquity the Greek terms *technê logôn* and *rhêtorikê,* and the Latin terms *ars dicendi, ratio dicendi,* and *rhetorica,* are all treated as more or less synonymous, and all later writers consider Isocrates to have been a teacher of "rhetoric," the "art of discourse," despite his non-use of those terms. Isocrates does occasionally use such cognate terms as *rhêtorikos* (oratorical) and *rhêtoreia* (oratory, eloquence), and he does declare at the end of *Against the Sophists* that his training program will "much more speedily" produce good intellectual and moral character than "eloquence" (*rhêtoreia;* 21), but that is not a disavowal of *rhêtoreia.* It only means that the development of good character precedes (and is a foundation for) the development of real eloquence—a principle reflected centuries later in Quintilian's famous assertion that only a "good man" (*vir bonus*) can be truly eloquent (*Institutio oratoria* 2.15.33–37, 12.1.1). Further, Isocrates immediately follows his remark with a declaration that he believes good character to be "especially" (*malista*) "stimulated and disciplined" by "the study of [exercise in] public discourse" (*tôn logôn tôn politikôn epimeleian; Against the Sophists* 21), or what, again, later tradition will recognize as "rhetoric." Rhetorical training develops good character, and in those with the requisite talent, discipline, and long-term commitment, it eventually will develop, too, Quintilian's *vir bonus dicendi peritus,* the "good man skilled in speaking" (12.1.1).

More problematic for my argument, however, is the fact that, as Roochnik observes, Isocrates nowhere in his extant writings explicitly calls what he offers a *technê logôn,* preferring such locutions as *logôn paideia, philosophia, epimeleia, askêsis,* or *diatribê* ("training, hard work, occupation," from *diatribein,* "rub, grind, wear away, spend time"), which seems consistent with his rejection of *tetagmenê technê.* But Roochnik offers two solutions. The first involves a bifurcation of *technê* as art into two main senses in fifth- to fourth-century Greek, which Roochnik derives from the Hippocratic writings and designates as "techne₁" and "techne₂."³² Techne₁ is the older of the two conceptions and is in essence the notion of *tetagmenê technê,* an "ordered art," craft, or science consisting of fixed, teachable rules and procedures that, if correctly applied by the competent expert, more or less infallibly produce the intended result. The art of a master furniture maker, for example, will be a techne₁: If he sets out to make a chair, and correctly executes the procedures for "making a chair," the outcome will always be a properly-made chair. Similarly, mathematics is a techne₁: If mathematical axioms and procedures are correctly applied, the result will always be an exact, correct calculation.

In contrast techne₂ is a "stochastic" *technê* that cannot promise an infallible result and consists not of fixed rules and procedures but provides a teachable set of precepts, principles, and methods that enable the skilled practitioner to aim at a desired result, methodically approach it, and achieve it with less-than-perfect but better than random regularity. Medicine, as the Hippocratic writings suggest, is a techne₂. It cannot infallibly cure disease or create health, but it can enable the methodical diagnosis and treatment of individual cases and can achieve better than chance results. So too is the art of war a techne₂ (though it may consist of various techne₁ *technai,* such as "how to build an earthwork"), as mastery of it renders the general more effective, or more resourceful, but cannot guarantee victory. Rhetoric or *technê logôn,* likewise, is a techne₂. It cannot infallibly produce persuasion, or whatever the intended effect is, in every situation, but it provides a set of principles and precepts that enable the properly trained *rhêtôr* to speak as well as possible within a particular set of circumstances.

This is, of course, the distinction made in Aristotle's *Rhetoric* (1.1.1, 14) and, three centuries later, in Cicero's *De oratore,* where Antonius argues that rhetoric is not an art "in the strict sense" but an art in a looser sense (2.28–33). It is also, Roochnik argues, the distinction made by Isocrates in *Against the Sophists,* when, almost immediately after denying that there can be a *tetagmenê technê* for effective speaking, he asserts that the proper training (*paideusis*) will make a speaker (with sufficient natural talent, character, and experience) *technikôteros,* "more artful" than he otherwise would be (*Against the Sophists* 12, 15). According to Roochnik, then, Isocrates offers a techne$_2$, while he avoids directly calling it a *technê.* This deliberate evasion is probably due, as Roochnik suggests, to the fact that techne$_1$ is the older and still-dominant conception of the term. Notably techne$_1$ is the notion that Plato applies in *Gorgias* and *Phaedrus* to deny that sophistic rhetoric is a *technê* at all. Isocrates has ample motivation for avoiding, or at least qualifying, the term, especially in his later writings, with Plato invoking techne$_1$ against him.[33] In short, by asserting that he offers not a *tetagmenê technê* but a *paideia* that renders speakers *technikôteros* (as well as cultivating good character), Isocrates implicitly adopts the techne$_1$/techne$_2$ distinction that will become more explicit in later writers on rhetoric.

The second solution that Roochnik provides is his observation that Isocrates does, in fact, repeatedly flirt with the term *technê,* in effect suggesting that what he offers is indeed some sort of art. This is evident already in the passage from *Against the Sophists* just discussed, but it appears most clearly in *Antidosis,* where Isocrates presents his central explanation of the "nature" and "power" (*phusis* and *dunamis*) of what he variously calls "philosophy" (*philosophia,* 175, 176, 181), "training [study/exercise] in discourse" (*tên tôn logôn meletên,* 177), and "education in discourse" (*tês tôn logôn paideias,* 180), and discusses its resemblance to "the other arts" (*tôn allôn technôn,* 178). In this web of locutions, *philosophia* is implicitly and deliberately identified as a type of *technê.* Isocrates then sets up a comparison between the twin arts (*technas*) or disciplines (*epimeleias*) devised for the cultivation of the body and the mind, namely, *gumnastikê* ("exercise, athletic training") and *philosophia* (180–181), which he says are "counterparts and complements, and homologous with each other" (*antistrophous kai suzugas kai sphisin autais homologoumenas,* 182). Here both *philosophia* and *gumnastikê* are identified as arts (*technai*) with parallel "natures" and "powers," while *technê* is identified with *epimeleia,* "discipline, exercise, study." Isocrates sums up the discussion by declaring, "These things are what I say regarding all the arts" (*kata tôn pasôn tôn technôn,* 189). Later, in claiming efficacy for discourse training, he asserts that, as in "all the arts and handicrafts" (*epi pasôn tôn technôn kai cheirourgôn,* 205), likewise in *philosophia:* All who have had a "true and intelligent guide" (*hêgemonos*) are seen to possess such a similar "ability in discourse" (*en tois logois tên dunamin*) that it is obvious that they have had "the same education" (*tês autês paideias*), since such similarity would be impossible had they not received a *diatribês technikês,* an "artistic discipline," and had thus acquired a "common habit" (*ethous koinou,* 206).

Isocrates, in sum, regards *philosophia* as a *technê* that consists of (or is formed by) *logôn paideia,* a "gymnastics of the mind" parallel to the gymnastics of the body, an "artistic training" in *logos* that cultivates a certain discursive *dunamis* ("ability, power, capacity, faculty") that renders its students—insofar as possible, for each individual—habitually "more artful" (technikôteros) in thought and speech than they otherwise would be, though it cannot infallibly produce excellent rhetors.[34] It is evident, then, that Isocrates has no objection to technê per se, but rejects only the notion of tetagmenê technê (or Roochnik's techne₁) as a paradigm for the technê he purveys.

But again, what sort of technê is it? The preceding arguments would seem to suggest not exactly a technê logôn, in the narrow sense of an art of speechmaking. That, apparently, would be a tetagmenê technê, a simpleminded how-to manual or "recipe book" that consists of fixed rules for different kinds of speeches, fails to understand the real sources of rhêtoreia, and, moreover, neglects the task of cultivating the intellectual and moral character without which genuine eloquence is impossible. Isocrates' philosophia, rather—his "art of rhetoric"— appears to be an art of producing rhetors, just as gumnastikê is an art of producing athletes or of training the body to be athletic. We see such a notion reflected, if glancingly, centuries later in the definition of rhetoric attributed to Dionysius of Halicarnassus: "Rhetoric is an artistic faculty of persuasive speech in public affairs, having the goal of speaking well."[35] Dionysius, like Isocrates (and Aristotle too), identifies rhetoric as a "faculty" or capacity (dunamis), but the key point here is that the faculty is said to be "artistic," perhaps in the sense of an instilled capacity for artful thought and speech, but also in the sense of a capacity artistically produced, that is, a capacity that is itself a work of artifice, a crafted construct.

A notion of Isocrates' technê as an art of producing rhetors still does not, however, preclude technê in the sense of a set of precepts, or even a handbook. Consider these passages:

> Abilities [dunameis], both in discourse [tôn logôn] and in all other endeavors, appear in those who are naturally talented [euphuesin] and those who have been exercised [gegumnasmenois] in practical experiences [empeirias]. Education [paideusis] makes such persons more artful [technikôteros] and more resourceful in inquiry [to zêtein], for it teaches them to take from a readier source what formerly they hit upon haphazardly; and although it cannot make those who lack talent [phusin] good debaters [agônistas] or speechmakers [logôn poiêtas], it can lead them to some improvement and can make them more intelligent [phronimôterôs] in many respects.

> But now that I have gone this far, I wish to speak more clearly on this subject. I maintain that it is not especially difficult to get a knowledge [epistêmên] of the forms [ideôn] from which we compose all spoken and written discourses, if one entrusts himself not to those who make loose promises but to those who know something about these things. But to choose from the ideai

what is required for each case [*eph' hekastôi tôn pragmatôn*], and to join them together and arrange them suitably, and not to mistake the opportune moments [*tôn kairôn*] but to embellish the whole discourse with fitting enthymemes and to speak in rhythmic, musical words—these things require much study [*epimeleias*] and are the work of a vigorous and lively mind. This requires, on one hand, that the student with the necessary talent [*phusin*] learn the forms of discourse [*eidê tôn logôn*] and be exercised [*gumnasthênai*] in their uses, and, on the other hand, that the teacher [*ton didaskalon*] explain these things as accurately as possible, so that nothing that can be taught is omitted; and for the rest he must himself provide such an example that those on whom the image is imprinted and are able to imitate [*mimêsasthai dunamenous*] quickly show more brilliance and grace than others in their speech. (*Against the Sophists* 14–18)

When they take students, the physical trainers [*paidotribai*] teach them the bodily figures [*schêmata*] that have been discovered for athletic contests [*agônian*], while those concerned with *philosophia* explain to their students all the forms [*ideas*] that discourse [*logos*] employs. When they have made them familiar [*empeirous*] with these things and have thoroughly discussed them, again they exercise [*gumnazousin*] them, and habituate them to hard work [*ponein*], and require them to combine what they have learned according to the needs of each particular case [*kath' en hekaston*],[36] so that they will grasp what they have learned more securely, and be in their judgments [*doxais*] more adaptive to *kairos*. It is not possible for the knowledge of forms [*tôi eidenai*] to encompass *kairos*, for in every case [*epi hapantôn tôn pragmatôn*] it escapes exact science [*tas epistêmas*], but those who most apply their minds and are able to observe [*dunamenoi theôrein*] contingency on most occasions usually hit the mark. (*Antidosis* 183–184)

What is most commonly noted in these and similar passages are Isocrates' stresses on "natural ability" (*phusis*) and "practical experience" (*empeiria*)—or "exercise" (*gumnasia*), "study/practice" (*epimeleia*), or "discipline" (*askêsis*)—as essential prerequisites for the development of the rhetorical *dunamis,* and his relative deemphasis of "education" (*paideia*) or theoretical "knowledge" (*to eidenai, epistêmê*) in the production of a rhetor. Natural ability provides the necessary raw materials that experience/practice will develop, and experience/practice across a range of particular situations cultivates the stochastic capacity to judge and creatively respond to the contingencies of *kairos,* a capacity that cannot be reduced to science and thus cannot be directly taught. As Isocrates goes on to say, either natural ability or experience alone can produce an excellent rhetor, a man "capable in both speech and action" (*deinon kai legein kai prattein*), and the two combined can make him "unsurpassable," but "I cannot say such things about education, for its power [*dunamin*] is neither equal nor comparable to theirs" (*Antidosis* 190–192). Indeed, one could "hear all about the principles of discourse," learn them with the utmost thoroughness, and practice diligently, but if any aspect of the necessary natural endowment is lacking, one will never speak effectively before a crowd (192).

Isocrates does allow that everyone has at least some natural capacity for *logos,* since it is part of our innate endowment as human beings (*Nicocles* 5–9, *Antidosis* 253–257), and he maintains that study and practice can "improve" the student of modest talents and make him "more intelligent" (*Against the Sophists* 15), just as, in general, "the study of public discourse" (*tên tôn logôn politikôn epimeleian*) cultivates good character before and on the way to *rhêtoreia* (21; see also *To Nicocles* 12). Most students of *politikos logos* will simply be "improved" and carry their enhanced articulateness, intelligence, and moral character into private life. From "all the schools" there really emerges only a small minority (Isocrates says "two or three") who will be competent orators or capable rhetoricians (*Antidosis* 201–204).

From this line of thought comes the opinion cited by Pseudo-Plutarch that "some say" Isocrates employed not "method" or *technê* but "exercise" (*askêsis; Isocrates* 838f), and likewise Photius' remark that "some say he relied more on training (*sunaskêsis*) than on art" (*technê; Bibliotheca* 260.486b). But Photius grasps Isocrates more truly. Isocrates relies "more" on natural ability and practical exercise / experience for the making of a rhetor, but preceptive *technê,* or direct instruction in "the elements and principles of discourse," also plays an essential role. To elide that aspect of his teaching—as does Pseudo-Plutarch—renders his notion of *logôn paideia* impossibly vague and consigns the student to the haphazard randomness that Isocrates says an "artistic training" should overcome.

As Isocrates says, it is the teacher's responsibility to explain "all" the principles of discourse "that can be taught" as thoroughly as possible (*Against the Sophists* 17). Or, as he put it in *Antidosis,* he must teach "all the forms (*ideas*) that discourse (*logos*) employs," making his students "familiar" (*empeirous*) with them and "thoroughly discussing" them (183–184). "Familiar," *empeiros,* can also be rendered as "experienced"—suggesting that the student acquires a knowledge of the elemental *ideai* from which all discourses are created through *experiencing* them, that is, by encountering, examining, and discussing examples of them. The teacher himself should provide a model, as Isocrates suggests, but the works of other authors should also be used. As Isocrates further says in *To Nicocles* (13), the student must read widely and critically in the "celebrated" authors, a list that would come to include not only poets and sophists but also orators, historians, and philosophers. This work is part of the dual project of cultivating character by expanding the student's intellectual horizon and learning the *ideai,* the fundamental elements of rhetoric. The student first comes to knowledge of these *ideai*—the things that can be taught—through hearing the teacher's explanations of them and through the careful reading and detailed discussion of sample texts. "Reading" would include both the private study/memorization of the text (as "homework") and the oral performance of it in the classroom ("reading aloud" by the student or teacher, or both), followed by critical analysis. Further, the student is to judge the weaknesses of what Isocrates calls the "lesser" examples, probably with the teacher's guidance, and "compete" with the better ones through imitation, and (at a more advanced level) through antilogistic refutation and defense of the authors' statements.[37]

This is the sort of activity we see portrayed in Plato's *Protagoras* and *Phaedrus,* in many of Isocrates' writings, and, much later and more systematically, in the *Progymnasmata* of Aelius Theon. Theon's basic classroom activities include the assignment of examples for study and imitation; memorization; preliminary remarks by the teacher on the genre of the text, its subject matter, situation, stasis, and so on; reading aloud by the teacher and/or students; "attending to what is read" through analytic/critical discussion; and paraphrase, elaboration, and "counterstatement" (*antirrhêsis,* "refutation"), depending on the level of the student.[38] These activities follow, at least in outline (and in some specifics), the basic pattern established already in Isocrates. In sum, the students with sufficient natural talent are to take the "imprint" of the *ideai* they have encountered in examples and "experienced" through reading/hearing, analytic discussion, and other activities, and those who have taken the imprint and have the ability to imitate will soon begin to show, as Isocrates maintains, "more brilliance and grace than others in their speech" (*Against the Sophists* 18).

Beyond this preliminary getting "familiar/experienced" with the *ideai,* there is, as Isocrates says, a second, and crucial, stage of training in which the student practices "selecting" which *ideai* should be used for particular "cases" (*pragmata,* "actions/affairs")—methodically, so as to "take from a readier source" what otherwise, with natural talent alone, would be "hit upon haphazardly"—as well as "combining" and "arranging" the chosen materials "suitably," according to the requirements and opportunities of the case in hand. Such a second-stage exercise is meant to cultivate, through practical and guided experience, that creative, kairotic sensitivity that cannot be directly taught but is the essence of skillful, even eloquent *rhêtoreia* (*Against the Sophists* 15–16, *Antidosis* 184).

The two stages Isocrates describes are clearly what later Greek rhetoric will call "preliminary exercises" (*progumnasmata*) and "declamation" (*meletê*): instruction and practice in the elemental *ideai,* and practice with the synthesis of those *ideai* in the composition of *logoi* for particular real or imaginary "cases." We can see in Isocrates' description of the components of declamation the outline of the Isocratean rhetorical *technê* that is invoked in Dionysius of Halicarnassus:[39] the *pragmatikos topos,* the domain of subject matter or invention, which includes the initial "inquiry" (*to zêtein*) into the case, the methodical selection and synthesis of the relevant *ideai,* and their suitable arrangement in argumentation (*taxis* or *oikonomia,* "management"), and the *lektikos topos,* the domain of style, which includes the embellishment of the discourse with "fitting enthymemes" according to *kairos* (for Isocrates treats the enthymeme as a stylistic feature as well as a form of proof)[40] and the composition of words in "rhythmic and musical" phrasing (the subject of Dionysius' treatise *On the Composition of Words*). If Quintilian is right that Aristotle's *Rhetoric* contained "more books" than that of Isocrates, and if Aristotle's contained three (as Quintilian would have seen it), it would seem that the Isocratean *technê,* if it existed, consisted of two books: one, perhaps, for the *pragmatikos topos,* and another for the *lektikos topos.* Written or not, there certainly was an Isocratean *technê.*

The Place of the *Technê* in the School

There is a question whether, or how, Isocrates (or any sophist) "lectured," or how the *technê* was presented. Did he lecture in the sense of narrating the contents of his *technê*? Was there a course of lectures on "the principles of rhetoric"? Or did he "discuss thoroughly" the *ideai* that appeared in the example texts or declamations that he presented to his students, or that were involved in their writing and speaking exercises?

In modern English translations of ancient biographies, it is common to read that someone "attended the lectures of" some sophist (or other teacher); however, the language of the original text usually says, literally, that he "heard" or "was a hearer of" the sophist. The verb *akouein,* "hear, listen to," can also mean, among other things, "understand, obey" a teacher's explanations and instructions.[41] Isocrates speaks of the rhetorician as both *didaskalos,* "instructor," and *hêgemôn,* "guide" (*Against the Sophists* 17, *Antidosis* 206), which suggests on one hand direct instruction and explanation of examples and on the other hand, "coaching" in writing and speaking exercises.

Quintilian, writing more than four centuries later, says that teachers of rhetoric "consider it their duty only to declaim, and to transmit the theory [*scientam*] and faculty [*facultatem*] of declamation" (*Institutio* 2.1.2), which again suggests both *didaskalos* and *hêgemôn,* closely tied to discussion of the rhetorician's declamations and the students' exercises. The sophist Libanius, in late antiquity, routinely uses the metaphor of a "chorus" (*choros*) for his school, implicitly defining himself thereby as a "chorus-master";[42] he also refers generically to rhetoric schools as *ergasteria logôn,* "speech workshops" (*Oration* 1 155). The same metaphor turns up in Cicero: *officina dicendi* ("speaking workshop"; *Brutus* 8.30).[43] These metaphors again suggest "leading" or "coaching" students in their exercises (through modeling, explanation, and guidance) more than a narration of rhetorical theory, though they do not exclude such narration.

Further, Libanius' letters to his students show him discussing their reading lists for "summer vacation" reading, which always consist of works by "celebrated authors," but in no case does he ever mention a rhetorical handbook.[44] Nor do the reading lists suggested by Quintilian, or any other rhetorician in antiquity, ever mention a *technê*. The focus seems to have been overwhelmingly on the critical analysis of example texts and explanation and coaching in writing/ speaking exercises.

"Transmitting the theory" that applied to the students' exercises was a basic part of the teacher's duties, but the modern idea of "lecturing," or a bald narration of theory, seems improbable. Consider the material realities of the ancient school. As Raffaella Cribiore's recent work has shown,[45] the typical school of rhetoric was a one-room affair with students of all levels present. Sometimes the room was large, sometimes small, and sometimes not a "room" at all but the shaded portico of some building, perhaps separated from public space by a partition such as a sheet. There were no distinct "courses"—"Invention 1A, Mondays 8:00–10:00 A.M."—no exams, no grades or diplomas.[46] Students typically studied with a rhetorician for up to four years or so, though some might stay for only one or two. (Isocrates says that his students usually stay for three or four years; *Antidosis* 87). The length of study would depend on family finances, what the student's ambitions were, the student's progress, or other circumstances. (Libanius seems to have taken on some economically disadvantaged students as "scholarship" cases; the successful ones rewarded him later with gifts.) As with Isocrates, a relatively small minority of students would reach the summit of *rhêtoreia* and become professional rhetors or sophists, while the rest would take their improved capacity for thinking, speaking, and writing into other careers. A sophist with a relatively large school might group students according to level. Libanius, whose school at its peak had over fifty students, and at its low points fifteen or less, divided them into groups called "symmories" (*summoriai*, "classes, companies"), though they all still met in one room.[47] A sophist with a large number of students might also, like Libanius, employ teaching assistants, and/or have older students tutor the younger ones, with the master's oversight.

The student population was fluid and mixed, and people came and went, sometimes returning after an absence of a year or more.[48] Instruction had to be tailored individually or at least adapted to "symmories" at different levels of development. The famous anecdote of Isocrates giving Theopompus the "bridle" and Ephorus the "whip," curbing the over-the-top verbosity of the former and curing the laconic flatness of the latter, illustrates the individualized nature of rhetorical instruction.[49] Under such circumstances, how would a sophist lecture? How would Isocrates have lectured? It has been estimated that Isocrates probably had no more than six to nine students in any given year—in one year there were only three—and again these would have been at different stages of instruction and development.[50] Would he, then, speak to the whole school, narrate principles of rhetoric that the older students had heard before, comment on readings that some had read and discussed before, or present a declamation and discuss it though some students were still at the "preliminary" level? Or would he circulate from group to group, or from student to student in those lean three-student years, "lecturing" to each in turn?

It seems most likely that the sophist—and Isocrates—"lectured" in the sense of providing commentary on the texts under study and the students' writing and speaking exercises. At the beginning levels, the first year or two, this would have included introductory prolegomena to the assigned texts, followed by reading aloud and "listening" and critical discussion focused on the particular rhetorical elements or *ideai* the teacher wished to emphasize. "Lecturing" would also have included preliminary remarks on the writing exercises the students were going to be assigned, the presentation of examples (model compositions), and the teacher's comments on and corrections of the students' work. At the more advanced levels, as the student progressed from progymnasmata to declamation exercises, this basic process probably continued.

As Raffaella Cribiore has noted,[51] among the Oxyrynchus Papyri there is a fragment (*P. Oxy.* 17.2086 verso) containing the right edge of a page of what appears to be a student's notes "jotted down" at a rhetorician's lecture: parts of twenty-six lines, and traces of a twenty-seventh, written probably in the third century C.E. on the back of a second-century set of scholia on poetry—that is, on some scrap paper from a discarded papyrus roll.[52] As the *Oxyrhynchus Papyri* editor remarks, the notes are written "in a sloping semicursive" hand, neat but seemingly rapid, with occasional abbreviations for titles or names, ligatures between some letters as in cursive writing, and some lines left blank or partially blank, suggesting notes. There also is an indecipherable mark, which I represent with "§" below, that is either a *paragraphos* of some kind (to mark a break or to highlight something), illegible writing, or a doodle.[53] What follows is a rough "translation." The open brackets represent the left and right edges of the papyrus fragment:

```
            }                          {
            } of the v. Timoc.         {
         } what [is] the correct       {
          } to have provided           {
          } whenever to them           {
            } [type?] of proof         {
          } we bring forth not         {
      } what has been confirmed        {
   } that [we?] not be suspected          {
```

```
} things narrated                      {
   } in deliberative speeches      {
      } as at length arous[ing?]    {
      }those hearing the matter    {
         }Philip. is indeed mine   {
         }                              {
         }[about?] headings        {
      }                              {
      } according to period {
      } epicheireme[s?] {
} §                      {
} and adjacent headings {
} timely the [first?] {
   } as Demosth. in {
} finally they put the {
} concerning the {
}or to dismiss hyp{
}[verb]ing          {
} [illegible] {
```

This fragment contains, with one possible exception, no complete sentence. Virtually no propositional sense can be made of it, and even the meaning of individual words or phrases can be difficult to determine without supporting context. But a few conjectures might be ventured, and some conclusions can be reached. The top line appears to be the beginning of the notes, as there is blank margin space above it, whereas the bottom edge of the papyrus contains traces of writing, which probably continued for a few more lines. At the top of the notes the subject appears to be Demosthenes' judicial oration *Against Timocrates*, with some focus on the uses of narrative in proof, or proof in narrative. Perhaps the idea is that a narrative should not contain disputed facts so "that we [will] not be suspected," and in order to "arouse" the audience (*akouontes to pragma*, "those hearing the matter"). There seems to be some comparison with the function of narrative in "deliberative speeches" (*sumbouleutikois*). Then the writer notes *Philip. esti dêta g' emoi*, which is the one complete clause in this document, perhaps meaning "Philip. is indeed mine," or "for me."[54] The abbreviation *Philip.* may be *Philippos*, "Philip," or *Philippikos*, "Philippic," as in Demosthenes' *Philippics*, or any inflected form of either word. Possibly it is a quotation, though it does not turn up in *Against Timocrates* or any of Demosthenes' extant speeches.[55] Possibly, though this is a mere guess, it may refer to a declamation exercise involving Philip and Demosthenes—for example, "Philip demands the Athenians surrender Demosthenes." Such themes were popular in later antiquity. Possibly it is a line from such a declamation—Demosthenes bravely declares that "Philip is my concern" or something to that effect—or a line that the writer would like to use. This is all speculation, of course, but I think the drift of these possibilities is that *Philip. esti dêta g' emoi* is probably the writer's "note to self," and that it records a reading assignment (for example, the *Philippics,* or one of them) or an intention to look further into the uses of narrative in Demosthenes' judicial and deliberative speeches (the writer being a good student) or the assignment of a declamation problem ("I get the one about Philip"). Or, if none of those, it records what the writer thinks is a striking line.

After this note to self, there is a blank space followed by what looks like a title—"[about] headings" (the papyrus shows *-ri kephalaiôn,* probably *peri kephalaiôn*)[56]—and then another blank space. Apparently the subject is now "headings," or topics, of invention, probably in connection with the "proof" section of an oration, which follows the narration in judicial speeches. Something is said about periods, probably about amplifying a proof by running through different headings period by period (in the papyrus, *kata periodon*), and something is said about epicheiremes, possibly the "working up" (*ergasia*) of proofs under different headings. This material is reminiscent of several subject matters discussed in books 3 and 4 of the pseudo-Hermogenic *On Invention*—including headings, proofs, amplification, and such stylistic concerns as periodic composition—but the treatment seems not to be systematic.[57] The discussion, rather, seems to consist more of commentary drawn from different parts of the rhetorical *technê,* though in general the subject seems to be the proof section of a speech. (*Against Timocrates?* The student's declamation problem?) Then there is another blank line, containing only the indecipherable mark ("§"), followed by notes on "adjacent headings" (*kephalaia sunora*), a reference to being "timely" (*eukairôs*), a reference to Demosthenes' procedure in some speech or passage (*hôs Dêmosth. en,* "as Demosthenes, in . . ."), notes that seem concerned with "final" procedures or headings (*teleutaion ethêke,* "finally he put"), and a note that may have to do with the alternative stasis of "dismissing the hypothesis" (in the papyrus, *ê exeinai hup-* , "or to dismiss the hyp- ").[58]

It is evident that several elements of rhetorical *technê,* what Isocrates might call *ideai,* are being discussed in the context of Demosthenic examples, perhaps mainly the example of *Against Timocrates,* and possibly in the context too of a declamation problem to be undertaken. The *technê* appears as immanent in the examples and problems under study, in particular manifestations, so that the student learns the *ideai* by becoming *empeiros,* "experienced," with them. It is also apparent, however, that such terms as "heading," "epicheireme," and "period" are being used as if already familiar. Our note taker seems to be a relatively advanced student who has heard those terms before.[59] It is probable that they have been introduced during the first stage of the student's training, during analytical-critical reading and progymnasmata, or that at the outset of second-stage training, in declamation exercises, the teacher introduced the *technē*'s main concepts and then has returned to them as needed, adding more complexity, detail, and additional concepts while the student worked through the analysis of examples and composed declamations. As Raffaella Cribiore remarks with reference to the "grammatical," or literary, education that preceded rhetorical training, instruction "proceeded in a circular motion, by revisiting previous material" (though "recursive" motion might be the better term: not a "circle" but an expanding "spiral").[60] Some such procedure seems to be reflected, too, in Cicero's *Topica* and *Orator,* which both begin with a rapid overview and then go through all the subjects addressed again in greater depth and detail.

A generally "recursive" procedure, however, does not necessarily imply a bald, preliminary narration in brief of the whole *technē*. If we take seriously Isocrates' analogy between athletic training and training in *logos,* it seems clear that there is no need for the trainer to prenarrate all the theoretical concepts embodied in the training, or even those that the trainee will eventually need to know. According to Cicero's Antonius, rhetoricians at the beginning stages of instruction are "like wet-nurses, who put only the most finely sliced pieces, chewed very small, into the mouths of baby boys" (*De oratore* 2.39.162); the precepts of the *technē* are introduced bit by bit, and the general framework is gradually built up. Moreover, in ancient schooling, the rhetorician was under no pressure to "deliver" a certain amount of "content" in a specified time; he worked individually with students, developing their capacities at their pace and according to their needs. As I think most teachers today will attest from their own experience, a "preview" of the technical concepts to be covered in a course has very limited value. It is very boring, since the student does not yet understand what is being previewed, and assures only that the student will, perhaps, remember and recognize the terms when they come back later, but little else. Further, the terms will be neither understood nor remembered until they are returned to, rehearsed, and handled repeatedly in practical experiences (*empeiriai*). In the case of our note taker, then, it is quite possible that no "preview" has been given, or only a very general one, and that the concepts he seems familiar with have been introduced entirely and repeatedly through the critical discussion of examples and exercises. In sum, the very fragmentary notes in this papyrus seem to confirm, or at least reflect, the "immanent" teaching of *technē* through commentary and discussion as the predominant form of sophistic "lecturing"—so that the various *ideai* emerge piecemeal, bit by bit, as relevant, and the whole *technē* comes progressively and slowly into view.

There is some probability that, in a sophistic school, and by implication the school of Isocrates, the preliminary discussion, reading/listening, and critical analysis of assigned texts, and the introduction of assigned writing/speaking exercises for individual students, generally took place in the morning. In the afternoon the sophist, and his assistants, if he had any, went over the students' work, in what modern pedagogy would call one-on-one conferences. Quintilian suggests that the teacher's declamations and the reading and analysis of texts can be delivered before the whole school, as a "banquet" from which each student takes what suits him, while only a "small time" (*modicum tempus*) is necessary to give each student his individual assignment for the day's work (*Institutio oratoria* 1.2.12).[61] Libanius in his *Autobiography* writes of his mornings being devoted to the same activities as "other instructors" (*didaskalois;* 108), and he remarks at one point that his school had so many students that "it was not possible to get through them all before sunset" (104); the context suggests that the number was more than thirty. That is, his mornings are normally devoted to *didaskalia* (instruction) and his afternoons to "going through" his students' work with them. In one of his letters, Libanius speaks of a former student whom he had "trusted" to share "the afternoon work"—he was one of the assistants or tutors that Libanius employed to help supervise the younger students' exercises.[62]

In *Oration* 5 (43–53),[63] Libanius mentions calling his students to school *prôiên,* "in the morning" (46), after several days of not meeting due to a festival of Artemis, which involved performances by boxers that his students could not resist. He was at that time holding school in the city council hall, the *bouleutêrion.* The students refused to come, claiming a premonitory fear, and Libanius excused them. With the morning instruction thus canceled again, one student seized the opportunity to go over his two-hundred-line composition with Libanius, and they had gone through forty lines when the entrance door suddenly collapsed, with large blocks of stone tumbling down—thus proving, Libanius writes, that the students' premonition was an intervention of the goddess, as many of them would have been killed. The point to note here, aside from the implication that Libanius' school was meeting in a space quite near the entrance of the *bouleutêrion* (portico, anteroom, main chamber?), is that he and this student were doing "afternoon work" that morning.[64]

In addition to "lecturing" and "conference," the sophist periodically declaimed, or gave "display" performances (*epideixeis*) of his own compositions, at least some of which would have been public; and there were, as well, occasions on which the more advanced students declaimed their compositions before their peers. Libanius refers to his own declamation performances as *theatra* (*Autobiography* 280). In late-antique and Byzantine writing *theatron* can mean either a "concert" performance (a "show") or the venue for such performance, from concert halls (*ôdeia*) to auditoria in public buildings, schools, or upper-class private houses. It seems that Isocrates restricted his performances to small groups of students, friends, and associates gathered at his school or in private houses, the sort of scene that, at the opening of Plato's *Phaedrus,* young Phaedrus has just come from, or the scene presented in *Protagoras,* in the courtyard of the house of Callias, where the sophist speaks and a discussion follows. Fifth- and fourth-century portrayals of sophistic activity, in Aristophanes and Plato, for example, suggest that such small-group performances were the norm for early-sophistic declamation generally, and not Isocrates only, though Isocrates was especially crowd-shy. He himself confesses to lacking the "confidence" required to speak in large public assemblies, and Pseudo-Plutarch reports an anecdote in which Isocrates was unwilling to admit to his *theatron* more than two persons, that is, presumably, two "guest" auditors in addition to his six to nine students. Zosimus, however, thinks that some of Isocrates' *logoi,* presumably those written as addresses to large assemblies, also were "displayed by others" (*epideiknuto di' allôn*) in larger venues.[65]

Suetonius mentions the rhetorician Marcus Antonius Gnipho, whose school Cicero attended "even when he held the praetorship," and writes that Gnipho "taught the precepts of eloquence on a daily basis, but declaimed only on market-days"; another teacher, named Princeps, gave instruction and declaimed on alternate days, and sometimes gave instruction in the morning and declaimed in the afternoon (*De grammatici et rhetoribus* 7.2, 4.6). Quintilian thinks the rhetorician should declaim on a daily basis—though this probably would include the presentation of models for analysis, including introduction, reading/listening, and discussion—and he describes the typical student declamation occasion (mornings? afternoons?) as a rambunctious event, with boys "standing up and exulting in applause" (*adsurgendi exultandque in laudando*) for their peers (*Institutio* 2.2.8–9). Being permitted to present a declamation to the school was a sort of "first publication" that resembled the sophist's public performances and was an honor. One was brought before one's classmates as a good example and a junior colleague of the master. Raffaella Cribiore notes that Libanius went over the drafts of his more advanced students' declamations, presumably making suggestions and corrections, and required a "final revision" and review before the student was permitted to declaim his composition "before the whole school"; the performance was then followed by discussion.[66] Quintilian, similarly, recommends that boys be allowed "sometimes" to declaim their compositions before the school and to "reap the fruit of their labor in the applause of many" as a reward, but only "when they have produced something more complete and polished" (*cum aliquid commodius elimaverint;* 2.7.5). The distinction here is with the declamations of beginners, which are sketched out in advance by the teacher (2.6.5).

It is, perhaps, risky to project the pattern of later sophistic teaching, and Roman as well as Greek, backward to Isocrates, even if one considers him the "teacher of all rhetoricians." But I think the pattern is, in general outlines, consistent with Isocrates' account of himself as teaching a philosophic *logôn paideia* that is a sort of *technê* but not a *tetagmenê technê*. It is an art of producing rhetors, and of cultivating intelligence and character, that supplements the indispensable elements of natural talent and practical experience with preceptive instruction consisting of the things "that can be taught"—the identifiable *ideai* from which "all discourses" are composed—delivered through the critical discussion of examples as well as exercise. Isocrates says, at the start of *To Demonicus,* "You desire education (*paideias*), and I undertake to teach others (*paideuein allous*); you are ready to philosophize (*philosophein*), and I direct (*epanorthô*) those who philosophize" (*tous philosopountas;* 3). This brief remark, placed at the start of what traditionally was listed first in the Isocratean canon, captures Isocrates' sense of the pedagogical contract. Isocrates presents two aspects of the teaching he offers to those wishing to "philosophize" (that is, to discourse on matters open to discussion): *paideia,* "education," which he elsewhere identifies with the preceptive or instructional aspect of *philosophia* (*Antidosis* 190–192), and *epanorthôsis,* "direction," in the sense of "correction" or "straightening" the student's work.[67] These two aspects correspond to "lecturing" or critical discussion of readings (in the mornings?) and going through his students' written work with them (in the afternoons?).

Finally, we catch a glimpse of Isocrates teaching and "declaiming" in the long and often-noted digression near the end of the *Panathenaicus* (200–265). Having nearly completed the discourse, he says, he was "revising" it (*epênôrthoun*) with "three or four youths" (*meirakiôn triôn ê tettarôn*) who were "accustomed to train with me" (*ethismenôn moi sundiatribein*), namely, his students (200). Then, while they were "going through" it (200), he decided to call in a former student likely to provide a useful counterperspective to his arguments. This person, having "read through" (201) the discourse beforehand, comes and engages Isocrates in a debate about the propriety of some of his claims, with the students present. At the end the students think Isocrates has debated well, but Isocrates is not satisfied that they have judged correctly (229–230). After stewing for a few days, he calls in a group of his former students, including his disputant, to ask whether he should revise and finish the discourse or abandon it. A reading is given (*anegnôsto ho logos;* 233)—this would have taken several hours[68]—and the assembled graduates declare it a successful *epideixis* (a "display" speech), but the disputant offers a shrewder analysis (233–263). This remarkable passage has been compared to the scene in Plato's *Protagoras* in which the assembled sophists dispute the propriety of some statements in a poem by Simonides, with Protagoras' students present (338e–347b); and it has been cited as the basis for arguments that Isocrates' pedagogy resembled the methods of the earlier sophists, featured group discussion, and was based on the analysis of his own writings.[69] Though that picture seems generally correct, one must qualify it by pointing out that Isocrates also stressed study of "all the celebrated poets and the sophists" in addition to the models he himself provided; and one might argue too that the scene in *Protagoras* is based on Isocrates, rather than the other way around, since Isocrates was Plato's main competitor and frequently his target, as in *Gorgias* and *Phaedrus*).

But a more important point is that *before* these sessions with his "graduates," Isocrates is "going through" and "revising" the text with "three or four youths" (*meirakia*) who are studying with him. He is "workshopping" the text with them, working through the process of creation, as he almost certainly does with their productions also. The term *meirakion* suggests a boy who has reached puberty but is under the age of twenty-one. Perhaps this particular group of *meirakia* is relatively young and at a less advanced stage of instruction, since Isocrates brings in others to do critique, refutation, and disputation, perhaps as a model for them, and their critical judgment seems limited, since Isocrates is not satisfied with their pronouncements. In sum, we see a teaching practice that seems to focus at low to intermediate levels on the analytic study and composition of discourse, examining and practicing the uses of *ideai*, and at higher levels on critical judgment and the disputation of issues.

I have spent time on these matters to frame the question of what role a written *technê*, a handbook, would play in such a pedagogy. One answer may be "Not much," but another would be "Not nothing." Alongside Plato's picture of Phaedrus carefully thumbing the pages of Tisias' *technê*, we place Libanius' (and Quintilian's and everyone else's) noninclusion of a *technê* in his recommended reading lists. It seems that a written *technê*, a handbook, was not a primary teaching material, but *technai* certainly were written, and evidently must have had a use. What, then, were they for?

Primarily a sophist might write a *technê*, or compile a collection of *technai*, for his own use. A written *technê* served as a reference guide or *aide-memoire* for teaching, in short, a "teacher's manual" or "toolbox" containing an organized, and thus memorizable and searchable, collection of "the things that can be taught" and a stock of explanations and examples—in essence, an inventional grid for commentary and guidance. Further, the sophist's written *technê*, or a collection of *technai*, could be made available to students as a "reminder" (*hupomnêma*) of their lessons or as reference and review material, not unlike the "outlines" and "hornbooks" sold in modern law-school bookstores.[70]

Some such notion is arrived at in the closing pages of Plato's *Phaedrus*, a dialogue all about the status of written speeches and written *technai*. As Socrates argues through the myth of Theuth (274b–278b), the written text cannot convey real knowledge of its subject matter but can function as a "reminder" for those who know and have had experience of the things referred to. Likewise, as noted in the preceding chapter, Cicero's Crassus in *De oratore* insists that text-book rules are of little use to anyone but the person with real, experiential knowledge: an *ars* memorializes and organizes what one has learned through training and experience and assists critical awareness and reflection by putting names to things. The "letter to Alexander" that prefaces the *Rhetoric to Alexander* presents the *technê* as just such a thing, a compilation of "reminders" (*hupomnêmata*) of the sophist's lessons for "Alexander's" use supplemented with materials from "the rest of the *technê*-writers, if anyone has written anything subtle on these same matters," including the author's own *technai* "written for Theodectes" and the rhetoric of Corax, or so he says (1421a–b).

A *technê* could also be compiled by the students themselves, from their notes. Thus Quintilian complains that there are two unauthorized "rhetorics of Quintilian" in circulation, one derived from notes taken by someone's steno-graphic slaves at a "discussion" (*sermonem*) of two days' duration—a sort of short seminar—and the other from notes taken over "many days indeed" (*pluribus sane diebus*) by some students who were "too fond of me" (*nimium amantes mei;* 1.Pr.7).[71] The *Rhetoric to Alexander* author suggests that his own *technê* derives from what "Nicanor explained to us" (*hêmin edêlôse;* 1421a). *Hêmin,* "to us," might be read as the authorial "we," but the author of this preface consistently refers to himself in the first-person singular. If *hêmin* is an inclusive we, the implication is that the author and "Alexander" have studied under "Nicanor" together and the *Rhetoric to Alexander* is a record of "Nicanor's" instruction (with supplements). Who "Nicanor" might be is unknown. The name is prob-ably fictive or a cover or corruption for some other name. But even if fictive, the idea that the author has written up the teachings of "Nicanor" as a mem-orandum of instruction and as a basis for his own *technê* seems to reflect com-mon assumptions about the sources, authorship, and purposes of *technai.* A similar case is Cicero's *De inventione,* which is generally thought to be a writeup from his schoolboy notes of his rhetoric teachers' lessons. In all such cases the written *technê* is a second-order production that, in the student's experience, follows rather than precedes the process of artistic training under a sophist's guidance and serves to reinforce that training or the conceptual framework it employs.[72]

A written *technê,* then, might be compiled by a sophist, primarily for his own use as a teaching resource, or, secondarily, as a review guide for his students, or eventually as a published review guide and/or teacher's resource for a wider audience. A *technê* also might be compiled by the students themselves as their own review guide; for use in their own teaching, should they become profes-sional rhetoricians; or for publication, should they wish to stake a claim to pro-fessional authority. Written *technai* seem to be primarily "reference material," while the sophist's "lectures"—his analyses and discussions of exemplar texts—and his "guidance/correction" of student work remain the fundamental medium of instruction. If that is correct, it seems that the primary audience for a published *technê* was other rhetoricians, as copies circulated from rhetorician to rhetorician, and from school to school, and some eventually found their ways into private collections and the great libraries while others disappeared. Quintilian, with his magisterial overview of virtually all the extant *technai* in his day, would be the perfect example of who and what the published *technai* primarily were for.

Did Isocrates Write the *Technê of Isocrates*?

Let us now return to the original question: Was there a *technê* of Isocrates? To grant Barwick his due, one must admit that there is no certain, irrefutable evidence that there was, unless and until a certifiably genuine *Rhetoric of Isocrates* turns up in a medieval manuscript somewhere or in a battered papyrus fragment. Nevertheless I think it probable that there was. In the first place, considering the observations already made in this discussion, it seems quite clear that there was an Isocratean *technê*, an art, in the sense of a body of precepts that probably included instruction in basic rhetorical *ideai*, exercised in what later rhetoric would call *progymnasmata*, as well as more advanced instruction in the creative use and combination of *ideai* in particular cases, corresponding to the later notion of "declamation" (*meletê*, "practice"). Further, the treatment of principles in this more advanced instruction probably was divided into what Dionysius of Halicarnassus would later call—citing Isocrates as the source—the *pragmatikos topos* (domain of inquiry, invention, and arrangement) and the *lektikos topos* (domain of style). There clearly was a teaching, a body of precepts and a training program, that Isocrates transmitted to his students, and they to theirs, and so on, so that Cicero's Antonius could declare him "the teacher of all rhetoricians."

But did Isocrates himself write a *technê*? Again, the evidence is equivocal. Even the ancients think so. Quintilian, who has seen and read something with a title like *Art of Rhetoric of Isocrates*, at one point cites it as the origin of the notion that rhetoric is a "faculty" (*dunamis*) for speaking persuasively, adding the qualifier "if indeed the *Art* which is in circulation is really his" (*si tamen re vera ars quae circumfertur eius est; Institutio oratoria* 2.15.4). Elsewhere, however, he cites it without any expressed doubt that it is genuine (for example, 3.5.18). Similarly, Zosimus mentions Isocrates' *technê* at the end of a discussion of the spurious works attributed to Isocrates, which he says "are not to be admitted alongside the received ones,"[73] but he argues too that Isocrates' *technê* did exist, on the grounds that Aristotle mentioned it in his *Sunagôgê Technôn*.

I think it plausible to probable that Isocrates wrote a *technê*, if only as a compilation of notes for use within his school. That does not seem hard to imagine for a man who lived so completely through the written word, a man so painfully shy that he could not speak in public but wrote and circulated his "speeches" in manuscript copy and existed in the public eye primarily as a text.[74] Dionysius of Halicarnassus, in the biographical note that begins his essay on Isocrates, writes, "Having inherited the discipline of discourse [*tên askêsin tôn logôn*] in a confused state [*pephurmênen*] from the sophists associated with Gorgias and Protagoras, he was the first to turn it from eristics and natural philosophy to political discourses [*tous politikous*], and he concentrated on and developed [*dietelesen*] the knowledge [*epistêmên*] from which, as he himself says [*hôs phêsin autos*], the ability to determine, say, and do what is beneficial comes to students" (*Isocrates* 1). The assertion that Isocrates was "the first" to focus rhetoric on "political discourses," a point that Pseudo-Plutarch makes (*Life of Isocrates* 837b), may seem to overlook the contributions of the early sophists. It may be true, however, that Isocrates was "first" to make the art's preeminent concern *politikos logos,* especially symbouleutic *logos* devoted to questions in political philosophy and policy—an emphasis that Aristotle echoes in his *Rhetoric* (1.1.10).[75] Isocrates may well have been the first sophist, or one of the first, to abandon or deemphasize the sort of metaphysical speculation that still can be seen in Gorgias and Antiphon.[76] Likewise the idea that Isocrates developed an *epistêmê* may sound un-Isocratean, until we recall that Dionysius meant a knowledge that supports beneficial deliberation, speech, and action in civic matters, or in other words a knowledge of the *ideai* of civic discourse, which Isocrates says can be obtained from a proper teacher (*Against the Sophists* 16). In short, Isocrates "developed" an *epistêmê* of the things "that can be taught" and, according to Dionysius, was the first to do so.

More important is Dionysius' assertion that Isocrates inherited the discipline (*askêsis*) of discourse "in a confused state" from Protagoras, Gorgias, and those associated with them. This does not mean that Isocrates' predecessors had made a mess of things, but that they had bequeathed to him a disparate collection of materials from different sources that no one yet had synthesized and organized. The fragmentary nature of the early sophistic *technai* is reflected in the *Phaedrus's* "review" of them (266d–267d): to Tisias and Gorgias is attributed a doctrine of the parts of an oration and the notion of proof from probability; to Theodorus of Byzantium the notions of supplementary proof and supplementary refutation; to Prodicus and Hippias something about speaking long and short and at appropriate length; to Evenus of Paros the notions of "insinuation" and "indirect praise"; to Polus such devices as "redoubled" speech, sententious speech, and imagistic speech; to Protagoras a treatise on *Correct Diction;*[77] to Thrasymachus of Chalcedon instructions on emotive speech and pathetic appeals; and so on. This fragmentariness is reflected also, if less clearly, in Cicero's brief overview of Aristotle's *Sunagôgê Technôn* (in *Brutus* 46–48): Tisias and Corax treated the parts of an oration and probability; Gorgias and Protagoras treated disputation on general themes, and Antiphon wrote "similar" things (and, as Michel Gagarin suggests, made some contributions to legal theory and was the first to write judicial speeches for others);[78] Lysias taught for awhile before taking up logography, and, as Pseudo-Plutarch adds (*Life of Lysias* 836b), he produced some *technai rhêtorikai;* and then Isocrates appeared. This account of a fragmentary, piecemeal accumulation of precepts is confirmed in the closing chapter of Aristotle's *Sophistical Refutations.* There, while "apologizing" for his work as only a beginning, he argues that "all other arts" (*allas hapasas technas*) have begun from small discoveries and developed "bit by bit" (*kata mêros*), and gives as his example rhetoric. This art, he says, was first developed by Tisias and other sophists, and since then "many men have contributed many parts" (*polloi polla sunenênochasi merê*), so that now "the art has a certain magnitude" or fullness (*echein ti plêthos tên technên;* 34/183b).

Both Dionysius and the apparent "plot" of Aristotle's *Sunagôgê Technôn* suggest that the piecemeal accumulation of sophistic *technai* of the late fifth to early fourth centuries B.C.E. reached a synthesis and completion, as well as a new departure, in Isocrates. As Dionysius states, Isocrates "developed" (*dietelesen*) the teachable knowledge that supports and helps to train the rhetorical *dunamis.* The verb *dietelesen* (*diateleô*) more specifically signifies "bring to an end, accomplish, complete, continue." Isocrates, then, "developed" the art in the double sense that he carried forward what he had received "in a confused state" from the fragmentary *technai* of his predecessors and brought it to an "accomplished" or "completed" state for the first time. He was the first to give the rhetorical *technê* what would afterward be, in the sophistic tradition, its basic form. Aristotle's remark that rhetoric has reached "a certain magnitude" or fullness (or "critical mass") reflects this sense of a culmination, as does his apparent placement of Isocrates last in the *Sunagôgê*'s evolutionary tale.[79]

The *Art of Rhetoric of Isocrates,* or whatever the title was of the work Quintilian read and Photius may have seen, could conceivably have been written by Isocrates himself, or like the "rhetorics of Quintilian" circulating in Quintilian's day, it could have derived from Isocrates' students, or one of them, as a writeup from notes of the teacher's *technê.* If Isocrates wrote it, he probably intended it for use within the school: his criticisms of those who teach *logos* as if it were a *tetagmenê technê* and who have published *technai* suggests a skepticism about the usefulness of a published handbook—though his objection may simply be that those *technai* are too rigid, too narrow, too simpleminded.

The ancient sources suggest dissemination through his students. Biographies mention that the young Demosthenes sought to become a student of Isocrates but could not afford the fee, so he offered to pay one-fifth for a fifth of the instruction. Isocrates declined, saying that his *technê* could not be cut in slices and sold like fish. So Demosthenes studied instead under Isaeus, who had been

Isocrates' student, and at some later point, as Plutarch records, he "secretly" (*krupha*) obtained the *technê* of Isocrates from Callias of Syracuse.[80]

While there is considerable doubt about the reliability of all such tales, this particular one may not be *completely* fanciful, though it probably is mostly fanciful, a sort of parable, or chreia. It derives from Plutarch and Dionysius of Halicarnassus as well as Pseudo-Plutarch, who drew from the third-century B.C.E. historian Hermippus of Smyrna and wrote, among other things, biographies of Isocrates' famous students, drawing his information from the fourth-century historian Ctesibus, who wrote from within living memory of Isocrates, Isaeus, and Demosthenes.[81] Dionysius, himself a generally solid scholar, remarks that Hermippus reports only two facts about Isaeus—that he was a student of Isocrates and a teacher of Demosthenes—but he considers Hermippus "accurate in other matters" and thus reliable if skimpy on Isaeus (*Isaeus* 1).[82] As Jan Bollansée has argued, Hermippus shares the penchant of most ancient biographers (for example, Diogenes Laertius) for piquant anecdotes, whether or not they are true. But the bare idea that Isocrates taught Isaeus and Isaeus taught Demosthenes is not a piquant anecdote.[83] To that is added, as ornament, such improbable anecdotes as young Demosthenes' encounter with Isocrates and Isocrates' remark about slices of fish. Perhaps the very paucity of Hermippus' factual information on Isaeus is evidence that he is not inventing beyond what was reported by his fourth-century sources.

But even if that tale about Isaeus is itself an apocryphal invention, it illustrates the ancient understanding of the probable means of dissemination for Isocrates' *technê*. Moreover, it is not difficult to conjecture a number of pathways for that dissemination. These would include Isocrates' adopted son Aphareus and Isocrates' student Cephisodorus, as both, according to Dionysius (*Isocrates* 18), wrote defenses of Isocrates against Peripatetic criticisms and seem to have been passionate about his reputation. Another possibility would be Isocrates of Apollonia in Pontus, whom Speusippus' *Letter* and the *Suda* describe as Isocrates' successor; or Naucrates, another student, whom Quintilian thinks was the first to use the word *stasis* as a rhetorical term and therefore must have written a *technê*. One might also name the historians Theopompus and Ephorus, or other less famous persons said to have been Isocrates' students, such as Lacritus of Phaselis (Demosthenes, *Against Lacritus* 15, 40). And so on.

Even if some, or most, of the anciently reputed "students of Isocrates" are apocryphal inventions, and some no doubt are, the basic point remains. Isocrates very certainly had students, some of whom went on to become rhetors or rhetoricians, some of them notable, and any of these could have been vectors for the transmission of the Isocratean *technê*.[84]

One might also consider the famous anecdote reported by both Cicero and Quintilian (and included in this chapter's epigraphs) that, when Aristotle began to lecture on rhetoric in the mid-350s, he said, "It would be shameful to keep silent and permit Isocrates to speak" (*De oratore* 3.141; *Institutio oratoria* 3.1.14). The point of this story is that Aristotle began to lecture on rhetorical *technê* specifically to compete with Isocrates, and that Isocrates' *technê* must therefore have been "speaking," circulating, already in public space. More than a decade later, the *Letter of Speusippus'* criticism of Isocrates for violating the principles of his own *technê* suggests the same. As Quintilian remarks, when Aristotle began his lectures, Isocrates was already old, and many of his students were themselves already eminent. In 355, in fact, he would have been eighty-one, would have been teaching for at least thirty-five years, and would have completed nearly all of his extant major *logoi* (all but *Antidosis, To Philip, Panathenaicus,* and six letters). In his letter *To the Children of Jason,* written about 359 and thus a few years before Aristotle's first lectures on rhetoric, Isocrates introduces a rhetorical principle that he "customarily" teaches in his school, and adds, "I would be ridiculous if, while I see others using what is mine [*tous allous horôn tois emois chrômenous*], I alone should refrain from saying what I have said before" (7–8). By 359, then, his *technê* already is in circulation and is being "used" and imitated by other teachers.

Even a fraction of the different possibilities suggested here would imply a wide dissemination, both of the original Isocratean *technê* and, eventually, of its various imitators and successors. I conclude, then, that there was a *Technê of Isocrates,* and that it probably was the ancestor of the later sophistic *technai.*

The student must learn the forms [*eidê*] of discourse and
become practiced in their uses, while the teacher must explain
them as thoroughly as possible, so as to leave out nothing that
can be taught.

Isocrates, Against the Sophists *17*

What Would It Contain?

This chapter is admittedly speculative, or, if you will, an exercise in probabilistic conjecture. I propose to consider what the *Technê of Isocrates* may have contained. The main sources of evidence are, on one hand, scattered testimonies by
other writers and, on the other, the fragments and traces of preceptive *technê* that
appear in Isocrates' extant writings. The *Rhetoric to Alexander,* moreover, emerges
as a fairly good index to the contents of the Isocratean *technê,* and indeed is
probably based on it, as Pierre Chiron has recently suggested.[1] I will proceed
according to the division between "preliminary exercises" (*progumnasmata*) and
declamation (*meletê,* "practice") and the main divisions that Dionysius of Halicarnassus has attributed to the Isocratean *technê:* the *pragmatikos topos* and the *lektikos topos.*

Prolegomenon: Philosophical Justifications and Definitions

If a *technê* has a "foreword," it is usually brief, and it is sometimes in the form of
a letter to a supposed recipient. It typically provides some general definition
of the art, extols its value, and lays out a few basic concepts. The "letter from
Aristotle to Alexander" that now prefaces the *Rhetoric to Alexander* is generally
considered a "forgery" (an ethopoiea) that was added to the text when it was
assimilated into the Aristotelian corpus, probably in the second century C.E.[2]
But the "letter" easily could have incorporated material from the original prolegomenon, if there was one, while changing the speaker and addressee. There
certainly isn't much about it that seems especially Aristotelian. It begins with an
encomium of *logos,* and of the art of *politikos logos* as "the mother-city itself of
good deliberation" (*tên mêtropolin autên tou kalôs bouleuesthai;* 1420a–1421a), and

follows this, in language reminiscent of Isocrates, with an exhortation to "hold fast to the philosophy of *logos*" (*tês tôn logôn antechesthai philosophias*). It ends with an injunction to keep the *technê* private lest "the Parian sophists" plagiarize it (1421a) and a note on the *technê*'s sources in the teachings of "Nicanor," the author's earlier writeup for Theodectes, and the rhetoric of Corax (1421b). Such material, especially the encomium and the exhortation, reflects the sort of thing that might be said in a sophist's opening lecture to his newly admitted students or in a preliminary interview. Perhaps the *Technê of Isocrates* would have been prefaced in some such way as well.

I am not going to go deeply here into the "philosophy of rhetoric" that would have been broached in Isocrates' prolegomenon, essentially because much has been said already, not only in the preceding chapter but also in the scholarship on Isocrates in general. Indeed, Isocrates' notions of *philosophia* and *logôn paideia,* and his beliefs regarding practical wisdom, civic virtue, civic education, politics, language, epistemology, and the role of eloquence in human culture, have been the predominant concerns of much of the published scholarship, especially the more recent scholarship.[3] Yet these matters of general philosophy would have been the concerns of only part of his prolegomenon, perhaps a few pages, and would have taken up little more than the first day or two in a three- to four-year course of study—although, of course, such matters would recur in the students' exercises. Isocrates' *paideia* was meant to cultivate the student's capacities through repeated practical experiences (*empeiria*) over a period of years, not through the narration of a doctrine.

The prolegomenon could well have begun with something like the oft-cited "encomium of *logos*" that appears in *Nicocles* (5–9, c. 370 B.C.E.) and is repeated verbatim in *Antidosis* (253–257, c. 354). It is conceivable that in both cases the passage has been lifted from Isocrates' *technê:* they have the feel of something patched in from somewhere else, as a set commonplace. Possibly they represent an update of an earlier version that seems to be reflected in *Panegyricus* (47–50, c. 380). In both the *Panegyricus* version and the *Nicocles/Antidosis* version, *logos* is portrayed as the distinctive human endowment and "the cause of the greatest blessings" (*pleistôn agathôn aition; Antidosis* 253) because through the power (*dunamis*) of *logos* people are able to reason and communicate, persuade one another, form communities, and institute laws and civic structures, so that, as the *Panegyricus* version concludes, to be a "Hellene" (a Greek) is a matter not of "common blood" (*koinês phuseôs*) but of a shared enculturation through *logos* (50).

To these ideas Isocrates might have added his views regarding natural talent, experience/exercise, *paideia logôn,* and the pursuit of *philosophia* much as they appear in *Against the Sophists*—supplemented with an exhortation to study hard, such as appears in *To Demonicus* and *To Nicocles.*[4] As Isocrates notes in *Antidosis,* these are the sorts of things he says "to those who wish to study with me" (186); the locution suggests some sort of preliminary interview. Zosimus describes *To Demonicus* and *To Nicocles,* which he says are assigned "to children" (*pros paidas*) as "recommending the truth to all . . . just as Hesiod does when he says to his brother, 'Work, childish Perses!'"[5] Aphthonius, in his discussion of the chreia ("useful anecdote") exercise, develops as his example the saying attributed to Isocrates that "the root of education is bitter, but the fruits are sweet," which echoes ideas expressed at *To Demonicus* 47 but does not appear verbatim anywhere in his extant writings. Something along these lines, then, may well have been said in his prolegomenon.

It is possible that some version of Isocrates' prolegomenon is parodied in Plato's *Gorgias,* which may have been written not long after Isocrates opened his school and published *Against the Sophists* (c. 390 B.C.E.). In Plato's dialogue, when Chaerephon asks Gorgias what art he teaches, Gorgias' student Polus answers, "Many are the arts (*technai*) that among humankind have been discovered experientially from experiences; for experience makes our life proceed by art, and inexperience by chance," and so on, leading to an assertion that Gorgias "partakes of the finest of the arts" (*metechei tês kallistês tôn technôn;* 448c). One can hear an echo of Isocrates' statement in *Against the Sophists* that his *paideia logôn* makes speakers "more artful" than they otherwise would be and enables them to discover ideas that they otherwise would hit upon by chance (15). One can also hear a heavily parodic echo of Isocrates' emphasis on experiential learning—and a distant echo too of the praise of *logos* as the source of most of the blessings of civilized life, which certainly would make an art of *logos* the best and finest of all arts.

As the discussion proceeds, Socrates declares rhetoric a "public worker of persuasion" (*peithous dêmiourgos;* 452e), a definition Gorgias accepts. Notably Quintilian attributes this very view to the *Art of Rhetoric of Isocrates* and adds that Plato's *Gorgias* "says the same thing" (2.15.3–5). Could that have been Isocrates' definition of "rhetoric" in his prolegomenon? While one may suspect that either Quintilian or his source has confused Plato's parody with Isocrates' actual opinions, it is in fact possible to extract this definition, as an implication, from Isocrates' actual statements. His "encomium of *logos*" explicitly praises it as the medium through which people form civil communities by persuading one another; and he explicitly speaks of *philosophia* as an "artistic" *dunamis* for accomplishing that work (for example, *Against the Sophists* 14; *Antidosis* 186, 206, 255–257, 271). If that is so, then an artistic *philosophia* would indeed be a *peithous dêmiourgos,* a "worker" or shaper (*ourgos*) of the shared "persuasions" (beliefs, opinions, faiths) of the public (the *dêmos*). So it is conceivable that Isocrates' prolegomenon would have said such a thing, at least in an early version. It is hard to imagine that a student or successor writing up a *Technê of Isocrates* would invent for him a definition of rhetoric/*philosophia* that had already been satirized by Plato.

But while Isocrates may or may not have used the *peithous dêmiourgos* metaphor itself, he may well have used the line that Plato and Speusippus pounce on, and that Pseudo-Plutarch cites as Isocrates' idea of the function of rhetoric: as an "artistic *dunamis* of persuasive *logos,*" it has the power to make great things small and small things great, old things new and new things old, and so forth. In this we hear some echo of his fifth-century sophistic predecessors, particularly Protagoras' notion of "making the lesser case greater" or Gorgias' notion of philosophic argument effecting swift reversals of belief (*Helen* 13).

Would Isocrates' prolegomenon have said anything about rhetorical genres? His notion of rhetorical invention as a "creative process" that involves selecting and combining *ideai* to meet the needs of particular occasions suggests that he regards genres as mixable and malleable. Perhaps he said something resembling *Against the Sophists'* critique of those who teach *politikos logos* as if it were a *tetagmenê technê.* As Robert Sullivan has observed, Isocrates employs *idea* and the related word *eidos* as technical terms quite flexibly, sometimes meaning genre and sometimes features of style, figures of speech, parts of a discourse, and in general the small and large "elements" or "forms" of which discourses are composed.[6] The *Rhetoric to Alexander* uses these terms in similar fashion, though it also uses the non-Isocratean term *genos* for the major genres of rhetoric (demegoric/deliberative, dicanic/judicial, epideictic).

Despite his flexibility, Isocrates does have some definite ideas about genre. For example, in the early *Busiris* (c. 390) and two decades later in his *Encomium of Helen* (c. 370), he faults another writer—Polycrates in *Busiris* and what appears to be Gorgias in *Helen*—for improperly handling the *idea* or "form" of the encomium and then offers a demonstration of how it should be done.[7] Or again, at the beginning of *To Demonicus* (3–5), composed in the late 370s, Isocrates differentiates "protreptic" discourse (exhortation on behalf of a specific course of action) from "parainetic" discourse (general advice, in this case a series of moral precepts). "Protreptic" is the *Rhetoric to Alexander's* term for symbouleutic discourse, or what it calls demegoric, in support of a proposition. Since Isocrates says the function of "parainetic" is to "give advice" (*sumbouleuein*), it appears that he regards both parainetic and protreptic as subdivisions of symbouleutic. This accords with his actual practice. *To Demonicus* and *To Nicocles,* for example, are parainetics, while *Panegyricus, Areopagiticus, On the Peace,* and others are protreptics. Zosimus reflects this division by calling the former parainetics (*paraineseis*), while Photius reflects the general category by referring to them all, parainetics and protreptics alike, as symbouleutics.[8]

In *Antidosis* (45–50) Isocrates says the specific "modes of speech" (*tropoi logôn*), meaning prose, are no fewer than those of poetry, and he mentions genealogies of demigods, "philosophizing about the poets," histories of wars, and the dialogues of "dialecticians" (*antilogikous*). But rather than attempt "to enumerate all the *ideai* of prose," he proposes to concentrate instead on his own concerns.[9] He then develops a contrast between writing speeches "about private contracts" (*peri tôn idiôn sumbolaiôn*), meaning speeches for petty lawsuits, and writing speeches that are "Hellenic, political, and panegyrical" (*Hellênikous kai politikous kai panêgurikous*). This phrase can be taken to mean "political"—or public or civic—speeches that address general or "panegyric" (festival) audiences on issues of broad Hellenic concern, which is the line taken in the best available English translations.[10] But however one parses that phrase, it appears that for Isocrates the realm of rhetoric divides into two very basic *ideai*: the judicial (dicanic) discourse exemplified in the law courts, with its relatively narrow concerns (judgment of specific acts by individuals), and what he calls "political" or "panegyric" discourse, with its broader concerns and audiences. Political discourse, in turn, subdivides into symbouleutic ("advisory"/deliberative) discourse with parainetic and protreptic subtypes, and more purely encomiastic discourse devoted not to advice and exhortation but to praise/blame and commemoration, as in *Evagoras* or *Panathenaicus*.[11]

In short, Isocrates reduces the "modes of prose" to what all subsequent rhetorical tradition will recognize as the three basic genera of *rhêtoreia*—symbouleutic, encomiastic, judicial—though Isocrates' arrangement of the categories seems fundamentally dyadic:

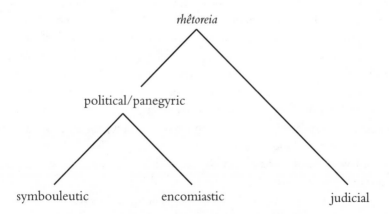

These basic *ideai* are of course the main categories represented in the traditional canon of Isocrates' extant *logoi* as transmitted in medieval manuscripts going back to Photius: the symbouleutics first, with the parainetics preceding the protreptics; the encomia second; and the judicial speeches third. To these probably should be added one more *idea*: the more "private" discourse of the letter, of which the Isocratean canon preserves nine examples and which

Isocrates probably taught.[12] Each of these basic types can incorporate a variety of *ideai,* depending on a discourse's purposes and situation, and they can incorporate one another. Encomiastic discourse is particularly suited to the amplification of values and beliefs in either symbouleutic or judicial; *To Philip* is a symbouleutic in the form of a letter; and so on. The Isocratean rhetor will regard each of the basic *ideai* as highly malleable and mixable, adaptable to specific situations, and capable of serving complex purposes.

An objection here is that Isocrates usually has been understood to despise the rhetoric of the courts, although according to the standard biography, he himself practiced it in his early career as a logographer. Would he have taught such discourse? The inclusion of six judicial orations in the Isocratean canon, three of which survive only as extracts, suggests that he did, especially if we assume that the canon represents the collection of model texts that he used with his students. Moreover, Isocrates' surviving judicial speeches are the only extant works he penned before he began his school, with the possible exceptions of *Busiris* and the *technê* itself. In 390, these texts and *Against the Sophists* would have constituted his whole portfolio, or all that we know of. If, as *Against the Sophists* argues, the rhetoric teacher must himself provide the paradigm for his students to imitate, what was Isocrates teaching to his students in that year?

That Isocrates taught judicial discourse is suggested, too, by the fact that three of his more famous reputed students—Isaeus, Hyperides, and Lycurgus—were active in the courts. Most of their preserved orations are judicial speeches concerned with lawsuits over private contracts, the very thing that Isocrates pooh-poohs in *Antidosis.* Whether any of these Attic orators were actually students of Isocrates may be disputed, but it is clear that at least one of his lesser-known students, Lacritus of Phaselis, practiced judicial rhetoric. Demosthenes' *Against Lacritus,* a commercial lawsuit over a broken contract, portrays Lacritus as a "student of Isocrates" (*Isokratous mathêtês*) and a "rascal sophist" (*kakourgos sophistês*) who paid Isocrates for instruction and now collects students and promises to teach them to escape from lawsuits (15, 39, 40, 41). Isocrates' own judicial speeches include such lawsuits: *On the Banker* (*Trapezeticus*), for example, is a lawsuit to recover a sum of money left on deposit with the banker Pasion, and *Aegineticus* involves an inheritance dispute.

One might invoke Isocrates' apparent declaration, in *Antidosis* (36–37), that—as it is usually rendered in English translations—he has never had anything to do with judicial discourse: an obvious falsehood, if that were what he meant.[13] If one translates more literally, however, what he actually says is, "I shall never be found to have been concerned *with such speeches*" (*peri tous logous tous toioutos*). What sort of speeches does he mean? In the passages leading up to this declaration, he is responding to the stock accusation leveled at sophists: that he trains young men "to gain advantage [*pleonektein*] in lawsuits contrary to justice" (30).

The word *pleonektein* can also carry the meanings of "defraud, be greedy, claim more than one's share," or in other words, to take advantage of someone and profit unjustly. Isocrates argues in reply that "no citizen has ever been harmed by my 'cleverness' or by my writings" (33). In short, he asserts not that he has never been involved with judicial discourse, but that he has never been involved with fraudulent, malicious lawsuits, or indeed with unjust, harmful discourse of any kind. He subsequently adds (37–38) that he has never appeared as a litigant in court or brought charges against anyone before the city magistrates. Those statements are essentially true, since all of his judicial speeches were written for others, since all his clients were, judging from the speeches, victims of unjust advantage taking, and since his only court appearance was as a defendant in the antidosis proceeding that prompted him to write the *Antidosis.*

In *Antidosis,* Isocrates does not really dismiss judicial discourse: after all, *Antidosis* is itself written in the form of a judicial discourse and is partly modeled on the *Apology* of Socrates. Rather, he dismisses *petty lawsuits,* especially malicious ones, as less conducive than the major forms of *logos politikos* to the cultivation of the intellectual and moral character required for genuine eloquence and good deliberation (see 48–50). Real eloquence arises from grand themes and requires a philosophic and poetic sensibility. This argument resonates with Isocrates' critique, in *Against the Sophists,* of those who teach *only* a narrow *technê* for judicial discourse. They deserve to be censured, he argues, because they have chosen to be "teachers of meddlesomeness and greed" rather than teachers of a *philosophia* that can benefit civil society (20).

Isocrates, in short, is open to the study and teaching of judicial discourse, as long as it is founded in the richer, more philosophic and poetic discipline of political-panegyric discourse—symbouleutic and encomiastic. Through these, he believes, it is possible to cultivate the sort of intellectual and moral character from which the capacity for genuine *rhêtoreia* can arise. It is possible that his prolegomenon would have said something along those lines and virtually certain that he directed at least some of his advanced students in the study of judicial speechmaking as a practical application of *philosophia.*

Finally, one may ask whether *Against the Sophists*—a polemical, programmatic statement of his pedagogical philosophy—could have been Isocrates' prolegomenon. The text as it stands seems clearly to have preceded something, though some have recently argued otherwise.[14] Isocrates breaks off just after announcing, "In order that I shall not seem to demolish the professions of others, but myself to claim more than is possible, I think that the very things by which I myself was persuaded will also make clear to others that what I say is true" (22). As David Mirhady has pointed out, Isocrates makes the same gesture in *Busiris* (9) and *Encomium of Helen* (15), precisely at the point where he turns from criticism of others to his demonstration of "how it should be done."[15] It is an *idea*, a "figure," for a particular type of transition. In *Against the Sophists*, what followed may have been a more complete elucidation of his pedagogical philosophy, very possibly with material that has been "replaced" by or reused in the later *Antidosis*; or an outline of his teaching program; or a version of his *technê*, which would have ceased to be used and recopied when it had been rendered obsolete by newer *technai*.

What is less often observed is that *Against the Sophists* not only ends as a fragment but possibly begins as one as well, though here the criterion admittedly is more subjective. The text seems to lack a proper introduction—the opening feels more like a transition than a proemium—as Isocrates abruptly launches into a critique of those who teach eristic (dialectic). It thus appears to be an extract lifted from some other context. Was it part of the prolegomenon? Considering the likelihood that Isocrates compiled his *technê* for his own use or for the internal purposes of the school—as "reference" material—and that *Against the Sophists* was intended for public circulation as a polemical manifesto and advertisement, and considering too Isocrates' promise to present the arguments "by which I myself was persuaded," I think it most reasonable to guess that the text it was extracted from was more like *Antidosis*, although the surviving fragment does contain some lines of argument that very probably would have been used in his introductory remarks to students.

It is possible that Isocrates' *technê* had *no* prolegomenon, or a very brief one, as in his extant letter to Alexander. But if he, or a student who compiled and published a *Technê of Isocrates*, did write a prolegomenon, one may conjecture that it contained an encomium of *logos*, defined rhetoric/*philosophia* as an artistic *dunamis* for persuasive speech and writing on public issues, argued in the manner of *Against the Sophists* for his notion of *logôn paidea*, recognized a broad division into political (symbouleutic and encomiastic) and judicial discourse, and centered instruction on the former.

[Pro]gymnasmata: Preliminary Exercises, *Ideai,* and the Foundations of *Philosophia*

As I argued earlier, Isocrates' younger students probably spent their first year or two studying the writings of celebrated authors and Isocrates' own *logoi* while doing what later tradition would recognize as progymnasmata. As I noted earlier, the earliest recorded use of the term "progymnasmata" is in the *Rhetoric to Alexander* (28 1436a): "When the common functions and uses of all the *eidê* are known to us, if we habituate and train [*gumnasômen*] ourselves to take them up as in the progymnasmata [*kata ta progumnasmata*], they shall supply us with great abundance [*pollên euporian*] in both writing and speaking." The author's diction and conceptual frame are reminiscent of Isocrates, and very possibly derived from him;[16] and the notion of "training" oneself through "preliminary exercises" (*pro-gumnasmata*), practicing the basic forms to automaticity, is mentioned in passing as something unproblematically familiar. The *Rhetoric to Alexander* has been dated to shortly or not long after 341 B.C.E., near the end of Isocrates' life (339/8).[17] If it is not an interpolation, the reference to progymnasmata suggests that some form of these exercises already was well established in Isocrates' lifetime, though his preferred terms, like those of Aelius Theon centuries later, are *gumnasma* and *gumnasia,* "exercise."[18]

In what follows I take the traditional list of progymnasmata, chiefly as it appears in Theon, as a rough heuristic for considering what might have been taught by Isocrates. If Isocrates was the "teacher of all rhetoricians," as Cicero writes, one can consider the classical set of exercises to have evolved from Isocratean prototypes. As George Kennedy observes, Theon's first-century C.E. handbook reflects a stage of development preceding the more or less standardized sequence of exercises that appears in the later handbooks of Hermogenes in the second century, Aphthonius in the fourth, and Nicolaus the Sophist in the fifth. At the same time Theon is more complete than the later handbooks, as he discusses teaching methods as well as the exercises themselves. As mentioned, Theon speaks of the exercises he discusses as "already transmitted," which suggests that they were more or less traditional by his time. Glancing references to the progymnasmata at earlier stages, mainly by Roman sources (for example, the *Rhetorica ad Herennium,* Cicero's *De inventione,* Quintilian, and Suetonius' *De grammaticis et rhetoribus*), do not provide a clear list and suggest a certain fluidity, but a significant number of the later-standard exercises appear and seem to have been established relatively early in the Hellenistic period—between the late fourth century B.C.E. and the Roman encounter with Greek rhetoric in the second and first centuries. These include maxim/chreia, fable/narration, refutation/confirmation, description, ethopoiea (speaking in character), commonplace, encomium, and thesis.[19] At least some of these early-established exercises probably go back to the fourth century B.C.E., and to Isocrates, if not earlier.

Maxim/Chreia, and the Parainetics

The later manuals differentiate the chreia and maxim exercises, but Theon lumps them together in a single chapter on chreia and places it first as the gateway to rhetorical instruction.[20] A chreia, he says, is a "useful" (*chreiôdês*) saying or anecdote: "Bion the sophist said that the love of money is the mother-city of all evil"; "Diogenes the Cynic philosopher, when he saw a boy eating delicacies, beat the boy's pedagogue with his staff." Theon makes efforts to distinguish maxim and chreia, but nevertheless does not treat maxim as a separate exercise.

This suggests that the distinctions are novel for him, and that at earlier stages any "useful saying" was regarded as a chreia, whether it took the form of a freestanding maxim or an anecdote. This seems to be Isocrates' attitude in *To Nicocles:* "Some of the poets of earlier times have left precepts that are useful for living" (*chrê zên;* 3). Isocrates is thinking of the maxims (*gnômai*) of the gnomic poets.

The point of the chreia is that it provides a prompt for moral-philosophical reflection that, as Theon says, is "useful" for the proper conduct of one's life. The young student is to draw the appropriate "lesson," explain its wisdom or truth, praise it, amplify it, contradict it, or simply restate it in various forms. These activities are "useful" in at least two ways. First (as Theon suggests), they help to cultivate the student's moral sensibility through performative repetition and reinscription of received wisdoms, and second, they build up over time an abundant supply of culturally authoritative moral-philosophical *topoi* that later may be invoked in complex discourse as premises for argumentation and deliberation.

It is possible that Isocrates' *logôn paideia* began with something along these lines. As I have already noted, Zosimus remarks that Isocrates' parainetics—*To Demonicus, To Nicocles,* and *Nicocles*—are meant "for children" (*pros paidas*), that is, for young students at the beginning of rhetorical instruction, and thus are "weak in expression" compared with his other *logoi*. Moreover, says Zosimus, they "deal with matters of character" that must come first in a student's training, just as a farmer must prepare his fields for planting by eliminating weeds and other things that ruin them.[21] They are *preliminaries.* Zosimus reflects how the Isocratean *logoi* actually are used in the schoolroom in his own time and how their pedagogical intentions are understood in the still-living tradition that he inherits.

As all readers of the parainetics recognize, each consists for the most part not of complex or extended argument, nor anything resembling a "treatise," but of a loosely organized collection of moral and political-philosophical precepts, following a preamble (though the preambles get progressively longer and more elaborate). *To Demonicus* addresses a wealthy young man on the threshold of adult responsibilities and offers guidance on how the private citizen may live honorably;[22] *To Nicocles* addresses, ostensibly, the young king of Cyprus on the threshold of assuming his kingly duties and counsels him on how to govern justly; and *Nicocles* presents an imaginary speech by Nicocles to his Cypriot subjects—supposedly delivered after Isocrates has spoken on the ruler's duties—in which Nicocles justifies the legitimacy of his rule and counsels his subjects on the duties of citizens to the sovereign power when it is legitimate, or, more precisely, on the necessarily cooperative relation between citizens and rulers in a successful, thriving state.[23] Along the way there are reflections on the nature of democracy, oligarchy, and monarchy, and the problems and advantages of each, as well as matters of piety, duty to parents, choosing friends, education, and so on. Notably it is Nicocles, the one destined to kingly power, who is told that he must become familiar with all the celebrated authors and make himself a critic of the lesser and a competitor of the greater, if he is to "rightly rule and properly govern the state" (*To Nicocles* 17). This is advice for any young man with political ambitions. Together, then, the parainetics offer the beginning student a primer in moral and political philosophy.

The other feature of the parainetics that is evident to every reader is that, as loosely organized strings of moral and political precepts, they are prose versions of the gnomic poetry of Theognis, Hesiod (in *Works and Days*), and others. These, with Homer and the lyric poets, were the traditional backbone of Hellenic education in the fifth and fourth centuries, the old-style education that Aristophanes caricatures as "Better Argument" in *Clouds*. Boys learned, recited, sang, and sometimes chorally performed at festivals, moralizing verses from the "celebrated" poets as an essential part of their civic enculturation. Indeed, many of the precepts Isocrates provides are paraphrases from gnomic poetry, Theognis in particular. Thus Isocrates' *logôn paideia* picks up where the traditional education of young boys leaves off, and with the kind of material that in later centuries would come to form the basis of the maxim and chreia exercises.

Isocrates' parainetics, despite their loose thematic organization, may have been easier for young students to memorize and recite than bare lists of premises organized by logical category, such as we find in Aristotle's catalogue of "particular premises," because of their quasi-poetic rhythmic style, their redundancy, and their relatively limited length: Instead of a moral-philosophical treatise, and instead of a comprehensive catalogue of maxims, the beginning student is presented with three "speeches" resembling the poetry of Theognis or Hesiod.[24] But the students probably did more than memorize and recite. First of all, the parainetics, like gnomic poetry, provided instructive sayings that could be critically discussed in school, as in the discussion of some gnomic lines from Simonides in Plato's *Protagoras,* and worked up in various writing exercises.

According to Theon, a student is "exercized" (*gumnazontai*) in chreias "by restatement [*apangeliai*], by inflection [*klisei*], by supplemental statement [*eiphônesi*], by counterstatement [*antilogiai*]; and we lengthen and shorten the chreia [*epekteinomen kai sustellomen*], and in addition we refute and confirm it" (*anaskeuazomen kai kataskeuazomen*).[25] At least some of these operations are exemplified in Isocrates' parainetics. I begin with "restatement." This activity, as Theon describes it, includes both verbatim repetition of the chreia and paraphrase, so that the student practices recasting the same idea in different terms. This could include taking a maxim from a poet and restating it in prose:

> Prefer to dwell with little wealth, as a pious man,
>> Than to be rich with unjustly gotten money.
> In righteousness is the sum of all virtue,
>> And every man is good, Kyrnos, when he is just.
>> (Theognis, *The Theognidea* 145–148)

Be more satisfied with honest poverty than unjust riches, for justice is much better than wealth . . . and while foul men may be wealthy, the depraved can have no share in justice. (*To Demonicus* 38)

The general point of restatement seems to be both familiarization with the language of the original statement, through reciting it or copying it in writing, and developing stylistic fluency, through paraphrasing and recasting the material in different ways.

"Inflection," in Theon, involves rewriting the same statement in different grammatical forms. It is thus an extension of the "restatement" activity, as well as of prerhetorical instruction in literary Greek (*grammatikê,* "grammar"). One of Theon's examples is the rather arbitrary process of converting singular forms to the obsolete dual, an ancient, "Homeric" form that had dropped out of everyday spoken Greek but was preserved in poetry and used as an ornament in literary prose.[26] The main point is to exercise the student's dexterity and fluency in managing the forms of the literate dialect as well as its vocabulary. There is no direct evidence of this grammatical kind of exercise in Isocrates' writing. For him it may not have been conceptually distinguishable from the "restatement" exercise, since grammatical analysis was fairly rudimentary in his day. (Consider Aristotle's discussion of grammar in *Poetics* 20–21, which is probably an advance over Isocrates, but still primitive.) It does seem likely, however, that Isocrates would have done something to promote syntactic fluency and variety, and enriched diction, at least when working with beginners.

Theon's next activity, "supplemental statement" or epiphonema (*epiphônêsis*), involves adding a suitable remark—one that "appropriately and briefly" affirms or explicates or demonstrates "what is said by the chreia."[27] Epiphonemas are everywhere in Isocrates' parainetics; they occur on virtually every page. One example will suffice:

[MAXIM:] Take care for everything that concerns your life, but especially the training of your intelligence [*phronêsin*];
[EPIPHONEMA:] for a good mind in a human body is a very great thing in a very small one. (*To Demonicus* 40)

This activity accomplishes at least two things. On one hand, it cultivates yet another form (*idea*) of "twofold statement," beyond the kinds cultivated by "restatement." On the other hand, it also begins to cultivate a habit of enthymematic invention, since the epiphonema is in essence either a "demonstration" (*apodeixis*) of the truth, value, or significance of the chreia's saying or a "conclusion" projecting a stance in response to it. Isocrates' parainetics, like gnomic poetry, provide plenty of examples of standalone maxims to which an epiphonema could be added, but epiphonemas themselves can be given further epiphonemas: "A good mind in a human body is a very great thing in a very small one, for . . ."

Paired with "supplemental statement," in Theon, is "counterstatement" or contradiction (*antilogia,* which he elsewhere calls *antirrhêsis*).[28] This is his illustration:

[CHREIA:] Isocrates said that teachers should be honored more than parents,
   for parents give us life, but teachers a good life;
[COUNTERSTATEMENT:] but a good life would not be possible, had our parents
   not given us life.

Theon leaves implicit the conclusion that follows from the counterstatement: "So let us honor our parents above our teachers" (or indeed all others). This activity is not yet an exercise in disputation, or what later tradition calls "refutation" and "confirmation" (*anaskeuê, kataskeuê*). It is an extension of the "supplemental statement" exercise but introduces the fundamental rhetorical principle of thinking in terms of opposing arguments—which, as Aphthnonius remarks, "contains within itself the art's whole force" (*ischus*).[29] In stasis instruction, the usual understanding is that an issue arises from the denial of a proposition—a counterstatement—which leads to arguments being marshaled on both sides according to the type of issue. The entire force of the art of rhetoric—the *impact* of its training regimen—lies in this fundamental activity.

Isocrates in various places expresses impatience with sophists who engage in captious disputation or uphold paradoxical arguments that contravene good sense or basic morality. In *Busiris* he faults Polycrates for praising the mythological villain Busiris, who, according to Polycrates, not only murdered but also ate his victims. The pressure to avoid captious or paradoxical counterstatements is especially strong in parainetic discourse, which is supposed to perform the moralizing functions of gnomic poetry. As Isocrates says in *To Nicocles,* "One should not seek novelties in this sort of discourse, in which it is impossible to say what is paradoxical, unbelievable, or alien to custom; rather, we should consider most accomplished that man who can gather the greatest number of ideas scattered in the thoughts of others and express them most elegantly" (41).[30] These considerations suggest that Isocrates may not have thought counterstatement appropriate to the chreia exercise. Clearly, however, counterstatement and antilogistic argument are part of Isocrates' *technê*; both *Areopagiticus* and *On the Peace,* for example, are counterstatements to fourth-century Athenian political ideology.

In the "encomium of *logos*" embedded in *Nicocles,* he also says that "with *logos* we contend concerning matters that are open to dispute" (8; see also *Antidosis* 256); and in the preamble of *To Nicocles,* where he ostensibly is speaking to a king, he presents a counterargument to the commonplace belief that a king's life is to be envied (2–6). From this perspective it appears that he would have included counterstatement in the chreia exercise, but with boundaries, restricting what was permissible to matters that were reasonably "open to dispute."

Through such activities as restatement/inflection, supplementary statement and counterstatement, then, chreia exercises based on the sayings of celebrated authors and Isocrates' parainetics would have accomplished several things. In addition to building up the beginning student's moral and political-philosophical commonplace collection, they would cultivate his familiarity and fluency with the literate dialect (and such figures or *ideai* as twofold statements, antitheses, and parallel constructions), and they developed basic habits of enthymematic and antilogistic invention—the foundations for a faculty of "argument on both sides"—as well as some judgment about what was reasonably "open to dispute" or not. All this would have been pursued through written compositions of small, easily managed compass, perhaps consisting of just a few lines.

The next component of progymnasmatic exercise, as Theon describes it, is "lengthening" and "shortening." Shortening involves taking a passage and reducing it to its essential gist—a process resembling what modern pedagogy would call "identifying the main idea." This would have little application to a chreia, unless the student started from an already-elaborated statement, such as a lyric poem or an argument from one of the celebrated sophists, and boiled it down to a line or two: "Protagoras said that man is the measure of all things." Lengthening involved taking a brief statement and expanding it with various kinds of detail. Theon's example is "Epaminondas [the Theban general], dying childless, said to his friends 'I leave two daughters: my victories at Leuctra and at Mantinea.'" This brief, anecdotal chreia is then expanded with narrative details that explain the meaning of Epaminondas' saying. Isocrates, in the preamble of *To Demonicus,* presents a nonnarrative expansion of a maxim:

> *No possession is more magnificent than virtue, or more lasting.* For beauty is destroyed by time or wasted by disease; and wealth serves wickedness more than nobility, giving license to indolence and summoning young men to pleasure; and strength with intelligence is helpful, but alone it is usually harmful to its possessors, adorning the bodies of those who train but overshadowing the care of their souls. But only virtue, when it grows purely in our thoughts, abides with us all our lives: it is better than wealth and more useful than good birth, making possible what is impossible for others, and bravely enduring what most people fear; and it considers laziness disgraceful, and toil honorable. This is easily learned from the labors of Hercules and the deeds

of Theseus, whose virtuous characters have cast such a stamp of glory on their works that not all time can cause what they have done to be forgotten. (3–5; emphasis added)

"Possession" here is *ktêma,* a "valuable thing" to have. The notion that virtue is the most magnificent and lasting of all valuable possessions proceeds through a set of *topoi,* subdividing the good things that one may possess into beauty, wealth, and bodily strength, each of which proves transient or actually harmful if not accompanied by intelligence *(phronêsis),* which in this passage seems closely related to virtue though not the same. Each of these statements is developed through brief restatement, counterstatement or epiphonema, and then the whole idea is restated, given a further epiphonema concerning laziness and toil (developed as an antithesis), and finally connected to the mythological examples of Hercules and Theseus. Through this sort of "lengthening" the beginning student can develop a short composition using the most basic elements of the chreia exercise.[31]

There clearly are some topics of invention at work here, such as a probably traditional *topos,* or set of *topoi,* that identifies the main good things that a person may possess as beauty, wealth, good birth, strength, intelligence, and virtue, as well as the "formal topics" or figures of subdivision and comparison, and what Aristotle *(Rhetoric* 2.23) would call the topic of "example" as a form of illustration or confirmation. Are all these topics *ideai?* The *Rhetoric to Alexander* would say they are. Robert Sullivan has suggested that, for Isocrates, *idea* and *eidos* signify formal features, such as the parts of an oration or figures of speech, but not topics of invention in the sense of substantive propositions, common beliefs, that serve as premises or starting points for arguments.[32] It is true that Isocrates' extant writings make no clearcut use of those terms to mean "inventional topic" in that sense. However, in *Nicocles* he does make reference to such qualities as beauty, temperance, justice, or time or condition of life as *ideai* by which people, or their words and actions, should be judged (30, 44). Elsewhere, in *To Philip,* he speaks of comparison *(antiparaballôn,* "putting side by side" to judge between greater and lesser) as an *idea* (143). *Ideai* seem to include both substantive and formal topics of invention.[33]

Isocrates probably would not have taught a comprehensive system of invention in the chreia exercise, at least not to beginners. It is possible, however, that he would have taught inventional topics as part of the *ideai* from which "all discourses" are composed and that he would have introduced some inventional *ideai* for the "lengthening" of individual chreias, depending on the particular subject matters that individual students were working with, as well as pointing out such *ideai* in the texts the students studied. At this stage of instruction, the point would not have been to teach an inventional system all at once, but simply to introduce the basic notion of inventional topics—the notion that there are frameworks of *ideai* associated with particular subject matters—and to give the student some elementary practice in their use.

A striking feature of Isocrates' little composition on the excellence of virtue is that, in certain general respects, it resembles the "speech of Lysias" that Plato has Socrates hold up to ridicule in *Phaedrus*, though the subject matter obviously is different, and Isocrates' composition is much shorter. Just as the "speech of Lysias" fails to provide explicit definitions of its focal subjects—"love" and "madness"—so too does Isocrates' mini- "encomium of virtue" not explicitly define "virtue" but loosely associates it with intelligence, courage, and toil. It invokes Hercules and Theseus as examples but does not explain exactly what the nature of their virtue was and why it made their deeds so glorious. Further, as Socrates says of Lysias' speech, Isocrates' composition displays a somewhat haphazard arrangement. It repeats ideas and does not systematically develop its *topoi;* intelligence, for example, is brought in alongside strength but not treated independently, though it seems to be one of the "possessions," like strength and beauty, that virtue should be compared with. The same could be said about "good birth," which is related to "wealth" but not the same. And what about courage? Or are intelligence and courage elements of virtue? Plato's Socrates would develop the theme more systematically: The goods that a person may possess are beauty, wealth, good birth, strength, intelligence, courage, and virtue, but virtue is superior to all these; virtue would then be defined, and the rest taken up and their comparative deficiency considered. This criticism may be leveled, too, at the loose structure of the parainetics in general. The argumentational and structural looseness of Isocrates' parainetics may be part of what Zosimus meant by their "weakness."

But Plato's criticism is unfair. The purpose of the chreia exercise—and the function of Isocrates' parainetics as models for his students—would not have been to teach argumentation, or even logical exposition, but to cultivate in the young student a certain degree of stylistic fluency and copiousness, as well as a basic habit of enthymematic and antilogistic statement, while steeping the student's sensibility in a collection of conventional moral and political-philosophical commonplaces: foundations for rhetoric/*philosophia,* but neither a philosophical treatise nor a complete rhetorical *technê*. For comparison, consider Desiderius Erasmus' popular Renaissance textbook, *De Copia,* which begins with techniques for stylistic abundance (famously including 150 ways to say "your letter pleased me very much") then extends these techniques to abundance of thought and finally to methods of argumentation.[34]

These observations suggest another dimension of Zosimus' justification of the relatively "weak" style of Isocrates' parainetics: they seem meant not only to be accessible for "children" at the beginning stages of instruction (boys of perhaps fourteen or fifteen), but also to be *imitable* by those "children." Isocrates' little composition-by-expansion on the excellence of virtue is a model for the kind of writing students might produce at the threshold of *logôn paideia*. Further, the sort of composition that Isocrates seems to be teaching to beginners via the parainetics is the very thing that both Speusippus and Pseudo-Plutarch cite as a central principle of Isocratean rhetoric and that Plato in *Phaedrus* satirizes as the art of "Tisias and Gorgias," namely, the art of making big things small and small things big, of saying old things in new ways and new things in old, and of speaking briefly or at length. In appears, in short, that Plato is satirizing the very first, most elementary lessons in Isocratean rhetoric/*philosophia* as if they were the whole of it, or of "sophistic" rhetoric in general.

One may doubt that Isocrates would have carried the chreia exercise into the more developed arguments of "refutation and confirmation" (*anaskeuê, kataskeuê*), at least at the beginning stage. Theon introduces this activity as *pros de toutois,* "in addition to these" (that is, to restatement/inflection, epiphonema/ counterstatement, and compression/expansion).[35] As he says explicitly at the outset of his treatise, amplification of what is already clear is easier than proof of what is unclear and thus comes first in rhetorical training while refutation/ confirmation should be saved for later.[36] Such an approach is reflected in the later manuals, which treat refutation/confirmation as a separate exercise, after maxim/chreia and fable/narrative. But insofar as rhetorical instruction was recursive and looped back to earlier matters and took them up in greater detail, the chreia could be returned to as a prompt for refutation and confirmation in more complex compositions, when reasonably disputable. It seems probable, then, that Isocrates likewise would have taken up disputation and argumentation later and at first would have confined the chreia exercise mainly to short "parainetic" or "gnomic" compositions that cultivated stylistic fluency, variability, and abundance; but chreias could, at a later stage, become the subject of refutation/confirmation exercises that set the stage for, and shaded into, the more advanced exercises.

Fable and Narrative

Isocrates' mini-composition on the excellence of virtue ends by invoking the mythological examples of Theseus and Hercules. This is an opening to the next type of exercise. Like the chreia, fables (myths) and narratives (histories) are to be worked up through the activities of restatement and inflection, expansion and compression, epiphonemas and counterstatements, and eventually refutation and confirmation. With fables, Theon stresses the placement of a "gnomic" epiphonema at either the end or beginning—the "moral of the story"—as well as the insertion, or "weaving in," of narrative digressions, which are historical examples that illustrate or confirm the fable or some aspect of it. Narrative, in turn, is supplied with a complex set of inventional *topoi* and stylistic virtues, such as clarity. The fable exercise thus continues the chreia's cultivation of stylistic fluency and abundance while further deepening the habits of confirmation (through the insertion and development of historical examples), enthymematic inference (by adding a "gnomic" epiphonema), and skeptical contradiction (through counterstatement). Moreover, these basic forms of argument, and, later, the more advanced activities of refutation/confirmation, also continue to develop "philosophic" habits of reflection on morally instructive tales while absorbing what can be said into the student's collection of moral and political-philosophical *topoi* for future use.[37]

While it is impossible to say whether Isocrates treated fable and narrative as separate exercises, and improbable that he would have treated them in the kind of detail that Theon does, they clearly are forms (*ideai*) that his *technê* is concerned with. In *To Nicocles* (40–50) he remarks that most people are unaffected by the maxims of the gnomic poets—they resist them as if they were being scolded—but are more responsive to fictional and mythological tales, such as Homer's, that delight the imagination and entrance (*psychagôgein*) the mind. While the truly intelligent, philosophical, and serious-minded person should not need such inducements to attend to the poets' wisdoms, says Isocrates, fables and narratives must be employed by the rhetor who wants to say something both useful and persuasive to audiences of ordinary people. Thus Isocrates' mini-essay on virtue ends by invoking the examples of Theseus and Hercules as a confirmation; in further rounds of development and expansion these examples could be unfolded as mythological narratives, lengthened or confirmed with historical-narrative digressions, and so on. In *Encomium of Helen* and *Panathenaicus* we find Isocrates engaging in lengthy mythological narratives: *Helen*, which is itself devoted to a mythological theme, digresses on Theseus, and *Panathenaicus* digresses on Agamemnon. His symbouleutic *logoi* also develop claims through narrative expansion of historical examples, as in *Panegyricus;* and of course the narrative is a fundamental component of his judicial speeches. (The narrative in judicial speech probably was treated in the earliest handbooks, and is an established feature of judicial argument well before Isocrates, as can be seen in Antiphon and Lysias.)

Among the handful of repeatedly cited fragments of Isocrates' *technê* in late-antique and medieval sources, we find instructions on the handling of narration. Here, for example, is Syrianus in the fifth century: "Isocrates, when he is teaching in his *Art of Rhetoric* how narration should be handled, says [*phêsi*] we should describe not only the action but also what preceded the action, what followed it, and the intentions with which each of the opponents did the thing in question; and the narration should be clear in its diction, its arrangement, or both. We should relate the bare fact without adding anything extraneous, as some people do who speak in simple and homespun language at the beginning, but afterward speak elaborately and undermine their arguments by laying on exaggerations and amplifications and all sorts of emotional appeals" (*Commentary on Hermogenes' On Types of Style* 25).[38]

The locution *phêsi* suggests that what follows is a quotation up to some unmarked point. Later, Syrianus repeats the statement about the parts of the action and the actors' intentions, with an added remark that "we must use what can be inferred from each" (170–171). Quintilian connects the advice about keeping the narrative clear, concise, and credible with the narrative section of an oration and attributes it to the "followers of Isocrates," while adding that "most writers" have adopted it (*Institutio* 4.2.31).[39] Isocrates says at the beginning of his narration in *On the Banker*, "I shall relate to you the facts, as well as I can, from the beginning" (*ex archês;* 3); this locution, coupled with the precept quoted by Syrianus, suggests the topic of narrative invention that turns up centuries later in the Hermogenic *On Invention* as "from beginning to end" (*ap' archês achri telous*): the subject matter is subdivided into parts, or episodes, and each is developed in chronological sequence.[40] This subdividing and developing—with expansions, suppositions, speeches in character, epiphonemas, and so on—can generate an entire historical narrative, a narrative in a judicial speech, or narrative illustrations, amplifications, and digressions in encomia and symbouleutics. From here, perhaps, begins the whole historiographic art of Ephorus and Theopompus. In sum, while the advice that Syrianus and Quintilian attribute to Isocrates may seem to be about narration in judicial speeches, it can also be applied to preliminary exercises in narrative as well—which, after all, are meant to cultivate the basic *idea* to be deployed in every kind of discourse, with adaptations suitable to *kairos*. Notably, Theon's account of the description exercise says that a description of events should address what preceded the event, what accompanied it, and what resulted from it;[41] this, and his emphasis on clarity, conciseness, and credibility, go back to Isocrates and his followers. Isocrates could have taught these things in his progymnasmata.

Refutation and Confirmation

According to Theon, refutation/confirmation can be applied to any progymnasma, is generally taken up after maxim/chreia and fable/narration, and forms the bridge to more advanced argumentation. The basic exercise begins with refutation; confirmation replies, in the manner of defense responding to prosecution. Theon gives fairly detailed lists of inventional topics for refutation. Those for chreias, for example, are the unclear, the redundant, the deficient (something important has been overlooked), the impossible, the incredible (or improbable), the false, the inexpedient (not beneficial or profitable), the useless, and the shameful. The student is to compose a brief, suitable introduction, then work through the topics in order, generating an argument from each wherever possible. Confirmation, in reply, uses the opposite topics, or those that are relevant; the chreia is clear, concise, complete, possible, probable, true, expedient, useful, and honorable. Refutation/confirmation of fable and narrative uses similar topics, though fables are permitted to relate untrue, impossible things, such as talking animals, and other topics relevant to narrative are added, such as whether the sequence of events is disordered. And so on.

At relatively early stages of instruction, refutation/confirmation would be an extension of the "lengthening" and "counterstatement" activities, and students would still be producing fairly simple, even mechanical compositions. The aim is not yet to generate sophisticated prose but to practice methodically running through inventional topics, developing resourcefulness in argument, and generating an abundance of things to say as well as rehearsing and deepening the habit of thinking and inventing in terms of opposing arguments while reflecting on morally instructive subject matter. The resultant composition may be little more than an inventory of possible arguments against and for a poet's saying or a fable. Theon remarks that later, as students become "more accomplished," the refutation/confirmation of chreias shades off into the thesis exercise, arguing a general, philosophical proposition, in which the student begins to produce something more like a real oration.[42]

It seems probable that Isocrates would have moved fairly soon to refutation/confirmation. It had been one of the mainstays of sophistic training at least from Protagoras onward: the activities of antilogy (statement and counterstatement, opposing arguments) and "making the weaker case stronger." It also seems probable that Isocrates' inventional framework would have been simpler than what we see in Theon and closer to what appears in the *Rhetoric to Alexander*'s treatment of "examination" (*exetasis*), a type of disputational (and mostly critical/refutative) discourse that can stand alone but usually, says the author, is incorporated in other types of discourse. The method of exetasis is, first, to produce a brief introduction that states a pretext for examination and then to consider the ways in which someone's words, actions, and/or intentions either contradict themselves or are contrary to justice, lawfulness, private or public advantage, the established "customs of good people," practicability (ease or difficulty), or probability (28 1445a–b; see also 5 1427b and 10 1430a). One then sums up with a concise restatement. Elsewhere, in his discussion of enthymemes, the author says they are developed by the same means as exetastic discourse; the exetasis is capped with a compact, enthymematic declaration in the form of an antithesis between the object of critique and what one affirms (10 1430a). If, for example, a gnomic poet declares that one should take no thought for money and sacrifice all for wisdom, one might charge that that is difficult to impossible to do and affirm a more moderate course. One might reply, in defense of the poet, by critiquing this "moderation" as laziness and reaffirming the virtuous austerity of wisdom in poverty, the advantages it confers on society, and so on. Clearly, exetasis provides a ready framework for short argumentative compositions in refutation and confirmation as well as a foundation for more elaborate disputation.

Notice that the exetasis of actions and intentions is echoed in Syrianus' report of Isocrates' instructions for handing narrative—one relates actions and the intentions of the actors and considers "what can be inferred from each"—while the exetasis of words has an obvious application to chreias. Isocrates' *Against the Sophists* exemplifies exetasis. The teachers of eristic (dialectic), he argues, are inconsistent in their actions (self-contradiction), teach what is either useless or positively harmful to their students (disadvantage), make impossible or dishonest promises (impossibility/improbability, injustice), and deserve to be scorned by people with common sense (the mores of the good); those who teach only judicial discourse cultivate nothing but "meddlesomeness and greed" (immorality, injustice, public disadvantage); and so on. Isocrates, in contrast, claims to make reasonable promises, to teach what is truly useful and effective, and to cultivate good character. This is, of course, a more advanced example, in which we see exetastic or refutative discourse developed into a thesis, or part of one, on the true philosophy of *logos;* but the core *topoi* are in essence those listed in the *Rhetoric to Alexander,* or very close to them.

Auxiliary Ideai: *Description and Comparison*

I am here collecting two exercises, or two *ideai,* that neither Theon nor the later handbooks present in just this sequence. They are, however, generally intermediate between the gateway exercises—maxim/chreia and fable/narrative, with restatement, expansion/compression, epiphonema/counterstatement, and refutation/confirmation—and the more advanced exercises of commonplace, thesis, encomium, and law.

Description (*ekphrasis*) and comparison (*sunkrisis*) may be dealt with quickly. They may or may not be independent progymnasmatic exercises with Isocrates, but they certainly are *ideai.* Description is a recognizable literary form and even an independent genre well before Isocrates: Homer describes Achilles' shield, in a famous passage from the *Iliad;* one of Alcaeus' elegies, composed in the sixth century B.C.E., memorably describes a hall of armor. The ecphrastic poem remains a functional genre into and through late antiquity, and the *idea* of ecphrasis is constantly available as a resource for literary prose. Theon treats ecphrasis, the use of vivid language and descriptive detail to bring the thing described "before the eyes," as already inherent in narrative as a form of amplification. Clearly it would have been essential not only to Isocrates' treatment of the narrative exercise but also to his treatments of the narrative section of a speech and of historiography as well. Theon, in his account of description as a separate exercise, gives more detailed instructions for the description of events, persons, places, and times, such as a season, a festival, or a time of day; but the basic principle, the *idea,* remains the same, deploying differently with different kinds of subject matter.[43] It is not hard to imagine that Isocrates assigned descriptions to his students, especially to writers of skimpy prose such as Ephorus: "Describe the Athenian fleet at Salamis, at dawn before the battle."

Isocrates in *To Philip* explicitly refers to comparison as an *idea,* though the word he uses is not *sunkrisis* but *antiparaballôn,* "setting side by side." This is what he says: "I can indeed rank what you already have accomplished above the deeds of your ancestors, and not with slippery arguments but in truth; for since you have subdued more nations than any Greek has taken cities, how would it not be easy for me to show, by comparing [*antiparaballôn*] you with each of them, that you have accomplished greater things than they? But I have chosen to refrain from that *idea,* for two reasons: because some do not use it in a timely way [*eukairiôs*], and also because I do not wish to make those who are considered demigods seem less than those now living" (142–43).

The function of comparison as Isocrates describes it here is essentially that given in Theon and the later manuals: to set things that are similar side by side to show which is the greater. One can magnify the greatness of a person's deeds, or of anything, by comparing them advantageously with examples already acknowledged to be great, as Isocrates says he could do with Philip's conquests. In the later manuals, comparison typically is associated with encomiastic discourse, and thus the comparison exercise follows the encomium, and, as Theon says, produces a sort of "double encomium." He goes on to give the advice that modern textbooks still repeat: Conduct the comparison either point by point or with two parallel accounts; an example of the latter would be Plutarch's *Parallel Lives.*[44] Clearly comparison to highlight greater and lesser is an *idea* that can be used in almost any discourse, and for many purposes.

There are other strategies of comparison inherent in the basic *idea.* Theon, in his discussion of topics for the thesis exercise, recognizes arguments from comparison with greater things, lesser things, similar things, and opposite things.[45] Likewise Aphthonius, in his treatment of comparison, defines it as discourse that "brings the greater or the equal together with what is set alongside" (*tôi paraballomenôi*), and he recognizes juxtapositions of "noble things [*kala*] with good [*chrêstois*], poor things [*phaula*] with poor [*phaulois*], good things [*chrêsta*] with bad [*ponêrois*], and small things [*mikra*] with larger" [*meizosi*].[46] Arguments based on comparisons of greater/lesser, similar, and opposite things are recognized, too, in Aristotle's discussion of "common topics" in the *Rhetoric* (2.23.1, 4–5 1397a–b; topics 1 and 4); notably, he treats arguments based on similarity and greater/lesser as variants of the same topic.[47] The *Rhetoric to Alexander* includes in its list of "common *ideai*" only arguments from similarity and opposition, and seems to associate them with argument from examples: "Examples [*paradeigmata*] are previous actions that are similar or opposite to those we are now discussing" (8 1429a). In its discussion of encomiastic discourse, however, it does treat "comparison" of greater and lesser things as a "method" (*tropos*) of amplification (*auxêsis;* 3 1426a), and he goes on to mention comparison of opposites as well, while thinking of both, again, in terms of examples. This treatment suggests that greater/lesser is a variant of the "common *idea*" of similarity, and indeed the handbooks generally emphasize that greater/lesser only makes sense when comparing similars—one cannot, for example, augment the greatness of Achilles by comparing him to Thersites, whom Homer portrays as a worthless character; one must compare him to, say, Hector, the greatest of the Trojans, or the other Greek heroes. The author's term for such comparison is *antiparaballein,* which echoes Isocrates.

In sum, it seems likely that Isocrates thought similarly: comparison is a "form" (*idea*) of argument and invention associated with argument by example; it includes comparisons of similars, greater/lesser, and opposites, and is useful especially for amplification of praise or blame in epideictic discourse, though it may perform evaluative and amplificative functions anywhere. The fundamental and recurrent idea of the enthymeme in ancient rhetoric—which clearly is a major *idea* for Isocrates—is that it sums up or "caps" an argument by stating the point in twofold form, usually in terms of opposition, contrast, or analogies and correspondences.[48] Comparison is a major argumentational resource in ancient rhetoric—or, for that matter, modern. Isocrates may have introduced the *idea* of comparison in connection with encomiastic discourse, just as he may have introduced description in connection with fable/narrative. But it seems likely that he understood both also as common *ideai,* "forms" or figures of argument and amplification, which "all discourses" may deploy according to need and opportunity.

Another Auxiliary: Ethopoiea

Speaking in character, or what Theon calls *prosôpopoiía* (literally, "face making" or "personification"), can be added to almost any exercise, from progymnasmata to declamation. It adds a layer of inventional complication and encourages the student to imitate voices and styles.[49] The exercise involves imagining what a certain character or character type would say in a certain situation; for example, what a man about to go away on a journey would say to his wife, or what the wife might say. As Theon points out, invention must take into account the characteristics of the speaker, the addressee, the scene (occasion and place), the subject matter, and the purpose of the speech (exhortation, lamentation, consolation, seeking forgiveness, and so forth). A young man, for example, should not speak like an old one, a serious subject should not be handled flippantly, and a seeker of forgiveness should not be imperious.

On one hand this exercise bridges from the poets and prose writers the student has been reading. Students might write in the manner of a stock character type or character from the stage, a mythological or historical personage, or a celebrated writer, depending on their level of advancement. One notable feature of this ethopoietic role playing—in addition to encouraging the student to imaginatively inhabit different subjectivities and positions—is that it generally promotes exuberant invention in young writers. (I think that anyone who has assigned ethopoietic exercises, as I have, will attest to this.)[50] This enables the student to more fully absorb and internalize the principles and *ideai* of the *technê,* as components of a new layer of rhetorical identity.

On the other hand, ethopoiea sets the stage for declamation. Ethopoietic speeches devoted to exhortation or praise within particular settings anticipate symbouleutics and encomia, and speeches of accusation or criticism, or justification in reply, anticipate judicial discourse, although the student is not yet held responsible for a full-fledged practical oration. The student is drawing chiefly from conventional character typologies and scenes (the husband's farewell) or well-known events (the banishment of Alcibiades) and is producing something more like the relatively short speeches of characters in history or drama. The main concerns of ethopoiea as a progymnasma are the representation of ethos, the expression of feeling, and the development of commonplaces—or what Aristotle in the *Poetics* calls the articulation of "thought" (*dianoia*)—in a style appropriate to the speaker, subject matter, and situation. In this way ethopoiea continues the development of the student's fund of moral and political-philosophical *topoi* (*ideai*), and of the student's stylistic fluency and sophistication, while introducing the principles of invention according to *kairos* and adaptation to audience.

It is highly plausible that Isocrates' first- or second-year students would have done some such exercise. Ethopoiea clearly is an inheritance not only from the poets but also from the sophists of the later fifth century. Gorgias' *Defense of Palamedes* is an ethopoietic declamation (Palamedes defends himself against Odysseus' charge of betraying the Greeks, in a situation drawn from Homeric myth), as are Antiphon's *Tetralogies* (unnamed, imaginary speakers accuse and defend, in an imagined situation that seems derived from the world of archaic poetry). Antiphon's pioneering work as the first professional logographer was ethopoietic also, as was the subsequent logography of Lysias; both wrote judicial orations "in character," in the voices of their clients. Ethopoiea was basic to the early sophistic enterprise, and probably was an exercise to which they set their students.

Isocrates' parainetic *Nicocles,* in which the young king addresses his subjects, is an ethopoiea. So too, at the level of declamation, are the symbouleutics *Archidamus* (the young prince Archidamus rises to address the Spartan assembly in the midst of a crisis) and *Plataicus* (a Plataean ambassador addresses the Athenian assembly, asking for help against Theban aggression.) And of course all of Isocrates' judicial speeches, which are specimens of logography like those of Lysias and Antiphon before him, are ethopoietic also. It seems reasonable to assume that some form of ethopoiea probably was included in Isocrates' progymnasmata.

Advanced Exercises: Commonplace and Thesis

Theon and the later handbooks treat the commonplace (*koinos topos,* or with Theon simply *topos*) as the amplification of blame or denunciation for convicted malefactors, or of praise for the good. If someone has been shown to be a tyrant or a temple robber, one dilates on the moral perversity of tyranny or temple robbery in order to drum up the jury's anger and disgust while calling for punishment. If someone has been shown to be a public benefactor, one dilates on the nobility of public benefaction and calls for a reward. Commonplace is associated in the extant handbooks mainly with the peroration of judicial speeches, though Theon observes also that "some" define it as a "starting point" (*aphormê*) for arguments (*epicheirêmata*), that is, as a technique for laying down and amplifying a premise in order to increase an audience's emotional commitment to it.[51]

Since the function of the commonplace is to intensify praise or blame, it resembles encomiastic discourse. The difference, as Theon explains it, is that encomium—or its opposite, invective—praises or blames a particular person or thing and can be an independent speech, such as a funeral oration or laudation of a city, whereas the commonplace amplifies an emotively resonant general concept, such as the depravity of tyrants, and is normally not an independent speech genre. However, in its assertion of general principles the commonplace also stands between the expanded chreia and the thesis. It differs from the thesis, as Theon points out, in that it simply intensifies an undisputed belief, whereas the thesis argues an assertion that is disputable—for example, whether the life of kings is to be envied. Hence the commonplace is more like an expanded maxim/chreia in that both are elaborations of an idea with which the speaker's audience and community can be expected to identify already.

As a school exercise the commonplace differs from the expanded chreia chiefly in the topics of invention that are prescribed. In Theon, as we have seen, the chreia is expanded mainly through techniques of restatement, supplementary statement, and counterstatement, whereas the commonplace employs a battery of topics that partially anticipates the longer list given for the thesis. Aphthonius, in contrast, assigns different sets of topics for the chreia, the commonplace and the thesis, giving the thesis the "final headings" (*telika kephalaia*) of lawfulness, justice, advantage, and feasibility. But presumably all the topics of invention and amplification introduced in earlier exercises remain available, as appropriate, for the thesis, since the instructional process is recursive and accumulative, building up a collection of *ideai* for copious invention.[52]

There is, in short, a continuum in the handbooks from the expanded chreia exercise to the commonplace and to the thesis. The commonplace adds more topics, while the thesis adds refutation/confirmation and still more topics—or culminates the collection of topics so far accumulated—while shifting the function from amplification of belief to disputation on general issues. With the thesis exercise the student arrives at philosophical debate and argument, or *philosophia* proper as Isocrates understands it. (The word *thesis* literally means a "position" to be argued.)[53]

Further, as the handbooks also note, theses divide into "theoretical" and "practical" questions (or what Aphthonius calls "political" questions). Theoretical questions generally are issues in natural philosophy or metaphysics, and are matters of knowledge, such as, "Is the world governed by divine providence?" Practical theses are questions in moral or political philosophy and are matters of choice and action (*praxis*), such as, "Should a man get married?" (The distinction is very much between questions of "is" and "ought.") Practical theses generally have a more obvious and immediate bearing on the concerns of civic rhetoric. Some such recognition is probably what we hear echoed in Dionysius of Halicarnassus' report that Isocrates turned rhetorical training away from the earlier sophists' concerns with "eristics and natural philosophy," that is, away from disputation of theoretical questions in science and metaphysics, and toward argument on the practical questions of political discourse, and of moral and political philosophy (*Isocrates* 1).

Isocrates may not have made clear distinctions between the expanded chreia, the commonplace, and the thesis, but he certainly employs commonplaces in his extant *logoi*. He also makes a conceptual distinction between the general issues of theses and the particular cases of hypotheses. Quintilian, in an apparent reference to Isocrates' *technê,* says that he defined a "cause"—*causa,* the Latin term for *hupothesis*—as "a definite civil question or a controversy involving definite persons" (*Institutio oratoria* 3.5.18). Quintilian's distinction between "civil question" and "controversy" reflects Isocrates' distinction between political (symbouleutic) and judicial issues, but both kinds of "cause" involve "definite" (*finitus*) circumstances and persons and are thus distinct from the "indefinite" (*infinitus*) issues of theses. In *To Nicocles,* as he is counseling the young ruler on how to choose and assess associates, Isocrates says,

> You should judge neither serious matters nor intelligent people by the standard of pleasure, but appraise them by that of practical usefulness [*epi tôn praxeôn tôn chrêsimôn*]. Moreover, since those who teach philosophy dispute about how to exercise the soul, some saying that students will become more intelligent through eristic disputation, others through political discourse, and others through some other means, but all agree that a well-educated person

whatever his training should show the ability to deliberate, you should disregard what is disputed and test [your associates] by what is agreed on. Observe them especially when they give advice in particular situations [*epi tôn kairôn sumbouleuontas*], or, if that is not possible, when they speak on general subjects [*kath' holôn tôn pragmatôn legontas*]. (50–52)

Isocrates here does not use the language of the later *technai,* as he frequently does not; the technical terminology has not yet crystallized. As I have noted, Aristotle remarks in his *Topics* that "problems" for dialectical debate—disputable general propositions, such as "All things are in motion"—"are now called theses" (*nun . . . theseis kalountai;* 1.11 104b). The specific terminology of thesis/hypothesis may belong to the generation after Isocrates. Nevertheless, what Isocrates calls "giving advice in particular situations" corresponds to (symbouleutic) hypotheses, while "speaking on general subjects" corresponds to theses and commonplaces.

If we imagine the deliberations of a ruler and his counselors, the act of "speaking on general subjects" most typically would take the form of a commonplace: the invocation and amplification of some general, philosophical consideration as a basis for making judgments about the particular situation in question. The commonplaces a man invokes are an index to his moral commitments, and thus Nicocles is advised to pay special attention to them. However, if the validity or relevance of that commonplace were challenged, the discussion would shift to refutation and confirmation, and a thesis, a philosophical debate, would emerge. Isocrates thus distinguishes the general and particular issues of theses and hypotheses and tacitly recognizes, or reflects in practice, the difference between thesis and commonplace but conceptually seems not to differentiate them sharply.

With Isocrates, then, there seems to be a sliding scale from chreia exercises to the commonplace and thesis. A "useful saying" can be developed and amplified as a commonplace or, when subjected to refutation/confirmation, as a thesis. He may or may not have had fixed sets of inventional topics to assign in these different exercises, though he probably worked in a recursive spiral from simpler tasks to more complex, from the amplification of a chreia to the argumentation of theses such as we see in the surviving extract of *Against the Sophists.* Indeed, that extract may have been preserved *as* an extract because it exemplified such argument. Through such a process Isocrates would have introduced the kinds of inventional topics listed by the *Rhetoric to Alexander* for exetastic discourse, and/or what it calls the "common *ideai*" for all genres of civic speech. These ultimately would include such things as the topics of the just, the lawful, the advantageous, the good (that is, the mores of the good and the honorable), the pleasant, the feasible, the possible, the necessary, and the past judgments of the wise, as well as examples (mythic and historical), comparisons (of greater/lesser, similars, and opposites) techniques of amplification (narration, description, accumulative restatement, subdivision), techniques of antilogistic and enthymematic statement (counterstatements and explanatory/inferential epiphonemas), and the dramatistic self-presentation of ethopoiea, and indeed anything else that came up in the course of the progymnasmata and in critical discussions of the student's readings.

Isocrates may also have had a notion of what the later handbooks call "final headings" (*telika kephalaia*) for "practical" theses. These involve the ultimate "ends" (*telê*) for which people choose and act. As he says at one point in *Antidosis*, "For the sake of pleasure or profit or honor, all do all they do; I see nothing that human beings desire outside of these" (217). Insofar as these three terms sum up the grounds of human motivation, they also sum up the range of inventional topics bearing on questions of choice and action in Isocratean moral and political philosophy: "Profit" (*kerdos*) sums up the advantageous, the feasible, and the possible (since there is no advantage in pursuing what is impossible or infeasible); "honor" (*timê*) sums up justice, lawfulness, and the good (or a reputation for being just, lawful, and good); and "pleasure" (*hêdonê*) sums up aesthetic desiderata (sensory pleasures, intellectual amusements). Isocrates' final headings align with those of Theon and Aphthonius as follows:[54]

Isocrates	Theon	Aphthonius
Honor (*timê*)	The good (*kalon*)	The just (*dikaion*)
		The lawful (*nomimon*)
Profit (*kerdos*)	the advantageous (*sumpheron*)	The advantageous (*sumpheron*)
	The necessary (*anankaion*)	The possible (*dunaton*)
Pleasure (*hêdonê*)	The pleasant (*hêdeon*)	

Note that Isocrates advises Nicocles to place profit ahead of pleasure in judging "serious matters and intelligent people," that is, people who give good practical advice are more valuable than those who are merely pleasant, and that elsewhere, as we have seen already, he echoes Theognis' ranking of honest poverty above unjustly gotten wealth: pleasure-profit-honor represents a hierarchy of "final" values.

Bridge to Particular Cases: Encomium and Law

In some sense neither encomium nor law is a "pro" gymnasma, since each corresponds to an actual genre of public discourse, each has to do with a specific case, and neither is mentioned in the scattered references to progymnasmata before the first century.[55] In the later handbooks they seem to be transitional between the other progymnasmata and the advanced study and practice of symbouleutic and judicial discourse in declamation. Encomium is praise of particular persons or things—or blame ("invective," *psogos*)—in contrast to the commonplace, which amplifies an emotively resonant general idea. The genre seems to have evolved from the funeral oration or memorial speech (*epitaphios*) and to have quickly proliferated into a family of subtypes related to different kinds of occasions for encomiastic discourse, such as those discussed in the third-century treatises on epideictic attributed to Menander Rhetor.[56] But the basic contours remained essentially the same. In essence one treats the origins, endowments, virtues, and deeds of the person praised or blamed, with the narration of deeds serving as amplification and proof of the virtues, or vices in invective; if the object of praise is not a person but, for example, a city, one makes suitable adjustments.

It is obvious that Isocrates gave explicit attention to the encomium. His *Busiris* and *Encomium of Helen* are both didactic treatments of how the *idea* of encomium should be handled, starting from critique of an example and proceeding to a demonstration of how it should have been done. These are perhaps the only works in the Isocratean canon that have such an overtly didactic function, though all, perhaps, are at least implicitly didactic and sprinkled with metacommentary. Notably, both end with gestures toward their incompleteness and suggestions that the student (or someone) take up what has been omitted:

> While there are many things to say, from which one could expand both the praise and the defense [of Busiris], I do not think it necessary to speak at length; for I am not putting on a display [*epideixin*] for others, but aiming to show you how each of these things should be done. (*Busiris* 44)

> I have passed over much more than I have said . . . [a list of possible topics is suggested] . . . Should anyone wish to finish these out and expand them, they will have no lack of starting-points beyond what I have said, from which to praise Helen. (*Helen* 67–69)

These gestures suggest the pedagogical approach recommended by Quintilian, centuries later, for students at the beginning of declamation: The teacher should develop the theme partway, providing not only a general outline but also a treatment of some parts and indications of the lines of argument to use in the remaining parts, leaving the student to complete what has been roughly framed (*Institutio oratoria* 2.6).

Beyond *Busiris* and *Helen,* Isocrates' canon provides two more encomia: *Evagoras*, a memorial *epitaphios* for the deceased Cypriot king, the father of Nicocles, and *Panathenaicus*, a praise of Athens, ostensibly written for or just after the Panathenaic festival of 342 B.C.E. Both are highly finished but also include reflective metacommentary on their own processes or on the *ideai* they employ. In *Evagoras,* for example, Isocrates says, "Of the many rulers in all of time, not one will be found who has attained a more glorious honor than Evagoras. If, then, we were to compare Evagoras' deeds with those of each of them, the account perhaps would not be fitting to the occasion, and there would not be time enough to tell it all. But if we select and consider the most illustrious of those rulers, our examination will not be deficient, and our discussion will be much briefer" (34).

This looks like instructional discourse directed to the student: a description of the compositional problem and of the strategic handling of it in the encomiastic comparison that follows. In *Panathenaicus,* as I have noted before, Isocrates includes a long "digression" on how he gathered some current and former students to critique his handling of the Spartans in the nearly completed draft, ending with the shrewder student's interpretation of the text as making covert arguments—thereby offering a lesson on what, centuries later, the Hermogenic *On Invention* will treat as "figured problems" in declamation (4.13) as well as an example of the "workshopping" of a draft in progress.[57] Finally, it should be noted that the surviving fragment of Isocrates' judicial speech *On the Team of Horses* is mostly an encomium of Alcibiades—in essence, an extract illustrating the use of encomiastic discourse in judicial argument.

The "law" exercise—more properly, "proposal of a law"—required the student to refute and/or defend either a proposed new law or an existing law. The model seems to be the classical (fourth-century) Athenian procedure for amending the constitution: Whoever wished to propose a change in the laws appeared before the panel of magistrates known as the Thesmothetes ("lawgivers"); the proposer of change acted as an "accuser" of the old law, his opponent acted as its "defender," and the Thesmothetes acted as "jury."[58] Thus although the "law" exercise does not seem to be mentioned as a progymnasma before Aelius Theon, it also seems to have very old roots that go back to Isocrates' lifetime. As Theon discusses it, the "law" exercise draws predominantly on the kinds of topics that appear under the "legal" stasis in classical stasis theory, such as ambiguity of law, conflicting laws, letter versus intent of law, and the rational extension of a law to analogous cases, as well as other topics that pertain more specifically to "constitutional" argument (for example, the law is unclearly written, it is disadvantageous, it is immoral and dishonorable). It is possible that Isocrates assigned a "law" exercise in some form. *Areopagiticus,* after all, is an example of just such discourse: a proposal that the Athenian constitution be amended, by restoring some key features of the older constitution of Solon, in order to correct the excesses and injustices of the post-Periclean radical democracy. (Those who take this text as representing Isocrates' political philosophy should consider that he would have asked his students to critique and reply to it, just as he shows himself doing in *Panathenaicus*.)

Assembling Predecessors' Contributions

One can only speculate, of course, on exactly what Isocrates' *progymnasmata* would have looked like, though it seems probable that he used a set of preliminary exercises that at least roughly prefigured what appears in the later handbooks—maxim/chreia, fable/narrative, refutation/confirmation, description, comparison, ethopoiea, commonplace, thesis, encomium, and possibly even law—and that through such *ideai* he introduced other, subsidiary *ideai,* such as resources for stylistic variety and copiousness, techniques of amplification (restatements, subdivision, examples), enthymematic "supplemental" statements or epiphonemas, counterstatements, topics of invention, and, at least in the later exercises, basic forms of discourse structuration (such as preambles and closing statements, corresponding to the prologue and epilogue of a finished oration). To all that would be added any other *ideai* pointed out in the students' reading and discussion of texts by "celebrated" authors and Isocrates' own *logoi*. In broad general outlines, we can see in this "preliminary" training a partial synthesis of what Isocrates inherited from the fragmentary *technai* of his early-sophistic predecessors: on one hand the various techniques of style, and the art of making new things old and old things new and speaking briefly and at length, that Plato satirizes in *Phaedrus;* and on the other hand the practice of disputation on "notable subjects," meaning theses, and probably commonplaces, which Cicero says Aristotle credited to Protagoras, Gorgias, and Antiphon as their signal contribution to the evolution of rhetoric as a *technê* (*Brutus* 12.46–48).

Two points should be briefly noted here. The first is that, in the progression from maxim/chreia and fable/narrative to thesis and encomium, the student would be given an introductory grounding in what Isocrates called *philosophia,* chiefly through articulating, amplifying, reflecting on, and disputing culturally resonant general beliefs, especially moral and political beliefs. The goal would be to cultivate not only mastery of basic *ideai* of style and argument, but also, and for Isocrates more importantly, to cultivate intellectual and moral character through repeated, performative iterations of and identifications with the values of the good and useful citizen. These are, in essence, the values summed up in the final headings of the thesis exercise in the later handbooks; in Isocrates' triad (in *Antidosis*) of the advantageous, the honorable, and the pleasant (practical, moral, and aesthetic goods); or in the *Rhetoric to Alexander*'s list of the common *ideai* used in all genres of civic discourse (the just, the legal, the advantageous, the good, the pleasant, the easy or difficult, the possible, the necessary, similars and opposites, and the previous judgments of the wise). The student who had spent a year or two continually rehearsing how to intelligently articulate and argue such values in copious, fluent, and effective ways in written compositions, and who had internalized them as a habitual mode of thought and affect—the ethos of Quintilian's *vir bonus*—would now be ready to pass on to the deliberation and argumentation of specific cases.

That last presumption is not as naïve as it may seem. As Isocrates says, no art exists that can create virtue, self-control, or a sense of justice in those who already are depraved (*tois kakôs pephukosi,* "the evil natured"; *Against the Sophists* 21). Nor can artistic brilliance be created ex nihilo, or even in those of modest talents, though the modestly endowed can be improved. The student must bring the requisite talent, virtuous intentions, and a desire to speak well—that is, a desire to truly give good counsel in well-formed speech—as well as a willingness to submit to instruction and hard work (*Antidosis* 186–192, 224–226, 274–282ff). *Paideia* can only work with and improve what exists already, and what exists already sets the limits of what can be achieved. But in those with the right aspirations and a proper work ethic, even with small talent, a great deal can be achieved.

The second point to note is that, in a sense, the Isocratean *logôn paideia* would be almost complete already at this stage. This certainly was true for the student who did not complete the full three or four year course of study, and returned to private life after a year or two. Such students, as Isocrates suggests, would go home with an improved ability to think and speak, and with a more highly cultivated sensibility, though they generally would not have an oratorical or political career. But that also would be true for students such as Ephorus, Theopompus, or Aphareus, who did perform as orators, but chiefly devoted themselves to literary careers: for example, Ephorus and Theopompus as historians, or Aphareus as a playwright. The progymnasmata, even in the relatively simple form that they probably took in Isocrates' *paideia,* provided a foundation for literary composition and philosophical disputation—in short, the philosophico-literary foundation that Cicero's Crassus and Antonius call for in the training of an orator.[59]

Technê I: The *Pragmatikos Topos*—Preliminary Inquiry and Invention

The student who had passed through Isocrates' progymnasmata progressed to "advanced" composition and declamation exercises on specific cases—symbouleutics and judicial discourses, as well as encomiastic discourses—and confronted the situational and inventional complexities of such cases. As Isocrates puts it, when students have become "experienced" with "all the *ideai* which *logos* employs," their teachers "exercise them again" (*palin gumnazousin autous*) and require them "to combine what they have learned according to the needs of each particular case" (*kath' hen hekaston*), so that "they will grasp what they have learned more securely, and be in their judgments [*doxais*] more adaptive to *kairos*" (*Antidosis* 183–184). This stage of instruction is what is generally thought of as "rhetoric" proper. With Isocrates, as I have noted before, the *technê* here divides into two main parts: the *pragmatikos topos,* the "domain of subject matter," and the *lektikos topos,* the "domain of style." The *pragmatikos topos,* in turn, has two main parts, which I will call "preliminary inquiry" and "invention," concerned, respectively, with the initial discovery and planning of subject matter and lines of argument and with the part-by-part development of the actual discourse.

Preliminary Inquiry

As Isocrates notes in his letter *To the Children of Jason,* one of the "most frequently repeated" of his precepts, and one of the most fundamental, is this: "I am accustomed to say to those who devote themselves to my *philosophia* that the first thing to consider is what is to be accomplished [*diaprakteon*] by a discourse and by its parts. And when we have discovered this and examined it thoroughly, I say the *ideai* are to be sought [*zêtêteon*] by which these things will be worked out and the goal we have set ourselves will be attained" (8).

   Diaprakteon, "to be accomplished," could also be rendered as "practicable"; the locution suggests both a canvassing of the possibilities of a discourse within a particular situation and an identification of its specific goals. (This suggests another likely source for Aristotle's definition of rhetoric as a "faculty" for observing "the possibly persuasive in each case"; *Rhetoric* 1.2.1). Once one has made a determination of the specific purpose of the discourse as a whole, then one can also determine what each of its parts—prologue, narrative, proof, epilogue—needs to do. At that point one must "seek" the specific *ideai,* the rhetorical "forms, figures," or resources, by which the purposes of the whole discourse and its parts can be achieved.

   As Robert Gaines has argued,[60] Isocrates' remarks suggest a two-part process for discourse creation, which Gaines calls "rhetorical intellection" and "invention" or what I am calling "preliminary inquiry" and invention. These two processes prefigure, as Gaines observes, the later division in rhetorical *technai* between stasis theory and invention, such as we see in the Hermogenic treatises *On Stases* and *On Invention:* the former is concerned with identifying the question at issue and canvassing the possible main lines of argument and counterargument on both sides, and the latter is concerned with the invention (*heuresis*) of the actual parts of the discourse. Such a division, it seems, was present already in Isocrates' treatment of the *pragmatikos topos,* the "domain of subject matter," in at least a rudimentary form. Considering Quintilian's report that Isocrates' student Naucrates was the first to use the word *stasis* as a rhetorical term, and the fact that it appears within a decade of Isocrates' death in

Aeschines' speech *Against Ctesiphon* (*Institutio oratoria* 3.6.3; *Against Ctesiphon* 206), the question arises whether Isocrates taught an incipient form of stasis theory in his treatment of preliminary inquiry.[61]

The development of stasis theory is generally credited to Hermagoras of Temnos, who was active in the mid-second century B.C.E. Hermagoras' *technê* is lost, but reconstructions of his system from extant fragments and references in later writers, chiefly Cicero in *De inventione,* suggest that it included both theses and hypotheses, and for hypotheses provided four main stases: issues of fact (conjecture), issues of definition, issues of evaluation (quality), and issues of procedure (objection or transference). The qualitative stasis also included "legal" issues, meaning questions of interpretation—letter versus intent, conflicting laws, ambiguity, and analogical extensions of a law—as well as "rational" issues regarding the evaluation of an act, usually with reference to ideas of justice, honor, and advantage. The procedural stasis involved objections to the formal constitution of a proceeding, for example, if a prosecution has been improperly brought, or should be transferred to a different venue. The system is generally regarded as oriented toward judicial discourse or derived from a model of judicial discourse; however, as Cicero points out (*De inventione* 1.9.12), Hermagoras' qualitative stasis included, under or alongside the "rational" substasis, headings for both symbouleutic and epideictic (encomiastic) discourse.[62] The point of the system was to work "dialectically" through the stases, starting from conjecture, until one arrived at the crux of the dispute. For example, one might acknowledge the facts asserted by one's opponent ("Yes, I killed the man") and acknowledge the opponent's definition ("Yes, it was murder") but dispute the "rational" question of how it should be judged ("The murder was justified"). Once one had identified the crucial stasis, the place where one was to make one's "stand," the system provided a set of headings that could be canvassed for possible lines of argument. It is important to note that stasis arises from the *denial* of a proposition, for example, "You did it" / "I did not." This process constitutes the preliminary inquiry, the "strategic" determination of what the aims of one's argument should be, before the "tactical" part-by-part invention of the actual speech.

Antecedents to Hermagorean stasis theory have sometimes been attributed to Aristotle—Quintilian, for example, sees some parallels (*Institutio oratoria* 3.6.23, 49)—though Aristotle never developed a systematic account of stasis, and seems not to have been greatly familiar with judicial procedures.[63] There is, however, a more obvious antecedent in the *Rhetoric to Alexander,* though the author does not use the term *stasis,* in its discussion of judicial discourse:

> The defense speech [*to apologêtikon*] is constituted in three ways [*dia triôn methodôn sunistatai*]. For either the defendant must prove that he did none of the things he is accused of; or, if he is compelled to admit them, he must

attempt to show that what he did was legal, just, noble, and advantageous to the city; or, if it is not possible to prove that, he must attempt to obtain forgiveness by attributing his acts to error or misfortune and by showing that little damage has resulted from them. You must define [*diorize*] injustice, error, and misfortune: establish injustice as doing an intentional evil, and say that the greatest punishments should be inflicted on such things; say that doing a harmful action unwittingly is an error; and establish not carrying out an honorable intention, when it is due not to oneself but to certain others or to luck, as misfortune. (4 1427a)

This passage clearly conceives of stasis as a series of possible positions that arise from a defendant's reply to an accusation, just as in the later treatments of stasis theory. The stases here are fact, quality (legal, just, noble, advantageous), and forgiveness; and in the discussion of defining injustice, error, and misfortune there is an incipient definitional stasis. Further, arguing that one's act of murder was "legal" involves legal interpretation and thus suggests an incipient version of the "legal" substasis of "quality." Hermagoras' system, so far as we know it, reorganizes this arrangement by making definition a separate stasis and by making the plea for forgiveness a substasis of "quality."

One can point to an even earlier antecedent of stasis theory, in the late fifth century B.C.E., in Antiphon's *Tetralogies* (though Antiphon too does not use the term *stasis*). As Michael Gagarin has pointed out, the *Tetralogies*—"fourfold arguments," two each by prosecution and defense, in three imaginary murder cases—are probably not intended as models of judicial oratory per se but as philosophical explorations of problems in legal argument.[64] The first tetralogy, as Gagarin shows, explores the uses and limits of probabilities (*eikota*) and evidence (*tekmêria*) in a case situated at the stasis of fact, while the second and third tetralogies are situated at the stasis of "quality" and turn on interpretive issues regarding the assignment of guilt. The framing of issues in these tetralogies prefigures the treatment of "stasis" in the *Rhetoric to Alexander* and could well be a source for it.

Between Antiphon and the *Rhetoric to Alexander* lies Isocrates and his generation. Isocrates certainly would have been aware of Antiphon—he was twenty-five years old when Antiphon was executed in 411 B.C.E.—and his own experience as a logographer in judicial cases, between 403 and 390, would have taught him much about stasis. He does not, of course, use the term: The word *stasis* and its variants do appear in his extant writings, but always with the ordinary meaning of "discord" or "civil strife" (for example, *Against Callimachus* 44). But his judicial *logoi* display an astute grasp of the *idea*. Of the three judicial *logoi* that survive complete, *On the Banker* is situated at the stasis of fact, *Aegineticus* at the stasis of quality, and *Against Callimachus* at the stasis of procedural objection. This distribution may well reflect what these *logoi* were used to teach.

On the Banker (*Trapezeticus*) involves a complicated story that, in simplified outline, is as follows. The speaker, a young foreigner from the Bosporus, claims that the banker Pasion has defrauded him of a large sum of money. The speaker was sent to Athens by his father on business and for the young man to "see the world," and on arrival he deposited the money his father had given him with Pasion for safekeeping. Political trouble ensued back home, and arrest and property-confiscation orders were issued there for the young man and his father. Pasion agreed to help the young man hide his money by pretending that the deposit did not exist. Soon things were straightened out at home, the arrest and confiscation orders were rescinded, and the young man asked Pasion for his money, at which point Pasion denied that he had it. After a series of further developments, the young man threatened to take Pasion to court. Pasion then begged not to be exposed, claimed that he was temporarily short of funds, and signed a memorandum promising to repay the money; this was sealed and placed under the care of a third party for safekeeping. After still more developments, the young man's friend Menexenus threatened to take Pasion to court on a related matter and thus expose his fraud. Pasion at first tried to get the suit called off, then suddenly began denying that he owed the young man anything, and insisted that the memorandum be opened. When it was opened, it was found to state that Pasion had no obligation. This complex situation illustrates what Isocrates means by determining precisely what is "to be accomplished" by a discourse within a particular situation. While the basic issue is a question of fact—whether the young man has in fact deposited money with Pasion and Pasion has defrauded him of it—the crucial issue, also a question of fact, is whether the memorandum has been tampered with. The young man must establish his claims on both of these questions, but especially the latter. As he says at the end of his narrative, "I think, men of the jury, that Pasion will base his defense on the altered document, and rely on it especially" (24). In the proof section of the speech, this issue is addressed mainly through the presentation of what are explicitly called *tekmêria,* "evidence," supported by witness testimony and interpreted through appeals to *eikos,* "probability." For example:

> But this is the greatest *tekmêrion* of all that Pasion was not released [from his obligation], but had agreed to repay the gold: when Menexenus brought the lawsuit against him, and the memorandum had not yet been altered, he sent Agyrrhius, who was friendly with both of us, asking me either to call off Menexenus or to annul the agreement I had made with him. And yet, men of the jury, do you suppose that he would have wished to annul an agreement with which he could irrefutably prove [*exelenxein*] us liars? But after the writing had been altered, he did not say these things, but appealed to the agreement concerning everything and asked for the memorandum to be opened.

I will provide Agyrrhius himself as a witness that at first Pasion was eager to annul the agreement. [Agyrrhius testifies.] (31–32)

While *eikos* is not explicitly mentioned here (it is repeatedly mentioned elsewhere), it clearly is appealed to in the question, "Do you suppose . . . ?" This appeal fits the *Rhetoric to Alexander's* definition of *eikos* as a statement supported by examples in the audience's mind (7 1428a). The jury is meant to recognize that Pasion's actions do not match what men would normally do with a document that would tell in their favor in an impending lawsuit.

The passage obliquely recognizes, in the term *exelenxein,* a third form of proof also, the *elenchos,* which is not Socratic "refutation" but what the *Rhetoric to Alexander* defines as a "necessary" argument that an opponent cannot deny: "an *elenchos* is what cannot be other than as we say" (13 1431a). If Pasion can produce a valid memorandum that absolves him of any obligation to the young man, that would be a decisive, "clinching" argument in his favor, an *elenchos,* and the young man's and Menexenus' claims against him would utterly collapse. The young man's witness-supported *tekmêrion,* the fact that Pasion at one point wished to annul the memorandum but later changed his tune, grounds a probability argument that the original document was not favorable to him and in the interim was altered. This argument is not a fully decisive *elenchos* because the young man cannot produce a witness to the forgery—but the probability seems high, and it renders Pasion's case, and his would-be *elenchos,* unpersuasive.[65]

Other types of proof mentioned in this speech include the "sign" (*sêmeion*). Again, this is not a "sign" argument as discussed by Aristotle, but something closer to the *Rhetoric to Alexander's* notion, namely, a kind of index that may produce something like full knowledge, or in other words a proof that is more than a *tekmêrion* but less than an *elenchos:* "one thing is a sign of another, not a chance event of a chance event and not anything of anything, but something that usually precedes, accompanies, or follows something" (12 1430b). Smoke is a sign of fire. Pasion says that the young man took a deposit or loan of three hundred staters (six hundred drachmas) from a person named Stratocles and calls it a sign that the young man had no money of his own; the young man counters by arguing that it actually provides a *tekmêrion* that Pasion had his money in safekeeping because Pasion stood as the guarantor that the young man would repay (*On the Banker* 36–37). Also included in this speech, of course, are types of what the *Rhetoric to Alexander* calls "supplemental" proofs (*epithetoi*): witnesses, documents and oaths (contracts, written agreements), and information extracted by "interrogation" (torture). The last of these is mentioned but not actually used, as Pasion refuses to surrender his slave, who was a witness to the original contract of deposit, for interrogation. This refusal, of course, becomes a *tekmêrion* against Pasion, because it suggests that he has something to hide.

In sum, *On the Banker* exemplifies not only the importance of identifying the crucial question at issue—and thus what the speech and its parts must accomplish—but also several *ideai* to be used in issues of fact: evidence (*tekmêria*), probabilities (*eikota*), signs (*sêmeia*), "necessary" proofs (*elenchoi*), and "supplemental" proofs (*epithetoi*) such as witnesses. These terms are all used as they are used in the *Rhetoric to Alexander.*

Aegineticus is about a dispute over a will. Like *On the Banker*, it is based on a complicated story. The speaker, a resident of Aegina, was made the adopted son and heir of his close friend, Thrasylochus, shortly before Thrasylochus' death. However, Thrasylochus' father, Thrasyllus, whose early life was spent as an itinerant soothsayer, had cohabited with several women in different cities and had left behind a number of illegitimate children. One of these, Thrasylochus' half-sister, claims that the will should be invalidated and that she, Thrasyllus' only surviving child, should be the heir. The stasis is therefore "quality": the existence of the will is not denied, nor its genuineness, nor any of the facts regarding the friendship between Thrasyllus and the speaker, but the plaintiff asserts that the will is illegal and unjust. As the speaker puts it, "They [the plaintiff's advocates] say that they do not doubt that Thrasylochus left the will, but they claim that it is neither honorable (*kalôs*) nor correct" (*orthôs;* 34).

The speaker's argument first addresses the question of legality or "correctness." There are possible complications here, because the will was written and executed at Aegina, where the trial is being held, but Thrasylochus and the speaker originally were citizens of Siphnos—they were driven into exile during civil strife, and resettled in Aegina—and the plaintiff is a resident of yet another city (which is not named, but may be Troezen). Thus there is a possible question about jurisdiction: whether the different cities' laws conflict, and if so, which should govern the legality of the will. The speaker has the will read out, followed by the inheritance laws of each city, and shows that the laws all agree with each other, and that the will is correct according to all of them. Hence there is no remaining issue at the "legal" subhead of the qualitative stasis, unless the plaintiff can argue, from intent versus letter, that the laws are intended to ensure the passage of an inheritance to blood descendants, which she apparently cannot or does not do. In consequence the plaintiff's available arguments are limited to the headings of the "rational" substasis, in particular the headings of the just and the honorable: is it right for a blood relative to be deprived of the inheritance, and for an "outsider" adopted at the last moment to inherit all?

Most of the speaker's argument, then, addresses the "rational" substasis. It details the longstanding close relations between Thrasylochus' family and the speaker's, and, especially, the speaker's many services to Thrasylochus and his family, often at great personal risk and cost, including getting them to safety during civil strife, running dangerous errands on their behalf, retrieving their fortune, saving the life of Thrasylochus' brother Sopolis in battle, and nursing, alone and with much difficulty, Thrasylochus during his long last illness. This is carried out—in the proof section of the speech—in the manner of narrative/descriptive amplifications in the encomiastic celebration of deeds (*ideai* practiced before in progymnasmata), all tending toward a recurring conclusion couched in terms of the just (*dikaion*). For example, "Who more justly (*dikaioteron*) deserves to possess this fortune than the one who helped to save it, and now has received it from its proper owners?" (20). In comparison to the speaker's many acts of selfless friendship are set the plaintiff's history of indifference and even hostility to Thrasylochus and his family. For example, "And when he was about to die, and she saw our fellow-citizens in Troezen preparing to sail to Aegina for the funeral, not even at that time did she come, but was so hardhearted and implacable that she did not see fit to come and mourn. Yet when less than ten days had passed she came to dispute about what he had left, as if she were related to his money and not to him" (30–31).

Just as comparisons can magnify encomiastic praise, here the comparison of opposites enhances the picture of the speaker's virtuous behavior and intensifies the "invective" (*psogos*) heaped on the half-sister, whose dishonorable record of unsisterly behavior invalidates the justice of her claim to familial rights. This comparison bolsters what Aristotelian rhetoric calls the speaker's apparent ethos, what the *Rhetoric to Alexander* calls the audience's "opinion of the speaker" (*doxa tou legontos;* 14 1431b)—and classes as a "supplementary" proof—and what Isocrates likewise calls "the opinion [*doxa*] the speaker gains among his fellow-citizens for being honorable" and considers indispensable to persuasion (*Antidosis* 278).

In the last part of the speaker's argument, corresponding to the refutation section of the classical oration, Isocrates deploys what the *Rhetoric to Alexander* (18 1432b) calls "anticipation" (*prokatalêpsis*), the preemptive reply to an argument that might be made by the opponent. Perhaps, the speaker says, the plaintiff will assert that Thrasyllus would feel dishonored if he could see his own daughter cast aside while an outsider inherits the family wealth (*Aegineticus* 42). After first dismissing the idea as legally irrelevant, the speaker argues that, in any case, and if the dead have any perception, Thrasyllus actually would approve. Several arguments are employed, mostly based on probability (43–46), including "Nothing is more probable (*eikos*) than that Thrasyllus would think well of those whose claims are based on a testamentary gift" (that is, because Thrasyllus received his own wealth in that way; 45). The whole argument, finally, is capped with a much-amplified enthymematic statement, a single sentence of 138 words, more or less in the manner recommended by the *Rhetoric to Alexander* (that is, draw the conclusion in the form of an antithesis): "Therefore, if you grant the inheritance to me, you will be well-regarded by [Thrasyllus], and by everyone else who has some interest in these matters; but if you are persuaded and deceived by this woman, you will do an injustice not only to me, but also to Thrasylochus who left the will, and to [his deceased brother] Sopolis, and to their sister who is now my wife, and to their mother, who would be the unhappiest of women," and so on (47–48), followed by a series of epiphonemas that further underscore the point (48–49).

Aegineticus thus illustrates judicial argument at the qualitative stasis, focused chiefly on the issues of legality and justice and employing several *ideai* of proof and amplification discussed by the *Rhetoric to Alexander*—*tekmêria* (the evidentiary facts), probabilities (*eikota*), comparisons, examples, "supplemental" proofs (the will, the laws, and the speaker's good ethos and the half-sister's bad one), enthymemes, and "anticipation"—as well as such elements from the progymnasmata as epiphonemas, encomiastic and invective discourse, and narration/description. In short, we see Isocrates selecting and combining *ideai* according to the needs of both the qualitative stasis and the particulars of the situation, the *kairos,* in this specific case.

Against Callimachus is striking as an early example of argument at the stasis of procedural objection—a stasis not recognized by the *Rhetoric to Alexander,* but firmly fixed, later, in the teaching of stasis theory from Hermagoras to Hermogenes. The full title of the speech is actually *Paragraphê against Callimachus. Paragraphê* means "exception to writ." When the speech was composed, this was a newly instituted procedure meant to support the amnesty (*amnêstia,* "forgetting") that had been declared after the restoration of democracy at Athens in 403 B.C.E. In essence, the amnesty forbade anyone to "recall" or pursue redress for wrongs committed during the brief oligarchic rule of the Thirty Tyrants, and their successors, the Ten, after the Athenian defeat in the Peloponnesian War, and in the civil strife that led to the democracy's restoration. The law of *paragraphê,* known as the "law of Archinus," established a procedure in which a defendant could challenge a writ of indictment (*graphê*) lodged against him as a violation of the amnesty, and, if he could prove that, get it thrown out; the loser would be subject to a fine equal to one-sixth of the damages in question. *Against Callimachus* appears to be one of the first cases that went to trial under the *paragraphê* law.[66] As the defendant says in his opening sentence, "If any others had contended before now on such a plea of *paragraphê,* I would begin my arguments from the facts themselves; but as things are, I must speak first of the law in accordance with which we have come together" (1).

As with *On the Banker* and *Aegineticus,* this speech too involves a complicated story. During the brief rule of "the Ten," Callimachus was deprived of a large sum of money by one Patrocles, who denounced him to the Ten for holding funds that belonged to an exiled democratic leader; the Ten ruled that the money was to be confiscated. After the restoration of democracy, Callimachus successfully sued Patrocles for the return of ten minas (one thousand drachmas; one drachma was a day's pay for a worker); he also sued Patrocles' friends, Lysimachus and the speaker. The speaker decided to avoid the dangers of a trial and settled out of court by an arbitration agreement, and paid two minas. Despite the agreement, Callimachus later sued the speaker again, this time for one hundred minas (ten thousand drachmas), an enormous sum. The speaker produced a witness to the arbitration agreement and Callimachus withdrew the suit, but after some interval and a change of magistrates, he sued again. It seems that the *paragraphê* law had been instituted during this interval, since the speaker now makes it the basis of his plea. One might assume that the speaker has an open-and-shut case, but the fact that Callimachus has been able to "persuade the magistrate" (12) to bring the case to court a second time suggests that the judgment may not have seemed obvious. The new law had not yet been tested by a trial, and there may have been some sympathy for people who claimed to have been robbed of money and property by the oligarchs—and some hostility toward those who might be linked to the oligarchs or their supporters, as in the speaker's friendship with Patrocles.

After his prologue, description of the *paragraphê* law, and narration of the basic facts that I have just outlined, the speaker devotes his argument to three main points: that Callimachus has no basis for a complaint; that even if he did, the amnesty and *paragraphê* laws ought to be upheld; and finally, that Callimachus is a malicious person who deserves no sympathy whereas the speaker has been a decent citizen and friend of the democracy. The first point arises as an "anticipation"—"I hear that Callimachus intends not only to tell lies about the allegations, but also to deny that there was an arbitration" (13)—a point of fact that is dealt with chiefly through what are explicitly called *tekmêria* and probabilities (*eikota*), as well as "supplemental" proofs (witness testimony). For example, Callimachus' former choice not to contest testimony that the arbitration had taken place is an "evidence" (*tekmêrion*) that he indeed acknowledged the arbitration at that time and is lying about it now; and it is "not probable" (*ouk eikos*) that Callimachus would have settled then for only two minas if, as he now claims, he actually was owed one hundred; further, agreeing to such a relatively small amount at the arbitration, after claiming such a large one, is a *tekmêrion* too that Callimachus was lying in the first place; it suggests that he was just making up figures as a bargaining tactic in blackmail (14–15). As for Callimachus' allegations, the speaker's narrative has already brought forth witnesses to testify that he had no role in the seizure of Callimachus' money. But even if there were no witnesses, the speaker says, the probabilities (*eikota*) alone make Callimachus' allegations unlikely. Since the speaker engaged in no injustices during the rule of the Thirty, even when many people were doing wrong and even were encouraged, or ordered, to do wrong, is it likely that he suddenly would have changed his ways when the oligarchy was at its end and people were repenting? (16–18).

The speaker's argument on the second point brings the focus to the actual stasis of procedural objection, or *paragraphê,* and begins from the topic of legality: "I think that I have proved sufficiently that I am not responsible for the confiscation of Callimachus' money; but that he had no right to bring a lawsuit over things that happened then, even if I had done everything he says, you will learn from the covenants [of the amnesty]" (19). The speaker then resorts to "supplemental" proof: he has the covenants (*sunthêkai*) of the amnesty and the supporting oaths (*horkoi*) read out and shows that the actions that Callimachus alleges are explicitly covered by the amnesty law. So Callimachus, he argues, is asking the jury to violate the city's oaths and covenants; his suit is illegal (20). As a matter of strict legality, the speaker's argument is completed at this point; his problem, however, is that the jury must *choose* to observe and enforce the amnesty. Thus he turns, first, to comparative examples that show the importance attached to the amnesty (in what the *Rhetoric of Alexander* calls the appeal to "previous judgments" and treats as one of the common *ideai*): Philon of Coele, who clearly had committed misdeeds on an embassy, when accused offered no defense but merely cited the amnesty and was acquitted; some of the most powerful men in the city lost a great deal of money and property but have not "dared" to seek redress as Callimachus is doing, and neither have any of the jurors (21–22). These arguments are followed by a series of counterfactual suppositions (contradictories) that appeal to notions of honor and justice, such as, "It would be shocking if you observed the oaths in your own affairs, but tried to transgress them for the sake of this man's malicious charges (*sukophantia;* 24) . . . You would be doing what is neither just (*dikaia*), nor worthy (*axia*) of yourselves, nor consistent (*preponta*) with your former judgments" (26).

These arguments are followed by a commonplace on the importance of observing covenants: "Consider [*enthumeisthe*] that you have come to pass judgment on very great matters; for you will cast your vote concerning covenants, and it has never been profitable to violate covenants, neither for you in relation to others, nor for others in relation to you. Indeed they have so great a power that most of life, both for Greeks and for barbarians, is governed by covenants; for by placing our trust [*pisteuontes*] in them we come to one other and trade for what each of us needs; through them we make contracts among ourselves and put an end to private quarrels and common wars. This is the one thing in common that all human beings employ continually. So it is everyone's duty to support them, and especially yours" (27–28). And so on, through an account of how the city saved itself from civil war and won universal admiration among the Greeks by the amnesty (29–32), so that the case ceases to be about Callimachus and the speaker only and becomes a referendum on the city's adherence to fundamental principles and its ability to live at peace. As the speaker says, "I do not think even Callimachus himself would deny that it is needful [*chrê*], beneficial [*sumpherei*], and just [*dikaion*] for you to decide about the covenants [of the amnesty] in this way" (35).

The third point in the speaker's argument follows this appeal to noble principles with an account of Callimachus as a bad citizen and then an account of the speaker's services to the city, a comparison of "opposites" as in *Aegineticus.* This includes a portrait of Callimachus' career as a "sycophant" (*sukophantês*) and one particular case, attested to by witnesses, in which Callimachus and his brother hid a servant girl and accused a citizen named Cratinus, with whom the brother was having a dispute over a farm, of murdering her. At the trial they produced fourteen witnesses to the murder, but Cratinus had found and retrieved the girl and brought her into court and revealed the utter falsity of Callimachus' case (51–54)—an *elenchos*, surely. With Callimachus' credibility and reputation thus destroyed, the speaker narrates his own heroic services to the city in the closing days of the Peloponnesian War (58–61) and concludes with an epilogue on how the jurors would do wrong to reward a sycophant such as Callimachus and to punish a good citizen such as himself while also violating their oaths and the covenants of the amnesty. "You should," he says, "remember these things and vote for what is just [*ta dikaia*] and beneficial" (*ta sumpheronta;* 68).

Isocrates' three complete judicial speeches, then, exhibit a sensitivity not only to stasis in some form but also to the specificity of the crucial issue in each case, and to the creative possibilities for selecting and combining *ideai* according to what is "to be accomplished" in each particular situation. *On the Banker* turns on a question of fact, but especially whether Pasion has tampered with the memorandum of agreement; *Aegineticus* turns on "qualitative" questions regarding the legality and justice of Thrasylochus' will, but especially whether the half-sister deserves to be the heir; and *Against Callimachus* turns on the "procedural" question whether Callimachus' lawsuit is prohibited by his former arbitration agreement with the speaker and by the amnesty law, but especially whether that law ought to be enforced. Issues of fact primarily call for arguments based on probabilities (*eikota*) and evidence (*tekmêria*), and other kinds of proof (*sêmeia, elenchoi,* "examples," "enthymemes"), as well as "supplemental" proofs (witnesses, documents, oaths, interrogation/torture, and the audience's opinion of the speaker). Qualitative issues, in addition, bring in topics of legality, justice, honor, and advantage, as well as such *ideai* as comparison, contradictories, narrative/description, commonplaces, and other forms of amplification. Judicial discourse will draw chiefly on topics of legality and justice, encomiastic on topics of the honorable, and symbouleutic on topics of the advantageous (including the profitable, the pleasant, the practicable, the possible, and the necessary), though the intelligent *rhêtôr* will select, combine, and use whatever suits the exigencies of his case.

We thus may attribute to Isocrates at least a rudimentary stasis system that looks something like this:

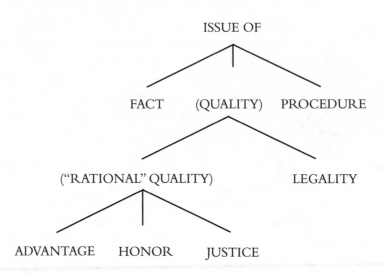

This representation probably is more systematic than Isocrates' presentation, and his own conception, really would have been; and the distinction between "legality" and "rational quality" probably reads in too much of later stasis theory. But something roughly along these lines, at least, is evident in his practice, in texts that he almost certainly used as models for teaching, and it is likely to have been addressed in his teaching of preliminary inquiry. Note that, in essence, the main "qualitative" headings correspond to the "final" or "ultimate" headings discussed in the later progymnasmata manuals and sum up the *Rhetoric to Alexander*'s common *ideai* or topics of invention to be used in all genres of civic discourse. Different genres and different situations will call for different selections from those *ideai,* while each genre also will have specialized *ideai* peculiar to its subject matter, such as, for symbouleutic, considerations related to "war and peace" or "revenues" (see *Rhet. Alex.* 2–5).

The Isocratean framework apparently lacks the *Rhetoric to Alexander*'s stasis of "forgiveness," which probably is subsumed under "justice." Isocrates' framework also lacks Hermagoras' and later theorists' stasis of definition. Isocrates seems not to recognize it either as a distinct topic of invention or type of argument. In *Antidosis,* in the course of a thesis on what can rightly claim the name of "philosophy," he proposes to "define and clarify" (*horisai kai dêlôsai*) what philosophy really is (270). However, Isocrates elsewhere invariably uses the verb *horisai* in its ordinary meaning of "delimit, outline, set a boundary to," and that may be all that he means here. Indeed he does not argue what *philosophia* really is on the basis of definitional or categorical arguments but on the basis of what is honorable and pragmatically advantageous. Likewise his argument about *philosophia* as a practice analogous to athletic training and other *technai* (*Antidosis* 180–189) is not a definitional or categorical argument but an argument from "similars." In general he seems uninterested in the methods of categorical argument, such as Plato and Aristotle were developing. (The nonappearance of definition in Isocrates' *technê* may be what motivates the critique of "Lysias's" speech in Plato's *Phaedrus* as lacking the method of definition, that is, collection and division, or genus/species.) Aside from this omission, however, Isocrates' basic framework for preliminary inquiry clearly prefigures the later, much more developed stasis theory of Hermagoras.

Isocrates' preliminary inquiry also includes a canvassing of facts in the subject matter, or case, that a rhetor plans to write or speak about. As he says, once the rhetor has selected a suitably honorable case (*hupothesis*) on which to exercise his powers, "then he will select from the facts [*praxeis*] that bear upon the case those that are most appropriate and especially useful" (*tas prepôdestatas kai malista sumpherous; Antidosis* 276–277). These somewhat oblique remarks seem to have symbouleutic or panegyric discourse, or history writing, primarily in mind. The basic point, however, is that the rhetor preparing a discourse must begin the process of preliminary inquiry with "research" into the subject matter of the case with an eye to what is relevant and useful. He must be thoroughly informed about the facts. One might compare Isocrates' remarks—made in passing, as an appendage to an argument about the character-building effects of *philosophia*/rhetoric—with Antonius' more direct account, in Cicero's *De oratore*, of his own process of preliminary inquiry: first he interviews his client in private and ascertains as fully as possible the client's version of the facts and what the real facts probably are; then he retires to his study and plays out an imaginary conversation between himself, the opposing advocate, and the judge, until he feels he has determined the true facts of the case, the available perspectives on those facts, where the points of contention or controversy are, and what most needs to be talked about, that is, what will advance the case, what will not, and what will positively hurt it; and at that point, the stasis is clear (*De oratore* 2.99–104). Antonius, of course, is thinking only of judicial argument, but the process easily can be generalized. The person preparing to write a history, for example, must consult the available sources of information—documents and eyewitnesses—and must consider the facts they provide from differing interpretive perspectives and ascertain their relevance and use on the way to identifying, as

Isocrates says, exactly what is "to be accomplished" by the discourse, or in other words the precise stasis of the case and its major lines of argument. And so too for encomiastic and symbouleutic discourse.

Invention: The Parts of the Oration

After the preliminary inquiry, the next stage of activity, or the next step in rhetorical training, is what the later *technai*, Hermogenes in particular, call "invention" (*heuresis*) of the speech itself and of its parts, or what the *Rhetoric to Alexander* calls the method of "ordering the arguments" (*tous logous*) in a discourse "part by part" (*kata merê*; 28, 1436a).[67] This is the signature approach of the early sophistic *technai* going back to Tisias and Corax, which is parodied in Plato's *Phaedrus* (266d–267a) and critiqued and reviewed in Aristotle's *Rhetoric* (3.13–19): instructions for the handling of the introduction (*prologos* or *prooimion*), narrative of the case (*diêgêsis*), proof or "confirmation" of the speaker's claim (*pistis*, or *kataskeuê* in later handbooks, and *bebaiôsis* in the *Rhetoric to Alexander*), "anticipation" or refutation of opposing arguments (*prokatalêpsis, dialusis, antilogia*), appeals to feeling (*pathos*), and "recapitulation" (*palillogia* or *epanodos*) and conclusion (*epilogos* or *peras*, "ending").

Dionysius of Halicarnassus attributes this part-by-part treatment of "the *prooimion*, the *diêgêsis*, and the other parts of the speech" to Isocrates and his followers (*Lysias* 16). *Prooimion* and *diêgêsis* clearly are part of Isocrates' technical vocabulary. As he says in *Panegyricus*, "I see that others, in their *prooimia*, soften up the audience and make excuses for what they are about to say" (13; see also *Panathenaicus* 33 and *Antidosis* 71). As I have observed, in *On the Banker* he promises to "narrate (*diêgêsomai*) from the beginning what has happened" (3), and surviving testimonia from Quintilian to Syrianus attribute to Isocrates specific instructions regarding narrative.[68] Beyond this point, however, things are less terminologically clear. Isocrates may be making a glancing reference to the "proof" section of a discourse in *Antidosis* when he argues that a speaker's reputation counts for more than "every form of proof" (*pan to tôn pisteôn eidos*), because these "serve only the part (*meros*) in which each of them is spoken" whereas a good reputation enhances the persuasiveness of everything the speaker says throughout the speech (280). Otherwise, however, Isocrates makes no explicit references that I can find to the "proof" section of a discourse, or to "anticipations," appeals to pathos, "recapitulations," or conclusions, though clearly his discourses have these parts, and he clearly has a technical vocabulary for types (*ideai*) of proof, such as *eikota, tekmêria, sêmeia, enthumêmata*, and so on.

Once again, the *Rhetoric to Alexander* is probably closest to Isocrates' teaching. Its instructions on narrative, for example—the narrative should be brief, clear, and convincing, and should narrate things in sequence (30, 1438a)—closely parallel those attributed to Isocrates. The same is true for its terminology for types of proof, as we have seen already, as well as its terminology for the common *ideai* to be employed for qualitative issues. Further, its precepts for handling the parts of a discourse are reflected in Isocratean practice. Let us take the example of *Archidamus*.

Archidamus is most probably a teaching text. It purports to be a straight-forward example of practical symbouleutic oratory delivered in a deliberative assembly on a question of war or peace, and it would have been a good model for introducing the genre. It is in the voice of the Spartan prince Archidamus and is set in the context of historical events: the peace treaty offered by Thebes to Sparta and its Peloponnesian allies in 366 B.C.E. Critical opinion varies on whether it is a real oration written by Isocrates for Archidamus to deliver in the Spartan assembly or whether it is a "rhetorical exercise," a declamation, written at some later time as an ethopoiea.[69] The question is irresolvable, though one might argue that the probabilities favor its being a declamation.

One might, for example, invoke Cicero's descriptions of Isocrates as a retir-ing schoolmaster (*Brutus* 8.32) whose discourses "neither fight in the battle-line nor use steel, but so to speak fence with a wooden sword" (*De optimo genere ora-torum* 6.17)—that is, are schoolroom exercises. Further, it is highly unlikely that a Spartan prince would want to deliver before Spartans a speech composed for him by an Athenian, or to be seen to be doing that, on an issue that involved the survival of Sparta itself; and the speech is composed in the Attic dialect, not the Doric dialect of the Spartans. There is also the problem of the time and care that Isocrates famously devoted to composing his *logoi,* and the fact that Archi-damus would have delivered his speech in reply to a Corinthian delegation in the course of an urgent deliberation. Would he have had time to send to Athens for a speech, wait a few days or weeks for Isocrates to compose one and send it back to him, and then rehearse and memorize it?

An intermediate possibility is that *Archidamus* was written in sympathy with Spartan concerns at that time and was meant to circulate as a pamphlet, perhaps to encourage Athenian aid; another, if weaker, possibility is that it was written as an after-the-fact literary representation of the speech that Archidamus actu-ally gave, if he gave one. One might add that the Spartans generally were not big on lengthy speeches. The bottom line, however, is that whatever *Archidamus* was originally, in Isocrates' school in later years it would have functioned as a declamation, a demonstration (*epideixis*) of symbouleutic speech composed "in character" and set in a particular historical occasion. In this respect it prefigures the historical declamations that were highly popular in later antiquity, and that are attested in papyrus fragments as early as the second quarter of the third cen-tury B.C.E.[70]

The situation of *Archidamus* is straightforward. Sparta's short-lived hegemony after the Peloponnesian War was brought to an end by the Thebans under the great general Epaminondas at the battle of Leuctra in 371. In the following years Theban armies repeatedly reinvaded the Peloponnese, harassed both Sparta and its allies, encouraged Sparta's serf populations, the Helots and Messenians, to revolt, and refounded the city of Messene, whose territory had been under Spartan control for centuries. At one point (in 369) Theban forces entered Sparta itself, an alarming development, since the city had never before been penetrated by hostile armies. The Spartans were facing the possibility of total destruction. In 366 Corinth and several other Spartan allies worn down by the Theban invasions began to sue for peace. The Thebans proposed a treaty that included the humiliating (for Sparta) requirement that Messene and its territory be independent—in effect depriving Sparta of a major source of its agricultural wealth and establishing a hostile, pro-Theban state on its western frontier. At an assembly held in Sparta to discuss the Thebans' terms, the Corinthian delegation urged that the proposal be accepted. *Archidamus,* then, purports to be the speech of young Archidamus in reply, urging that Sparta refuse the terms and resolve to fight for Messene. (This is, in fact, the choice they made.)[71]

The *Rhetoric to Alexander* offers the familiar precepts for the *prooimion*. It is "a preparation of the listeners" and "a summary statement of the subject-matter" to ensure that "they will know what the speech is about and will be able to follow the case" (*parakothoulôsi têi hupothesei*) and "to exhort them to pay attention and to make them well-disposed to us" (29, 1436a). Concerning goodwill, the discussion focuses especially on the problems of overcoming "prejudice" (*diabolê*) against the speaker himself, the subject matter (*to pragma*), or the speech (29, 1436b–1437b). Prejudice against the speaker is aroused by past misdeeds or present problems, and of present problems, "the first is age," when the speaker seems too young or too old to be addressing a deliberative assembly. The subject arouses prejudice when a speaker "advises acting against those who have done no wrong, or against those who are stronger, or making a shameful peace"; and the speech arouses prejudice when it is "long or oldfashioned" or otherwise "unpersuasive" or offputting. *Archidamus* illustrates these problems: Archidamus is by Spartan custom too young to be addressing the assembly and apparently has never addressed it before, he is proposing war against a stronger adversary, and the idea that Sparta might prevail seems prima facie unlikely.

The *prooimion* begins, from its opening sentence, by addressing the problem of age: "Perhaps some of you are astonished that . . . despite my youth I have come forward to give advice on matters that even my elders hesitate to discuss" (1). The *Rhetoric to Alexander* recommends that a young man justify his speaking by invoking its necessity because of a lack of good advisors, the special interest of a young man in the issue (particularly when it is a question of war), his own qualifications by virtue of nature and training, and the argument that "if he is wrong [*hamartonti*] the misfortune is his own, but if he is right [*katorthôsanti*] the benefit is shared in common" (*koinê hê ôpheleia;* 29 1437b). That is exactly what Archidamus does, and in that order. He first complains that "none of those accustomed to address you have spoken in a manner worthy of the city," so that it would be "disgraceful" for him to keep silent merely for the sake of custom (*Archidamus* 2); next he maintains that young men have a particular right to speak on questions of war, since "they will bear the greater part of the dangers" (3); then he maintains that "it is not by the number of our years that we differ from one another with respect to practical wisdom [*to phronein eu*], but by natural ability [*phusei*] and by training [*epimeleiais*]," and he adds that it is strange that young men like himself are thought fit to lead armies in the field[72] but not to give advice on issues of war and peace (4–5); and finally he asserts that "when we [young men] are right [*kathorthôsantes*] in these matters we benefit you all [*hapantas humas ôphelêsomen*], but when you think us wrong [*diamartontes*] we may look foolish but we cause the state no harm" (5). The language of this last argument is remarkably similar to that of the *Rhetoric to Alexander.*

Archidamus then turns to the problem of prejudice against his subject matter. The *Rhetoric to Alexander* suggests using "anticipation" (*prokatalêpsis*) and placing the blame on necessity (*anankê*), fortune (*tuchê*), circumstances (*kairoi*), advantage (*sumpheron*), or the facts (*pragmata*). Archidamus announces his position: "Formerly we struggled to rule over others, but now we must struggle not to do what others command, which is a sign [*sêmeion*] of liberty, for the sake of which nothing is too terrible to be endured, not only for us, but also for others who barely retain their manhood yet still claim at least a little courage [*arête*]. As for me, if I must speak for myself, I would rather die right now and not comply with this order, rather than live many times my allotted span and vote for what the Thebans propose. . . . May no one persuade you to bring upon our city such disgrace" (7–8, 10).

This argument, backed up with its maxims about liberty and manly courage, in effect refers Archidamus' stance to "necessity" by suggesting that there is no honorable alternative for a Spartan, and particularly not for Archidamus himself, who is, as he says, a descendant of Hercules and of kings (9). It also portrays the present state of affairs as a "misfortune"—"we seem to have been unfortunate (*dedustuchênai*) in our war against the Thebans"—brought on "by incorrect leadership" (*dia ton ouk orthôs hêgêsamenon*), meaning tactical and strategic errors on the battlefield (9). Archidamus, then, presents his position as a necessity caused by "fortune" and "circumstances," while implicitly suggesting also that there is no necessary reason why the Thebans should continue to be successful, or for the Spartans to submit to their demands without a fight. As he says, "In our souls we still are unconquered" (9–10). Having, then, "anticipated" objections that he is proposing action against a stronger adversary and that the probabilities for success are low, he turns against those who counsel peace: "And yet our allies all too eagerly have advised us that we must give up Messene and make peace! It is right for you to be much more angry with them than with those who revolted from you at the start" (11). And so on for several hundred words (11–14). This passage works to generate prejudice or resentment against the Corinthian position and anyone who seconds it by presenting it, in the *Rhetoric to Alexander*'s terms, as "making a shameful peace." With this the *prooimion* comes to a close and Archidamus wishes for the ability to adequately state his case and thereby serve the city (15).

Aristotle maintains that narrative (*diêgêsis*) "as people describe it" properly belongs only to judicial speeches, and that making it a division of the symbouleutic speech is "ridiculous" (*Rhetoric* 3.13.3), but the *Rhetoric to Alexander* recommends that, in symbouleutic discourse, after the *prooimion* "it is necessary that we either report or recall to mind what has happened before, or clarify the present state of things,[73] or forecast what is going to happen" (*Rhet. Alex.* 30, 1438a). That is, a symbouleutic discourse needs a narration of the past, present, or future facts to which the proposed policy or course of action is a response. It will, in essence, state the problem for which the proposal is a solution and provide a frame for the arguments to follow. And as the precepts attributed to Isocrates and those of the *Rhetoric to Alexander* both suggest, it should narrate things in sequence, and should be brief, clear, and convincing (30, 1438a–b).

Archidamus offers a narrative not of the present situation but of the past, in order to establish the justice of Sparta's claims to Messene and the injustice of the Theban demand and to lay some groundwork for an argument concerning the probabilities of success. As he says, "First, I think I ought to explain to you how we acquired Messene, and the reasons why you settled in the Peloponnese when anciently you were Dorians; and I will start from the earliest times, so that you may understand that they [the Thebans] are attempting to steal from you this country, which you acquired no less justly than the rest of Lacedaemon [the territory of Sparta]" (16). This account draws on a complex network of myth and proto-history that I will not attempt to spell out here, other than to note that the descendants of Hercules were supposed to have settled among the ancient Dorians in northern Greece, and then—at the behest of the god Apollo through the oracle at Delphi, and on the legalistic grounds of claims to ancient kinship—to have moved into, conquered, and settled with Dorian help the territories of Argos, Sparta, and Messene in the eastern and southern Peloponnese, setting themselves up as kings from whom the Spartan kings still claimed descent. Sparta conquered Messene later, after the Messenians overthrew and killed their Heracleid king. The surviving Heracleids of Messene appealed to their brother-kings in Sparta, offering their land in return for vengeance, and Apollo's oracle gave approval.[74] As hard to follow as Archidamus' patchwork of legendary material may seem to a modern reader, the narrative indeed attempts to be sequential, brief, clear, and convincing—and of course much of it would have been familiar to fourth-century readers. He more than once remarks that he is passing over material that is not directly relevant: "Concerning, then, what was ours from the beginning, I have not gone into detail; for the present occasion [kairos] does not allow me to narrate mythology [muthologein], and it was necessary to speak more briefly than clearly about these things. Nevertheless, even from what has been said I think it is clear to all that we came to possess the land that is acknowledged to be ours no differently than the land that is in dispute" (24).

Remarks such as this can be read as "paraliptic" gestures, mentioning or acknowledging something by setting it aside, but they also can be read as paideutic commentary in which the teacher directs attention to how he is handling a particular compositional problem. Such remarks are part of what Cicero portrays as "fencing with a wooden sword" in school, as the master conducts a demonstration for the class. In this case the problem is keeping complicated mythological material under control for the sake of brevity and relevance in narrative. Here the goals of brevity and clarity conflict, as the shortened account cannot fully tell the story of how Sparta came to possess Messene, and the determining consideration is what suffices for the narrative to make its point convincingly. The mythological material is authoritative, and need only be invoked in an abbreviated, incomplete form.

Arthur Walzer has suggested that *Archidamus* is a companion piece to *On the Peace,* forming an "antilogy"; the two *logoi* respond to a similar occasion, a peace treaty, but in different circumstances and in opposite ways—against and for— thus forming an object lesson in the role of *kairos* and the situatedness of practical deliberation and judgment.[75] Similarly, Archidamus' narrative can be viewed as an object lesson in Spartan ideology, exploring how a Spartan could view as reasonable an argument that Messene is an inalienable part of Sparta, a possession granted in perpetuity to the Heracleid kings by divine decree and acquired by justified conquest. As Archidamus observes, the Spartans have "to this day" observed the ancient oaths and covenants they made with the Heracleids and Apollo, have prospered, and will continue to prosper "if you stay constant" (22), whereas the Messenians broke their covenants and in consequence were punished by the god with conquest and enslavement in perpetuity (22–23). This argument also warrants an inference that by yielding Messene to the Thebans, the Spartans would break their covenants and therefore could expect a similarly wretched fate. Thus the Theban demand is really an attempt to weaken and destroy Sparta itself, anyone who counsels accepting the treaty is a traitor, and war is necessarily the only option. At the same time, the narrative warrants an inference also that the Spartans will prosper, despite recent setbacks, if they keep their ancestral covenants with the Heracleids and Apollo by fighting for Messene.

Archidamus tops his narrative with historical reminders that long possession is normally recognized as incontestable possession: Sparta has possessed Messene since early times, and even the Persians and Athenians have always recognized Sparta's right to this possession (26–27, 29–31). These recognitions, along with the ancient oracles, function as further proofs—what the *Rhetoric to Alexander* calls "previous judgments"—of Sparta's rightful ownership. Alongside these he sets what amounts to an argument from opposites or contradictories that the Thebans are unjust: they would restore to Persia some territories that the Persians controlled for only a short time, and they have razed two Greek cities, Thespiae and Plataea, to the ground while seeking to deprive Sparta of Messene (27–28). These facts are evidence (*tekmêria*) that Theban behavior violates accepted norms of justice and that their intention is simply to injure and humiliate Sparta. The argument of the whole narrative is then summed up with a recapitulation (*palillogia*), capped with an assertion that "any one of these facts is sufficient to refute (*dialusai*) the arguments" of those who say that Messene should be independent, and marked off with a transition that also may be paideutic commentary: "I could perhaps say more about our acquisition of Messene, but I consider what I have said enough" (32–33).

Archidamus then turns to the confirmation section of his speech (*bebaiôsis*), which is by far the longest part (34–106). The *Rhetoric to Alexander* suggests that the *bebaiôsis* of a symbouleutic speech should confirm the speaker's position with proof (*pistis*) of the facts given in the narrative, and with considerations of the justice (*to dikaion*) and advantage (*to sumpheron*) of the course of action in question, as well as other common *ideai* such as honor, legality, possibility, practicability, or pleasure (32, 1438b–1439a). It also suggests, in its discussion of the particular subject matters (*pragmata*) of symbouleutic discourse—religious ritual, legislation, constitutional reform, alliances, and so forth—that issues of war and peace involve mainly the questions of justice and advantage, and particularly, as a subset of advantage, questions regarding the probability of success (2 1425a). "Success," it says, "is always due to the favor of the gods, which we call good fortune, or to manpower and strength, or to material resources,[76] or to good leadership, or to good allies, or to advantages of locality" (2 1425a). Such things are to be confirmed through probabilities and evidence (for claims of fact), as well as examples, comparisons, maxims, enthymemes, and the like (for claims of justice, advantage, and probability of success; 32, 1438b–1439a). Archidamus' *bebaiôsis* is composed of a selection and combination of several of these elements.

The "facts" of Archidamus' narrative are not really disputable, at least in Spartan eyes, so there is no need to prove them. The *Rhetoric to Alexander* recommends that, in such a case, the speaker should skip the proof (*pistis*) of the narrated facts and proceed directly to the topics of justice and advantage, which Archidamus does. Further, since the issues of justice and honor have been dealt with in the narrative already—the Theban proposal, as well as Theban behavior in general, is unjust, and to accept such an injustice would be fatally dishonorable—all that really remains are the questions of advantage and probability of success. Archidamus thus proceeds to those questions and begins his argument as an "anticipation" (*prokatalêpsis*) or refutation (*dialusis*) of the opposition's basic stance: "Those that advise us to make peace say that men of practical intelligence should not hold the same attitude toward things in good fortune and in bad, but always should deliberate with a view to the present and accommodate themselves to circumstances, and should not presume to things beyond their power, and should seek not justice [*to dikaion*] in times like these but expediency [*to sumpheron*]" (34).

This is the fundamental principle, or "maxim," behind the Corinthian argument that Sparta should accept an unjust peace for the sake of self-preservation, or in other words sacrifice justice for advantage. It is a line of argument listed by the *Rhetoric to Alexander* for advising against a war (2 1425a). Archidamus' reply does not dispute the question of Theban superiority—he yields, in essence, the topic of "manpower and strength" (*Rhet. Alex.* 2, 1425a). Instead he offers what might be called a counter-commonplace on the indispensability of justice: "On their other points I agree with them, but that anything could be more indispensable [*proourgiaiteron*] than justice no-one can persuade me," and so on (35). The word *proourgiaiteron* can also mean "more serviceable, profitable, useful," and Archidamus' reply in essence is that justice cannot be sacrificed for advantage because justice is the most advantageous thing of all; it is, as he points out, the fundamental aim of the laws on which all civil society depends, indeed, the one advantage without which cities cannot prosper or endure, and wars are most often won not by those with the strongest army but by those whose cause is just (35–36). "Justice of the cause" trumps "manpower and strength" as a source of success in war.

This point is further developed by an argument from probabilities that, in attempting to trade land for peace, Sparta would be sacrificing a certain good (justice) for an uncertain one (safety). Giving up Messene without a fight does not prevent, and indeed invites, further harm: "For I think you know that everyone is accustomed to negotiate with those who defend their rights, but with those who too readily submit to demands, they always add more to what they originally had in mind, so that those of a warlike disposition obtain a better peace than those who easily come to terms" (39).

Having thus disposed of the central principle of his opposition's argument as a "kick me" piece of cowardice unlikely to get good long-term results,

Archidamus announces that he will "abandon" (*aphiêmi*) the subject and take up "the simplest of my proofs" (40). This is, in essence, an argument—relating to the topic of "possibility"—that frequently the weaker force defeats the stronger and "the besiegers are destroyed by the besieged" (40). This may be a version of the *Rhetoric to Alexander's* topic of "advantages of locality" for questions of war and peace, that is, the military precept that the defender has an advantage over the attacker if the defender occupies a suitably defensible position. It also resembles, faintly, what Aristotle describes as the topic of "things that are thought to have happened but are incredible" (*Rhetoric* 2.23.22), though Aristotle thinks that the very improbability of an asserted fact can work as a proof that it must really have happened. From the viewpoint of the *Rhetoric to Alexander,* however, Archidamus has asserted a proposition that does not immediately carry probability in the audience's mind and that therefore needs to be substantiated with examples, or what Aristotle calls "induction," *epagôgê* (*Rhetoric* 2.23.11). Archidamus thus declares that he can illustrate his claim with "many examples" (*pollois paradeigmasi*), the most famous of which are the Athenians' glorious fifth-century victories in defense of their city over seemingly invincible Persian forces and their later downfall after acquiring an empire and attempting to lord it over the other Hellenic states (41–43). These and other examples (44–47) are briefly narrated.

The series is broken off with a suggestion that it could go on all day and is capped with a confident assertion, "Whoever sees that such reversals have occurred and thinks that they will not occur with us is extremely foolish" (48). In other words, because such things have happened, the Spartans should *expect* the pattern to repeat. Thebes' position as the dominant power in Greece actually gives the Spartans an advantage. This argument from examples may seem too optimistic, but it is backed up with an appeal to the notion that "states repair such disasters [as Sparta has suffered] with good government and experience in war"; and of course Sparta has the best government of all and is more experienced in military matters than anyone (48). This appeal to superior leadership and experience, in essence, amounts to the *Rhetoric to Alexander's* topic of "good leadership" in its list of things that contribute to success in war. There is an unacknowledged problem here, since Archidamus already has attributed Sparta's setbacks on the battlefield to "erroneous leadership." The truth was that Sparta had no leaders who could match Epaminondas.

Archidamus' next main line of argument, which also is introduced through the gesture of "anticipation" or reply, responds to the charge that what he proposes is highly doubtful: "Some people denounce war and talk at length about its uncertainty [*apistian*], and use many other *tekmêria*—especially the things that have happened to us—and are amazed that anyone sees fit to trust [*pisteuein*] in a course of action so difficult and so perilous" (49). This too is a line of argument suggested by the *Rhetoric to Alexander* for advising against a war (2 1425a). Archidamus' answer is a commonplace: "Those who are doing well should set their hearts on peace, for in peace they may safeguard their present condition for the longest time; but those who are unfortunate should set their minds on war, for from the confusion and upheaval they may more quickly change their fortunes" (49–50).[77]

From this he develops a mixed argument that, on one hand, it would be foolish for Sparta to do the opposite—to seek a status-quo-maintaining peace when their fortunes are at low ebb—and that, on the other hand, it would be shameful not to live up to the many examples of Spartan prowess, in which "one Spartan alone" was often enough to overcome a greatly superior force (50–57). Thus the topic of "manpower and strength" is partially addressed, through an argument that Spartans in the past have always been unbeatable; one Spartan is worth an army. The topic of "honor" is then invoked with an argument from comparison. "What people do we know," he says, "who after losing a single battle and experiencing one invasion were so cowardly that they agreed to everything demanded of them?" (56). Once again there are problems. Archidamus' evocation of *tekmêria* in the form of past instances of Spartan prowess does not really respond to the present problem of Theban superiority in "manpower and strength" and "good leadership," and his presumption that the past predicts the future is undercut by his own statements that things may change with time and circumstance. So far, then, his argument rests chiefly on appeals to topics of justice and honor, while the topics of advantage and probability of success are only partially and somewhat weakly addressed.

This problem seems to be recognized in the next phase of Archidamus' argument, which again begins as an "anticipation" or reply: "Some think nothing of these things, but overlook all the shamefulness and recommend what will bring the city to disgrace. And they are so eager to induce you to give up Messene that they have dared to talk at length about the weakness of our city and the power of the enemy, and they call upon those who oppose them to answer where we expect help to come from when we urge you to go to war" (58).

This demand raises the topic that the *Rhetoric to Alexander* calls "good allies" (*summachôn arête*) in its list of sources of success in war. Archidamus' first reply is that Sparta's "greatest and surest ally" is "doing what is just" (*to ta dikaia prattein*)—yet another rehearsal of his central argument so far—because it is "probable" (*eikos*) that "the favor of the gods" (*hê tôn theôn eunoia*) will side with those whose cause is just. "Favor of the gods" is also a topic from the *Rhetoric to Alexander*'s list. To this he adds, again, such "allies" as the Spartan virtues of good government, self-control, courage, and a sense of what is honorable and shameful, as well as the inconsistency and unsteadiness of Sparta's enemies and the likelihood that they will make mistakes (59–61), so that "there is no reason to fear our enemies because they are many" (60). The Spartans are just and virtuous and can expect the gods to favor them, while the Thebans are unjust and corrupt and cannot be expected to enjoy success for long. This argument, in itself, may not be as weak as it seems to a modern mind. It reiterates a traditional if archaic topic in Greek religious thought that frequently recurs, for example, in Pindar's odes, and therefore has some authority.[78] Nevertheless it still is a weak answer to pragmatic concerns about such things as actual military alliances and other material resources necessary for success in war.

That weakness is addressed with a more pragmatic argument about "help from the outside" (60–69): The Athenians will not permit Sparta to be destroyed and will come to help; so will the tyrant of Syracuse and the king of Egypt, the potentates of "Asia"—the rulers of states in what is now Turkey— and the pro-oligarchic Hellenic states. Moreover, even the prodemocratic states of the Peloponnese, sick of years of democratic misrule, will stand with Sparta. The critique of democracy's excesses provides an interesting inside view of Spartan or oligarchic political ideology, but as a whole Archidamus' argument about likely allies is problematic.[79] If it were true, of course, it would make a very strong case for confidence. However, none of it is backed by any firm evidence. It is all an appeal to *eikos* without *tekmêria* or any "supplemental" proofs, and there is no discussion of what resources any of the potential allies would be able and likely to commit. Archidamus is arguing what easily can be seen as wishful hope. Moreover, his argument obviously resembles arguments that, according to Thucydides, were made in favor of the Athenians' Sicilian expedition during the Peloponnesian War: the various Sicilian states are sick of Syracusan domination and will quickly ally themselves with Athens. As things turned out, however, the Sicilian states did not turn and the Athenian expedition ended in complete disaster. Every educated Greek of Isocrates' time knew that story well, most would have read Thucydides, and indeed, Thucydides probably was included in the reading lists Isocrates gave his students. Another problem with Archidamus' argument about allies is the fact that the prooligarchic states that supposedly will rally to Sparta's side are in essence the very ones now urging Sparta to accept the Thebans' terms.

Archidamus rounds off this argument by returning, again, to the topics of justice and honor. Even if, as he says, "none of these things should come to pass and we fail to get any help from anywhere," Sparta still should refuse the Thebans' terms and should "consider how we shall fight in a manner worthy of ourselves" (70–71). He then proposes, and discusses at great length (72–86), how the Spartans could carry on the war even when abandoned by all potential allies.

They should abandon the city, send parents, wives, children, and everyone not capable of military service to safety (in Sicily, Cyrene, and Asia), and with the remaining army wage a guerrilla war. The model for this proposal is very obviously the famous Athenian strategy during the second Persian invasion more than a century before (c. 480 B.C.E.): the city was evacuated, and the Persians (who occupied and ravaged the empty city) were drawn into a decisive naval battle in the straits of Salamis near Athens, where the hugely outnumbered Athenian fleet won a spectacular victory. Indeed Archidamus explicitly invokes the example: "It would be most terrible of all if we, knowing that the Athenians abandoned their own country to defend the freedom of all Greeks, should lack the courage to leave our city for the sake of our own salvation" (83). As the *Rhetoric to Alexander* observes, this is an argument from comparison—setting "similars" side by side—in which an example is invoked as an analogy for the present state of affairs or a proposed action. The problem with Archidamus' argument here is that he fails to consider how the example is nonsimilar: the Athenians had spent more than a year building up their navy, and their strategy was deliberately designed with the idea of staking everything on a single naval battle. Archidamus, on the other hand, simply proposes taking to the hills and fighting hit and run, without taking into consideration the material resources the Spartans would need to carry on the fight or how they might win a decisive victory. He does suggest that the guerrilla army would be able to live off the countryside and be "at home" wherever it encamped, and he maintains that such an army, mobile and with no city to defend, would be terrifying to the Thebans and would "easily" prevail (81). The unstated example here is probably the story of Xenophon's *Anabasis,* in which a Greek mercenary force of ten thousand men, stranded in the middle of the Persian empire, successfully fought its way home. But the ten thousand did not defeat the Persian empire or liberate any Greek territory, and on their return they were obliged to put themselves in service to the rulers of Thrace and Sparta. Moreover, Xenophon portrays the success of the ten thousand in Persia as a result of the superiority of Greek to "barbarian" culture, but Archidamus' guerrilla army would be fighting Greeks, indeed, the militarily preeminent Greeks at that moment, and the guerrilla force would be provisioning itself by pillaging Greeks in a countryside increasingly stripped bare. In sum, Archidamus does not very fully consider the material differences in the explicit and implicit examples he uses as models for what he proposes. He sounds very much like a young man inspired to emulate the glorious examples he has read about in school without thinking too much about the details.

Archidamus does qualify his proposal by maintaining that it is a worst-case scenario and that Sparta is more likely to obtain a more "honorable and secure" peace if it simply signals its willingness to fight to the last in the manner he has outlined (87). So to some extent his proposal is a dangerous negotiating bluff, though the idea that Thebes will make a better deal with an almost suicidally intransigent Sparta may be the best argument he has. At the same time this qualification returns him to the topic of honor, which he then uses to excoriate the advocates of peace, again, as shameful cowards: "I would like to hear from these men what sorts of things they think we should fight and die for" (88), and so on. What follows is a series of "digressions," often in the form of further "anticipations" or responses to ideas, generally focusing on the theme of honor, and reiterating the themes of Spartan valor and hope for the future (88–106). He then concludes briefly (107–111) with an enthymeme that sums up and caps the general argument—"If we are willing to die for our rights we will not only be renowned, but will be able to live securely for the rest of time; but if we fear the dangers, we will bring upon ourselves a lot of trouble" (107)—followed by a short commonplace on exchanging one's mortal body for deathless fame (107–109), a pathetic evocation of "your parents and children . . . exhorting you not to disgrace the name of Sparta" (110), and a reminder that Sparta has never been defeated when a king from his family was in charge (111). This sequence of "digressions," emotional appeals, and closure is a textbook illustration of the principles for handling these parts discussed in the *Rhetoric to Alexander.*

I have focused some attention on the problems of Archidamus' arguments in the "confirmation" section of this speech because they are evidence that Isocrates meant *Archidamus* as an object of schoolroom critique. In its recurring appeals to notions of justice and honor and its evocations of the glorious Athenian stand at Salamis and Xenophon's heroic ten thousand, the speech has an undeniable emotional appeal that would have been especially strong for the morally earnest, mentally lively young men Isocrates preferred to teach. At the same time, if he taught the sorts of topics (or *ideai*) that the *Rhetoric to Alexander* gives for symbouleutic discourse on questions of war and peace, those topics would have enabled his students to better see that Archidamus may speak stirringly on the topics of honor and justice, but also that, regarding the sources of success in war, his arguments are rather weak. He adequately addresses only the notion of "favor of the gods" as a result of the justice of their cause and the good fortune likely to result from it, as well as "advantages of locality," in the sense that defenders have an inherent advantage over attackers, and perhaps also in the sense that a mobile guerrilla army would have tactical advantages, though it would lose the advantages of entrenched defenders. But on the other key topics—manpower and strength, material resources, good leadership, and good allies—his arguments are weak and often amount to little more than wishful thinking and youthful zeal. By focusing attention on such things, Isocrates would have been able to teach lessons not only about the handling of "confirmation" in symbouleutic discourse but also about preliminary inquiry, since it would show that "probability of success" is the crucial stasis, as evidenced by the concerns that Archidamus repeatedly replies to, and since the topics of "sources of success in war" provide a guide to the sets of facts about which anyone arguing war and peace would need to be well informed. By applying such topics as heuristics, those of a resourceful and inventive intelligence will be able to more methodically discover the possibilities of their subject matter and find arguments that the untrained person would hit upon only randomly (*Against the Sophists* 15).

Archidamus might also be read as a pamphlet written and circulated roughly contemporaneously with the events of 366 or shortly after. In that case one might argue that the evident weakness of its argument is meant as part of an emotional appeal. The speech presents a credible mimesis of an impassioned young man ready to rush to the barricades in a noble if hopeless cause and fight and die with his honor intact. Such an effect might motivate sympathy with Sparta's plight and persuade Athens, and other states where the text was circulated, to come to Sparta's aid. And of course Athens did come to Sparta's aid, at the battle of Mantinea in 362.[80] If *Archidamus* was written after 362, it would have been composed with the purpose of justifying Athens' actions. Still, whatever the date of its original composition was, in Isocrates' school in later years it would have functioned as an ethopoietic declamation, presenting a heroic speech by a Spartan prince in the desperate circumstances of 366. As such it might have provided occasion for discussing the uses, force, and value of emotional appeals in practical deliberation, compared with the uses, force, and value of such proofs as probabilities and evidence, or the relative weight of such topics as justice, honor, advantage, and probability of success.

In *Panathenaicus,* in what are nearly his last written words, Isocrates portrays his "more serious and philosophical" *logoi* as "instructional and artistic" (*didaskalikous kai technikous*) and contrasts them with discourses written purely for "display" (*epideixeis*) or for "trials" (*agōnas;* 271). Likewise, in the long digression in which he portrays a gathering of present and former students to critique his nearly finished draft, his most astute critic observes that Isocrates develops "ambiguous arguments" (*logous amphibolous*) that are "capable of being taken different ways and contain many issues for debate" (*pollas amphisbêtêseis;* 240). *Archidamus* appears to be such a discourse. It opens issues for rhetorical-critical discussion and debate, as well as issues for debate and declamation on the subject matter of the speech itself. Having examined the problematics of Archidamus' situation and the strengths, weaknesses, and omissions of his speech, students would be prepared to compose their own speeches on the theme or similar themes in different circumstances, that is, different set problems for declamation. Moreover, as I think the foregoing analysis has made apparent, the *technê* by which Isocrates has composed the speech, and by which he would have led his students through a critical examination of it, very probably was close to what we find in the *Rhetoric to Alexander's* treatments of both preliminary inquiry and invention (the handling of the parts of the discourse from proëmium and narrative to confirmation, digressions, and ending). *Archidamus* and the *technê,* then, illustrate for us what Isocrates means by saying that his *logoi* are instructional, artistic, serious, and philosophical. It is philosophical and serious in opening the problems of how to deliberate and speak on questions of war and peace, and in its empathetic exploration of Spartan ideology; and it is artistic and instructional in opening up the principles of the *technê* for discussion and practice.

Technê II: The *Lektikos Topos*—The Domain of Style

The second main part of Isocrates' *technê* had to do with *lexis* or style, or what the *Rhetoric to Alexander* calls *asteia legein,* "urbane [sophisticated, elegant]) speaking" (22, 1434a). If it occupied a second book, it may have been a short one— to judge by the *Rhetoric to Alexander,* which devotes seven of its thirty-eight chapters to the topic, occupying just two of its twenty-five pages in the standard Bekker edition. Aristotle's treatment of *lexis* in the *Rhetoric* and *Poetics* is longer and represents a later and more developed stage in stylistic theory, though it too is fairly rudimentary compared with the later *technai.* I will treat Isocrates' *lektikos topos* fairly summarily here.

The surviving fragments from Isocrates' *technê,* preserved in later testimonies, include a small handful of stylistic precepts, which I partially quote and partially paraphrase:[81]

Avoid hiatus: do not juxtapose and combine vowels that do not support blending (*krasis*), seem not to join your speech together evenly, and do not go smoothly and steadily by the ear.
Avoid repeating the same syllable at the end and beginning of adjacent words, as in *eipou̲s̲a̲ saphê* ("she spoke clearly").[82]
Do not put the same conjunctions close together, and make what follows immediately correspond to what precedes: for example, "those things are so, yet these are otherwise";[83] or again, the *men* and the *de,* and the *hôs* and the *houtôs.*[84]
Let the whole speech (*logos*) not be prose (*logos*), for that is arid; nor in verse, for that is obvious; but above all let it mingle every rhythm.
Use words that are metaphorical, or beautiful, or (sparingly) invented, or familiar.

These precepts fall into two main concerns. The first is what later tradition calls *sunthesis,* which includes the euphonious and rhythmic "composition" of words in phrases, clauses, and longer syntactic structures, and, as an important part of that, the relation of prose rhythm to poetic meter.[85] The second main concern is diction, including "metaphor" or tropes, "beautiful" words and neologisms, and "familiar" diction. What "beautiful words" means is less than clear, but it may have something to do with euphonious sound, semantic resonance, poetic diction, or all three.

In *Against the Sophists,* after his brief description of choosing and combining *ideai* to compose a speech suitable to its *kairos,* Isocrates adds that the able rhetor must "embellish the whole speech with fitting enthymemes, and speak in words both rhythmic and musical" (16). That sentence's thumbnail account of the *topos lektikos* suggests, on one hand, the highly polished and sometimes excessive use of quasi-poetic, rhythmically balanced constructions for which Isocrates was famous—in which the phrase or clause is the unit of prosody instead of the line of verse—and, on the other hand, a conception of the enthymeme as not only a form of proof but also a stylistic element for capping and "embellishing" a line of argument with an "urbane" and striking statement of the point. This too was a recognized element of Isocrates' stylistic practice. Zosimus, after remarking on Isocrates' "Gorgianic" penchant for similar endings (*homoioteleuton*) and parallelism (*parisôsis*), and his "clear, ethical, and persuasive" style, says, "He uses enthymemes constantly: before he completes a thought, he weaves in another enthymeme" (*Life of Isocrates*). The enthymeme in this sense, as a stylistic element, is a figure, an *idea,* along with *parisosis* and *homoioteleuton.* Further, in both *Antidosis* and *Evagoras,* Isocrates compares prose style with that of poetry, observing that poetry has more freedom in its use of diction and "metaphor" and that its meters and rhythms give it a psychagogic persuasiveness unavailable to prose—while claiming also that his own discourses, especially the political-panegyric kind, are "more poetic and varied in style" and use "enthymemes that are more impressive and original" and "other figures (*ideais*) that are more striking and more numerous" than in common practice (*Evagoras* 9–11; *Antidosis* 47).

Such scattered and brief remarks do not clarify very much, but they do suggest, again, a stylistic teaching focused on diction, composition, figures of parallelism and repetition, and enthymemes and other figures of thought such as paralipsis and aporia, which frequently recur in Isocrates' *logoi.* Most of Isocrates' stylistic teaching probably was a synthesis of things inherited from his sophistic predecessors, such as Protagoras' *Correct Diction,* Gorgias' stylistic practices, Polus' treatment of "redoubled" speech, and so on. Notably these matters are reviewed in the *Phaedrus* after the parts of the oration and methods of proof—suggesting that this was the order of treatment already in early sophistic teaching.[86] But perhaps the best index to the Isocratean *topos lektikos* is, again, the *Rhetoric to Alexander.*

The *Rhetoric to Alexander* begins its account of "urbane" style with suggestions for the use of enthymemes and maxims—state half of an enthymeme so that the audience fills in the rest, mix maxims into the different parts of an oration—and then gives methods for lengthening a speech, making it brief, speaking at "moderate" (*mesos*) length, and fitting the style to the character of the speaker (22).[87] The next chapter (23) introduces the "composition of words" (*sunthesis onomatôn*), beginning with the joining of vowels and consonants at the end and beginning of adjacent words and the marshaling (*taxis*) of words in particular sequences.[88] This chapter's concern with word-by-word and phrase-by-phrase prosodic "flow" overlaps with Isocrates' precepts concerning hiatus, repeating syllables, and rhythmic phrasing. Next (chapter 24) the author gives six methods for handling "twofold statements"—that is, constructions of the form "X is not only Y but also Z," "X is not Y but Z," "X is neither Y nor Z," "X is Y but not Z," "X is Y but Z is not," and "X is not Y but Z is"—all of which are useful for building complex sentences with rhythmically cadenced as well as logically balanced construction, such as "This city is not only pre-eminent in the arts of war, but also unequaled in the accomplishments of peace." The next concern (chapter 25) is methods for keeping one's meaning clear: Use plain, non-ambiguous diction; avoid elision of juxtaposed vowels when that may confuse;[89] use definite articles where needed; avoid confusingly transposed sentence structures, that is, extreme hyperbaton; and use both parts of a paired construction, as in "on one hand . . . on the other hand," in which we hear an echo of the Isocratean precepts regarding keeping conjunctions together or apart and making what follows correspond to what precedes. The next three chapters treat antithesis (26), *parisôsis* (parallelism; 27), and *paromoiôsis* (parallelism with similar-sounding words; 28), all of which are useful, again, for "twofold statements" in balanced structures and are reminiscent of Isocratean, and Gorgianic, practice.

Elsewhere (chapters 18–21, following the discussion of types of proof) the *Rhetoric to Alexander* discusses such figures of thought as anticipation (*prokatalêpsis*), "postulations" (*aitêmata,* calls to the audience to pay attention, judge fairly, and so forth), "recapitulation" (*palillogia*) in various forms, and irony (*eirôneia,* including paralipsis and saying the opposite of what one means); but aside from the treatment of clarity there is almost no discussion of diction, or of the relation between prose rhythm and poetic meter.[90] It seems probable that the Isocratean *lektikos topos* did address those concerns, at least briefly, but otherwise its treatment of style probably was similar to that of the *Rhetoric to Alexander* and, indeed, could well have been a source for it.

One impression that is hard to escape is that most if not all of these stylistic matters could have been introduced through the progymnasmata, as well as the critical discussion of readings. Certainly such matters as compressing or lengthening a statement, developing a statement through epiphonemas, counterstatements and "twofold" statements, the uses of enthymemes and maxims, diction

and metaphor, and various figures of speech and thought, and speaking appropriately in character, are progymnasmatic concerns. It is perhaps significant that
the *Rhetoric to Alexander's* discussion of urbane style follows its discussions of the
common *ideai,* the inventional topics for the main genres of civic discourse, and
the forms of proof and figures of thought. The whole treatise actually seems
to come to a general conclusion after its treatment of style—"That is enough
about these matters," and so on, through a brief recapitulation of everything that
has been taught so far (28, 1436a). Moreover, this passage ends with the *Rhetoric
to Alexander's* one reference to progymnasmata: if we have learned these things
in the progymnasmata, they will supply us with great abundance (28, 1436a).
Then the author takes up a second *technê* devoted to the invention of the parts
of an oration and the practice of declamation. Perhaps this apparent division
into two *technai* is what the author means when he says, in his prolegomenon,
that he has combined what "Nicanor taught to us" with the *technê* of Corax and
an earlier treatise of his own (1421a–b). Perhaps the *technê* of "Nicanor" is that
of Isocrates, while that of "Corax," and the author's earlier work, is an early-
sophistic type of *technê* organized by oration parts.

It is also possible, or probable, that these stylistic matters—or what Isocrates
sums up as the composition of words in phrases and larger structures that are
"both rhythmic and musical"—would be revisited at more advanced stages of
instruction and practice. Yet Isocrates may not have said a great deal about them
in his *technê.* His pedagogical philosophy, after all, assumes an ideal student of
ready wit who can take the imprint of the stylistic models set before him, and
can quickly come to imitate and absorb them, while the teacher explains the
limited amount of what can be explained and comments on the student's writing and speaking (*Against the Sophists* 17–18). Dionysius of Halicarnassus, in a
similar vein, describes the style of Lysias as having a "charm" that cannot be adequately described or directly taught but that can be felt and learned through
patient study (reading and criticism) and practice (imitation and declamation).
Out of this activity develops, in later antiquity, the much more sophisticated
analysis of prose style as a main focus of rhetorical instruction, such as we see
in Dionysius of Halicarnassus' *On the Composition of Words,* Cicero's *Orator,* and
Hermogenes of Tarsus' *On Types of Style.*

On Isocrates' *Technê:* A Short Conclusion

In this and the preceding chapter I have speculated at some length on the possible existence and likely contents of a *Technê of Isocrates.* On the first of those
points there never can be certainty, admittedly, and on the second point there
can only be conjecture. It does, however, seem virtually certain that there was a
technê in the sense of an art, method, or collection of precepts that informed
Isocrates' *logôn paideia,* his teaching of rhetoric/*philosophia.* It was the conceptual

apparatus by which he led or "coached" his students through a set of exercises from progymnasmata to declamation. It was meant to cultivate in them a developed moral and intellectual sensibility and the capacity to deliberate and speak and write effectively on issues in civic and private life. Further, given the admittedly skimpy available evidence, I do think it likely either that Isocrates wrote a *technê* or that his students compiled a *Technê of Isocrates,* and that it was disseminated and imitated until it eventually was superseded by the more developed *technai* of later generations of successors, such as, most notably, the *Rhetoric* of Hermagoras. Antonius-Cicero's remark that Isocrates is the "teacher of all rhetoricians" is probably more than hyperbole.

Regarding the likely contents of Isocrates' *technê,* I think that Dionysius of Halicarnassus is probably correct when he describes them as both a synthesis of the previously disorganized collection of specialized *technai* left by Isocrates' late-fifth-century predecessors and a new departure (*Isocrates* 1). The newness may have inhered, as Dionysius suggests, in Isocrates' primary focus on "political" or civic discourse as opposed to dialectical disputation (eristics) and metaphysical speculation, which truly would mark his *technê* as the beginning of what forever afterward has been understood as "rhetoric." Signs of such a shift, however, can be seen already in Gorgias and Antiphon, as well as Plato's portrait of Protagoras. The newness of Isocrates' *technê* may have inhered, too, in its organization under two main headings or "domains," the *pragmatikos topos* and the *lektikos topos,* and possibly in his assembly of an organized set of progymnasmata for the beginning stages of instruction and practice. In sum, he seems to have developed a *paideia* that first cultivated the student's familiarity and skill with a progressively larger and more complex set of *ideai* in progymnasmata, including the foundations for moral-political *philosophia,* and then practiced the student in creatively recombining those elements according to the demands of particular, practical situations, or facsimiles thereof, in declamations.

But what seems most original in Isocrates' *technê,* if it truly was original with him, as he claims, is the addition of preliminary inquiry to the *pragmatikos topos:* the identification of the key question(s) at issue and what the discourse specifically must accomplish, and the methodic searching, selection, and combination of the relevant *ideai* and topics of invention, so that the student of able wit can learn to be more artful and resourceful in inquiry (*pros to zêtein*) and can more readily discover what otherwise would be hit upon haphazardly (*Against the Sophists* 15; *To the Children of Jason* 8). This is the essential method—a training apparatus—for developing skill in what Isocrates calls the "creative process" of inventing and composing discourse (*Against the Sophists* 12), and it appears to be the root of what all later rhetoric, from Hermagoras to Hermogenes, will treat as stasis theory. Isocrates may justly claim to be the first to explicitly incorporate the teaching of preliminary inquiry, or "stasis" in a rudimentary form, in a rhetorical training system.

While I do not claim that my conjectures are correct in every detail, and while they cannot be confirmed with certainty, I do think them probable in general outline. That general outline looks a lot like the *Rhetoric to Alexander,* the later handbooks, and what was to be more or less the standard sophistic rhetorical *paideia* for the rest of antiquity. There were, of course, better and worse sophists, and undoubtedly some were the sort of small-minded hack that Isocrates critiques in *Against the Sophists,* those who teach rhetoric as if it were a *tetagmenê technê,* an "ordered art" consisting of rigid rules or recipes to be mechanically and mindlessly applied, or those who teach only judicial discourse as a tool for the would-be sycophant. A papyrus of the first to second century c.e., a letter from a student to his father, complains that there are no decent rhetoric teachers to be found in Alexandria but only "trash" who ruin the talents of their students.[91] The fault of such people is not that they teach a *technê* but that they teach it stupidly, misunderstanding its nature and its better purposes. Even Isocrates' *technê* can be taught stupidly, as if it were a *tetagmenê technê.*[92] One cannot draw a sharp distinction, as is often done, between a philosophical tradition in sophistic rhetoric descended from Isocrates and the technical tradition of the handbooks. The two traditions are one and the same. Isocrates' *technê* was, I think, the ancestor of the later *technai.*

FOUR

In the Garden of Talking Birds

Declamation and Civic Theater

I ask you to consider that—if what I say is worthy of the
senate house—you hear me in the senate house itself.

Apuleius of Madaura, Florida *18*

The "Sweet Garden"

Consider the following passages:

Rhetoric was discovered and came forward as a safeguard of justice and a
bond of human life, so that matters would not be decided by hands, by
weapons, by seizure, by numbers and size, or by any other inequality, but that
reason should determine justice peacefully. This is the very origin and nature
of rhetoric: its purpose is to save all human beings, and by means of persuasion to ward off force. . . . If I must speak briefly, rhetoric is nothing other
than practical intelligence [*phronêsis*] combined with the power of speech,
so that one not only can discover what is best, but also can persuade others.
. . . Rhetoric manifestly is a sort of philosophy. (Aelius Aristides, *Defense of
Rhetoric* 210, 302, 305, second century C.E.)

Rhetoric is a discipline [*askêsis*] of discourse that exercises the *rhêtor* in evenly
balanced cases. (Anonymous prolegomenon to Hermogenes' *On Stases* [c.
tenth century], as quoted in Christian Walz, ed. *Rhetores Graeci*, 7.1:49)

I was not yet ten years old (or perhaps I had just reached that age), and one
night a dream lifted me up and transported me into the open sky. I do not
know whether or not I was hunting, but it seemed to me that I was pursuing two musical birds, one of which resembled a parrot, and the other
unquestionably was a magpie, and they both went in beneath the fold of my
robe! At this my spirit was lightened and gladdened, and I frequently petted
them and grasped their wings. But the birds said, "Neither rule tyrannically,
in the way of men, nor seize power by force: rule, master, according to law!
Rather, accomplish this by reason, and stay and converse with us. And should

you persuade, then rule over us; but if not, give us back the freedom of our wings." It seemed to me that what they said was wise, and as I grasped each one firmly by the wings on either side, I exchanged arguments with them as if we were philosophers. And then and there the veil that birth casts over the soul was lifted from me. (Michael Psellos, *Encomium of His Mother* 6c–d [eleventh century])

On this side [of the forecourt of the church], then, there are the open shrines of the Muses of the *logoi,* toward the east . . . Here the grammarians teach their lessons, and books are opened up for the first lesson to be explicated, and the young beginners are constantly reading their lessons and pacing up and down the enclosure of the portico, while others are carrying armloads of papers and reciting orally from memory what is written in them, which they have imprinted in the tablets of their minds through constant reading, and still others who are more advanced in years and learning carry writing tablets in their hands and loudly speak their themes [*problêmata*] from the beginning, part of which they have derived from the materials in their hands . . . And full of children are the seats, and full the benches, and from everywhere without the church there is a twittering of children, as if from some sort of musical birds, and the church echoes with them from within, not like an echo heard in the mountains, and not discordant, but a harmonious and most sweet sort of echo, as though one heard angels singing. . . . [And] around the forecourt of the church is a swirling crowd of children, youths, men, and old men, composed of all kinds thrown together—some inventing questions for each other concerning letters and accents and the rules of short and long syllables and nouns and verbs, and others concerning figures of speech and all the manifold forms of enthymemes and epenthymemes, and of clarity and forcefulness, and others put forth problem and question in a dialectical manner . . . So there is a twittering clamor of voices around the forecourt and the watertrough, like all sorts of sparrows crowding in around springs and pools, and not a little confusion and noise is raised by their mingled cries, as one thing and another is put forward by the students or by the teachers for joint examination, and some strive to maintain their own opinion, while others contend that the truth is otherwise. (Nicolaus Mesarites, *Description of the Church of Holy Apostles at Constantinople* 8.1–2, 11.3, 42.1, 43.1 [late twelfth century])

These four passages embody a set of familiar attitudes concerning the discipline of rhetoric. On one hand, it is a *technê* of exercise, or what the anonymous prolegomenon calls an *askêsis* (discipline, regimen),[1] that cultivates the student's discursive powers through declamation and disputation in "evenly balanced cases." On the other hand, it is a kind of *philosophia* concerned with cultivating practical wisdom (*phronêsis*) in public and private affairs, especially in questions of justice, action, and moral preference. With Aelius Aristides, this pragmatic philosophical project is portrayed as virtually a holy calling, a mission to "save" all human beings from the injustices of force in unequal power relations—to move them, in Isocratean fashion, from the realm of primitive bestiality, mere assertion, and violence to the civilized life of reason, law, and deliberated communal assent. In the *Sacred Tales,* Aristides records how the healing-god Asclepius appeared to him in dream visions over a period of years, saving him from debilitating chronic illness to answer this holy call.[2]

The eleventh-century Byzantine rhetor-philosopher and proto-humanist Michael Psellos also presents in his semiautobiographical *Encomium of His Mother* what he claims is a dream vision he had when he was almost ten, when he was precociously advancing through the traditional curriculum from "grammar" (*grammatikê,* that is, "literary study") toward rhetoric. Apparently he did not take up rhetorical training proper until the age of fifteen or sixteen, which was the normal age for that, probably because it involved participation in adult affairs, including traveling with a judge responsible for "no small part" of the Byzantine Empire's western regions (Thrace, Macedonia, Greece) (15a)—a sort of internship. But it is probable that, by the age of ten, his quickly advancing literary studies already included prose writers, especially orators and historians. Psellos' educational and professional trajectory eventually would lead him from his relatively humble origins to eminence as a *rhêtôr* and to the imperial circle, culminating in his appointment as "Consul of the Philosophers" (*hupatos tôn philosophôn*), that is, "head professor" or superintendent of the schools of secular higher education in the capital, or at least those under some form of imperial sponsorship (a collection of salaried teachers sometimes referred to by modern scholars as the "university of Constantinople").[3]

Psellos' purported dream is clearly an invention. It equally clearly is an allegory of his experience of the classical *paideia,* which had not substantially changed since late antiquity. The two birds, a parrot (*psittakos*) and a magpie (*kitta*), represent the verbal arts (*logoi*)—as Psellos himself remarks, noting that they had voices "both musical and human" (6d).[4] More specifically, as birds of mimicry they represent the grammatical curriculum, which involved large amounts of memorization, recitation, and imitation, or what Nicolaus Mesarites describes as students "imprinting" canonic literature "in the tablets of their minds" through "constant reading" (that is, reading aloud, rehearsal, and recital). One can read the birds' "flying in" under young Psellos' robe and his seizing them as his internalization and mastery of the language and thought of the authors he has studied. Likewise one might read the birds' prompting him to engage in reasoned persuasion and to "rule according to law," and the dream debate that follows, as representing the transition to rhetorical-philosophical training, especially the progymnasmata of refutation/confirmation and thesis, and the "evenly balanced cases" of declamation.

Notably, Psellos portrays the whole dream episode, and thus his experience of rhetorical education, as lifting him into the "open sky" (*eleutheron aera,* literally the "free air") and as bringing him to a revelation he rather platonically describes as a "lifting of the veil" from his sleeping, childish soul—an intellectual and spiritual awakening. Similarly, when he later mentions his study of rhetoric at age sixteen, he says that he had taken it up "with gratefulness" (*sun chariti*) and associates it with his first ventures outside the city walls into the "open country" (*hupaithron,* literally "under the sky"; 15a). It is hard not to note the sense of liberation and exhilaration. Grammatical study emphasized correct reading and interpretation, worked through explication, memorization, and recitation, and often enforced its lessons with corporal punishment. Nicolaus Mesarites describes the elementary grammar teachers as men who "fuss over syllables and spend their whole life chopping up words and squeezing and scraping and polishing little phrases, [and] who beat young boys and because of this power exalt themselves as lords [*hupsêloi*] and are full of arrogant pride" (*Description* 8.1); the arithmetic teachers (described at 10.2–3) are even worse. It is doubtful that young Psellos, excellent student that he was, ever got a beating from his elementary teachers. Still, his dream allegory clearly suggests that his encounter with rhetoric brought him to a "revelation" or vision of the possibilities of rhetorical culture as a realm of freedom where reasoned persuasion, dialogue, and the rule of law replaced tyrannical coercion, violence, and the usual "way of men."

Something of the mood of Psellos' dream vision appears as well in Mesarites' *Description of the Church of Holy Apostles.* Holy Apostles was originally built by the emperor Constantine I, contained his tomb and those of many subsequent Byzantine emperors, was one of the chief shrines of Byzantium, and in the late twelfth century housed a school in its forecourt.[5] The speech, a highly elaborated version of the progymnasmatic description (*ekphrasis*), was written to commemorate a visit of the Greek Orthodox patriarch (probably John X Camaterus, not long after his accession in 1198).[6] It begins by "viewing" the surrounding neighborhood from the church roof, then descends and guides the patriarch through a roughly "omega"-shaped tour (Ω) of the church itself, beginning and ending with the school in the forecourt. The first view of the school concentrates on the elementary subjects. These "open shrines [*môseia*] of the *logoi*"—grammar, arithmetic, and music—are housed in the "portico" (*stoa,* a covered colonnade) surrounding the forecourt, and in essence are open-air teaching spaces protected from sun and rain. The second view, at the end of the speech, focuses on the higher subjects (rhetoric and philosophy), which are located at the water trough and portico adjacent to the church itself. In other words, advanced secular learning, which the Byzantines called the "external wisdom," occupies the church's front porch. One thinks of Libanius' rhetoric school at the *bouleutêrion* (city hall) of Antioch, probably also in a portico near the entrance.

Despite the beatings handed out occasionally by the elementary teachers, Mesarites observes that every passerby, seeing the things he has described, "wishes to become a student and to be a child through life and a learner" (11.1), or to send his children to the school, or other family members or even friends. Mesarites does not quite present the secular verbal arts as holy callings or as liberatory, soul-awakening enterprises—indeed, his description focuses on them simply as modes of exercise accompanied by some technical study. The elementary students recite their lessons and memorize their texts, and the more advanced do composition exercises, discuss "enthymemes and epenthymemes" and types of style (*saphêneia* and *deinotês*, "clarity" and "forcefulness"), and engage in disputation and declamation.[7] Nevertheless, Mesarites endows this scene of exercise with a quasi-paradisal imagery of children's voices, twittering birds, pools and fountains, the rustling of sparrows, and angel song echoing faintly through the church. Further, though he does not embrace it as does Psellos, Mesarites too suggests the potential for freewheeling debate. The disputation of the advanced students around the water trough generates a loud discussion, and, as Mesarites goes on to say, the arguments become increasingly animated; but all will be settled when the patriarch arrives, for he, good shepherd that he is, will kindly act as judge and solve and explain all points of disagreement (43.2–4).[8] In this way Mesarites maintains the traditional Byzantine view that the centrifugal, heretical potentials of secular rhetoric/philosophy, the "external wisdom," are to be kept safely within the bounds of Orthodox belief; but he also notes that the centrifugal potential is there, since the scene at the water trough presumably is a daily, perennial event. But what is important in Mesarites' description, for my purposes, is the overarching sense of "paradisal" pleasure attached to what is, after all, a scene of exercise and toil in a paved courtyard surrounded by a portico.

It is easy to dismiss Aristides', Psellos', Mesarites', and all such representations, going back at least to Isocrates, as ideological fantasias, idealizations, or propaganda for a less exalted reality—stories that rhetoric has liked to tell to dignify itself as something more than just a practical training regimen. Certainly Mesarites is aiming more to please the patriarch and to spread a good image of Holy Apostles than to give a true report. (The emperor Alexius III recently had opened the imperial sarcophagi at Holy Apostles and removed the gold and jewels they contained, to meet a financial crisis; Mesarites has a stake in showing that all is well again despite that desecration, and his description makes it seem as if nothing has happened). And certainly people desired and sought *paideia,* and rhetorical training in particular, for reasons other than to save all human beings from the inequities of power, to philosophize about general and specific issues in civic and private life, to experience the exhilarating freedom of intellectual open skies, or to enjoy the paradisal pleasures of being in school. Not every student was a Psellos, or an Aristides or a Cicero. In the Roman-imperial and Byzantine worlds, a limited degree of *paideia* could be adequate for upper-class respectability and for finding a salaried place in the civil service or on some magnate's staff, and many students, and their parents, had no intention to reach the heights of rhetoric or to study with a sophist longer than it took to acquire the necessary basic skills: for them, rhetoric was simply vocational training, a ticket to a white-collar job and a chance for some upward mobility.[9]

Moreover, despite their claims to purvey a *technê* and *philosophia* of the discursive power that made civil society possible and mediated all thought and action—the art of all arts, the best and most noble—sophists and rhetoricians themselves often occupied a precarious if respectable social position. Unless they happened to be independently wealthy star performers such as Herodes Atticus or Aelius Aristides,[10] they typically were dependent on private fees, even when fortunate enough to hold a hard-to-get and usually modest municipal or imperial salary; they constantly faced the possibility of losing students to competitors; they might be viewed as social inferiors by wealthy parents and their children; they might have trouble getting paid or getting students to do their work; and, in general, through most of rhetoric's history they were subject to the real inequities of power under absolute autocracies. As Raffaella Cribiore has put it, teachers in antiquity "stood on shaky ground, often battling against economic hardship and insecurity."[11] Libanius, who held the municipal chair of rhetoric in Antioch in the fourth century C.E., complains in *Oration* 31 (*For the Teachers*) about the inadequate public support for his school and the grinding poverty of his teaching assistants.[12] Likewise, Libanius complains in *Oration* 62 (*Against Critics of His Educational System*) that "[students] sleep, snore, drink, and get drunk, and hold high revelry, and make it plain to teachers that unless they put up with any and everything, they will go off to somebody else, and their fathers won't stop them. . . . [Teachers of rhetoric] see the profession despised, dragged down deep, and without reputation, influence, or income, but instead of this, involving a grievous servitude, with many as their masters—fathers, mothers, attendants, the students themselves. . . . Who will look at me and wish to enter this profession? I am held to be lucky, but my life is more miserable than that of prisoners, for I am ordered about and needs must both dislike and court the same people" (25, 32, 33).[13]

That things remained more or less the same in the Byzantine world is attested by a collection of letters (122 in all) from an anonymous tenth-century schoolmaster who appears to have taught both grammar and rhetoric and to have squabbled frequently with parents, students, former students, and rivals, usually over money. We see it too in the twelfth-century letters of the scholar and rhetorician John Tzetzes, who for obscure reasons was denied an official teaching post and constantly was faced with poverty.[14] Wayne Rebhorn has commented on the very similar situation in the Renaissance: while rhetoric portrayed itself as "the emperor of men's minds," actual teachers of rhetoric occupied a subordinate position in society, often were regarded with suspicion, and wielded little power.[15] One could say that things have ever been so, down to the present time.

Nevertheless, without denying that the stories rhetoric tells about itself can be discounted, one can argue too that Psellos' and Mesarites' portrayals of the *experience* of rhetorical education ring true, or at least reflect what that experience was like for the right sort of student. Consider the case of Gregory Antiochus, a midlevel Byzantine bureaucrat of the later twelfth century (about a century after Psellos, and a generation before Mesarites).[16] Gregory's family were not aristocrats; he portrays himself as belonging with "small businessmen" (*mikremporoi*) and as dwelling as far below the nobility as a "grain of millet" beneath the "heavens."[17] His father was, however, wealthy enough to send him to school, and he studied rhetoric under the leading teachers of his day: Nicholas Cataphloron, Nicholas Hagiotheodorites, and Eustathius of Thessalonica.[18] His training must have been fairly thorough—he seems to have stayed at rhetoric school for as much as ten years, and thus probably had started a career as a professional rhetorician (that is, as a teaching assistant)—but he says that, because of financial pressures, he was forced to leave the school and seek employment in civil and private service. After some obscure difficulties early on, Gregory was fairly successful, moving from secretarial work in the imperial chancery, and a stint in private employ, to legal administration as a circuit judge and, perhaps, to the senate, making his way slowly upward. A number of orations, mainly panegyrics, have been preserved under his name. Successful as he was, however, Gregory repeatedly portrays his bureaucratic work as "slavish servitude," consisting of "days and nights" of "hardship and toil" in a "hell of stupidity"; and he frequently complains about his meager pay and his poverty.[19] In contrast he looks back fondly to the rhetoric school as "the sweet garden" (*to gluku kêpion*) where, like Adam, he once enjoyed the fruit of the trees of knowledge and experienced freedom but could not stay.[20] In recalling the "sweet garden" of rhetorical training as a place of freedom and intellectual stimulation he echoes Psellos; in portraying it as a sort of paradise he anticipates Mesarites.

Lucian, writing at the height of the Second Sophistic in the second century C.E.—when the conditions for rhetoric presumably were better than in Libanius' day, or in medieval Byzantium—presents a somewhat different picture that never-theless resonates with those discussed.[21] In *The Dream, or Lucian's Career,* he re-counts a dream vision that he says determined his choice of career when he was in his teens. Like Psellos' dream it is an obvious allegorical contrivance, and he openly admits as much, but it nevertheless may reflect his actual experience and represent his understanding of the motives, purposes, and effects of rhetorical training and education (*paideia*): he says that he has told the tale to encourage young men to "pursue the better thing and stick to [higher] education" (18). When Lucian was done with his elementary schooling, he says, his father delib-erated what career the boy should be directed to. Lucian's was a family of respectable but modest means in Roman Syria; and his father's main concerns were focused on what craft (*technê*) would be "best, easy to learn, suitable to a freeborn man, affordable to get started in, and sufficiently remunerative" (2). Since the father's brother was a respected sculptor already, and several genera-tions of the family had been in that business, sculpture was the choice. On his first day at his uncle's shop, however, young Lucian made an expensive mistake, ruining a slab with an erroneous chisel cut, and was beaten for it; he went home humiliated, bruised, and in tears. And so that night, he says, quoting Homer, a "divine dream came to me in my sleep, / out of immortal night" (5; *Iliad* 2.56–57).

The "divine dream" is a humorous rewrite of the *Choice of Hercules* (between vice and virtue) attributed by Xenophon to the sophist Prodicus.[22] In Lucian's version, he is approached by two women representing Sculpture and Paideia, the one callused, shabbily dressed, covered with marble dust, and somewhat inartic-ulate, and the other good looking, dignified, elegantly clothed, and well spoken. Each extols her virtues and asks to be chosen. Sculpture promises that "you'll eat like a king and have sturdy shoulders" and practice the noble art of Phidias and Praxiteles (7–8), but Lucian, of course, chooses Paideia. Among the win-ning arguments that Paideia presents are these: on one hand, if he chooses Sculpture, he will in fact be "only a worker [*ergatês*], one of the populous crowd, always cowering beneath the eminent and paying court to the man who can speak, living a hare's life, being a windfall for the stronger" (9). On the other hand, if he chooses Paideia, she will introduce him to the "wondrous deeds and words" in classic literature and will "ornament" (*katakosmêsô*) his soul with all the virtues: self-control, justice, piety, mildness, reasonableness, intelligence, patience, love of the beautiful, and a passion for what has grandeur. Most impor-tant, she will endow him with eloquence, dress him in fine clothes, and make him esteemed and honored everywhere; crowds will listen to his speeches open-mouthed, and wherever he travels people will point him out and say, "There he is!"; he will even attain a kind of immortality, as cultured people will read and discuss his *logoi* after he is gone (10–12).

Here one could say some obvious things about social class in the Roman world. Suffice it to say that Lucian seems to both reflect and satirize boy-Lucian's desire not to be one of the "populous crowd" of nobodies who work with their hands, his wish not to be beaten, and his dream of rising in the world, attaining wealth and fame, and enjoying the finer things. Unlike Aelius Aristides, his contemporary, boy-Lucian does not so much dream of rhetoric as a means of saving "all human beings" from injustice but dreams of it mainly as a means of saving himself from his middle-class origins in a provincial outpost of the Roman Empire, and particularly from his uncle's sculpture shop.

But there is another dimension to this dream. Like Psellos' dream, it associates a kind of freedom with becoming educated in rhetoric while frankly recognizing the realities of power in the Roman world. The *ergatês* who cannot speak lacks agency in the sense that, in Kenneth Burke's terms, his position in society reduces him to the status of a virtual "thing" that cannot "act" but only "move," being pushed about by arbitrary forces.[23] As a "windfall for the stronger," he is merely a human resource to be employed in their designs; his exercise of freedom is mostly limited to evasion and escape, where possible, "living a hare's life." He "cowers" beneath the eminent for protection and must court "the man who can speak" to speak for him. He is mired in the brute, inarticulate creation that, in Isocrates' as well as Aristides' stories, rhetoric would rescue all humanity from. The *ergatês* does, of course, exercise an agency within the context of his work—the sculptor makes deliberated choices, and designs and executes a sculpture according to his purposes, within the constraints and opportunities afforded by the material conditions of his work—but this is the agency of the private individual, the *idiotês,* the nobody, acting within his house or shop and powerless against the forces outside his door. The "man who can speak," by contrast, exercises a more expansive though not unlimited agency as a *politês,* a citizen (literally a "public man") empowered to act and speak effectively in civic space and so to mediate by *logos* the conditions of social existence for himself and others.[24] In this respect he is, at least to a degree, the sort of figure that Aristides posits.

One might argue that, to this point, the frequently, though not always, cynic-satiric Lucian is aiming to deflate the pretensions of rhetoric and of *paideia* by exposing the fundamentally mundane motives that led boy-Lucian to be persuaded by Lady Paideia's sales pitch—the sheerly practical motives that probably led most to take the path to rhetoric, in hopes of rising above the "hare's life" of the *idiotês.*[25] But the dream continues. Once boy-Lucian chooses Paideia, she rewards him with a ride in her chariot drawn by winged horses through the sky and reveals what is in store for him. That is, the chariot ride discloses what Lucian's rhetorical education *actually* would reveal to him, as opposed to the desires that motivated his choice originally, though he fulfilled those desires as well. As he says, "I was lifted up on high [*hupsos*], surveying cities and nations and peoples from the very east to the very west, and like Triptolemus sowing something broadcast over the earth" (15).[26] Once again, through a "dream imagery" of flight through the open sky and sublime (*hupsos*) revelation, there is a sense of liberation, intellectual awakening, the expansive knowledge of the sophist who "knows (or surveys) everything," and, with Lucian, a sense of acquiring agency or power as an author who not only "can speak" in civic space but also can disseminate a beneficial *logos* "broadcast" over the world and thus, like Aristides as well as Triptolemus, pursues a sacred calling. Lucian seems serious about this, or at least serious enough to encourage the young men in his audience to stay in school.

The contrast between boy-Lucian's mundane motivations and the loftier aspect of the rhetorical *paideia* appears again in Lucian's *Teacher of Orators*.[27] The speaker counsels a youth (*meirakion*) who wants to become an orator, and as with boy-Lucian, the motive is to join those who once were "nothing at all" (*mêden ontes*) but rose to fame and wealth and entered high society through public speaking (2–3). The speaker observes that there are two roads to this goal, a long, difficult road, and a short, easy one. In *Choice of Hercules* fashion, again, each is personified and speaks on its own behalf. Long Road is a hardened, sinewy, old-fashioned figure—think of the famous portrait-statue of Demosthenes—and represents the full rhetorical education in the tradition of Isocrates: a thorough, rigorous training measured in Olympiads, that is, four years, which involves close study and imitation of the classic authors, constant exercise, and "hard work, lack of sleep, lots of water, and living lean" (9). Many fall by the wayside. Short Road, a foppish, soft-skinned libertine, advocates skipping most of the preliminary education (*propaideia*) that Long Road requires—literary and rhetorical-critical study of the classics and the progymnasmata—as well as disciplined declamation (14, 17). Short Road advises, instead, that the would-be orator be completely shameless, speak whatever comes into his mind without stopping, and dwell on easy themes while dismissing difficult ones as unworthy of his attention; he can hoodwink the ignorant by dressing fashionably and displaying other trappings of success, sprinkling his speech with antique expressions, using obscure and high-falutin' terms wherever possible, adopting a singsong delivery, maintaining a claque to applaud, and so forth, and he is to make connections with the influential by being willing to do anything at all for them, including sexual services (15–23). This will bring him the sort of success that he desires.

Lucian's satire is fairly brutal, and at least some of it can be dismissed, but what is clear is that the "short road" that many students in fact took consisted of a briefer stay at rhetoric school, perhaps a year or two, and conveyed a more superficial training that still could be sufficient for getting a civil service job, or even to try cases in local courts.[28] A less prejudicial, first-century C.E. version appears in Dio Chrysostom's *Discourse* 18, *On Training in Speech* (*Peri Logou Askē-seôs*). Dio addresses himself to a wealthy and perhaps *nouveau riche* man who apparently has had little schooling but now wants a quick course in rhetoric so he can enter politics, probably participation in the local *curia,* the city council. Because of the press of "business" (*to prattein;* 5) he lacks the time and inclination for the long road's thorough, demanding regimen, which Dio says he would recommend if the man were very young. The shorter, easier route that Dio prescribes consists mainly of an abbreviated reading list drawn from the traditional canon—a few of the classic poets, orators, historians, and philosophers—with a preference for those that are easier to grasp and imitate: Hyperides or Aeschines rather than Demosthenes; Xenophon rather than Plato or Thucydides. Isocrates is not even mentioned. In fact, says Dio, Xenophon alone is enough as far as the classics go (14), and for the rest, the "more recent" orators will be more useful because they are much easier to grasp, critique, and imitate (12–13). Further, Dio recommends that his addressee *not* do traditional composition or declamation exercises; instead he should "very occasionally" dictate to a secretary, so as to cultivate a habit of speaking his thoughts without hesitation (18). If he does write, he should take a speech from his reading and paraphrase it and/or compose a speech against it; but the best exercise of all is simply to read the speech aloud (18–19). In sum, the short road, as Dio describes it, is an abbreviated *paideia* that combines some limited literary study with a few elements of the progymnasmata—reading aloud, restatement, and counterstatement—and aims mainly at developing some ability to speak in public with a modicum of fluency and confidence and a thin veneer of culture. That will be enough for the rich man's purposes.

Other short roads would develop, not to rhetoric but to bureaucratic careers. In the fourth century Libanius had to contend with competition from shorthand schools, law schools, and Latin schools (Latin being the language of Roman law), forms of vocational training that developed specialized practical skills required for civil service or secretarial jobs and that may have been quicker, surer ways than rhetoric, and the broad, humanistic *paideia* that went with it, to get those jobs.[29] The point, in sum, is that the more sheerly practical, mundane motives that led boy-Lucian and most others to take the path to rhetoric could be fulfilled with a relatively limited practical education, even a nonrhetorical education, though a Lucian might lambaste it as the short and easy way to the "hell of stupidity" and "slavish servitude" in midlevel administration where Gregory Antiochus spent his life, not to mention the moral corruptions of toadying to the powerful and the various kinds of graft and bribery that Roman officials could indulge in. (Which was not much of an escape, either, from the "hare's life" of the *ergatês*.) But the point is also that the *experience* of rhetorical education itself delivered, at least for certain students—perhaps especially those who took the long road—what Lucian, Aristides, and Psellos portray as a revelation of something more philosophical and sublime, or what Mesarites and Gregory portray as the student's life in a quasi-paradisal "sweet garden" of talking, disputing, declaiming birds.

The larger point is that such portrayals of the experience of rhetorical education fuse two images that all too easily are thought of as distinct: on one hand an "Isocratean" sophistic tradition that treats rhetoric as an intellectually liberating philosophic endeavor, even a holy calling, devoted to practical questions in politics and ethics, and to a vision of civil community; on the other hand a "technical" sophistic tradition, represented by the *technai*, that treats rhetoric as a regimen of exercise in the methods of handling certain types of public discourse. (And alongside these there is the other philosophical tradition of rhetorical study descended from Plato and Aristotle and carried on in the later philosophic schools.)[30] As I suggested earlier, however, the Isocratean and technical traditions both descended from Isocrates and in truth were one and the same. Thus the Academic Charmadas attempted to refute rhetoric's philosophical status by observing that he found no political philosophy or any other kind of philosophy in the rhetoricians' "little books" devoted to the technicalities of introductions, narratives, and so on (as Cicero's Antonius reports in *De oratore* 1.85–86). What Charmadas did not understand was that rhetoric's philosophical activity operated through its regimen of exercise informed by the precepts of the *technai*—in particular, the arguing of "evenly balanced" cases in declamation.

This chapter, then, is devoted to declamation, understood as a philosophical practice in the Isocratean mode, both in the classroom and in the theatrical public performances of the sophists—a practice capable of producing the sort of experience that Lucian, Psellos, Mesarites, and Gregory portray. Further, as I hope to show later in this chapter, *as* such a practice, declamation functioned too as a kind of "civic theater" that rehearsed the student, performer, and audience in an experience of democratic culture, even when such culture was unavailable or unthinkable as a realistic practical possibility.

I begin, however, with consideration of the *technai* as a frame for that activity. In particular I examine the pedagogic use of stasis theory in Quintilian and Hermogenes.

The *Technai* Revisited

As noted earlier, rhetorical *technai* could have a variety of functions.[31] First of all, and primarily, they might serve as a resource for the teacher—a compilation of the "things that can be said" to students doing exercises[32]—and might be made available to students as a "reminder" or supplement to the teacher's orally delivered instruction. For example, Philostratus mentions that his own teacher, Proclus of Naucratis, "had a library [*thêkê bibliôn*] at his house, which he made available to his students to fill out what they had heard" (*es to plêrôma tês akroaseôs; Lives of the Sophists* 2.21 [604]).[33] It should be noted that while *bibliothêkê* is the standard Greek term for "library," *thêkê bibliôn* suggests a more modest sort of library: literally a "chest" or "case" (*thêkê*) "of books" (*bibliôn*). We probably should imagine a sort of box or cabinet containing a number of papyrus scrolls. These would be Proclus' personal collection of *technai*, which could consist of his own teaching notes or some other *technai* that he relied on and invited his students to consult to "fill out" his oral teaching. He probably possessed other boxes of books as well, such as the works of the poets, historians, orators, and so on that he used in his teaching.

Technai might also be produced and published as hornbooks or as memoranda of instruction meant to be used as study aids or review guides. This seems especially true for *technai* that appear to have been intended as quasi-literary works, sometimes with dedicatory "letters" or prefaces attached, such as the *Rhetoric to Alexander,* the *Rhetoric to Herennius,* or Cicero's *On the Parts of Rhetoric.* The dialogue comprising *Parts of Rhetoric,* for example, begins with his Cicero's son's statement that "I am eager, father, to hear from you in Latin what you have imparted to me in Greek about the theory of speaking" (*de ratione dicendi;* 1). What follows is a concise review in dialogue form. Similarly, the *Rhetoric to Herennius* purports to have been written for a friend who wishes "to have knowledge of rhetoric" (*cognoscere rhetoricam;* 1.1); the term *cognoscere* suggests gaining an intellectual grasp of the art that Herennius already has been practicing in exercises. The relation between author and reader, and the intended use of the text, becomes clearer in the preface to book 3: "You will learn the principles [of rhetoric] both with me, when you wish, and also sometimes without me, by reading, so that nothing will impede your ability to make equal progress with me in this useful art" (3.1).

The *Rhetoric to Herennius,* in short, is another "Proclus' bookcase" item; it can be used as a hornbook to summarize and supplement what a student has heard from his teacher while working on declamation exercises. Finally, the *Rhetoric to Alexander* purports to be a "memorandum" (*hupomnêma*) of what "Nicanor explained to us," supplemented with materials from the author's own writings and the rhetoric of "Corax" (pr. 1421a–b).

As noted earlier, a *technê* might be written or compiled by the rhetoric teacher's students from their notes. That is possibly the case with the *Rhetoric to Alexander* and is clearly the case with Cicero's *De inventione* and the unauthorized "rhetoric of Quintilian" that Quintilian says his students circulated (*Institutio*

1.pr.7–8). The case is similar with the so-called *Anonymous Seguerianus,* a text of the late second or early third century, which appears to be an advanced student's compilation of notes from the *technê* of "Alexander, the son of Noumenius," a rhetorician of the mid-second century, supplemented or "filled out" with material from other sources.[34] The *Seguerianus* writer appears to be attempting to assemble a comprehensive treatment of rhetorical teaching on the parts of an oration derived from his preferred authorities. He seems thoroughly familiar, too, with the canonic orators. For example, in his discussion of proemia he notes that their topics are derived from the persons and facts involved in the case, and he then gives some highly abbreviated examples, such as "From oneself, like Demosthenes in *Against Conon,* 'having been insulted'; but if you speak on someone else's behalf, this too should be signified, as Lysias has done, saying 'Archippus here is my friend, judges.' From the opponent, as in *Against Meidias,* 'the insolence.'" (7)

This procedure is fairly common in the *Seguerianus.* The truncated quotations from Demosthenes and Lysias, and the non-identification of the particular speech the Lysias derives from, as well as the non-identification of Demosthenes as the author of *Against Meidias,* presuppose not only an advanced writer but also an advanced reader who can instantly identify the passages in question and probably reproduce them more or less from memory.

Such student-compiled texts suggest a retrospective effort to gain a comprehensive mastery of the lore and the literary exempla that the student already has become acquainted with. It also suggests the prospective function of acquiring such mastery in order to become, oneself, a teacher. In this function, the truncated quotations may be meant as references to examples that can be used in teaching. The *Seguerianus* writer, if he is setting up as a rhetorician, has attempted to produce a text that may serve as the master scroll in his, and possibly other rhetoricians', box of *technai.*[35]

The *Anonymous Seguerianus'* attempt to assemble lore from various sources, in particular its refutations of "the Apollodoreans,"—followers of the influential first-century rhetorician Apollodorus of Pergamon—suggests also another type of motive, namely, to participate in debates over rhetorical doctrine, make a contribution to rhetorical lore, or assert oneself as an authority.[36] The most obvious example of that motive is Quintilian, whose *Institutio oratoria* is a quasi-literary text addressed chiefly to rhetoricians on the question of how an orator should be educated from early childhood to retirement. Quintilian offers a thorough survey of the lore current in his time, with critiques of various opinions, adjudications of controversies among the sources, and his own views and recommendations. But the motive appears in many *technai.* In the opening pages of Hermogenes' *On Stases,* for example, we find this:

Now the division [into heads] of questions that have a valid issue must be discussed. To speak about the genre and style of declamation-problems is irrelevant at this point—for presumably the reason we learn the genres and styles is so that we will use the appropriate types of style when we practice with declamation-problems, for example, judicial speech in a judicial style, deliberative speech in a deliberative style, epideictic speech in an epideictic style, and each adapted suitably to the given subject-matter. But for those who have not yet studied the basic [*psilês*, "bare"] division of questions into what are called heads, and who do not know what are called the stases of declamation-problems, it obviously is impossible to have a good understanding of any of the aforementioned things. So to teach the types of style before these other matters is totally senseless.[37]

Clearly, Hermogenes here is speaking *to* fellow teachers *about* students, concerning what to teach when: his opinion is that there is no reason for a teacher to discuss judicial, deliberative, and epideictic types of style before the student has learned the inventional handling of the types of issues and their heads in preliminary inquiry. The reasons for this opinion become apparent in Hermogenes' *On Types of Style* (*Peri Ideôn*), where he offers a very complex analysis of twenty types of style—each consisting of the "thought" to be expressed and the appropriate "method" (the figure of thought) and stylistic features (diction, figures, clauses, word order, cadence, and rhythm) for expressing it—all culminating in a discussion of "practical" and "panegyric" styles in the final chapters.[38] Thus he argues that there is no point in bothering with such stylistic issues before the basic generation and development of "thoughts" has been mastered by the student. Hermogenes, in short, is arguing a point in pedagogical philosophy for an audience of fellow rhetoricians.

The rhetoric attributed to the third-century (?) rhetorician Apsines of Gadara, which discusses the parts of an oration, presents a similar kind of motive in its opening remarks on proemia: "As for me, I would praise and accept [what our predecessors have said], but perhaps I also can add to the common store something neither useless nor unprofitable, by which we will more readily and more opportunely get a proemium" (1.2).[39] This suggests an address to fellow rhetoricians, and an intent to make some contribution to the accumulated lore concerning "what can be said" to students doing exercises—and thus to present himself as an authority. Apsines occasionally speaks as if addressing students, as in, "We have provided you with the topics of refutation; when you know them you will easily find plenty of refutations" (5.21). But as Malcolm Heath suggests, such locutions may be stylistic echoes of schoolroom talk, preserved fragments from students' or stenographer's notes compiled into the text without stylistic assimilation, or artifacts of composition by dictation.[40] Apsines much more commonly uses a generic "we" or "you," as in, speaking of the "preparation" or "forecast" statement that precedes narration and proof, "We start from a promise when the hearers are expecting a certain heading that clearly limits the question at issue, and you claim that you are hurrying to it and would gladly make a beginning from it, but it is necessary to talk about something else first" (2.20).

He also uses, less commonly, a generic third-person mixed with others: "I have no objection to someone saying too that Lysias unfolds his narratives in the nominative case, while Demosthenes uses oblique cases according to the thought, and Lysias employs plain narrations while Demosthenes adds some interpretation to them—and [I likewise have no objection] if you wish to understand too that in narratives one should not use up all the facts at the start, but use them with moderation, and that sometimes one should not narrate when the narrative would work against us, and that whenever some facts are on our side and others against us, what is on our side should be narrated and what is against should be challenged and refuted with counter-arguments" (3.1–2). In this example Apsines appears to be speaking mostly to fellow rhetoricians. He has "no objection" to someone, that is, the rhetorician, saying certain things about Lysias' and Demosthenes' uses of narrative (*eô de kakeino legein,* literally "I would allow [someone] to say this"), or "if you wish to understand" (*ei de boulei mathein*) certain other things about narratives.

Two other features shed light on the intended audience and purposes of Apsines' *technê*. First, as with the *Anonymous Seguerianus'* abbreviated examples, Apsines makes frequent and usually abbreviated references to declamation problems, as if the reader is expected to be familiar with them. For example (speaking of the proemium "from result"), "Let there be, as examples, the Athenians tried on behalf of the Potidaeans, and Aeschylus [tried] on behalf of the Eumenides, and the person [tried] on account of the plague among the Scythians, and in all [problems] where there is some great and acknowledged wrong" (1.54). Such abbreviated references can be found on virtually every page. Aside from the obvious implication that the precepts Apsines offers in his *technê* are meant for use in declamation problems, the point I wish to emphasize here is that Apsines assumes a reader familiar with a large repertoire of declamation problems—that is, a rhetoric teacher.

The second feature is the long list of what Apsines calls "theorems" (*theôrêmata*) for proemia. There are twenty-eight in all, some discussed at length and others more briefly. This list is probably what Apsines thinks he is adding to the "common store" of rhetorical precepts. The list has no apparent logical order, and most entries after the first are introduced simply with the word "another" (*allo*), as in the second entry: "Another. We will praise the listeners when they have performed some noble act, and . . ." (1.11). The locution is sometimes varied, with "another theorem" (*allo theôrêma*), or "yet another theorem" (*eti ge mên kai allo theôrêma*), and the like; but the simple "another" is most common. This clearly is "teacher's resource book" material. It reads like a file cabinet to which things have been added over the years—notes for the handling of particular types of declamation problems. It would be unendurable, and unrememberable, if delivered all at once in a lecture. And it makes for tedious reading if one attempts to read it straight through. But it can be drawn from selectively, depending on the declamation problem a student is working on.

In sum, Apsines' *Art of Rhetoric* seems to have been written or compiled primarily as a teacher's resource book and, perhaps secondarily, as a contribution to rhetorical lore, and it could have functioned, as well, as a "Proclus' bookcase" item, a supplemental resource, for the more diligent student who wished to "fill out" the instruction delivered in the schoolroom. In this it seems fairly representative of the ancient rhetorical *technai* generally.

The broader point of this discussion (both here and in chapter 2) is that the *technai* are not exactly textbooks or works of theory in the modern sense. They are not textbooks in the sense that they are not a primary medium of instruction. Not every student would have consulted "Proclus' bookcase" or acquired a *technê* for his personal use, and it is conceivable, even likely, that most students neither possessed nor consulted a *technê* at all. This would be especially true for students who did not intend to become professional rhetoricians, or aimed only at enough proficiency to get a bureaucratic job—or those whose main interest was extracurricular carousing.[41]

The *technai* are not theory in the modern sense either, insofar as they are not a systematic account of the principles of persuasive speech, or even a system of rules for creating such speech. This point is tricky and easily overstated and misinterpreted; it needs some clarification. As Cicero's speakers recognize in *De oratore*, the precepts of the *technai* indeed originate from the "observation and collection" of "what eloquent men did spontaneously" (*quae sua sponte homines eloquentes facerent*)—the imitable features of their discourse, derived from close study of their written texts—but those precepts, or those imitable features, do not themselves constitute eloquence or a methical procedure for producing it (1.146). To put it differently, and again as Cicero's speakers tend to put it, any orator who attempted to argue in court or assembly simply by following the "rules" of the *technai* would be acting very foolishly, like a mere schoolboy who fails to perceive the difference between parade-ground exercises "with a wooden sword" and real-world contestation. Nevertheless Cicero's speakers all consider the "rules" of the *technai* and the declamation exercises they accompany to be essential for the training of an orator. And that is the point: the precepts of the *technai* are an apparatus for doing declamation exercises. The exercises cultivate in the student a habituated rhetorical *dunamis* in simulations of rhetorical situations, and that *dunamis,* carried forward into real, practical experience, will or can develop further into a capacity for "spontaneous" eloquence in real occasions. As I have said before, the art of rhetoric is not as much an art of producing speeches as it is an art of producing speakers through its regimen of exercise. Let us, then, consider an example: the pedagogic function of stasis systems in Quintilian and Hermogenes.

Stasis Systems: Simulations for the Inexperienced

Malcolm Heath has argued that Hermogenes' stasis system emerged as part of a second-century C.E. "transformation" in Greek argumentation theory.[42] As Heath suggests, the earlier versions of stasis theory, in particular, that of Hermagoras of Temnos (c. 150 B.C.E.), seem to have associated "the familiar framework of issue-theory (the types of issues) with a diagnostic apparatus designed to help the orator identify and focus on the crucial argument in a given case," though the evidence is fragmentary and inconsistent.[43] As we have seen, Isocrates' own treatment of preliminary inquiry probably performed such a function, albeit in a rudimentary way compared with later stasis systems. We have observed such a procedure too in Cicero's Antonius' account of his approach to the analysis of a case: interview the client, ascertain the facts as well as possible, then play out an imaginary, point/counterpoint debate between the opposing advocates and the judge, through which the crucial question at issue will emerge (*De oratore* 2.102–105ff.). Eventually, however, as Heath argues, the "Hermagorean apparatus . . . broke down entirely," so that, when we turn to the Elder Seneca's *Controversiae* (first century B.C.E.) or the *Lesser Declamations* ascribed to Quintilian (second century C.E.?), it appears that the Hermagorean stasis system has become merely "a loose collection of potentially useful topics" for each type of issue, and has come to play little observable role in the process of invention.[44] The second-century "transformation" in Greek theory, then, attempted to reorganize those "loose collections" of topics as "ordered sequences" of headings that could "provide the speaker with a ready-made outline of his case." Eventually the system of Hermogenes of Tarsus proved to be the most "pedagogically effective" of the new systems,[45] and it enjoyed a millennium of dominance in the schools of Byzantium.

The notion that Hermogenes' system reflected a change in stasis pedagogy seems undeniable, and Heath's very thorough analysis of that system is persuasive.[46] But stasis pedagogy probably always was in flux. Seneca the Elder, writing a few decades after Cicero and recalling the declaimers of his youth, speaks of what for him were the "old" and "new" methods of "dividing" an issue into its constituent topics (*Controversiae* 1.1.13). There is, moreover, a slippage in the narrative laid out above. We move from a second-century B.C.E. Hermagorean system said to be useful *for the orator,* but which "breaks down" within a century or two, and then, two centuries after the breakdown, is replaced by the more *pedagogically effective* Hermogenean system and its competitors.

There is little doubt that Hermogenes' system came to be preferred by teachers, mainly in the Greek East, but was it more useful for the orator? And did the Hermagorean system "break down" for the orator? Here some version of Cicero's Antonius might remark, a little hyperbolically, "What capable, eloquent orator was ever at a loss over how to analyze, prepare, and argue his case for lack of the right stasis system from the schools, or for lack of those ready-made, tinkertoy outlines of Hermogenes?" Was Cicero crippled by not having read Hermogenes? Were any of the Attic orators crippled by not having read Hermagoras? Let us recall that Isocrates' *Against Callimachus* apparently treats a stasis that then was novel (*paragraphê,* "exception to procedure"). It did not appear in the *Rhetoric to Alexander's* embryonic account of stasis, and so far as we can tell it did not become part of any formalized stasis system before Hermagoras.[47] Yet Isocrates argued that stasis quite effectively. The real-world orator, if truly capable, does not proceed according to the schoolroom prescriptions of either Hermagoras or Hermogenes but improvises according to the *kairos* of his situation while deriving his inventional *dunamis* from an array of internalized habits cultivated long ago in school and further developed through practical experience. The "transformation" narrative, in sum, is more persuasive if it is conceived not as a progress from less to more adequate argumentation theory or as an improvement in real-world practice, but as a progress from a less to more effective *pedagogical apparatus* for exercising students in declamation—or, simply, as a change in pedagogy that reflected the changing needs of the students that rhetoricians confronted in the schoolroom at different times and places.

One may question, too, whether the older, Hermagorean type of system "broke down" even in pedagogical practice. After all, it seems to have remained in use in schools for hundreds of years, from the mid-second century B.C.E. to the second century C.E., long after its supposed breakdown. Another problem is the question whether the change Heath observes is really a change at all, or simply a difference between Roman and Greek pedagogical traditions—Hermogenes seems rather fussy for Roman preferences. He certainly does not appear to have replaced Hermagoras in the Latin tradition. Cicero, the *Rhetoric to Herennius,* and Quintilian remained the dominant Latin authorities through antiquity and into the Middle Ages. In Alcuin's eighth-century *Rhetoric of Alcuin and Charlemagne* we find Alcuin still rehearsing the Hermagorean system, with a patchwork of quotes from Cicero. This suggests that Hermagoras never "broke down" at all in that tradition, but simply was adapted in various ways.[48]

Perhaps the first thing to note is the multiplicity of stasis systems recognized by Quintilian, in his overview of the then-current lore (*Institutio* 3.6). His review includes everything from "one-issue" systems to "eight-issue" systems, with representatives in each category, with the exception of the mostly hypothetical one-issue systems, of which he finds no actual example (3.6.29–31). Some of these systems are plainly the products of philosophical theorizing, such as the Stoic Posidonius' classification of all issues under two basic stases (3.6.3), an arrangement that seems designed for theoretical elegance more than practical utility. Most of the systems Quintilian mentions, however, are clearly the products of rhetoric schools and show that there were differences from teacher to teacher in how the classification and "division" of issues was presented.

Despite their differences in presentation, most systems reflect the basic set of issues generally attributed to Hermagoras: three "rational" stases (fact, definition, quality), plus the "legal" stases (letter and intent, analogy, conflicting laws, ambiguity), plus the stasis of procedural objection. The legal stases are sometimes treated as extensions of definition, or definition as one of the legal stases, and procedural objection likewise is sometimes subsumed under the legal stases. Some rhetorical authorities treat as stases what others treat as subheads of more general stases, and some treat the more general stases not as stases but as "types of questions." One could argue that this diversity of treatments, as well as the underlying agreements among them, reflects not a breakdown but the continuing vitality and flexibility of the underlying Hermagorean model, as it evolved in pedagogical practice with different teachers in different schools. In essence there were individual differences in approach to the *pedagogical presentation* of stasis and the assignment of exercises, more than substantive theoretical differences or differences in real-world rhetorical practice. Rhetoricians in the Hellenistic period did not slavishly follow the system of Hermagoras, but used it as a resource and adapted it to their own teaching, according to what seemed useful in their particular experience.

Quintilian, interestingly, in the presentation of his own view, says that he used to teach that there were four main types of issue—fact, definition, quality, and law (including procedural objection)—but has now come to agree with Cicero's view that there are only three issues (fact, definition, quality) and a broad distinction between legal and rational "questions." In Quintilian's view "questions" or "types of actions" (*formae actionis*) are not yet "issues" (or "stases"); in disputes over questions of both law and equity (what the law requires and what reason says is right), the crucial point to be decided always will resolve into an issue of fact, definition, or quality (3.6.63–82, 86–91; the discussion is fairly convoluted).[49] However, says Quintilian, "for those instructing beginners" (*instituentibus rudes*), "it will be helpful to employ, at first, the broader principle" of four issues (3.6.83–85). Theoretical elegance, even correspondence to truth, is less important than pedagogical utility at a given stage of instruction.

In book 7 of the *Institutio oratoria*, Quintilian discusses the process for the "division" of a case (7.1.34). As he presents it, division is a matter of generating questions through a process of assertion and counterassertion until one arrives at the crucial issue. The order of questions generated through this process will differ from the order of arguments in the actual speech, says Quintilian, and he stresses that the process should not be rushed, or approached with a set method, but patiently and painstakingly worked out. (7.1.40). This denial of a set method for division is important. In Isocratean fashion, the student is to approach the process as a "creative activity" requiring the exercise of ingenuity according to the *kairos* of the given case: the precise issue and its available arguments arise not only from the specifics of the declamation problem but also from the interplay of opposing arguments in preliminary inquiry. Also important is Quintilian's denial that the sequence of questioning in division, and the arguments discovered, provides an "outline" for the speech: rather, it produces an inventory of available heads of argument, or available arguments, to be used in whatever sequence will be strategically and tactically most effective.

Quintilian then offers a worked example, based on a declamation problem "from the school" (*de schola*) that, in his opinion, is "neither especially difficult nor novel" (7.1.41). This is the problem: "[The laws:] Whoever fails to appear in defense of his father on a charge of treason shall be disinherited. A person convicted of treason shall be exiled, together with his advocate. [The case:] A son who was a skilled speaker [*disertus*] appeared in defense of his father on a charge of treason; his brother, who was an uneducated farmer [*rusticus*], did not appear. The father was convicted and went into exile with his advocate. The farmer brother became a war hero, and as his reward chose restitution for his father and brother. The father returned and died intestate. The farmer son claims a part of the estate. The orator son claims it all for himself" (7.1.42).

Quintilian observes that people who think themselves too "eloquent" to bother with the niceties of school exercises will pounce on the sympathetic and unsympathetic qualities of the two brothers—humble-modest-brave farmer versus greedy-glib-ungrateful orator—and will develop some flashy *sententiae* from the contrast, but will not have a strong case (7.1.43–44). Similarly, "those who aim higher but focus on what is obvious" will observe not only that the farmer son is more deserving, but also that the key "question" on which the case will turn is "letter and intent" (7.1.44–45). The letter of the law favors the orator son, but one can argue that its intent favors the more deserving *rusticus*. But this is still a superficial analysis, since it has not located the specific propositions, and thus the specific stasis, by which one could argue most effectively for letter or intent. In contrast, "he who follows nature" (*qui naturam sequetur*) and is patient and thorough will proceed as follows: "[He] will certainly consider that the farmer son first will say, 'Our intestate father left us, his two sons, and I claim a share by the law of nations' [*iure gentium,* that is, the natural law followed by all peoples]. . . . He will then elaborate lightly on the common law of all men as just. Next, obviously, we shall ask what is the reply to such a reasonable assertion. It is obvious: 'There is a law that requires a man who did not appear in defense of his father on a charge of treason to be disinherited; you did not appear.' This statement is necessarily followed by praise of the law and denunciation of those who do not defend their fathers" (7.1.46–47).

Let us note briefly that Quintilian has each of these statements—the farmer son's opening claim and the orator son's reply—followed by a sort of commonplace, one amplifying on the justice of the "law of nations," and the other on the wickedness of sons who fail to aid their fathers in the hour of need. This is part of the exercise, even if both arguments ultimately will play no role in the finished version of the student's declamation. What the student does here resembles a progymnasma, either the maxim or the commonplace exercise, depending on how fully it is developed. The point is to start compiling an inventory of possible arguments, beginning from the "natural" starting point in the more or less inevitable first clash of claim and counter-statement. Quintilian then continues:

> So far we have been occupied with what is obvious. Let our thought turn again to the petitioner. Unless one is utterly dull, he surely will think the following: "If the law obstructs the claim, there is no dispute, and a trial is futile. But that there is a law, and that the farmer son did what it punishes, is beyond doubt." So what shall we say? "I was uneducated." If there is a law, it includes all men, and this argument is useless; let us then ask whether the law can be invalidated in some respect. What else (if I may repeat) does nature allow, when the letter of the law is against us, but to investigate its spirit? So the general question is whether the letter or spirit should prevail; but regarding law in general, this question has been perennially disputed without any satisfactory resolution. We must ask, then, concerning the particular law on which the trial is based, whether something can be found which opposes a literal interpretation. "Then, is anyone who fails to appear in defense of his father to be disinherited? Anyone without exception?" *Now the arguments will spontaneously suggest themselves.* "Even a child? And someone away from home? And someone on military service? And someone who was away on an embassy?" Now we have made a great advance: it is in fact possible for someone not to appear in his father's defense and be his heir. (7.1.48–50; emphasis added)

Quintilian's example goes on for several more pages (7.1.51–61), continuing the basic process of assertion and reply and exploring at length what the two sons can say on the question of letter and intent in this particular case. After his exploration of the legal question, Quintilian more briefly examines the "remaining" matters of equity (*reliqua aequitatis*) or "which of the two makes the juster claim" (7.1.62–63).

The first point to note is that the process Quintilian illustrates resembles what Cicero's Antonius more summarily describes: an imaginary point/counterpoint between opposed positions, and a judge, discovering whatever arguments can be derived from each position regarding the persons, actions, and laws involved in the problem. Second, the key legal issue emerges, as it does with Antonius, from this point/counterpoint exploration of the initial question. For example, it emerges that the issue is not simply "letter and intent" but more specifically whether the law in question applies to all cases uniformly, without exception, and, if there are exceptions, whether the farmer-son's nonappearance at his father's trial falls into the excepted category. Third, once the key, specific question has been arrived at, according to Quintilian, arguments will begin to "spontaneously" suggest themselves—or will, at least, for the person whose natural wits have been sharpened and made more resourceful through study and exercise. And fourth and finally, the pursuit of the more refined, specific question brings the dispute to questions of what "failing to appear in your father's defense" means, and thus to the stasis of definition, just as Quintilian says. (That is, all questions, rational or legal, ultimately come down to the stasis of fact, definition, or quality.)

It should be noted, too, that the *Lesser Declamations* ascribed to Quintilian show a similar pattern. Most of these declamations consist not of a finished speech but of a statement of the problem followed by "rough draft" treatments of certain parts or aspects of the case, often accompanied by the teacher's "discussion" (*sermo*) of selected points. That is, the truncated "declamations" presented in this text are mainly rehearsals of particular arguments or sketches for the "confirmation" (proof) section of an oration. As such they embody what Quintilian says should be done with less advanced students, that is, the teacher should suggest the lines of argument to use, rough out some particular arguments, and have the student finish up the rest (*Institutio* 2.6.5).

The treatment of stasis and the process of division in both Quintilian and the *Lesser Declamations* suggests that, rather than an orderly, methodical system of stases and subheads that "broke down" into a "loose collection of potentially useful topics" for each stasis, the Hermagorean system was from the start a relatively loose affair. It never did provide ready-made "outlines" or a rigid procedure. It required the student to exercise his wits by imaginatively constructing a "conversation" or debate between opposed positions, and assumed that the logical sequence of the conversation would not necessarily correspond to the argumentational structure of the finished declamation. Once this initial inquiry was complete, an inventory of possible arguments had been compiled, and the key stasis had been identified, the precepts for generating the different parts of an oration and managing one's proofs took over. It appears, then, that the Hermagorean system required the student to approach the preliminary inquiry into the stasis as what Isocrates would call a "creative act" (*poiêtikon pragma*). It also, if Cicero's Antonius is to be believed, put the student through a fairly realistic simulation of what a practicing orator would really do.

A notable feature of the Hermogenean system is its continuity with the progymnasmata, which—though they probably go back, in some form, to the early sophists and Isocrates—by Hermogenes' time had begun to take on what appears to us now as their canonic form, as exemplified by Aelius Theon and especially by Aphthonius.[50] There are of course differences among the surviving progymnasmata manuals, but one key point in common is that, especially in the more advanced exercises, they generally prescribe a fixed set of headings to be taken up in order. The progymnasmata, in short, provide the student with a "ready-made outline" for a speech.

Aphthonius, for example, notes that the commonplace is "like a second speech [for the penalty phase in a trial] or an epilogue" and as such does not naturally have a proemium, but for the sake of the exercise it should be given one. This is a structural prescription. Then, in the body of the speech, "you put *first* the heading from opposition [*ek tou enantiou*], *then* bring on the exposition [*ekthesis*]—not to instruct the listener, for he knows [the facts], but to inflame him. *After this* you bring on a comparison, setting the better thing beside what is denounced; *then* the so-called gnomic heading, attacking the doer's intention; *then* a digression, pointedly reproaching his past life; *then* rejection of pity, *and to complete* the progymnasma the final headings [*telika kephalaia*]: legality, justice, advantage, possibility, honor, and result" (emphases added).[51]

For the thesis exercise, similarly, Aphthonius prescribes an "opening" (*ephodos,* "approach, entry") in place of a proemium, followed by some of the final headings: legality, justice, advantage, and possibility. Theon prescribes for the thesis a much longer list of headings (which he calls *topoi*), which seems to require some selection as appropriate to the question under debate, but as with Aphthonius, he expects the student to more or less work through the list in sequence.[52] The process of speech production is parsed into a structured sequence of "envelopes" constituting an abstract outline for a speech.

Now compare Hermogenes' treatment of the "division" of stases with the progymnasmata. Let us take the first stasis, "conjecture," the issue of fact, which Hermogenes treats most fully. According to Hermogenes, a conjectural issue arises when a set of facts is invoked as evidence that a crime has taken place: "You were discovered burying a slain corpse in a deserted place; you committed murder." The issue is "conjectural" if the defendant denies that he has buried a slain corpse, or that his doing so is evidence of the crime alleged. A

normal conjectural issue, then, is divided by Hermogenes into the following
sequence of headings, which I outline in abbreviated form:[53]

Objection (*paragraphikon*): In some situations the defense may simply call for
dismissal of the case, on the grounds that the charge is ill formed or legally
improper in some way, or *prima facie* groundless; four topics are given. For
example, a dissolute son's father disappears and the son is charged with
murder; he objects that there is no proof that his father has been killed,
so there is no basis for a trial.

Demand for proof (*tôn elenchôn apaitêsis*):[54] If there are witnesses, the defense
must argue that they are unreliable; four topics are given. If there are no
witnesses, the defense must demand that witnesses be produced, with regard
to the topics of narrative (who, what, when, where, how, why); the prosecution will argue that proof from facts is more reliable than witnesses.

Motive and capacity (*boulêsis kai dunamis*): Both prosecution and defense must
explore the motives and capacities of the persons involved in the case, using
the topics of encomium (family, upbringing, education, age, mental and
bodily nature, occupations, deeds, and fortune). Did the accused have reasons, and the ability, to do as alleged? Is the prosecution malicious?

Sequence of events (*ta ap' archês achri telous,* literally "the matter from beginning to end"): The prosecution must construct, demonstrate with supporting evidence, and amplify (where appropriate) a coherent story. The
defense will try to refute the story, or to make it seem doubtful. The topics,
again, are those of narrative, as in the "demand for evidence." In some cases
the defense will also construct a story (a counternarrative), but that is not
usually necessary. If only the prosecution constructs a story, according to
Hermogenes, the rest of the headings belong to the defense; but if both
prosecution and defense construct a story, the subsequent headings will
fall to both. (But see "Retort.")

Counterplea (*antilêpsis*): The defendant may argue that the acts alleged in
the sequence of events are permissible (and hence are not suspicious). For
example, a rich young man maintains all the disinherited sons in the city,
and is charged with plotting tyranny; he argues that it is permissible to
maintain whomever one wishes.

Retort (*metalêpsis*): According to Hermogenes this is "always opposed to
counterplea." In essence, if the defense enters a counterplea, the prosecution
will respond either that the act is not permissible, or (if permissible) that it
is not permissible *in that way* or under those particular circumstances.

Transposition of cause (*metathesis tês aitias*): The defense explains away the
key part(s) of the sequence of events by providing an alternative cause or
motive. For example, the man found burying a slain corpse in a deserted
place and accused of murder argues "in the manner of a thesis" that giving

burial to the dead is honorable. (This entails a reinterpretation of the sequence of events: he came upon the corpse, and decided to bury it out of respect for the dead, the laws of piety, and so on.)

Persuasive defense (*pithanê apologia*): What the prosecution alleges in the sequence of events as evidence of a crime is shown to be evidence for the defense; this can be used only when there is no necessary connection between the known facts and the alleged crime. For example, a man is observed gazing at the acropolis and weeping and is charged with intending to make himself tyrant; he replies that, had he been intending to make himself tyrant, he would not have wept (that is, he would have concealed his feelings and ambitions). Thus his weeping is proof that he was *not* intending it. In cases where there does seem to be a connection between the fact and the alleged crime (for example, a boy who uses cosmetics is accused of being a male prostitute), a "persuasive defense" cannot be used. "My use of cosmetics is itself a proof that I am not a prostitute" will not fly. But the defense can use other arguments that weaken the connection, in the manner of transposition of cause: "Not every boy who uses cosmetics is a prostitute; there can be other reasons."

Common quality (*koinê poiotês*): An "epilogue or second speech" done in the manner of a commonplace, with a summation of the argument. For example, the prosecution delivers a commonplace on the evils of male prostitution, calls for righteous indignation, and sums up its case against the defendant; the defense delivers a commonplace on the misery of unjust prosecution, calls for pity, and sums up its case in turn. Hermogenes notes that the final headings of the legal, the just, the advantageous, the possible, and the honorable are available to both sides.

This division of the conjectural issue prescribes a sequence of headings very much in the manner of a progymnasma. But it is more complex; in essence, a "gymnasma" with more moving parts and more variable outcomes. The topics of individual progymnasmata, such as narrative, thesis, encomium, and commonplace, are absorbed as components of particular headings. The headings themselves constitute a prefabricated sequence that simulates the exchange of arguments that might take place in a preliminary hearing—or, they codify the process of "imaginary conversation" that Cicero's Antonius describes and Quintilian illustrates—and, as Heath has suggested, they provide the student with a virtually "ready-made" outline for a speech.

As Heath further observes, the sequence of headings for conjecture divides into a primary phase (headings 1–4) concerned with the asserted facts and a secondary phase (headings 5–9) concerned with the interpretation of those facts. For example, in the case of the corpse-burier the primary phase is concerned with whether the defendant has in fact buried a slain corpse as alleged by the prosecution; the secondary phase is concerned with whether the act of burying the corpse (if that is what he did) is persuasive evidence that he has committed murder.[55] One might interpret this two-phase sequence as a series of fall-back positions: first, try to get the case dismissed; failing that, raise doubts about the witnesses and evidence; failing that, show that you had neither the motive not the ability to do as alleged; failing that, raise doubts about the prosecution's narrative; and so on. Hermogenes, however, seems to have intended that *all* the headings be used, or as many of them as possible, and generally in the given order. He does say that, in certain circumstances, it will be better to transpose a heading to a different place in the sequence, and sometimes not all the headings can be used; but the given sequence is assumed to be the "natural" one.[56]

Heath provides a detailed analysis of Libanius' *Declamation* 44—a case of a general accused of conspiring with a tyrant, on the grounds that he put to death a foreigner who tried illegally to enter the citizens' assembly with some urgent warning, shortly before the tyrant seized power. The proof section of the general's speech more or less runs through all of Hermogenes' headings of conjecture, in order. He does not use exception but hints at it, in an opening remark that it is strange that he should be put on trial, and he cannot use the persuasive defense, since he cannot believably say that his execution of the foreigner proves that he was not complicit with the coup. Instead he substitutes, as evidence of his innocence, a discussion of his longstanding loyalty to the city and his behavior when the tyrant was overthrown, a kind of transposition-of-cause argument. Finally he concludes with "common quality" (a commonplace on "malicious accusers"), emotional appeals, and a summation.[57]

One might ask, Why does Libanius use this rather formulaic, mechanical procedure? (He uses it with great artistic skill, but it still is formulaic.) If the general has made his case on the primary headings of demand for proof, motive/capacity, and sequence of events—thus refuting the prosecution's claim that he has done what is alleged—why does he need to go through the secondary headings, showing that what he has not done is not criminal? Libanius portrays the general as responding, point by point, to the prosecution's charges, which follow the Hermogenean sequence of headings for conjecture. He thus embodies in the declamation itself the "dialogic" process of investigating the stasis and its divisions that Hermagoras, Cicero, and Quintilian treat as *preparatory* to the declamation, or to an actual oration. In doing so, Libanius in effect presents his students, and others, with a virtuoso display of what can be done with Hermogenes' headings of conjecture. But why do it in a declamation? Why not enact the sort of inquiry process that Quintilian illustrates?

As Raffaella Cribiore has suggested, most of Libanius's students did not stay with him for long. Some, pursuing the short road to rhetoric for one reason or another, probably stayed for no more than two years. Others, treating Antioch as a stepping stone between the provincial schools where they received their elementary education and the more prestigious schools in cultural centers such as Athens, also moved on.[58] If that is true, it follows that Libanius worked mostly with beginning to intermediate students. In that case *Declamation* 44, and others like it, probably should be regarded as a highly developed, literary rendition of a middling-intermediate type of declamation exercise that Libanius had his students do: produce a composition in which you work through the possible arguments at every heading prescribed for the relevant stasis. As such, Libanius's declamation parallels his also highly developed and polished renditions of the progymnasmata.[59] It shows what can be done with the Hermogenic formulae and how lifelike, and entertaining, the result can be.

In sum, Hermogenes' treatment of stasis is a pedagogical apparatus that appears to be designed for use with beginning to intermediate students of declamation. For every stasis he prescribes a formulaic sequence of headings that resembles a progymnasma (but is more complex), and that walks the student through the dialogic inquiry process that Quintilian, Cicero, and, presumably, Hermagoras approach as a looser, more intuitive, more realistic activity. Hermogenes' approach, however, clearly would have been more pedagogically effective, especially for the less advanced, less experienced student. It may have been particularly useful for students coming from provincial elementary schools or sojourning for a time in second-tier centers such as Antioch, especially if they had little experience to tell them what real-world argumentation in courts and council halls was like, or deliberations in a popular assembly, as in fourth-century B.C.E. Athens. Such students may have had few "intuitive" resources to draw from.

As Isocrates says, the essential prerequisites for formal training in rhetoric (*paideusis*) are natural ability (*phusis*) and practical experience (*empeiria; Against the Sophists* 14–15). It is less likely that a student who lacks the relevant *empeiria,* however talented, will come to the point at which arguments will "spontaneously suggest themselves," as Quintilian suggests, without explicit guidance. Hermogenes' ready-made outlines provide the sort of aid that Quintilian provides to the neophyte student: rough out the headings to be addressed, suggest some lines of argument, and set the student to working out the rest. Whereas Quintilian's approach seems closer to what an actual, practicing orator would do, Hermogenes provides a *simulation* that bridges neatly from the progymnasmata, is accessible for the beginning to intermediate student, substitutes for the *empeiria* the student lacks, has some verisimilitude, and is pedagogically ingenious.

Perhaps, then, the Hermogenic apparatus replaced the older Hermagorean one not because the Hermagorean apparatus had broken down but because the Hermogenic apparatus more effectively met the needs of Greek-speaking students in the later Roman Empire—students whose sociopolitical reality was different from that of students in Hermagoras' day and who brought a different set of experiences, expectations, and rhetorical "intuitions" to the school. In late antiquity the looser Hermagorean apparatus may still have been a more realistic simulation of what an orator actually did, but too "advanced" for the beginner in declamation.

What Hermogenes is aiming at can be seen in the opening pages of *On Stases*. He devotes his first three pages (in the Rabe edition) to classification of the types of "persons and actions" (*prosôpa kai pragmata*) involved in any civic question (*politikon zêtêma*).[60] There are seven types of persons that "can be examined" (*dunasthai exetazesthai*) and yield material for argument, and two types that do not; and three types of actions that yield material, and one type that does not. The seven types of persons are, in descending order of "strength" or productiveness: "determinate and proper" persons (historical personages such as "Pericles" or "Demosthenes," or characters from myth or poetry, such as Odysseus), relatives (for example, father/son, slave/master), the despicable (dissolute, adulterer), "characters" (*ta êthika;* farmer, glutton), types that combine two appellations (rich youth), types that combine person and act (a boy who wears cosmetics), and types whose names are "simple" appellations (general, politician), which are the weakest source of material that still is usable.

All but the first type are abstract categories—nouns. Hermogenes obviously is thinking of the sorts of "persons" who populate the problems for declamation exercises. Both the historical/literary personages and the abstract character types, like the types outlined in Theophrastus' *Characters* or invoked in the commonplace exercise, are stock figures or stereotypes from literature, history and comedy in particular, whose distinctive characteristics and background stories are implicit already in their names.[61] If one brings "Demosthenes" or "Alcibiades" or "honest farmer" or "Xanthias the crafty slave" on stage, or into a declamation exercise, each comes preequipped with a conventionalized and expected set of characteristics. The types of persons that do not yield material for declamation are the "indeterminate" person ("someone") and "wholly equivalent" persons, as when two "rich youths" bring charges against each other. In the latter case, says Hermogenes, whatever can be said about one can be said about the other, so that all arguments based on person cancel each other out.[62] There is a fixed set of *topoi* attached to the character type "rich youth," deriving from the nouns of which it is composed.[63]

Something similar happens with the three types of actions that yield material for argument: acts for which the agent is charged (the corpse-burier is accused of murder), acts for which the agent and the person charged are different (a foreign city erects a statue of a hero, so the hero is charged with treason), and acts that are "intermediate" (*metaxu*) between these two. The one action type that yields "no act to be judged" (*pragma ou krinetai*) is, again, equivalent actions.[64] For example, a rich man and a poor man both have beautiful wives, and each sees the other coming out of his house, so they bring charges of adultery against each other. Since there is no difference in the actions on either side, all arguments based on act are available to both sides and therefore cancel each other out. There may, however, be some basis for argument arising from the differences between the persons in this case. But if the persons are equivalent as well—two rich young men with beautiful wives see each other coming out of each other's house—it is not possible to make any arguments at all. Without any differing arguments, there is no issue to decide, no stasis, and no material for a proper declamation.

Hermogenes sums up the criteria for determining whether a civic question "has stasis" (*sunestêke*): "One must determine from these [persons and actions] which questions have stasis and can be divided [into heads], and which do not have stasis. For when there is both a person and an action to be judged, or at least one of these; and when there are persuasive arguments on both sides that are different and have strong proofs; and when the jury's verdict is non-obvious and not predetermined but can be brought to a conclusion, [the question] has stasis."[65]

These requirements for a case to "have stasis" look like a prescription for an ideal democratic forum in which disputes are settled through the free exchange of reasoned arguments before unprejudiced judges, rather than through violence or coercion, arbitrary authority, or what Michael Psellos calls the "usual way of men." This sort of exchange, this sort of forum, is what the declamation student is to be exercised in. Hermogenes then lists some representative types of questions that are "without stasis" (*asustata*), such as the "one sided" (*monomeres*) question in which one side has no strong arguments or the "wholly equivalent" question with identical persons and actions—as well as questions that are "nearly without stasis" (*engus asustata*) but "are declaimed on anyway" (*meletômena de homôs*).[66] This latter type includes the "unbalanced" case that is nearly but not completely one sided, and the case that is "flawed in invention." Hermogenes' example for "flawed invention" is a deliberative problem derived from Thucydides' account of the Athenians' disastrous Sicilian expedition in the Peloponnesian War: "After [the arrival of] Nicias' letter, someone proposes that Cleon be put in command [of the expedition]." The problem with this problem is its historical anachronism: Cleon, in fact, was already dead when Nicias wrote his letter. Nevertheless one still could declaim on the problem as if Cleon were alive. The problem would thus become an exercise in historical speculation. If the impetuous, demagogic Cleon had not died and had been put in command of the Sicilian expedition instead of the reluctant, overcautious Nicias, would things have gone better?

At this point there are a number of things to say. First and most obvious, as the case of Cleon and Nicias' letter clearly indicates, Hermogenes is thinking of "civic questions" not in real-world contexts but in declamation exercises, especially how to determine whether a proposed declamation problem has stasis and can be divided and declaimed on. The sources of stasis are "differing" or conflicting arguments that arise from stock character types and types of actions, either in imaginary situations (for example, the man discovered burying a corpse) or in episodes (real or contrived) from history or literature (for example, Nicias' letter). It is hard to see how a "wholly equivalent" case like that of the two rich young men who see each other leaving each other's house could ever occur in actuality. There would always be *some* difference in persons and acts, some difference in the arguments available to either side. Such a precisely identical situation could only occur in the imaginary, delimited world of a declamation problem. And would a "wholly one-sided" case be impossible to argue in real-world practice or give no grounds for invention? Such a case, it seems, would be a prosecutor's dream; one could hammer away at the hapless defendant, amplifying the seriousness of the crime and working up the judge's indignation and disgust in order to secure the severest punishment available. Likewise a defendant with an indefensible case will try to minimize its badness and make a bid for mercy; there is always *something* to say. Why not declaim on a *maiestas* (lese-majesty) case, in which a citizen caught red-handed plotting to overthrow the emperor is tried before the emperor himself? In the real world such cases were common under some emperors, usually the less popular ones, such as Nero and Domitian. But such a case is not, with Hermogenes, fit to be declaimed on, unless it involves an issue that reasonably could be decided either way, or is argued before unprejudiced judges with open minds.

Further, who needs to decide whether a given declamation problem has stasis? Neither Cicero, nor Quintilian, nor the anonymous teacher in the *Minor Declamations,* nor the Elder Seneca, nor anyone else concerned with declamation, ever discusses having the *student* determine whether a stated problem has stasis. Invariably the student's job is to determine what the stasis *is* and to "divide" it and generate material for a speech, either through the dialogic procedure of Hermagoras or through the "ready-made outlines" of Hermogenes' sequences of headings. It always is assumed, in short, that the problem given to the student has a stasis. Hermogenes' concerns with the characteristics of declamation problems that have stasis are considerations for the teacher who is constructing or choosing declamation problems for students to work with. Hermogenes is addressing himself to other rhetoricians. *On Stases* is a source book for the teacher who is supervising a student's declamation exercises. In turn the relatively inexperienced, beginning-to-intermediate student is provided with a guided, simulated experience of inquiry and argument on a disputable civic issue in a rhetorical forum that admits free debate before unprejudiced judges.

As a simulation, the declamation exercise appears as a sort of game. A modern comparison might be an educational video game in which the student takes on a role, a character, and must complete some sort of complex problem-solving task that simulates a real-world situation. (Imagine a video game in which the player is a lawyer preparing and arguing a case. How would you design it?) This game experience is what Michael Psellos and others from Lucian onward describe as revelatory and liberating, or that Mesarites and Gregory Antiochus describe as a sort of paradise, a "sweet garden" where the student of rhetoric declaims and engages in what Aelius Aristides, like Isocrates, would call *philosophia.*

It may have been the declamation game's simulation of free debate and civic contestation that fundamentally mattered most to students like these. Psellos in his eleventh-century *Synopsis of Rhetoric,* a rapid review in verse of the Hermogenic corpus, gives a quick overview of the stases but focuses attention on the criteria for a problem that "has stasis" and the ideal of free debate and reasoned judgment. About a century later, John Tzetzes likewise briefly overviews the stases, also in verse, and focuses on those criteria and that ideal, devoting more words to them than does Hermogenes. Notably both Psellos and Tzetzes also stress the ancient Protagorean notion of "making the weaker argument stronger." As Psellos puts it, "The ability of the rhetor is revealed when he takes up a case that is weak in some way, and by the power of reasoning strengthens it and prevails" (*Synopsis* lines 19–21).[67] At the same time neither scholar discusses Hermogenes' division of the stases, beyond noting that each stasis is divided into headings "in some way" (Psellos, *Synopsis* line 74). Perhaps Psellos is omitting those details for the sake of brevity, or because they are more of a concern for the teacher than the student, or because his addressee, the young emperor-to-be Michael VII Doukas, does not want or need to bother with them. But avoidance of detail is not necessarily the motive. In his overview of *On Types of Style,* Psellos systematically and even tediously runs through the particular features of each type. In the eleventh and twelfth centuries Hermogenes still provided the basic apparatus for rhetorical instruction in the schools of Byzantium—after a thousand years of continuous use—but apparently his particular apparatus for division had declined in interest or was considered a technical matter for the teacher's use. Meanwhile the fundamental game of antilogistic disputation in the imaginary civic space of declamation, and the *idea* of stasis, and the process of preliminary inquiry that it serves, remained the primary sources of appeal.

Civic Theater

What Hermogenes and his predecessors had in mind, evidently, was declamation as not only a complicated simulation/game but also a kind of theater. One speaks in character, in a fictive scene, addressing both the audience in the scene and the audience of the declamation, whether that audience is a teacher and/or one's fellow students or the audience gathered in a *theatron* or an *odeion* to hear a professional sophist's public performance. As Donald Russell has suggested, the characteristic setting for declamation problems is a fantasy city that he calls "Sophistopolis," a city with a democratic constitution, freedom of speech, and a vibrant cultural life.[68] It is, in essence, a theatrical civic space, an idealized image loosely based on Athens in the fifth and fourth centuries B.C.E. and populated by stock character types and famous worthies from history and literature. For centuries students continually rehearsed, entered into, performed, and experienced that imaginary democratic scene, even when it bore a tenuous relationship to real political conditions under Hellenistic kings and Roman emperors.[69] However much things changed, the theatrical world of declamation sustained a fictive but remarkably stable parallel reality.

The theatrical or dramatistic nature of the declamation game is reflected in a "lecture" by an unknown teacher of (probably) the second century C.E. titled *On Mistakes Made in Declamation* and misattributed in the manuscript tradition to Dionysius of Halicarnassus.[70] This text seems to be an introductory lecture meant for students at the beginning of an "intermediate" course in declamation. The students, or the intended audience of the written text, are not complete neophytes, since the lecture presumes a good familiarity with technical vocabulary. Probably the students have acquired this knowledge through the reading and discussion of exemplar texts, through progymnasmata, and perhaps through beginning declamation exercises. Early on the teacher says that those who handle "character" (*êthos*) incorrectly are "many and near" (10.3), apparently meaning the students he is addressing. And at the end of the lecture (10.19) he says that he has omitted a great deal, which will be taken up later in "our meetings," that is, during the course of their work together on declamations. These things seem to imply a student audience at an early stage in declamation: students, perhaps, of about seventeen or eighteen years of age.

The teacher leads off with faults in the handling of character (*êthos;* 10.1–3). Some, he says, "make their speeches without character," assuming that the case is all about the specific act (*pragma*) at issue; apparently they treat the persons as mere names. Others, more significantly, fail to attend to the "mixture" of characters—this seems to mean what Hermogenes calls "dual appellations" (rich youth, heroic foreigner, and so forth)—so that they produce "simple," transparent characters that are based on what's familiar to them, or what the teacher calls "naked" characters. (This is especially a problem when speaking as "Demosthenes" or some other historical figure whose known history provides a mixture of character qualities.) The complexity of "mixed" characters gives rise to the complexity of what the teacher calls mixed, "woven-together" purposes and acts.[71] A rich youth should differ from a poor youth, a dissolute youth from a dissolute rich old man, an orator son from a farmer son, and so on. In short, the students err in speaking naïvely as just themselves with name tags, rather than entering fully into the "persons" of the case and rendering them as complex, three-dimensional characters.

Still more important, and a deep cause of the mistakes just cited, is the students' failure to adopt the sort of "philosophic" character that the teacher attributes to both Plato and Demosthenes, saying that it pervades their writings and gives each of them *megaloprepeia* (magnificence, high-mindedness). Heath interprets this as the overall moral character of a discourse, in essence the moral compass of its author, embodied in judgments of the ethico-civic quality of persons and actions.[72] The anonymous teacher most explicitly associates this philosophic *êthos* with a capacity for reasoned analysis and moral judgment, or "measure," and for putting characters into dialectical relation: Demosthenes speaks to, say, the tyrant (Philip of Macedon), or the orator engages his opponents, just as Socrates engages his interlocutors in Plato's dialogues. What this seems to mean is a capacity for empathic insight as a foundation for critical judgment. This capacity is what enables the declaimer to more effectively enter into and develop complex characters for the persons of the declamation problem, discover and assess the strongest arguments on both sides, and speak with regard to each (and *kairos*) in a fitting manner. "Philosophy" enables the declaimer to analyze the problem richly, understand its deeper issues, and produce high-minded eloquence.

The teacher's lecture goes on to other matters: errors in "thought" or judgment (*gnômê;* 10.4), "artlessness" (*atechnia*) in the presentation of arguments (10.5–6), errors in style (*tên lexin hamartêmata;* 10.7–11), and the most common mistakes in the "parts of the case" (*tôn tês hupotheseôs stoicheiôn*), meaning the handling of the prologue, narrative, proofs, and epilogue (10.12–18). Much of this discussion goes back to the capacity for "measure" supplied by "philosophic" character—the capacity for being neither "artless" in the "naked" presentation of arguments, nor inappropriate in the use of description, embellishment, brevity and length, nor mechanical in the management of heads of argument, and so on. Interestingly, the teacher remarks that a cardinal type of artlessness is using all the prescribed headings mechanically, "in ABC order" (*kata tên taxin apo tou* A *heôs* Ω, "following the order from alpha to omega"), rather than adapting them "according to the requirements of the dispute" (*kata tên chreian tou agônos;* 10.6). That must have been a recurring problem with the

Hermogenic framework. Further, says the teacher, some of the headings supplied "in the sophists' exercises" (*en tais tôn sophistôn diatribais*) are foolishly unrealistic and should be skipped (10.16).[73] In all of this we hear refracted echoes of Isocrates' identification of rhetoric as *philosophia,* his emphasis on discourse as a "creative act," and, probably quite consciously, his use of the "spelling" metaphor (here an "alphabet" metaphor) for the rigidly rule-bound approach to *technê* that he rejects. We also can recognize a presumption that the headings of argument prescribed "in the sophists' exercises," both foolish and otherwise, are an apparatus for declamation.

My point for now, however, is the implicit stress in this teacher's lecture on declamation as an exercise in civic theater in which success is defined as fully realizing *in performance* the complex rhetorical and philosophical potentials of the fictive situation given in the problem: its persons, actions, attendant circumstances, and deeper significance. The successful declamation reembodied and enacted the philosophico-rhetorical ideals of Sophistopolis. It argued general civic and moral questions through the *agôn* of a specific case with "arguments on both sides." In declamation the successful student ceased to be "himself," or the still-childish, artless self that had come from the grammar school to the rhetorician, and instead assumed the *êthos* and the speech of the rhetors of Sophistopolis—the characters of the exercises, from "Demosthenes" and "the tyrant" to "rich man" and "poor man." In this way, as Psellos says, the "veil" was lifted from his childish soul and he took to the intellectual "open sky."

Hibeh Papyrus 1.15, found in a Greek necropolis in Middle Egypt (where it was used as mummy wrapping), may be an example of a student's declamation exercise.[74] Grenfell and Hunt, the *Hibeh Papyri* editors, who remark with disappointment that it is "only a rhetorical composition," date it to roughly the middle of the third century B.C.E. (c. 280–240). This makes it one of the earliest surviving examples of declamation, and perhaps the earliest example of a student's declamation. It is a fairly substantial fragment, containing four mostly legible columns, or about 93 near-continuous lines, "carefully written in a handsome hand of medium size,"[75] as well as traces of other columns, for a total of 165 lines. If we recall Libanius going over a student composition consisting of 200 lines, we may guess that Hibeh Papyrus 1.15 represents possibly half to three-fourths of the complete text. The readable remnant appears to be from the "proof" section of the speech, and its exhortative quality suggests that the speaker is heading toward his conclusion; if that is correct, the text may not have been much longer than the 165 attested lines. That this composition probably is student work is suggested in part by its "frequent confusions between *i* and *ei,*" and by other spelling mistakes that one would not expect in a professional sophist.[76] The systematic *i / ei* confusion suggests that the writer—a young Greek in a provincial town in Hellenistic Egypt, roughly 175 miles south of

Alexandria—speaks an "iotacized" version of *koinê* ("common," demotic) Greek that has lost the *i / ei* distinction preserved in the literate dialect (classical Attic Greek), and he has not yet fully mastered it despite having graduated from grammar to rhetoric. This confusion suggests a learner, as do the other spelling mistakes. That the writer is a student, and has gone over his composition with his teacher, is evidenced also by the fact that, as Grenfell and Hunt note, "The text has been corrected with some care, apparently by the original scribe." Someone had to point out those mistakes for the writer to correct them.[77]

The speech is set in the historical context of the Lamian War of 323 B.C.E., in which a combined Greek force of Athenians and their allies tried to throw off Macedonian domination after the death of Alexander the Great. This is relatively recent history—about fifty to eighty years before the declamation's composition—but not exactly "current events" either. Athenian independence was not a realistic possibility when this writer wrote, a non-issue outside the garden of declamation. The speaker appears to be Leosthenes, an Athenian general who had assembled a large force of unemployed mercenaries at Taenarum, at the southern tip of the Peloponnese, and upon Alexander's death joined to it the Athenian and other forces. Leosthenes then was put in command and marched north to Thessaly, where he won some impressive victories against an initially overmatched Macedonian army led by Antipater, the regent of Macedon and Greece. Leosthenes was, however, killed in action during the siege of Lamia. After that the rebellion bogged down and the Athenians and their allies finally were defeated at the battle of Crannon in Thessaly in 322. In what remains of the declamation it appears that Leosthenes is speaking just after the death of Alexander and urging the Athenians to seize the opportunity to regain their liberty. The speech is thus set in the moment of decision to launch the Lamian War.

What follows is a translation of the surviving readable text in its entirety.[78] Dashes represent the only "punctuation"—also dashes—inserted in the original, probably to indicate pauses in delivery, which suggests that the text was meant as a script for performance. As is normal for written texts at this time, the papyrus has no other punctuation and no spaces between words. I have inserted some commas to clarify the syntax between dashes. Ellipsis points indicate gaps in the papyrus.

> . . . you will have more pleasing allies, and will make it clear to all that the city's character is so far from doing evil to any Greeks who do no wrong— that it leaves unpunished even those who clearly have committed crimes, on account of its benevolence—but consider especially, by the gods, men of Athens, that to delay in the present circumstance is hardly profitable—for the opportunities arising from this change[79] are likely to be fleeting—seize them

then, and stop listening to those who call slackness safety—and do not be afraid . . . your salvation, but be brave and make resolutions by which no one will ever . . . (col. 2, lines 26–51)

. . . it is proper for you to imitate . . . and to consider that I hardly would station myself at Taenarum—and I am inferior to no . . . in the city— willingly to take on such dangerous affairs, if I did not know how pressing the moment is, and that the moment of our salvation is at hand— . . . (col. 3, 55–66)

. . . and humbled, I assume—as no-one could foresee the outcome—but now indeed I foresee the future, and summon you to action and the destiny which . . . not let drop—and I entreat especially the younger men among you who have had, since childhood, an adequate military training—to be strong in their thought, and to employ their own bodies in a timely demonstration of their virtue—so that your quietude at other times is not attributed to cowardice but to caution—and may we not, men of Athens, go into action without your power, and may you not be compelled in any way by us either to do what others command, or to go into battle with inferior forces . . . (col. 3, 70–75, and col. 4, 76–99)

. . . and make use of . . . and choose the safety in right conduct, securing your own salvation with greater numbers—since it is unworthy, men of Athens, of the daring deeds at Marathon and Salamis for us to persevere in totally giving up the hegemony—or in thinking that it will ever come to you of itself and without your making any effort—I then, since it was a general's duty not to consider his personal safety or election prospects, but your salvation, accordingly have put myself forward on behalf of the common liberty . . . (col. 5, 101–122)

Those with much experience in teaching first-year writing at colleges and universities will recognize some familiar characteristics of student writing, aside from the spelling mistakes. One, though it is less apparent in translation, is an occasional awkwardness or immaturity of style stemming probably from an incomplete control of the literate dialect and its customary locutions. For example, "You will have more pleasing allies," the first line of the surviving text, renders *eu arestoterous summachous exete*.[80] The form *arestoteros*, of which *arestoterous* is the accusative plural, is unrecognized in the Liddell-Scott-Jones lexicon and unattested in the Theasurus Linguae Graecae. It occurs only in this papyrus. It appears to be a rare comparative form of the adjective *arestos* (pleasing, satisfactory), but in classical Attic Greek *arestos* is not normally used in the comparative. In fact, there is no attested use at all of this word in the comparative form aside from this papyrus. Further, the writer's rendering of the comparative, for which one would expect *aresterous* (in the accusative plural needed here), seems to be mixed with the superlative, *arestatous*. In short the writer's *arestoterous* is a form akin to "pleasingester" or "more most pleasing." Moreover, this construction is formed on the phrase *eu arestos,* "well pleasing," so that the resulting locution is something like "well pleasingester" or "well more most pleasing"—or if we just read it as a comparative, "well more pleasing." Either way it is a clumsy collation of redundant intensifiers, a little like "way more better." Either this locution has not been corrected by the teacher or the student has not entered the correction. Perhaps the teacher has decided to let it slide for now, focusing instead on the more-pervasive and systematic *i / ei* confusion. Such a choice would be recognized today as good pedagogical practice. In any case the phrase exemplifies the typical stylistic nonsophistication of young writers not yet at home in the literate dialect.[81] "Persevere in totally giving up" probably falls in this category too. The dashes/pauses also are evidence of this awkwardness; some do suggest a heightened "oratorical" delivery, but others cut oddly across the logical and syntactic structure of what the speaker says. As Grenfell and Hunt remark, "The phraseology of the papyrus is somewhat colorless."[82] This young writer from Hibeh, like most young writers, is stylistically immature.

Another indicator of student writing is the argumentation. The writer runs fairly quickly through a series of points, each of them a likely one to use, so the student has done some passable preliminary inquiry. In general he is working the *topoi* of advantage, honor, and military capabilities, or feasibility, but he does not develop any of his points very fully or clearly indicate the transitions between them. Transitions mostly are marked by a mere *kai,* "and," although *kai* is also used in places that are not transitions, where it simply indicates some added remark. Thus the main points all seem run together. The writer also loops back to points already raised, which may be a good tactic in protreptic (exhortatory) discourse, but here gives a feeling of disorder rather than either logical development or emotional force. A good comparison, which suggests how the subject matter might have been more fully and artfully developed, is Isocrates' *Archidamus.* One might say that this student commits the errors of artless presentation discussed by *On Mistakes in Declamation.* It is possible that he has had some training in preliminary inquiry—or, in the third century B.C.E., a rudimentary form of stasis analysis—but has not been trained yet in the handling of the parts of an oration and the management of proofs. If that is correct, he is about half way through the curriculum outlined in the *Rhetoric to Alexander.*

With those observations in mind, consider again how long this declamation may have been. Such jumbled, underdeveloped argumentation usually cannot be sustained for long. Thus I think it likely that the complete text was not greatly longer than the 165 attested lines, perhaps 200 at most. Each column consists of about 25 lines, so there may have been about eight columns. As the translation of column 2 shows, a column rendered in English is roughly equivalent to one hundred words. (Column 2 has about ninety-five words in Greek, but lacunae make the exact number uncertain.) Thus, if there were eight columns in the original, this composition was about eight hundred words, which in English would be, typed in 12–point font and double-spaced, a paper of just two and a half pages. If it were twice that long, it would be five pages. Those lengths are drastically shorter than the surviving texts of real orations, or of public declamations by professional sophists—again, compare *Archidamus* or the declamations of Libanius, Aelius Aristides, or Polemo.[83] Those lengths, too, are typical today for student papers in first-year college writing classes.

So this student is starting to look familiar. He probably is about seventeen to eighteen and has recently graduated from progymnasmata to declamation. He possibly has had some training in preliminary inquiry, but not yet in the management of an oration. His "Leosthenes" is perhaps a C-plus paper by modern standards, but it is a reasonably promising start for a beginner. In any case his teacher did not assign grades. The student probably received some praise for his use of the inventional *topoi* for deliberative/protreptic discourse, and some stylistic correction that addressed mainly his *i / ei* confusion. His management of proofs probably was deemed good enough for the time being, with the proviso that later he would be expected to do more.

But leaving aside the question of how well this student has done, the more significant question is *what* he has done. What, in Hellenistic Egypt between 280 and 240 B.C.E., under the rule of King Ptolemy II Philadelphus and his lavish court,[84] motivates a declamation exercise in which a young man in a provincial rhetoric school impersonates Leosthenes exhorting the Athenians of the previous century to liberate themselves from Macedonian rule? It is not enough, I think, to invoke the usual argument that historical declamation themes permitted both declaimer and audience to glory in a Greek past more splendid than the present, or to bask in the poignance of Athens' last hurrah as an independent power. That explanation makes more sense if applied to the period of the Second Sophistic—the "renaissance" of Greek culture under Roman rule in roughly the second century C.E.[85]—though even for that period such an explanation is incomplete. Moreover, it is an explanation only of public "concert" performances by professional sophists, not declamations in school. Ptolemaic Egypt in the third century B.C.E., when the Greeks ruled most of their known world and Rome was just a blip on the horizon, would have felt little need to look nostalgically back to better days; they were in a heady time.

One can only speculate, of course, but one motive for choosing this problem, and one reason why the student may have enjoyed it, was that it was set in an historical moment of high drama where speech and judgment were highly consequential. The sense of high stakes emphatically foregrounds the elements in the rhetorical situation that the declaimer, in character, must attend to. This foregrounding heightens the pedagogical effectiveness of the exercise and enhances its philosophical depth. As in Isocrates' *Archidamus,* Leosthenes speaks in a desperate situation, exhorting his countrymen to fight for their freedom or die honorably in the effort. The important difference, however, is that the student and his contemporaries know that Leosthenes died and the rebellion failed; it accomplished nothing. This knowledge is part of the dramatic tension of the scene in which the declamation is to be spoken. It provokes, among other things, a question regarding how Leosthenes should be judged. Is the self-sacrificing heroism of Leosthenes a thing to be admired and imitated—is it better to die for freedom rather than live peacefully, prosperously, and comfortably in subjugation?—or is Leosthenes a fool or just mistaken? Should the Athenians have taken up the war against their Macedonian overlords, as they in fact did? How would a Leosthenes argue, and how should such argument be weighed? What would have made him persuasive in that context? Certainly the student gives Leosthenes some admirable qualities. He is motivated more by devotion to the common good, as he understands it, than by personal gain, and he is willing to put himself at risk while resisting the inexorable course of history.

One interesting feature of the student's effort is that his Leosthenes, like Isocrates' Archidamus, relies heavily on appeals to national honor and to shame. If the Athenians "cautiously" decline to seize the moment they will be "unworthy" of their ancestors' glorious deeds at Marathon and Salamis, and the young men's unwillingness to commit their own bodies to the struggle will be deemed not "quietude" but "cowardice." This seems to be the core of his argument; the question of the rebellion's likelihood of success is met only by sketchy statements of optimism that are not backed up with any meaningful analysis of feasibility, resources, or probable outcomes. While appeals to shame and patriotic zeal are endemic to ancient Greek culture, one can also reflect that such appeals, if Leosthenes indeed successfully argued in that way, led the Athenians to pursue a doomed, quixotic policy of resistance to the new order that Alexander had brought, an order that in Ptolemy II's Egypt probably looked rather good, at least to members of the educated classes.[86] The missing analysis, in this view, is what the Athenians should have been persuaded by but were not.[87]

Leosthenes is a complex and interesting character to recreate, his situation presents intriguing, clearly defined problems for inquiry and invention, and his argument as recreated by the student raises complex philosophical (rhetorical, civic, ideological) issues in historical retrospect. Perhaps most interesting is the exercise's assumption that the case could have been argued either way, for or against, and that things could have been decided otherwise. As "theater" in the "sweet garden" of the school, even if the school is a curtained-off space in a portico, the declamation transpires in an alternative world where lost or unpursued possibilities remain in play. The fateful decision has not yet been made, the die is not yet cast, and the debate remains forever open, forever in suspension.

The standard ancient and modern objection against declamation is its tendency toward "unreality."[88] The locus classicus is Quintilian's critique of "corrupted" declamation based on unreal themes (*Institutio oratoria* 2.10, 5.12, 8.pr., 10.5). Quintilian's objection applies more to judicial declamations, in which he is primarily interested, and his precise worry is the theatrical tendency to ham it up and engage in poetic flights of fancy that might occur on stage but could never occur in court—much as the author of *Mistakes in Declamation* censures inappropriate, purple-patch descriptions and amplifications that might be suitable to poetry but are irrelevant to the issue being argued. Deliberative declamations that recreate history, such as Leosthenes exhorting the Athenians to war, may be less susceptible to Quintilian's complaint, but even these are by definition fictive, inherently theatrical, and potentially subject to the same excess. Quintilian's solution is to keep the declamation problem as realistic as possible, up to and including having the student declaim on actual cases from the courts. But the fundamental problem is not the declamation problem per se. The main concern is the verisimilitude, the probability, with which the fictive or historical *hupothesis* is realized in performance. That has more to do with the teacher's guidance and the student's proclivities.

The tendency of modern rhetorical pedagogy goes a step further than Quintilian, generally preferring that students write on actual current issues using subjects derived from their immediate lifeworld, such as diversity-sensitive admissions policies at your university, the "Barbie" image in contemporary culture, and so on, or more distant national or world affairs. By this standard even "Leosthenes Addresses the Athenians" is an exercise in unreality.[89]

Pace Quintilian, there is little evidence that "unreal" declamation themes failed to provide effective training.[90] There is little evidence, either, that using "real" cases in declamation was ever very popular, either with students or with teachers.[91] On the contrary, the declamation manuals that survive are overwhelmingly full of "unreal" problems. Indeed some of them, especially the judicial problems, seem highly melodramatic, as in "The Case of the Pirate Chief's Daughter": "A man captured by pirates wrote to his father about a ransom. He was not ransomed. The daughter of the pirate chief made him swear to marry her if he was released. He swore. She left her father and followed the young man. He returned to his father, and married the girl. An orphan appears. The father orders his son to divorce the pirate chief's daughter and marry the orphan. The son refuses and is disinherited" (Elder Seneca, *Controversiae* 1.6).[92]

Here the options are to take up the son's case, suing for restitution and arguing that it is neither legal nor just for his father to disinherit him, or to defend the father's legal and moral right to disinherit his disobedient son in these circumstances. The romance-novel quality of the problem's plot affords plenty of opportunities for colorful descriptions of the son's capture and his life among pirates, the pirate chief's daughter's love—rough but tender and true-hearted, she—the scene of his swearing, their travels together, the orphan's intrusion, and so on, all in the speech's narrative, to say nothing of the kinds of arguments possible for the proof section of the speeches on either side.

But problems such as these, as melodramatic as they may seem, are perhaps no more bizarre than the real cases studied in first-year torts in law schools today. For example, "A man carrying a package was attempting to board a car of a moving Long Island Railroad train. As he seemed unsteady and about to fall, two conductors employed by the railroad, one in the train and one on the platform, caught and helped him onto the train, but caused him to drop his package. The package, which contained fireworks, exploded when it hit the tracks. The shock of the explosion caused a set of scales at the far end of the platform to fall down. The falling scales struck and injured a woman, Mrs. Helen Palsgraf. Palsgraf sues the Long Island Railroad for damages for her injuries."

This 1928 case, *Palsgraf v. Long Island Railroad Co.*, was a landmark that established notions of "proximate cause," negligence, and the limits of liability and can be found in any torts textbook. (The opinion, from the New York State Court of Appeals, was written by Benjamin Cardozo, who later went on to the Supreme Court.) It does not, to be sure, have the melodramatic qualities of "The Pirate Chief's Daughter," but it sounds as contrived as a Rube Goldberg contraption and is imaginable as a scene from a Buster Keaton movie. Here is another: "A 12-year old school child reached his foot across the aisle and kicked another child in the right shin with the toe of his shoe. The second child at first felt nothing, but later experienced sharp pains in his knee. The problem became progressively worse, and within six days it was determined that the child had permanently lost the use of his right leg. Apparently he had had an unknown, pre-existing condition which was triggered by the kick. The injured child's family brings a charge of intentional battery."

This case from textbook torts, *Vosberg v. Putney*, was decided by the Wisconsin Supreme Court in 1891; it turns on the question of what "intentional" means.[93] Again there is a Rube Goldberg quality. The real is sometimes stranger than fiction. Indeed it is likely that the cases that establish precedents will be bizarre, precisely because their circumstances press the rational boundaries of the law and bring on complex philosophical problems. (Think, again, of the concatenation of circumstances in Antiphon's *Second Tetralogy,* which prevents a straightforward application of the supposed legal rule.) Further, like "The Pirate

Chief's Daughter," both Vosberg and Palsgraf are set in an historical otherworld somewhat removed from the student's immediate experience in the twenty-first century: catching the train in 1928; a midwestern schoolroom in 1891. What matters is not the "realism" or contemporaneity of the case, but the principles involved and how to reason about them, though the circumstances are entertaining and help to make the principles and reasoning more memorable.

Now, to look at things from the other end, it is also possible that "The Pirate Chief's Daughter," and the like, has its origins in a real but now-forgotten case, an oddity whose historical particulars have faded away while the basic structure of the rhetorical problem remains. Or at least it is composed of familiar-enough elements to be a recognizably plausible scenario. Pirates and fugitive lovers may have been the stuff of Greek romance, but pirates, abductions, and ransomings were not uncommon in the ancient Mediterranean, nor were problematic fathers, disobedient sons, and disinheritings. Neither was sex unusual. It actually seems quite likely that most declamation problems not derived from history or myth have sprung from actual situations or circumstances. So the question of "reality" or "unreality" in declamation seems moot. What matters, again, is the quality of the student's handling of the problem, and the cultivation of habits of reasoning, analysis, argumentation, and speech suitable to civic discourse.

Michael Winterbottom has argued that the fictionality of declamation was its cardinal advantage as a pedagogical device.[94] It freed students from the daunting and sometimes dangerous complexities of serious real-world issues and encouraged them to play with the inventional possibilities available within a problem's set parameters, which, as in "Daughter," typically consisted of a sharply limited set of facts. My own experience with declamation in the writing classroom is consistent with Winterbottom's argument. For several years I have experimented with ancient declamation problems, virtually unchanged. I am constantly astonished at how well the ancient problems work, and I have gained an appreciation of the subtle art by which they have been designed. Students get caught up in the game, and just as Winterbottom suggests, they throw themselves into the imaginary situation, often with exuberance. Perhaps not surprisingly, they usually produce papers that are far better written and livelier than their usual "academic" stuff; it helps to speak as a character in a fictive but sharply defined rhetorical situation.

In declamation exercises the student was (is) also freed from the pressure to discover the "correct answer" to the problem. This is plainly an advantage of the declamation problem over the cases recorded in a Torts textbook, as a device for cultivating resourceful reasoning/judgment and rhetorical invention in students of seventeen to twenty years of age. In the case of torts, each case has already been decided, and it is the student's job to correctly recognize and understand the legal reasoning on which the decision rests. Likewise with the actual current issues favored by modern writing instruction: not only does the student usually lack authoritative adult status, knowledge, or sophistication, but the presence of real emotional investments (if the issue is truly "live") also makes it a minefield for the student wary of transgressing the teacher's (and other students') heartfelt commitments.[95] Alternatively, some students with strong opinions on the matter will tend to engage in aggressive, talk-radio kinds of bloviation, neither engaging seriously with contrary positions and evidence nor examining or developing their own thought; this is a common problem.[96] With a properly constructed and properly taught declamation exercise, however, it is clear that there are *supposed to be* "strong arguments on both sides," that the decision is not obvious—indeed, it remains forever open, though it has the potential to be decided either way—and that the object of the game is to explore the argumentational possibilities on either side as fully as possible. Further, because the student is playing a role, his or her youthful ego is not at stake, and it is possible to both play with lines of argument and to reflect on them as well, just as "Leosthenes Addresses the Athenians" invites reflection on Leosthenes' *êthos,* his use of *topoi,* and so on.

In sum, declamation exercises enabled the student to engage in what Isocrates, Aelius Aristides, and others would call *philosophia* while "theatrically" performing in the imaginary civic space of Sophistopolis, at a distance from the passions of the actual event and having some fun in the process. Through declamation, rhetoric's regime of "exercise in evenly balanced cases" in a fictive parallel reality, students both cultivated through performance their rhetorical capacities and entered the "sweet garden" of practical *philosophia* and a democratic civic imaginary, where students like Michael Psellos, Lucian, and Gregory Antiochus experienced a kind of revelation and intellectual liberation.

Nicias Writes Again: Aelius Aristides' "Sicilian Orations"

Recent studies of ancient declamation have generally focused on its role in identity formation and ideological reproduction. Maud Gleason and Erik Gunderson, for example, have discussed the role of declamation and rhetorical culture in general in the production and politics of masculine identity in the Roman world; and Simon Swain has argued that Second Sophistic declamation—meaning Greek declamation in public "concert" venues and the literary representation of those performances in the first and second centuries C.E.—was a way of asserting and maintaining a sense of Hellenic identity, based on an idealized image of the glorious Greek past, within and against the pressures of Roman domination.[97] These analyses are generally persuasive, but they nevertheless seem incomplete as an account of declamation.

In the first place, *everything* played a role in the formation and dissemination of ideologies of gender and social identity, from works of literature to the most mundane, everyday social interactions.[98] All of Greek education cultivated a sense of Hellenic identity, as did all Greek social life. As Isocrates put it, to be a "Hellene" was to share a certain *paideusis,* a certain process of education/ enculturation (*Panegyricus* 50).[99] The recitation of a poem, an imperial pane-gyric, or a work of history or philosophy in properly "Attic" classical Greek, adorned with learned evocations, echoes, and allusions to canonic literature, placed both the speaker and the educated audience in a ritual space where the past and present were contemporaneous; and everyday interactions with Romans and Greeks taught every Greek to feel their Greekness, and every Roman their Roman-ness likewise.[100] Greek declamation, or Latin declama-tion for that matter, certainly embodied ideas of and attitudes toward gender, Greekness, and Roman-ness, as did everything else, but those were not the only or even the primary reasons for declamation's appeal, either as a school expe-rience or as a form of entertainment.

There is little doubt that declamation was popular, in ways that often are dif-ficult for the modern mind to comprehend.[101] As the Elder Seneca shows, grown men could enjoy revisiting their school days, recalling the declaimers they had heard and indulging in declamation themselves, for both exercise and recreation: "It is, I admit, pleasurable to me to return to my old studies and look back on better years" (*Controversiae* pr.1). As Suetonius reports, Cicero, when Praetor, still visited the school of Marcus Antonius Gnipho to practice declaim-ing in Greek (at the age of forty), and in the last year of his life (at age sixty-three) he practiced declaiming in Latin with the Consuls Hirtius and Pansa, playfully calling them his "students" (*discipulos*) and "grown-up schoolboys" (*grandis praetextatos*). We must assume that, between these attested instances, declamation was a lifelong recreation for Cicero and his friends, as was the schoolish disputation portrayed in *De oratore* (when he had time for it). As Sue-tonius also says, Mark Antony and the future Augustus Caesar "kept up the habit of declaiming" (*repetisse declamandi consuetudinem*), "even during the war at Mutina" (*ne Mutinensi quidem bello omisisse*), presumably when they had some down time. Julius Caesar declaimed in public on three occasions, and "a large number of orators" (*plerique autem oratorum*) performed and published declama-tions (*De grammaticis et rhetoribus* 7.2, 25.3). The Elder Seneca mentions that the orator Latro declaimed before Augustus and his associates, including Maecenas and Agrippa, in private concert, and that the politician Asinius Pollio, who celebrated a triumph in 39 B.C.E., declaimed in private gatherings and later instructed his grandson in declamation (*Controversiae* 2.4.11, 4.pr.2–3). Declama-tion was a competitive game that the well educated continued to enjoy, both as performers and as discerning spectators.[102]

What about the public "concert" performances of Second Sophistic sophists? Surely they attracted sizable audiences and were enjoyed. But it will help to recall what sort of audience. An informative example is Philostratus' account of Alexander Peloplaton's performance at Athens, in the Odeion of Agrippa, also called the Agrippeion, in the center of the Agora near the South Stoa (*Lives* 2.5 571–57).[103] On arriving at Athens, Alexander Peloplaton ("Clay-Plato") announced that he would give a declamation performance in the Agrippeion. On learning that "all" the young men, probably the young men studying rhetoric, had retreated with the eminent sophist Herodes Atticus to his country estate at Marathon, twenty-six miles away, Alexander wrote a letter asking Herodes to send his Hellenes and to come himself. Herodes accepted, but on the day of the performance Herodes was late, and because the audience already there was getting restive, Alexander decided to start. Herodes appeared a little later, and Alexander cleverly worked back into the speech the parts Herodes had missed, without noticeably repeating anything. The theme, which the audience had chosen, was "Seeing that city life has ruined their health, the speaker advises the Scythians to return to their former nomadic life," a fantasy problem. After the performance Herodes and his advanced students held a critical discussion in which Herodes reproved the bad judgment of one student (who quipped, "I hear the clay but not the Plato") and praised Alexander as a "more sober Scopelian." Herodes then did a declamation in return, again on a theme selected by the audience: "The wounded Athenians in Sicily beg their retreating comrades to put them to death"—a quasi-historical problem. More discussion followed, in which Alexander praised Herodes and Herodes rewarded him with gifts.

This anecdote suggests that the prime audience for a "concert" performance was students and aficionados of rhetoric. Alexander needs Herodes' Hellenes—the young men studying rhetoric—for the performance to be worthwhile. The Odeion of Agrippa is estimated to have held up to a thousand spectators.[104] Could Herodes have had a thousand students, even if he did have "all" the rhetoric students in Athens? Could he accommodate a thousand students at his Marathon estate? Even if the students camped out in the neighborhood and gathered to hear him in his private *theatron,* it seems unlikely. The scanty ruins of Herodes' sprawling estate suggest no structure as large as a thousand-seat *odeion;* his *theatron,* presuming that he had one, would have been at most a largish lecture hall. Comparable structures in Athens, such as the so-called Omega House, which probably was a sophist's school in the fourth century C.E., would barely accommodate fifty, a number that aligns with Libanius' numbers in his very best years.[105] Even if one credits Herodes with double that number, which is far too many for an individual teacher (Libanius employed assistants), Herodes' Hellenes would only fill the few front rows of the Agrippeion's auditorium, leaving Alexander to declaim to a nearly deserted hall. But that does not make sense. Lucian's *On the Hall* suggests that a well-known sophist could expect a decent audience of cognoscenti, or what he calls the "distinguished" (*beltistoi*) and the "educated" (*pepaideumenoi*), and perhaps some "ordinary" spectators (*idiôtai*) too. Alexander Peloplaton certainly was a well known sophist. Philostratus says that his arrival in Athens created a stir, and that his performance was eagerly anticipated. He very probably drew a good crowd.[106]

If we give Herodes one hundred students, which is a stretch, and assume that Philostratus' "all the young men" means all the best rhetoric students, perhaps we can allocate another two hundred students to the lesser sophistic schools, Omega House size and smaller, scattered around the city, though that is an optimistic guess. Then there were the philosophic schools, where there might have been another two or three hundred, optimistically speaking, with at least some interest in attending a notable sophist's performance. We now have the building at most half full with students. The upshot is that, if Alexander declaimed to a reasonably full house as seems likely, then at least half of the audience must have consisted of nonstudents, that is, of mostly educated upper-class adults with an appreciation of rhetoric and of declamation. (Some of these, of course, could have been other teachers.) Philostratus describes the audience as choosing the theme for each sophist, presumably by informal show-of-hands voting, or the like, on a short list of proposed alternatives; who did the proposing is not clear. One can assume that the audience, or at least those that voted, knew enough about the proposed alternatives to have a preference. Alternatively, if the audience was shouting out titles of declamation problems for the sophist to pick a "winner" from, one ends with the same inference. Further, Philostratus' account suggests, though it does not explicitly say, that the audience remained through the critical discussion between Herodes and his students, and through Herodes' subsequent speech as well, since they chose its theme. If that is correct, it seems that the discussion was part of the entertainment—and that the whole event was a sort of public "seminar," a bit like a master's class at the Actors' Studio today.[107]

The point, in sum, is that Alexander Peloplaton's audience probably was typical for "concert" declamations, although the performance itself was unusual, yielding an anecdote that Philostratus thought worth mentioning. That audience was composed primarily of students of rhetoric, and former students—educated people who enjoyed or had enjoyed the civic theater of declamation and its *philosophia,* in the "sweet garden" of the school.

My claim is that while public declamation certainly had multiple sources of appeal for its audiences, including its enactment of "Hellenic" identity and/or models of masculinity, its fundamental and distinctive sources of appeal were two: first, its "theatrical" recreation and rehearsal of an imaginary civic space where issues could be freely and rationally debated "on both sides" before unprejudiced judges, and second—for the experienced cognoscenti—the technical (artistic) proficiency with which the performance was carried off. Philostratus, for example, reports that Alexander's audience was deeply impressed by his ability to work back in the parts of the speech that Herodes had missed, without noticeably repeating anything; that is, they were discerning enough to notice his non-noticeable repetitions. That is technical appreciation. Further, the appeal of any particular declamation lay in its rendition of practical civic *philosophia* within a specific *kairos:* the ways in which it played out, interpreted, and judged the ethico-political issues inherent in the rhetorical situation set up by its problem.

I will close this chapter with a quick look at one example: the Sicilian Orations of Aelius Aristides (Orations 5 and 6 in the Aristidean canon).[108] The two orations form a set, arguing both sides of the case. The case is a familiar one, derived from Thucydides' account of the Athenians' disastrous Sicilian expedition in the Peloponnesian War. The situation is roughly as follows. The effort to conquer Syracuse has bogged down, things have taken a turn for the worse, and the Athenian position is no longer tenable. Nicias, the only remaining general of the original three, who was against the expedition from the start and has constantly proceeded with extreme caution, reluctance, and delay—writes to the Athenians, informing them of the situation, asking to be relieved of his command, and telling them that they must either withdraw their forces from Sicily or send a relief force at least as large as the original expedition, which itself had been unusually large and costly (Thucydides 7.8). It is probable that Nicias wanted the Athenians to recall the expedition, but rather than explicitly say so he proposed an alternative so extreme that, as he supposed, they would consider it unthinkable.[109] Thucydides strangely does not report the Athenians' deliberation in response to Nicias' letter. He says only that "when they had heard it" (*akousantes autês*), they neither recalled the expedition nor removed Nicias from command but appointed new generals to assist him and resolved to send the relief force (7.16).

As everyone in Aristides' audience knew, the ultimate results of that decision were catastrophic: total loss of all the expeditionary forces, Athens' eventual defeat in the Peloponnesian War, and the beginning of the end of Athens' significance as a political and military power. Thucydides' language makes it seem as if there was no deliberation at all before that fateful choice, but there must have been some. This silence is what the declamation problem exploits. As a school exercise, and like the themes proposed for Alexander Peloplaton and Herodes Atticus, it would have taken some such form as this: "On receiving Nicias' letter, the Athenians take counsel." The declaimer's task is to insert himself into this consequential situation and to give advice on either side of the question—to recreate what both sides would have said, or should have said, to the Athenian Assembly.

We do not know when Aristides composed his Sicilian Orations, or where or when they would have been performed.[110] He toured and declaimed throughout his career (c. 148–180), and these orations probably were part of his repertoire and underwent periodic revisions. We do know that he declaimed at least once in the *bouleutêrion* (council hall) of Smyrna, his home city, in 167; and that in 176 he declaimed again in Smyrna before the emperor Marcus Aurelius, his entourage, and local dignitaries, when Marcus was touring his Asian provinces. It seems likely that that performance was in the *bouleutêrion* also. Clearly Smyrna's *bouleutêrion* doubled as an *ôdeion,* as was the practice in many cities, and would have been the place for state occasions. If it was anything like the still-visible and well-preserved *ôdeion-bouleutêrion* of nearby Ephesus, which seated well over a thousand, it would easily have accommodated an audience comparable in size to that faced by Alexander Peloplaton in Athens.[111] Philostratus' account of the declamation before Marcus Aurelius adds that Aristides asked permission for his "students" (*gnôrimoi*) to be in the audience; Marcus agreed, saying that it would be "democratic" (*Lives of the Sophists* 2.9 582–583).[112] This item shows, among other things, that in Aristides' case as in Alexander's, there was an assumption that students constituted a primary audience for declamation, and that public declamation, even in a command-performance concert for an emperor, retained at least a trace of the schoolroom *epideixis* from which it had evolved. Marcus' remark, too, is significant in its assumption that a "democratic" gesture would be appropriate for the occasion. We still are in the space of civic theater, in its "democratic" parallel reality.

Let us imagine, then, that Aristides delivered his Sicilian Orations in Smyrna, in the city's *ôdeion-bouleutêrion,* to an audience of students, connoisseurs of rhetoric, and local dignitaries (and/or persons of *paideia*), as well as "ordinary" spectators who enjoyed theatrical performances. Such a setting, or one similar to it, is at least possible. Aristides certainly assumes an educated audience: one must be familiar with Thucydides' account of Nicias' letter and its circumstances to fully understand the speakers' references to various details, such as the Egestans' money. (Egesta or Segesta, an initially pro-Athenian city-state in Sicily, encouraged the Athenian invasion by promising to fund the war, but never delivered.)

Aristides' first speech, *On Sending Reinforcements to Those in Sicily,* argues for the decision that the Athenians actually made, though for the most part it is an argument against withdrawal. Essentially the speaker argues that the original decision to send the expedition was not mistaken and must not be reversed; that, despite recent setbacks, things generally have gone well and there is no cause for despair; that sending reinforcements will solve all problems (indeed their mere appearance will accomplish almost everything, 5.45); that success will bring great rewards, while retreat will create great dangers to the state; and that it would be foolish and shameful to give up now. This summary list of topics does not reflect the actual structure of the speech, however, and in fact that structure is something of a problem. C. H. Behr, the editor and English-language translator of Aristides, and Laurent Pernot each provide a structural outline of the speaker's arguments, and neither outline resembles the other at all.[113] Pernot's, which is more rhetorically informed and seems better, is a list of the final headings employed: *justice, possibility, advantage, possibility, advantage, honor, results.* The recycling of topics that Pernot notes, or what might be called the recursivity of the speaker's arguments, is one of the speech's key features. But it is even more recursive than Pernot suggests. Instead of presenting his arguments one by one, the speaker "scatters" and mixes them, so that his key points repeatedly get made and the weaknesses of his reasoning are less apparent.

After the proem and partition (5.1–2), in which he dismisses the secondary question whether Nicias should be removed from command and focuses on the primary question of withdrawal, the speaker begins with reassuring arguments that the present problems are no cause for despair. The Athenians have succeeded in almost every way, and the recent setbacks are merely the results of bad luck and minor mistakes that easily are remedied (5.3–5). This *topos* (that is, of possibility) then gives way to the argument—a key to the speaker's strategy—that the original decision could not have been wrong, so that it would be improper, and in fact shameful, to reverse it now (5.6–8). This argument is premised, first, on the patriotic, even jingoistic notion that Athenians are "the wisest of the Greeks" (*sophôtatoi tôn Hellênôn*) and the best at practical deliberation (5.6), and second, on the belief that the decision to invade Sicily was deliberated as fully as possible: "What argument was not spoken among us?" (*tis logos ouk errêthê par' humin;* 5.8). If Athenians deliberate a matter thoroughly, their decision cannot be wrong. This ideologically determined impossibility of error permits the speaker to cast shame on the proponents of withdrawal as acting "like children" who foolishly give up when faced with the slightest difficulty. The speaker then turns to a digression (5.8–10) on the question whether Sicily's size and diversity make it difficult to conquer and still more difficult to control, an objection raised by Nicias in the original debate and raised again by him in his letter. The speaker's reply is a reiteration of the arguments made then by Alcibiades: the mixture and disunity of the peoples of Sicily, a mere "rabble," will make them easier to conquer and control once Syracuse has been defeated (Thucydides 6.17). Since these arguments were deemed persuasive then by the wisest of all Greeks, they could not have been wrong and remain true now. With this mixture of appeals the speaker has now set out the main themes with which he will weave the rest of the oration: the impossibility of error; the possibility (and advantages) of success, and the shame (and harm) of changing one's mind and giving up.

In the next major segment (5.11–16) the speaker returns to his opening theme, the reasons not to be discouraged, under the guise of giving proofs of the correctness of the original decision: things have generally gone well up to now, one setback after much success should not discourage, and sending a second expedition will easily solve the present problems and make Athens' success complete. This last point is, perhaps, more asserted than proven. The Syracusans, he says, took courage and their fortunes improved when Gylippus, the Spartan general, recruited and brought them reinforcements, so Athenian reinforcements will reverse the situation. The speaker ignores that Gylippus will still be there, coordinating help for the Syracusans. But his hopeful logic leads him, again, to arguments that, given how well things mostly have gone and what a difference the reinforcements will make, it would be shameful to withdraw (5.17–19). Indeed, he says, the Athenians will be seen by all other Greeks as guilty of poor judgment and cowardice (5.17), and nothing should be chosen that is shameful (5.18). Moreover to retreat would be inexpedient; by leaving the unconquered Syracusans behind them, the Athenians will be threatened with retaliation (5.19.)

The speaker next returns, with a lengthy development (5.20–39), to the idea that the current problems are not serious and that success is possible if the Athenians will persist. This time, however, the arguments are made not under the guise of proving the original decision correct but now maintaining that nothing has substantially changed; that the expedition is as essential as ever to the Athenians' overall strategy in the Peloponnesian War; that on many past occasions the Athenians have endured and overcome problems at least as great as the present ones, including the desperate situations they faced in the Persian Wars; and that, despite Nicias' arguments that Sicily is large, diverse, and difficult to conquer and control, its size and diversity are in fact the main features that make it conquerable and controllable. This latter argument (5.36–39) is itself an expansion of the earlier digression (5.9–10) on the conquerability of Sicily. In these passages the speaker does much to minimize the problems by maintaining that "we've seen worse before" and thereby stokes Athenian confidence in the ultimate correctness of their policy, but offers little analysis of the actual current circumstances.

The expanded argument about Sicily's conquerability takes on a curious tone. The speaker invokes the example of the Persian king's ability to rule effectively over an empire that he does not in fact have the material means to control. The king, he says, "enslaves and controls all by means of fear" because when many are enslaved everyone fears everyone, just as in a household with many slaves each is kept at odds with all, so that they are incapable of cooperative action or resistance. All can be dominated and terrorized by inflicting punishment on one of them, or one at a time. So too then Sicily, with its disparate and disunited peoples. More brutally cynical even than Alcibiades' argument about the Sicilian "rabble," the speaker's argument here is a fairly naked statement of the ideology of empire—or of a form of empire that squares with tyranny, which in the world of declamation is universally an evil. It also is a representation of what Thucydides portrays as the Athenians' loss of their virtue in the Peloponnesian War, their betrayal of the democratic ideals voiced by Pericles in his funeral oration. The fact that the speaker invokes the hated king of Persia as a model is significant. The speaker in this speech makes repeated appeals to shame, but cannot perceive the shamefulness of what he says here.

But this is not the end. The speaker caps this section with reiteration and expansion of the earlier argument (5.19) that retreat would leave revengeful enemies in place and expose Athens to retaliation. Here (5.40–41) he makes the point more explicitly that the undefeated Syracusans would be motivated to attack Athens. My students circa 2005 were quick to perceive a resonance between this argument about "results" or consequences and the rationale made for the Iraq War that "if we don't fight them there we'll have to fight them here." Aristides' audience would have known that the hypothetical Syracusan revenge expedition never came, but they also would have had to judge how probable that argument would have seemed to the deliberating Athenians, how reasonable it would have seemed as grounds for fear, and what a contrast it presented to the jingoistic, imperialistic hubris of the arguments about Athenian infallibility and Sicilian conquerability.

These arguments are followed by an extended appeal to shame (5.42–44): "Shall we ourselves recall so great an army without accomplishing a thing, an army that will not have had to return in accordance with a truce, but—I am ashamed to say it—will be seen in flight? . . . Shall we not feel ashamed before this sun? . . . For they [the army] will return to nothing other than silence and the boatswain's call, well nigh ashamed before the sea." And so on. This urgent emotional appeal to shame at the imagined sight of the nonvictorious grand army coming home in miserable silence, seen by all to have cut and run, is quite effective, and makes it possible to imagine how the deliberating Athenians *in that moment* may have found that thought intolerable, especially in light of the patriotic pride already stirred in them as the "wisest of all Greeks." This passage is followed by an exhortation to not give up, reiteration of the assurance that the mere appearance of the reinforcement expedition will accomplish virtually everything, and a final contemptuous rejection of Nicias' concerns, since they were rejected at the first debate (5.45–47). This completes the proof section of the speech. A brief epilogue (5.48–49) repeats the main contentions: retreat will be an irreparable disaster, but sending reinforcements will accomplish all and at worst will not prevent retreat if that becomes necessary later—an assurance that of course proved tragically untrue.

Aristides' first oration thus presents his audience with a palpably specious but nevertheless effective speech, one that makes it possible to understand, or imagine, how the Athenians could have been persuaded to make the choice they made. Notably the argument depends heavily on the emotive force of repeated appeals to, on one hand, patriotic pride and imperialist ambition, and on the other hand, and especially, to shame and fear. Meanwhile it is actually rather short on practical analysis of the situation. Indeed, practical analysis is largely precluded by the idea that "our original decision and the analysis it was based on could not have been wrong and cannot be rescinded now." The speaker does not in fact have many arguments, but the "recursive" structure of his speech—its scattering and repetition of the same arguments—makes it *seem* as if there are more, while permitting him to keep reiterating and amplifying his central emotional appeals. In these respects the speech is much like the anonymous student's "Leosthenes" but is more effectively handled. It is a demonstration, on Aristides' part, of how "the weaker argument," or in this case a really terrible argument with catastrophic consequences, can be made "stronger," or at least to seem so for a time. In this way it also is a demonstration of how political deliberation can go awry.

The second speech, *For the Opposite* (*Eis to Enantion*), can be treated more summarily. In essence it is a refutation of all the first speech's major points. Notably it begins, in the proemium, by invoking (like Isocrates) the necessity of frankly speaking what an audience may not want to hear, on the grounds that "when it is up to you to examine and choose whichever of the arguments you wish, the right thing is not to avoid the choice, but to put them side by side and see which is the better" (6.2). Aristides, or his speaker, thus takes the view suggested by Thucydides that the Athenians did not really deliberate but were driven by reasoning like that of *Oration 5*: they did not do the "right" (*orthos*) thing and believed what they wanted to believe. Thus the speaker first takes on what he calls "the last part" of his opponent's argument, namely, the idea that what has already been deliberated and decided cannot be reconsidered, since the Athenians could not have decided wrong. (This idea does appear "last," in 5.47, though obviously it is a repeated point and the backbone of that whole speech.) The *Opposite* speaker takes the pragmatic view that circumstances, not decrees, determine a policy's wisdom and success (6.6) and that "if it will not be possible for those that have erred regarding what is best to change their plans according to the circumstances, then the ability to learn from experience (*para tôn pragmatôn*)—that most human quality—will be destroyed, so that the failure (*kakopragia*) will necessarily be endlessly repeated" (6.8). After elaborating this point awhile (6.9–10), the speaker then argues that the Athenians have "erred regarding what is best" by developing precisely what the previous speaker has failed to provide, an analysis of the current situation (6.11–17). Things have not gone as expected, he argues, and indeed if the Athenians had correctly forecast what has actually happened they would not have sent the expedition. Athenian capabilities are badly overstretched and their resources are nearly exhausted.

Having thus assessed the situation, the speaker turns, at length (6.18–27), to the possible consequences should anything go wrong:

> May you not, O Athenians, be afflicted with folly, nor may you deceive yourselves, like people who shut their eyes so that they do not see what they do not wish. (6.18)

> So then . . . if now the same thing as before should happen, and you be eager to send reinforcements and in whatever number he [Nicias] should wish, and they should fall into the same difficulties—No, by God, may it not happen! May it not happen, O Zeus and all the gods! And I wish not only that it not happen, but not even to fear that it happen! (6.22)

> For if . . . we should be defeated in just one, one naval battle—and may all the gods turn this on the sons of the Syracusans and those who sympathize with them—not only will we not be in control of matters there, but we will not find even a way to escape. (6.26)

The speaker's mixture of aposiopesis and apostrophe underscores the urgency of the dread he seeks to communicate, and his dire, almost unspeakable predictions—the things that, as Aristides' audience knows well, actually will happen—are supported by his analysis of Athens' parlous, overextended situation.

Having made these arguments, then, the speaker devotes the rest of his speech to refutation of the first speaker's specific claims, almost in grab-bag fashion: the Syracusans will not be paralyzed with fear by the sight of the reinforcements (6.28–29); the invasion is not consistent with the original Athenian strategy for the Peloponnesian War (6.30–32); the majority of the Sicilian states will not come over to Athens' side (6.33); it makes no sense to avoid pitched battles at home, per the original Athenian strategy, but to commit to warfare far away in Sicily (6.34–35); it is not shameful to retreat when circumstances require it but shameful to persist in a losing strategy (6.36–42); the advocates of reinforcement are inconsistent in claiming that retreat is shameful but still will be possible later (6.43–44); a retreat will neither damage Athens' reputation nor expose it to dangers, while sending the reinforcements involves much greater risk (6.43–49); Syracuse will not send a revenge expedition against Athens (6.50–51); and sending reinforcements risks a complete catastrophe, as suggested already and as happened once before when the Athenians invaded Egypt in 459 B.C.E. (6.52–54; this example offsets the first speaker's examples of obstacles overcome). To this is tacked on an oddly disconnected, one-line final point: "And perhaps you all know that there is plague at the place where the camp is" (6.54). The speaker then briefly concludes (6.55–56).

These are, of course, the sorts of arguments that should have been made, and should have persuaded them, had the Athenians truly deliberated the choice that Nicias' letter presented. And, of course, Aristides can invent these arguments and his cultured audience can judge them with perfect 20/20 hindsight, having read how it all turned out so very badly in Thucydides and other historians. But perhaps this double declamation's point is not (or not only) the obvious one that the Athenians should have heeded arguments for withdrawal, or that they should have been more critical of their own "ingenuous and cunning," self-blinding rationalizations, including the ideology of empire. The first part of the second speaker's argument makes an eloquent general case, a thesis, for the importance of true deliberation, meaning deliberation that opens itself to arguments on both or all sides, and for the need to be able to change one's thinking and one's plans when circumstances prove one wrong. This argument is powerfully underscored by the speaker's emotive evocation—with aposiopesis and apostrophe—of the possible, and actual, dreadful outcomes of the Athenians' persistence in their mistake. This thesis on the need for true deliberation, then, seems to be Aristides' deeper point. This point, however, is brought to its forceful conclusion at the midpoint of the speech, where it is buried, and what follows is a miscellany that, while true, as events would prove, disperses and depletes the emotive force of what preceded it. The curious final "throwaway" remark about plague in the camp could possibly be considered a coup de grâce, and perhaps the audience is meant to think the *speaker* sees it that way, but its real effect is to heighten the sense of miscellaneousness, as if it had been tossed in apropos of nothing because the speaker happened to think of it just then. And it is left without elaboration, a "naked" remark, as the author of *Mistakes in Declamation* might say.

This is not to say that Aristides—who made a point of his meticulous preparation, never declaimed *ex tempore,* and probably revised his Sicilian Orations many times—has blundered or composed haphazardly. Rather, Aristides has meticulously created a portrait of a stumbling speaker, one who speaks with truth on his side but fails to follow through effectively—or two portraits: the first speaker is wrong both ethically and pragmatically, is blinded by his own ideologically driven rationalizations, and recommends what will prove to be a catastrophic mistake but connects with his audience's sense of identity and closes with a powerful emotional appeal; the second speaker speaks the truth, argues more logically, and has an even more potent emotional appeal available but expends it quickly and finishes weakly. The question then is, if the Athenian Assembly *had* deliberated on that occasion, and if they had heard speeches such as these, which would have been the more persuasive? Given such speeches, what response would have been reasonable for them to make in that specific moment? Aristides' performance of the two speeches likely was followed by discussion of issues such as these, certainly in private with his students (who were not numerous), and very possibly in the Smyrnaean *ôdeion-bouleutêrion* that I am imagining. Aristides has made the weaker argument stronger, and the stronger argument weaker, not only to prompt rhetorical-critical reflection on the speeches themselves, but also to pose a problem (or set of problems) in rhetorical philosophy regarding the ethics and the pragmatics of deliberation and of symbouleutic (advisory) speech. Significantly, he does not offer a doctrine on these matters but what Hermogenes might call an "evenly balanced" case from which further issues and arguments can emerge.

The *Rhetoric of Alcuin and Charlemagne,* written in the eighth century by Alcuin, a scholar from England at Charlemagne's court, is composed in a catechistic question-and-answer format (*disputatio*) and is a sort of searchable database of review material, like Cicero's *Parts of Rhetoric.*[114] For the most part it is a patchwork, a *cento,* of quotations lifted from Cicero's *De inventione* (plus a few bits from the fourth-century rhetoric of Julius Victor) parsed into segments by "Charlemagne's" questions. But not entirely. As Alcuin is reviewing Cicero's stasis theory, with illustrations from ancient declamation problems, Charlemagne interrupts to ask, "How many persons are there in a court of law?" (*Quot personae solent in iudiciis esse?*). Alcuin replies, "Four: the accuser, the defendant, the witnesses, the judge" (*Quattor: accusator causae, defensor causae, testes, iudex*).[115] Then in reply to Charlemagne's next question he briefly describes the function of each, and a little later he must describe where each of these persons sits.[116] This is new material; it is not from Cicero. Three centuries after the collapse of the western Roman Empire, Charlemagne, or the intended reader of the dialogue, who reads Latin, has never seen a court of law. No such thing exists. But he, or the students that Alcuin teaches, can encounter one in the parallel world of rhetoric's civic theater.[117]

As Isocrates said, to be a Hellene is to share not a common "blood" (*phusis,* "nature") but a certain *paideusis,* an enculturation. The true Hellene is a *pepaideumenos,* an "educated person." As the Hellenic *paideia* settled down, this meant at the most basic level training in *grammatikê,* the art of letters, alongside other basic studies such as mathematics, geometry, music, and astronomy. To be a Hellene was to be steeped in all that, but especially in classic literature—including poetry and prose, philosophy and history, and the orators—and to be fluent or at least competent in the literate dialect, classical Attic Greek. Further, for rhetorical education or what Isocrates called *logôn paideia* or *philosophia,* the *pepaideumenos* was to be a certain kind of educated person, one trained to exercise responsible, intelligent reasoning and judgment in practical deliberations in private and public life, and, for those with the necessary gifts and sufficient practice and instruction, to be a *rhêtôr,* an orator, capable of effective speech in public, civic space. This is what is meant, in Philostratus' anecdote about Alexander Pelopla-ton, when Herodes Atticus refers to his students as his Hellenes.

That identity, a rhetorical self, was cultivated through incessant exercise in the "sweet garden" of the school through reading, recitation, and rhetorical criticism; through the progymnasmata; and most especially through the civic theater of declamation, all framed by the preceptual material contained in the rhetorician's *technê.* In the school's declamatory theater the student entered, and performa-tively re-created and experienced, the parallel reality of Sophistopolis, the imagi-nary democratic city where Demosthenes, Pericles, Rich Man, Poor Man, the Tyrant, the Hero, the Pirate Chief's Daughter, and other characters all lived and spoke. It is this endlessly repeated reenactment of that democratic space—even when real democracy was in decline, absent, or simply unthinkable—that seems the most significant. That democratic theater began long before, and continued long after, the "Greek renaissance" of the Second Sophistic, and indeed contin-ued right through the Middle Ages, if sometimes in attenuated forms, and after. Undoubtedly the rhetorical *paideia* continued to cultivate general abilities in reasoning, speech, writing, and practical judgment that were valuable for civil service under kings and emperors. But the disjunction between the theatrical world of declamation in the school and the political realities outside the school sometimes must have seemed striking, as we see in Gregory Antiochus' twelfth-century contrast between the "sweet garden" of rhetorical study and the "hell of stupidity" in imperial bureaucracy. In short, the rhetorical *paideia* preserved, at least in its long-road versions and especially in the civic theater of declama-tion, an experience of a democratic imaginary, an ideal that frequently was unavailable from the real or contrasted with it sharply but could also be carried back into it. That is, it seems to me, the point of Michael Psellos' allegorical dream of talking, disputing birds in the "open sky," *eleutheron aera,* the "free air."

FIVE | Dionysius of Halicarnassus and the
Notion of Rhetorical Scholarship

A poor relation.
Ulrich von Wilamovitz-Moellendorff, "Asianismus und Atticismus" (1900)

A small soul.
Eduard Schwartz, "Dionysios von Halikarnassos" (1905)

A dumb schoolmaster.
Eduard Norden, Die antike Kunstprosa *(1915)*

The great Dionysius of Halicarnassus.
Aelius Theon, Progymnasmata

Dionysius the Under-Appreciated

Dionysius of Halicarnassus is often described as one of the leading "literary" critics of antiquity, although he was in fact a rhetorician. More precisely, he was a Greek sophist from Asia Minor. (Ancient Halicarnassus is modern Bodrum, on the western coast of Turkey.) Dionysius lived and worked at Rome between 30 and 7 B.C.E., and probably longer, a period corresponding closely to the reign of the emperor Augustus (27 B.C.E.–14 C.E.). During his time at Rome Dionysius learned Latin, made contacts with Roman and Greek intellectuals, took students, researched the history of Rome, and wrote probably everything that we now have from him.[1] His preserved works include seven critical "essays"—the introduction to a two-volume treatise *On the Ancient Orators* and its first three chapters (on Lysias, Isocrates, and Isaeus), an essay on Demosthenes (which may be part of the same work), and essays on Thucydides and Dinarchus—as well as his famous treatise *On the Composition of Words* (*Peri Suntheseôs Onomatôn*) and three letters on rhetorical-critical topics. He also wrote a twenty-volume history of the early Roman republic, *Roman Antiquities,* which he describes as his life's work (*Rom. Ant.* 1.7.2) and probably considered his masterpiece. About half—the first ten and a half books and scattered fragments of the rest—remains.

Also surviving are a few fragments and a partial epitome of a three-volume work *On Imitation,* which he may not have completed. His lost works include a discourse *On Behalf of Political Philosophy* (mentioned at *Thucydides* 2), two more chapters from *On the Ancient Orators* (on Hyperides and Aeschines, mentioned at *Ancient* 4 and *Isaeus* 20), a treatise on the genuine and spurious orations of Demosthenes (mentioned at *Demosthenes* 57), and probably other unattested writings. There also are a number of probably falsely attributed works preserved among his writings, including the lecture *On Mistakes Made in Declamation* discussed in chapter 4, another lecture *On the Assessment of Speeches,* and a handbook (*technê*) on epideictic oratory.[2] Dionysius is one of the most fully attested ancient sophists available to us now, and he represents an advanced stage in the development of Hellenistic rhetoric.

As the first three epigraphs to this chapter suggest, however, Dionysius has not received a lot of respect from modern scholarship, despite his high reputation in antiquity and the Middle Ages in Byzantium. German *wissenschaft* at the turn of the twentieth century sets the keynote: Wilamowitz calls him a "poor relation," that is, to advanced literary criticism, with misguided judgment and no ideas of his own (an *armen Gesellen,* literally "a poor fellow worker"); Schwartz likewise labels him a "small soul" unequal to the great issues of his day; and in 1915 Norden trumps them both by dismissing Dionysius as a "dumb schoolmaster." Dionysius does get a more positive assessment from W. Rhys Roberts, who in his 1901 edition, translation, and commentary on Dionysius' critical letters, finds him an excellent critic and an able defender of good taste, though sometimes overly concerned with the details of style.[3] Maximilien Egger's 1902 book-length study of Dionysius adopts the mixed but mostly German judgment that "this writer, scarcely philosophical, timid, without imagination, is passionate about his work. The study of rhetoric or of history is for him a serious matter"—which seems to assume that neither is, but nevertheless gives Dionysius some credit.[4] Roberts and Egger represent a sort of minority position, a counterweight to the magisterial Germans, but even they find fault.

The German view prevails in Earnest Carey's 1937 introduction to his Loeb translation of the *Roman Antiquities,* which is organized around the sneering thesis that "unfortunately, in spite of [the] high ideals [of classical historiography] which Dionysius tried to keep before him, his *Antiquities* is an outstanding example of the mischievous results of that unnatural alliance between rhetoric and history which was the vogue after the time of Thucydides" (that is, beginning with the followers of Isocrates).[5] Dionysius commits the sins of wishing to give the reader pleasure, being "biased," and spoiling the factual narrative with lengthy fabricated speeches on opposing sides at almost every important crisis. The speeches in Thucydides and other historians, and Plutarch's essay *On the Malice of Herodotus,* suggest the absurdity of those judgments.

Stephen Usher's somewhat more Eggerian introduction to his 1974 Loeb translation of the critical essays includes the unpromising remark that "rhetoric, as Plato knew, was too important a subject to be left to the rhetoricians," and he goes on as if nearly everything worth knowing about rhetoric derived from Aristotle, Theophrastus, the philosophical tradition, and Alexandrian philology. Usher acknowledges the "originality" of Dionysius' analysis of style, however, and considers him an Isocratean and therefore a cut above the tedious "technical *minutiae . . .* of practical handbooks,"[6] although Dionysius does in fact engage in such *minutiae,* and his "originality" is probably impossible to judge because the evidence from the Hellenistic age is so sparse and fragmentary (besides, it is a modern concept that may be irrelevant to him). In short, Usher considers Dionysius something better than a "dumb schoolmaster" with nothing but borrowed ideas and a narrow intellectual horizon, but the evaluation still is mixed.

The standard attitude of the twentieth century toward Dionysius' critical writings was pithily summed up by Stanley Frederick Bonner in 1939:[7] "Rhetoric . . . overhangs the critic like a cloud; sometimes it descends and darkens a whole essay; at other times it seems to lift, particularly when the critic is engaged upon some form of original research. But it cannot be said that there is any gradual improvement. . . . Nor indeed can any permanent improvement be reasonably expected; so closely interwoven were rhetoric and criticism in the ancient world."

As with history, any intellectual activity infected or "clouded over" by rhetoric is spoiled. Bonner's study, which has long been the definitive account, at least in English, of Dionysius' critical writings, was devoted to the rather unpromising question of how much Dionysius "freed himself from the shackles of the rhetorical system" and whether his essays showed any "gradual improvement" in his methods. "Improvement" meant, in essence, movement toward a post-Victorian model of literary criticism "freed" from "practical purpose" and devoted to sensitive aesthetic appreciation supported by detailed close analysis, as well as by historical and comparative considerations. The argument that answered this question involved the mostly impossible problem of deciding the compositional sequence of Dionysius' extant works and then attempting to observe his spiritual progress from rhetoric to aesthetics, as if all the essays had the same purpose, and indeed as if they all were *essays*—as opposed to instructional manuals, lectures, and the like—and embodied the stages of a romantic *Bildung* in which a Walter Pater–like spirit was struggling to manifest itself. In Bonner's view, as later in Usher's, Dionysius did sometimes manage to achieve a greater degree of sensitive "contact" with the authors that he studied and did develop highly refined techniques of stylistic analysis and explication that sometimes transcended the supposedly mechanical procedures of traditional rhetorical analysis.

But, after all, Dionysius never could quite escape the rhetorical clouds that loomed across his intellectual skies.[8]

A rhetorician might well reply that those clouds were, after all, a good thing—why should a critic, why should rhetorical studies, aspire to "freedom" from practical purpose, or in other words to uselessness?—while adding that Bonner's argument amounted to little more than an exercise in prejudice and was, for that reason, absurd. However, it is also the case that Bonner's argument bears a curious resemblance to the persistent modern view that has perhaps its best contemporary articulation in John Bender, David Wellbery, and Dilip Gaonkar: classical rhetoric is inadequate to a hermeneutic of "rhetoricality" (the effects of figurality, the subtle play of meaning and affect, the trace of ideology, social forces, and so forth) in every and any sort of discourse, because it offers a system of practical precepts meant to guide not the sensitive reception and critique of discourse but the production of a few set types of civic oratory.[9] As Bonner says, Dionysius' "rhetorical bias" leads him to stress "those characteristics of the authors under consideration which are likely to prove of service to his pupils; the great writers of Greek poetry and prose are throughout criticised for their rhetorical, not their inherent value.... All writers form a single quarry from which he may draw material for the all-important study of effective public speaking."[10] Again, the rhetorician might want to say, "Well ... good!" But the key point is that Bonner, Bender and Wellbery, and Gaonkar, as do many others, conceive "classical rhetoric" in more or less the same terms: a set of precepts for public speaking. Is such a conception adequate to Dionysius?

Then there is the testimony of this chapter's fourth epigraph—Aelius Theon's reference to "the *great* Dionysius of Halicarnassus" (emphasis added)—the praise of an actual rhetorician. But what Theon meant is opaque. There also have been, more recently, Emilio Gabba's book-length 1991 study of Dionysius as a historian in the *Roman Antiquities* and Casper de Jonge's very detailed study of Dionysius as a linguistic theorist "between grammar and rhetoric," both of which are highly sympathetic, but neither treats Dionysius specifically as a rhetorician.

In what follows, then, I hope to contribute to the rehabilitation of Dionysius as an important but understudied figure who deserves our fuller attention. In particular I wish to consider him as an example of what it may mean to do rhetorical studies per se, that is, as a rhetorician rather than as something else. It is obvious, of course, that ancient rhetoric was oriented toward a discursive realm rather different from that of modernity or postmodernity—though ancient culture certainly was pervaded by "rhetoricality"—and it is obvious too that the modern rhetorician works in a different institutional context that favors *wissenschaftlich* research (philology, hermeneutics, aesthetics, theory) and for the most part addresses teaching as an afterthought. Nevertheless it may be argued that Dionysius embodies, in his particular circumstances, a basic paradigm for the rhetorician's work, and one that merits our attention now. I begin with some general perspectives, then turn to an extended analysis of Dionysius' extant writings.

Dionysius on Rhetoric

Dionysius' definition of "rhetoric" appears in one of the surviving fragments of *On Imitation,* preserved as a quotation in Syrianus: "Rhetoric is an artistic faculty of persuasive discourse in political matters, having the goal of speaking well." Citations of this definition by Byzantine scholars—Aphthonius, Planudes, and Sopater—repeat it verbatim but suggest that it continued: "according to the possibilities," that is, in any given case.[11] Clearly Dionysius thinks of rhetoric as an art of persuasion, not simply an art of elegant expression or a grammar of figurality. To "speak well" means to speak persuasively, or as persuasively as a given set of circumstances will permit. "Having the goal of speaking well" partly anticipates Quintilian, while "faculty" (*dunamis*) and "the possibilities" (*to endechomenon*) echo Aristotle's well-known definition.[12] But Dionysius is no Aristotelian, and his definition probably owes more to Hermagoras and the tradition that Hermagoras embodied.[13] Dionysius is, of course, well aware of Aristotelian and later Peripatetic rhetorical theory, especially Theophrastus' work on style, just as he was well aware of Stoic, Epicurean, and Academic theory, and indeed, of the full range of Hellenistic and Roman work on rhetoric and grammar, including the literary and linguistic scholarship of Callimachus and other Alexandrians, and he is willing to use some of them, or parts of them, or none or all of them, in various combinations.[14] He may well have been familiar with Cicero's works, including the *Orator,* which develops an analysis of prose rhythm that probably derives from Hellenistic sources (the sophists that Cicero studied with in Asia) and bears a resemblance to Dionysius' analysis in *On Composition.* Dionysius is, in short, eclectic, and like Kenneth Burke he is willing to "use all that is there to be used," depending on his purposes in any given case.[15]

In this eclecticism he agrees with Cicero's Antonius and Crassus in *De oratore*: the rhetor, and the rhetorician, should lend an ear to the philosophers when they speak on matters relevant to rhetor's or the rhetorician's concerns, though the rhetor/rhetorician need not *be* a philosopher, or be committed to any one school, or aim at a completely systematic, self-consistent theory. As a sort of Gramscian organic intellectual, or as a pragmatist, Dionysius is more interested in using any and all ideas that "work." As he says, for example, in *On Composition,* he first turned to the philosophers' handbooks (*technai*) on dialectic and their accounts of "logical" word order to see whether they offered the rhetoric teacher useful precepts for sentence construction in prose, and concluded that they offered "nothing helpful . . . for civic discourse" (*politikos logos*) and wrote very bad prose themselves, especially the Stoics (4). Then he attempted to formulate for himself the rules of "natural" word order in order to define a "starting point" (*aphormê*) for a systematic teaching of style—things such as "nouns precede verbs" or "adverbs follow verbs," as Alexandrian grammarians might propose. But he quickly discovered that all such rules, even if correct (as linguistic descriptions of normal Greek word order), had no relation to what were obviously good or bad specimens of style in poetry or prose. So he gave up and conceded that though some very general prescriptions might be given— for example, sentence construction generally should seem natural and be accessible, a principle that Thucydides violates—such prescriptions are not a matter of systematic or even logically coherent rules. It all depends on context (*kairos*), what is possible or available (*to endechomenon*), and appropriateness (*to prepon*; 4–5).

As that anecdote hints—with its step away from what Isocrates calls *tetagmenê technê*, a "rigid art" with invariant rules, toward an embrace of prose style as a "creative act" responding to *kairos*—Dionysius' key allegiance is to Isocrates, or to the sophistic rhetorical tradition of which Isocrates is the fountainhead and representative figure. In his *First Letter to Ammaeus*, Dionysius presents an extended refutation of a Peripatetic claim that Demosthenes learned the rules of eloquence from Aristotle's *Rhetoric*. He doesn't want, he says, "all who are serious about public discourse" to think that Peripatetic theory encompasses all there is to say, or that nothing important was discovered by the older sophists or by Isocrates and his followers, seven of whom are named (2).[16] He then goes on to demonstrate that nearly all of Demosthenes' important speeches were delivered before Aristotle wrote the *Rhetoric*, which Dionysius consistently refers to as "Aristotle's *technai*," thus leaving Isocrates and his followers, Isaeus in particular (2), as the most likely source of the great orator's rhetorical instruction. Further, as I also noted earlier, in the chapters comprising *On the Ancient Orators* Dionysius does not proceed according to the canons of Aristotelian rhetoric but, as he says, according to those of Isocrates and "those belonging to his school" (*Lysias* 16), that is, the *pragmatikos topos* and the *lektikos topos*, the "domains" of subject matter and of style, each with its respective subdivisions.[17]

In his introduction to *On the Ancient Orators*, Dionysius subtly but emphatically affiliates himself with Isocrates by celebrating the return of what he calls *hê archaia kai philosophos rhêtorikê*, "the ancient, philosophical rhetoric," which he portrays as having been displaced by a "mindless" prostitute rhetoric from Asia (1). Just as Isocrates in *Against the Sophists* claims to be rescuing the study of *logos* or "philosophy" from the discredit into which recent sophists have brought it, so too does Dionysius hail the return of philosophical rhetoric from its supposedly long decline. Dionysius' story clearly is connected to the Atticist-Asianist controversy of the time—the "pure" style and moral earnestness of the Attic orators versus the supposed vulgarity and excess of the Asiatic style—a controversy connected to sociopolitical anxieties and the claims of Athens to cultural centrality in the Roman world. (Athens was the Roman Empire's quintessential "university town," where the well-off young man could go to complete his education, but it also was in competition with other centers.)

But for Dionysius the philosophical quality of the better rhetoric does not, in fact, inhere particularly in its Atticism, though he is certainly an Atticist. In the Second Sophistic, "Asiatic" style would continue to have widespread appeal; prominent sophists in the second century C.E. such as Aelius Aristides typically regarded rhetoric as philosophical and identified themselves as Atticists yet essentially practiced an Asiatic style that featured rhythmic composition, short clauses, parataxis, and moderately "learned" diction not too far removed from common speech. As Lucian satirically suggests in *Teacher of Orators,* Atticism was sometimes merely a matter of sprinkling one's speech with a few antique expressions in order to seem more learned. For Dionysius, rather, the philosophical quality of rhetoric is grounded, as with Cicero, largely in an *eleutherion paideuma,* a "liberal education" acquired in youth and sustained into maturity consisting chiefly of literary studies: the canonic poets, historians, philosophers, and orators, and the literary dialect they constitute. The bad rhetoric, by contrast, is largely devoid of such education and the concerns that go with it, or so he portrays it.

In *On Composition,* for example, as Dionysius is explaining the nearly poetic rhythm of a passage of Demosthenes, he turns aside to anticipate "an attack against this very idea [that Demosthenes' rhythms could be so carefully composed] from people with no experience of a rounded education [*enkuklios paideia*], and who practice the vulgar sort of rhetoric" (*to agoraion tês rhêtorikês meros;* 25), or more literally, "the vulgar part [*meros*] of rhetoric." The adjective *agoraios,* "vulgar, common" (from *agora,* "town square, marketplace") suggests, on one hand, the "vulgarity" of marketplace harangues. On the other hand, it also suggests, and is a term for, courtroom oratory, though perhaps not an elevated kind. Thus Dionysius, like Isocrates, has lower esteem for the oratory of the courts, and especially that of the "sycophants" (*sukophantai*) who make their living as freelance accusers, profiting from "lawsuits contrary to justice," as Isocrates puts it. Both Isocrates and Dionysius favor a higher and more philosophical rhetoric that reflects the better ideals and purposes of a liberal *paideia.*

But the notion of courtroom oratory as belonging to "the vulgar part of rhetoric" may simply reflect Dionysius' awareness that most judicial cases in his day involved petty, mundane disputes between private individuals and generally offered limited scope for the eloquent expression of high ideals or the contestation of grand issues. A typical case, for example, might be a dispute over a contract or a will. As Tacitus' speakers remark in *Dialogus de oratoribus,* ordinary civil and criminal legal cases normally were not heard in open-air courts before large juries and crowds of onlookers, as in the high-stakes political trials of Cicero's day, but generally transpired in small, drab recitation halls before a single judge or magistrate, where dramatic gestures and high eloquence were out of place. We know that Aelius Aristides in the second century C.E. went to court several times to be exempted from appointments to civic office, and in his *Sacred Tales* he mentions lawsuits with his neighbors—presumably property disputes—but those speeches were not preserved, probably because he considered them too mundane. All forty-six of his surviving speeches are symbouleutics, encomia, "prose hymns," or panegyrics.[18]

The notion of the "marketplace harangue," moreover, reflects another aspect of "the vulgar part of rhetoric" and suggests a further Isocratean attitude. As Isocrates says at *To Philip* 12, to harangue (*enochlein*, "disturb, annoy") an indiscriminate crowd (*ochlos*) with some political proposal "is to speak to no one at all" (*pros oudena legein estin*) because the crowd is not empowered to enact what the rhetor recommends and may be too ignorant even to intelligently judge his argument.[19] (Think, today, of the devotees of the most egregious talk-radio blowhards and blog conspiracy theorists.) Isocrates' remark, aside from being flattery to Philip, may reflect a late-career disillusion with the Athenian *dêmos* as the plaything of demagogues and incapable, as a body, of deliberating sensibly. But it also may reflect a more general, practical attitude that serious discourse on "political matters" is best addressed to those most able to evaluate it and most empowered to take action. With Isocrates that view is a pragmatic adjustment to the problem of dealing persuasively with absolute monarchs, such as Philip of Macedon, and their counselors.[20] For Dionysius it would clearly be relevant to the practical realities of power and political deliberation in the Roman Empire.[21]

Dionysius' contrast between the "ancient, philosophic" rhetoric with its Attic style and the "senseless" rhetoric that lacks *eleutherios paideuma* and practices an *agoraios* style probably boils down to a contrast between what Raffaella Cribiore calls the "long" and "short" roads to rhetoric: a complete rhetorical training founded on a full-scale liberal education in classic literature, including the orators, and lasting for many years, versus an abbreviated training in public speaking that lasts only a year or so. From this point of view, the contrast is not so much between educations that differ in kind as between those that differ according to time in school, depth and extent of study, and the motives of the student. "Short-roaders" still could get a basic training adequate to speak in the local courts or city council, or get a job in civil bureaucracy or on a rich patrician's staff. Dionysius' tale of the "Attic Muse" displaced by an "ignorant" Asiatic whore in effect identifies Asianism with the short-road education and takes a position much like that of Lucian in *Teacher of Orators:* The short-roader is a flimflam man, a pretentious phony, a demagogue, a marketplace haranguer, a sycophant, a toady—the sort of person more interested in gaining and exercising power than in practical wisdom, good deliberation, the true advantage of the *polis,* or high eloquence. The proper governance of the state, as Dionysius' tale suggests, depends on a philosophical rhetoric grounded in the long-road *enkuklios paideia,* as well as the qualities of character, the virtues, that it both requires and cultivates in the student. This position is consistent with Isocrates (for example, *To Nicocles* 13 and *Antidosis* 93–97, 207–208, 224–231, 274–280) and with Cicero's *De oratore.*

What Dionysius means by philosophical rhetoric may be glimpsed in the surviving text of *Roman Antiquities.* He aims, he says, to explicate the motivations of events because

> I assume that such lessons [*mathêseis*] are a necessary and excellent thing for virtually all people, but especially for those that occupy themselves with philosophical speculation [*philosophos theôria*] and political affairs [*politikai praxeis*]. . . . [Hearing such narrative is pleasurable] for men in politics [*politikôi andrasi*], among whom I place also those philosophers who consider philosophy a discipline [*askêsis*] not only of fine words [*logoi*] but also of fine deeds [*erga*]. . . . But aside from their pleasure, they also gain from this sort of experience [*empeiria*] the ability to render great service [*to megala ôphelein*] to their cities in necessitous situations [*anankaioi kairoi*], and to guide them as willing followers to the advantageous by means of speech [*logos*]. (11.1.1, 4)

The philosophical politician here is clearly one who takes a "theoretical" interest in observing "political affairs" and practices "philosophy" by doing rhetoric in practical civic life. This interest manifests itself, in part, in the study of history and the "lessons" it teaches rather than abstract political theory such as one might find in Plato's *Republic* or *Laws,* or in Aristotle's *Politics.* From the observation of political action and its motivations and outcomes in specific circumstances derives a kind of experiential knowledge (*empeiria*) that combines with one's accumulated personal experience to cultivate the *phronêsis* required for giving good, effective, advice in critical situations where decisions must be made. "Philosophic" rhetoric, then, is rhetoric as Dionysius defines it: an "artistic faculty" of persuasive discourse in "political" or civic matters (*en pragmati politikôi*), having the goal of speaking as well as possible.

Dionysius' self-identification with Isocrates has other implications, too, for his notion of rhetoric. For example, while he clearly is committed to the study and teaching of practical deliberative and judicial oratory—his criticisms of the styles of Isocrates and Thucydides center on their suitability to real-world argument in council halls, assemblies, and courts of law—it is also clear that, like

Isocrates, he understands rhetoric as essentially an artistic faculty of effective discourse and practical deliberation *in general*. Symbouleutic or "advisory" discourse is rhetoric's preeminent form, and the philosophic—liberally educated, fully trained—rhetor advising his city well is rhetoric's paradigmatic scene, but rhetoric is not limited to the genres of practical civic oratory. As a general political-philosophic discourse art that concerns itself with questions in civics, ethics, justice, and public policy, rhetoric manifests itself also, even most fully, in panegyric discourse and in such literary forms as history, philosophy, and poetry.[22] The perspective here is that of the twelfth-century scholar Gregory of Corinth, who classifies Plutarch's *Moralia* and the sermons of Basil the Great as "symbouleutic" discourse.[23] When Dionysius says that "rhetoric" is "an artistic faculty of persuasive discourse *en pragmati politikôi*," what seems to be meant is not "political matters" in the narrow sense of political "affairs" (*praxeis*) but, more broadly, "political subject matters" (*pragmata*). And these may be addressed in virtually any kind of discourse, prose or poetry, practical or epideictic, in fluid mixtures of the basic *ideai* from which all discourses are composed, according to the rhetor's purposes and the possibilities that *kairos* makes available.

We do not know whether Dionysius considered poets and philosophers to engage in enthymematic argument, but since he considers historians in those terms (for example, *Letter to Gnaeus Pompeius* 3), and since Aristotle clearly considers poets in those terms as well, it seems likely. Isocrates at one point compares panegyric prose and poetry by suggesting that both employ enthymemes "more ample and original" than those of practical orations (*Antidosis* 47). And indeed it is arguable that, with the fading political importance of the forum and the courts under the principate, discourses such as the *Roman Antiquities,* Virgil's *Aeneid,* or the lyrics of Horace were among the most important and influential genres of "political" discourse in Dionysius' world.[24] Insofar, then, as Dionysius is to be understood as an Isocratean, it seems clear that for him "rhetoric" is an "artistic faculty of persuasive discourse in political subject-matters" that manifests itself, as rhetorical practice, across the spectrum of practical, panegyric, and literary discursive genres, as well as private conversation, letters, and even one's inward thought. (Not to mention things such as the graffiti, advertisements, and imagery festooning the walls of Roman city streets, electioneering such as Cicero describes in his essay to his brother Quintus, and so on.)

A first conclusion might be, then, that conceptions of classical rhetoric as an art limited to giving rules for the production of a few types of practical civic orations, and as more or less the same thing as Aristotelian rhetoric, are inadequate to Dionysius, and indeed to the classical rhetorical tradition generally, insofar as the main line of that tradition descends from Isocrates and through "the genuine teachers of this art" in the Hellenistic age to Dionysius and beyond him to the Second Sophistic and late antiquity.

Rhetorical Education

Notably, Dionysius' definition of rhetoric makes it an *artistic faculty* of persuasive discourse on "political" or civic matters. That is, he does not say that rhetoric is a faculty of *artistic discourse.* Perhaps I have put excessive weight on that locution, but as I have been suggesting throughout this book, it seems to consider the *dunamis* of rhetoric as a faculty artistically produced or fashioned. "Rhetoric" is an art or discipline not so much of producing speeches, but an art of producing rhetors capable of creatively constructing or improvising effective discourse according to the constraints and possibilities in particular situations.

Like Isocrates, Dionysius considers this faculty not to be the product of a *tetagmenê technê,* a rigid set of rules, or even of a handbook's worth of precepts, though such precepts are not useless and in fact perform an essential role. As he says, for example, in a discussion of Demosthenes' rhythmic composition, "Will anyone come to know precisely the nature of harmonious prose composition [*logôn emmelous harmonias phusis*] from a few precepts and a brief explanation? Far from it!" (*Demosthenes* 50). What is required for this knowing, as in all other aspects of the rhetorical *dunamis,* is an extended education that resembles, as Isocrates would put it, athletic training (gymnastics). In Demosthenes' case, "when lengthy training [*hê chronios askêsis*] had created a great habitude [*hexis*] in him, and had produced strong impressions of what he had constantly been practicing [*ta aiei meletômena*], then he could with ease and from habit [*hexis*] produce it" (52).

Dionysius here is holding up Demosthenes as a paradigm of rhetorical, and stylistic, training: how did he acquire his impressive mastery of prose composition? *Ta meletômena,* "things practiced," derives from the verb *meletaô,* "exercise, practice, train, rehearse, take careful thought for, study," and is related to the noun *meletê,* "care, attention, practice, exercise," and "declamation." Here, with respect to the acquisition of stylistic habits, Dionysius seems not to mean declamation only but "practice" in general, in the sense of rehearsal with close attention to what one is doing. What is thoroughly rehearsed leaves deep memory traces ("strong impressions") and habituated practices related to those traces.

What Dionysius means is partly explained in his next few sentences with an analogy to the acquisition of literacy in grammatical instruction (*grammatikê*), which he has chosen, he says, because it is the "most familiar" (*phanerôtatê*) art of all and "very wonderful" (*thaumasiôtatê;* 52); that is, it is familiar to anyone who comes to the threshold of rhetoric from the grammatical *paideia* (that is, all literate people), and it is "wonderful" because Hellenistic grammatical studies have made great advances.[25] The acquisition of literacy in the ancient world started from small elements and worked up to larger ones.[26] First, the basic "letters" (sounds/phonemes) of Greek or Latin, then their combinations in syllables, then words, then sentences, and so on. At all stages the elemental skills were practiced to automaticity. The student learned to read slowly and haltingly, at first. There were no spaces between words and punctuation was nearly nonexistent in ancient texts, so that the beginner had an arduous task just to identify and read out the words one by one, or to tell where phrases or sentences began and ended. Later, as the student grew more adept, it became possible to read whole phrases, sentences, and larger units with ease. At this level the student could start learning more complex technical matters, such as the parts of speech, inflections, the rules of versification, archaic dialects and vocabularies in the poets, and so on up to larger interpretive schemes, such as allegorical reading and the interpretation of subtexts in "figured" discourse, so that eventually it was possible to read with a thorough understanding.

Reading well, then, was not a matter of consciously applying rules to the decoding of sequences of letters as meaningful discourse but a matter of possessing a flexible, habituated *dunamis* built up with time and practice, a *dunamis* that adroitly enacted the rules but no longer needed to consciously think of them. So, as Dionysius says, "Some such thing must be supposed to occur in the case of this art [*technê*] [of prose composition] also: beginning from small and petty precepts [*theôrêmata*], with time one's habitude [*hexis*] increases to easily master them, so that it instantly will conceive, with discernment and without stumbling, what it is to do."

"It" (*autê*) is ambiguous here; it could mean "art," but more probably signifies "habitude," the artistically cultivated *dunamis* of prose style, or of rhetoric more broadly, which must instantly intuit and execute what it should do. Once the *theôrêmata* or "precepts" for style have been absorbed as habitude, one can unfalteringly and instantly enact them, choosing the apt words and deploying them strikingly, just as Demosthenes does. But one starts by learning and practicing with "small and petty" rules in repetitive classroom exercises, and then proceeding to more and more complex kinds of reading and composition, and higher-order rules, and so on.

In general, students are to exercise and develop their intellectual and discursive powers by reading, engaging critically with, imitating, and practicing political discourse in various discursive genres. In such a framework, the terms of rhetoric function not as a prescriptive calculus—not as recipes for particular types of speeches—but, more descriptively, as a means of informing the "gymnastic" process by enabling the student to reflect more analytically and consciously on what he is reading, critically engaging with, imitating, and practicing. It enables him to put names to what he feels, and to make increasingly fine distinctions. And as we have seen, for Dionysius the vocabulary to be used is not limited to the terms of Aristotelian rhetoric, or for that matter the terms of the *technê* tradition. Analytical vocabulary can be drawn as needed from a wide, eclectic variety of sources.[27] The larger purpose is to produce a person capable of intelligent, ethically responsible deliberation as well as persuasive speech and writing in every facet of public and private life.[28]

How this process was to work with Dionysius may be glimpsed in a few passages. In one of the surviving fragments of *On Imitation,* he says, "Three things will furnish us with excellent habitude [*hê aristê hexis*] in political discourses, and in every art [*technê*] and branch of knowledge [*epistêmê*]: a ready nature, careful study, and laborious exercise" [*phusis dexia, mathesis akribês, askêsis epiponos*].[29] "Excellent habitude," again, suggests a cultivated *dunamis,* a crafted "nature" (*phusis*), built up through rhetorical education from the inherent talents, physical endowments, and moral proclivities of each particular student's given nature.

What "careful study and laborious exercise" means is evident in *Lysias,* where Dionysius is summing up his discussion of Lysias's style, in particular what he calls its "grace," *charis.* This grace, he says, cannot adequately be described or analyzed, but it can be felt and can be learned (*Lysias* 10). The way to do this, he says, if I may translate rather literally, is "for a long time and by extended practice and nonlogical felt experience to discipline one's nonlogical sense-perception," just as a person who wishes to acquire musical ability must train his ear (10).[30] From this we can understand at least two things: the experiences of reading and recitation at the advanced or transitional level of grammatical study and continuing through the beginning stages of rhetorical training and beyond—think of Libanius' summer reading lists for his students and the classroom performance and analysis of texts as a constant component of rhetorical education—and imitation and original composition, from the beginning to the more advanced levels of rhetoric, from progymnasmata to declamation.

By "reading," moreover, we should understand reading out loud, or in other words, oral interpretation or delivery. The significance of this is evident in what Dionysius says in *Demosthenes* about the different effects of reading—performing—the writings of Isocrates and Demosthenes:

> Whenever I read one of the discourses of Isocrates, whether those written for lawcourts and assemblies [*dikastêriai kai ekklêsiai*] or those . . .[written for festival gatherings?] . . . I become serious in mood [*en êthei spoudaios*] and have great steadiness of mind, like those who listen to libation-songs played on reedpipes or to Dorian or enharmonic melodies. But whenever I take up a discourse of Demosthenes, I am enraptured and transported hither and thither, partaking of one emotion [*pathos*] after another . . . every emotion that is disposed to rule over human thought. . . . It is not possible for anyone to run through [Demosthenes' discourse] just as he pleases, as the words themselves teach how they must be delivered, . . . and all that the style is meant to produce is shown upon enunciation. (*Demosthenes* 22)[31]

For Dionysius and for the tradition he represents, "reading" as oral interpretation means entering into the ethical and pathetic mood(s) of the discourse being read, its patterns of thought, its characteristic style(s), its voice, or what Dionysius frequently calls its *charaktêr,* its "stamp." (*Charaktêr* means "stamp" in the sense of an image stamped on a coin, an impress.) To read out the words, with their appropriate sound values, tonal textures, rhythms, and significance, is to perform or reenact, if briefly, the Isocratean, Demosthenic, or other character embodied in the discourse of the text.

As Dionysius further suggests, it takes a long period of study—reading/ performing and analysis—before one can thoroughly know or inhabit the Demosthenic, Isocratean, Lysianic, or other *charaktêr,* just as sculptors and painters need prolonged close study of the masters' works before they can with confidence recognize and take the impress of their *charaktêr* (*Demosthenes* 50). "Imitating" Demosthenes is not so much a matter of copying as of inhabiting the master's ways of thought and speech. As the author of the Pseudo-Dionysian lecture *On Mistakes Made in Declamation* puts it, "The one who imitates Demosthenes is not the one who speaks Demosthenes, but the one who speaks Demosthenically" (19). One can speak Demosthenically, with the true "stamp," without using Demosthenic catch-phrases, reproducing his stylistic tics or mannerisms, or even repeating his ideas.

Thus, to acquire the "grace" of Lysianic style, or the distinctive *charaktêr* of Isocratean or other eloquence, one must literally rehearse it, repeatedly and over a long period of time, by means of oral interpretation, recitation, imitation, and original production, in order to internalize its "feel" as part of one's own discursive competence. This is to be done with the full range of models considered in *On Imitation:* poets such as Homer, Hesiod, Antimachus, Panyasis, Pindar, Simonides, Stesichorus, and Alcaeus; dramatists such as Aeschylus, Sophocles, Euripides, and Menander, and all the comedians; historians such as Herodotus, Thucydides, Xenophon, Philistus, and Theopompus; philosophers, including the dialogues of Xenophon, Plato, and Aristotle; and orators such as Lysias, Isocrates, Lycurgus, Demosthenes, Aeschines, and Hyperides.[32] The object, ultimately, is not to cultivate just one specific *charaktêr* but to achieve a distinctive personal synthesis. As Dionysius argues in *Demosthenes,* the great orator developed his own rhetorical *charaktêr* as a synthesis of the best features of the Lysianic, Isocratean, Thucydidean, and Platonic *charaktêres.*

For Dionysius, "nonrational felt experience" is key to the training of habitude, though it can and should be supplemented by *technê.* As he puts it, in the context of examining the characteristics of Thucydides' discourse, in both style and subject matter, "I concede that the common person is not a worse judge of many things than the practitioner of art [*ho technitês*]—those things apprehended by nonrational sensation [*alogos aisthêsis*] and by the emotions [*pathê*]—

and that every art [*technê*] aims at their criteria and from them takes its start" (*Thucydides* 4).

This is not far from what Cicero has Crassus say, in *De oratore*, regarding the natural receptivity of the human ear to prose rhythm and the role of technical precepts: Everyone can feel the rightness or wrongness, or effectivity or failure, of a rhythm, but few can explain the sources of that feeling, and fewer still can achieve an effectively rhythmic prose in actual performance (3.195–197). To put it differently, the student who is able to read (orally interpret) a text properly, can—more or less by instinct—*feel* its *charaktêr*, such as the indescribable grace of Lysias, the balanced seriousness of Isocrates, or the overwhelming passionality of Demosthenes, before and even without an art to provide an explanation. Art will imperfectly explain as much as can or needs to be explained and will give the student a greater ability to name and describe what he perceives in a discourse (and thus make his perception sharper), but it is the ability *first* to feel and experience what the explanation explains that makes the explanation intelligible and useful. Experience is primary, *technê* secondary and supplemental.

Two things should be noted at this point. First, though the passages above, and most of Dionysius' extant critical writing, have mainly to do with matters of style and thus represent only a part of his concerns as a rhetorician, his notion of *acquiring the character* of Lysianic, Isocratean, Demosthenic, and other types of eloquence through repeated rehearsal is consistent with the broader notion of ethical development that appears in Aristotle's *Nicomachean Ethics*. Aristotle conceives of *êthos* as a matter of "habit," *hexis,* a predisposition to respond with particular moods, emotions, or behaviors to particular kinds of situations. Such predispositions have a kind of logic to them, insofar as one's perceptions of a situation and responses to it are mediated by cognition, but Aristotle considers the process to operate quickly and below the level of conscious awareness, and thus to have the effect of instantaneous nonlogical "feeling" or intuition. Thus, as Aristotle says (*Nicomachean Ethics* 10.9), it is not possible to make a person good by means of moralizing lectures, for that person will respond only to what he already can respond to, and in the ways that he already habitually responds. However, the attitudinal and emotional predispositions constituting a person's *êthos* can be trained by guiding that person, particularly when young, to the repeated enactment of ethical choices and emotional behaviors until they become habitual. This, then, appears to be the sort of process by which Dionysius would have his students acquire the characters of various kinds of eloquence.

Second, let us note too that Dionysius does not limit this notion of acquisition through rehearsal and habituation to matters of style. We see this, for example, in *Lysias,* as Dionysius is turning from the *lektikos topos* to the *pragmatikos topos:* "Now, as for habit [*hexis*], I will examine what is characteristic of Lysias' treatment of subject matter [*tis ho pragmatikos esti Lusiou charaktêr*], following the account of his style [*lexis*]" (*Lysias* 15).[33] By "characteristic treatment of subject-matter," Dionysius here means Lysias' habitual methods of argumentation, though the locution itself is broad enough to include, for example, methods of historical narration and argument in Thucydides or Theopompus. That he means methods of argument in this case is clear from what follows, as Lysias' characteristic invention, arrangement, and presentation of arguments, and his use of pathos and ethos, are discussed, as well as his handling of the standard parts of the oration. The word for "habit" here is again *hexis*, and it suggests that, as with methods of stylistic composition, methods of argumentation must also be acquired through repeated critical engagements with, and rehearsal and reembodiment of, a rhetor's characteristic ways of reasoning. Later in the same essay, Dionysius sets out to clarify what he calls "the *charaktêr* of his [Lysias'] proofs [*apodeixeis*]" in the oration *Against Diogeiton* (*Lysias* 50).

So rhetorical training in both style and argument requires the "ready nature" that Isocrates considers an essential prerequisite and develops that nature through "careful study" and "laborious exercise." "Careful study" appears to be the activities of reading—oral interpretation and classroom commentary—while "laborious exercise" suggests imitation and original composition in pro-gymnasmata, declamation, and other exercises. While "careful study" alone is insufficient to produce a rhetor, it performs a crucial mediating role. As Isocrates suggests, students who have a sufficiently "ready nature" and are "able to imitate" the exemplar texts that have been presented and explained to them will quickly absorb the exemplars' characteristics and quickly show in their speech a "greater brilliance and charm" (*Against the Sophists* 17–18). Similarly Dionysius seems to assume a process by which "ready nature" nonlogically perceives the discursive *charaktêres* of the authors it reads/performs with close attention, comes to understand them yet more deeply and analytically through "careful study," and more fully absorbs them as part of its developing rhetorical *dunamis*, its performative competence.

In one respect Dionysius' pedagogical approach seems unusual. The standard sequence of rhetorical instruction is generally presumed to have been the *pragmatikos topos* first and the *lektikos topos* second, such as we see in the traditional Hermogenic sequence of *On Stases*, *On Invention*, and *On Types of Style*. As we have seen, Hermogenes argues that there is no point in discussing types of style before the student has mastered stasis analysis and the creation of whole orations in different genres. Yet the sheer fact that Hermogenes feels the need to argue the point suggests that it could not be treated as self-evident. In *On Composition*, Dionysius begins the instruction by saying,

> There are two disciplines [*askêseis*] concerned with virtually all discourses [*logoi*]: one concerned with the thoughts, and one with the words. The

former may be considered especially the concern of the *pragmatikos topos,* and the latter the concern of the *lektikos topos.* All who aim at speaking well [*to legein eu*] are equally serious about both of these studies of discourse [*theôriai tou logou*]. But the knowledge that guides us regarding the subject-matter [*ta pragmata*] and prudential judgment [*phronêsis*] in it comes slowly and is difficult for the young; indeed it is impossible for those at the age of beardless boys [*ageneia meirakia*]. A grasp of the subject-matter belongs more to an already mature understanding, and to an age disciplined by grey hairs, augmented by much examination [*historia*] of speeches [*logoi*] and deeds [*erga*] and by much experience and suffering of one's own fortunes [*pathê*][34] and those of others. But the love of splendid utterance is natural to those in the flower of youth: every young mind [*psuchê*] is thrilled by the bloom of style [*ho tês hermeneias hôraïsmos*], and takes to it by certain nonrational impulses [*alogoi tina hai hormai*] that are very like inspiration. (*On Composition* 1).

Dionysius is saying this, ostensibly, to a seventeen-year-old boy who recently has begun his rhetorical studies, a *meirakion* named Metilius Rufus who is celebrating his first birthday since reaching *andrôs hêlikia,* the "age of manhood," or sixteen. In this passage we hear the locutions of an introductory lesson, parsing out the main divisions of rhetorical study and discussing their importance. Notably, Dionysius considers the *pragmatikos topos* to require mature knowledge and experience, "augmented" by historical study "of speeches and deeds"—the subject matter of the *Roman Antiquities*—and thus to be difficult for young students to handle well. Rhetorical training should begin, instead, with what comes "naturally" to the young, what they can do well at and enjoy, namely, the "nonrational" experience of impressive utterance, the striking turn of phrase, the "bloom" of a memorable stylistic flourish. This is the bedrock and starting point for all rhetorical theory, criticism, and instruction.

One is reminded of Plato's Phaedrus, a young man, perhaps no older than Rufus, in love with Lysias' style, who declares that he would rather be eloquent than rich (*Phaedrus* 228a) but fails to notice the problems with Lysias' argument until the more grownup Socrates points them out. Or the young Hippocrates in *Protagoras* who wants to study with Protagoras, knowing only that he is a famous sophist and that a sophist is a "knower of wise things" (by the tautological rationale that a *sophistês* knows *sophia*) and most importantly is "a master at making awesome speakers" (*epistatês tou poiêsai deinon legein;* 312d).[35] Again, the young man's attraction is to impressive utterance, without much exercise of phronetic judgment because he lacks the requisite knowledge and experience. He wants to learn to say awesome things like Protagoras does. Closer to home, Isocrates remarks that those who wish to study with him are "seized with emulous esteem" (*philotimôs diatetheien*) for "speaking well" (*pros to legein eu*); again, they wish to say wise-sounding, impressive things (*Antidosis* 278), though they do not yet possess the mature wisdom from which such statements can arise. What strikes such students first, what is most immediately accessible and attractive to them, and within their competence, is the outward stylistic face of the discourses they admire and wish to imitate. It is, in fact, this attraction to beautiful and impressive utterance that first identifies these *meirakia* as good candidates for rhetorical, and philosophical, training; these are the ones who quickly will absorb their models and zealously seek to emulate them. Perhaps more to the practical point, Aelius Theon remarks, as noted earlier, that instruction should start with what is easier, and that it is easier to amplify an undisputed statement than to demonstrate a disputed one, so that progymnasmatic exercises should at first be limited to techniques of amplification and stylistic play—for example, for "working up" a chreia—and should later move to refutation and confirmation exercises.[36]

One thinks, too, of Isocrates' apparent pedagogical progression from his parainetics and exercises in the stylistic manipulation of gnomic sayings—bits of authoritative wisdom to be amplified and restated in different ways—to more advanced kinds of discourse and more serious political deliberations on matters open to dispute. Both Isocrates and Dionysius, then, seem to presuppose a transitional phase of training that corresponds to the early-stage progymnasmata and focuses mostly on the *lektikos topos,* followed by gradually deepening studies in the *pragmatikos topos* (and declamation), perhaps followed by a return to the *lektikos topos,* and so on, in a widening spiral. One might, for example, "spiral" back at a later stage to something like Hermogenes' advanced study of "types" (*ideai*) of style, since these involve a synthesis of all aspects of the *lektikos topos* (diction, figures, rhythm) and are keyed to the "thoughts" or subject matter they express and, in the final chapters of Hermogenes' *On Types of Style*, to the decorum of practical and "panegyric" genres. Such studies are more appropriate to students who already have gained some expertise, through declamation, in the *pragmatikos topos,* as well as the different components of the *lektikos topos.* It seems that Dionysius' concern in the transitional phase is with establishing some basic habitual grooves for the composition of cadenced, dignified-sounding, well-shaped sentences, or what modern psychology might call a behavioral "envelope" for prose rhythm (into which other stylistic features can be placed), or in other words a nonrational, subconscious "feel" for it. If that is correct, what he was eliciting from his younger students was by modern standards quite extraordinary.

However that may be, the striking fact is that Dionysius' *On Composition,* which usually is regarded as his crowning achievement in "literary criticism," is clearly positioned at the beginning phase in rhetorical instruction, or as Casper de Jonge puts it, "between grammar and rhetoric."[37] It suggests a pedagogical sequence, though not a chronological one, imperfectly reflected in

Dionysius' extant writings: *On Composition* first, and the *Roman Antiquities* last, insofar as that text corresponds, probably, to a later, more advanced stage in the rhetor's education—the historical knowledge that augments practical intelligence and personal experience. Between these texts lie the "essays" of *On the Ancient Orators,* and the *Demosthenes* and *Thucydides,* while the letters' place is more ambiguous.

Rhetorical Criticism: The "Essays" and Letters

So what is the function of rhetorical criticism for Dionysius? If the central practices of rhetorical training involve rehearsal through reading, analysis, imitation, and exercises in original production, from progymnasmata to declamation, then a central issue for the rhetorical critic, and for the student, becomes the question of what to rehearse and internalize—or more precisely, which aspects of which models to acquire and for what reasons and which to avoid. This seems to have been the burden of discussion in the second book of *On Imitation,* which offered an inventory of recommended models, with commentary on which aspects of which were useful to imitate. The first book explained the general theory of imitation, while the third, which may never have been finished, was devoted to particular methods of exercise (*Letter to Gnaeus Pompeius* 3.1). The whole text seems clearly to have been intended as a resource for the teacher, a *technê;* in the classroom, the various models and their different virtues and limitations would have been examined in greater detail. That sort of examination is exemplified in the surviving critical "essays."

Rhetorical criticism, then, was the business of the "careful study" that intervened between "ready nature" (or talent and inclination) and the "laborious exercise" of imitation, emulation, and practice. Thus, for example, we hear in *Lysias* not only that Lysias's prose has a certain plain-style grace that is well worth acquiring but also that it lacks the emotive power of Demosthenes. It is best for narrating events and representing moral character (*êthos*) but not especially good for strong conclusions and emotional appeals. In matters of argumentation, Dionysius recommends that "readers of Lysias should imitate his invention and choice [*heuresis* and *krisis*] of enthymemes," but not his ways of "arranging" and "working up" arguments (*taxis* and *ergasia*), for which better models can be had from other writers (*Lysias* 13, 15).[38] On the other hand, the sophist and historian Hegesias of Magnesia, whom Dionysius describes as the "high priest" of contrived style and foolish invention, is not to be imitated in any way (*On Composition* 4, 18). Such judgments are generally backed up with examples, analysis, and argument in varying amounts, depending on Dionysius' audience and his purposes. This is the characteristic pattern of his criticism, and this pattern itself becomes an imitable, rehearsable model, on one hand for his students' critical engagement with the texts that they are studying, and on the other hand for rhetoricians using Dionysius' texts as resources for their own teaching.

One can certainly disagree with Dionysius' judgments, some of which seem wrongheaded now and were controversial in his day as well, such as his critique of Plato's style in the *Menexenus* (*Demosthenes* 23–30), which he is forced to defend in his *Letter to Gnaeus Pompeius.* The ancient objections, however, are not the same as the modern ones. Modern readers object that Dionysius fails to recognize that the funeral speech in *Menexenus* is intended ironically as a parody of the genre, but Pompeius also seems not to notice the parody and simply objects that Dionysius' criticism is disrespectful to the revered philosopher. Dionysius' point is that not everything in Plato needs to be so piously regarded, and that, in fact, Plato does not provide good models for funeral orations. But Dionysius' treatment of Plato is, in truth, rather catty: "O gods and spirits, where is that rich Platonic fountain, those grand constructions gushing forth? Does the wise man's mouth, that twelve-spouted spring, flow by such a trickle and talk such trifles?" (*Demosthenes* 28). This tone is really what Pompeius objects to. But whatever one thinks of Dionysius' specific judgments, the salient feature of his rhetorical criticism is precisely its orientation toward weighing and deciding the quality, desirability, or usefulness of various forms of rhetorical practice, with an eye to identifying what may best serve the purposes of the rhetor, or a rhetorical education meant to cultivate the possibilities of good deliberation and effective intervention in the various forums of public and private discourse.

One striking feature of Dionysius' critical writing is that, unlike most modern rhetorical criticism from Wichelns onward, it often displays surprisingly little interest in a detailed analysis of the historical contexts of specific texts. If he pays any attention to that at all, he generally contents himself with what might be found in a standard "hypothesis"—such as was used in school texts as a "headnote" for an oration or as the set problem for a declamation exercise—briefly outlining, often in a few sentences, the basic circumstances of the case.[39] Dionysius certainly is aware of the situationality of discourse, and of the overwhelming importance of timeliness, or *kairos,* to rhetorical effectivity. Indeed one of his favorite adjectives for inept rhetoric is *akairios,* "untimely." Moreover, Dionysius does display impressive powers of historical and philological scholarship, or of grammatical-hermeneutic analysis, when it suits his purposes, for example, when making judgments about the relationship between Aristotle's *Rhetoric* and the speeches of Demosthenes, or about the probable authorship of speeches attributed to one or another "ancient orator." And as the *Roman Antiquities* makes obvious, he certainly is capable of painstaking historical research. It's not that he can't do it. It's just that, for his purposes, he often is not interested in a rich hermeneutic of a text's particular function within a specific historical moment, insofar as the specifics of that moment are not generalizable or transferable to the present and are thus of no real relevance for current practice. Nor is Dionysius interested in formalistic, aesthetic appreciation as an end in itself, as if criticism were an exercise parallel to wine tasting, though he certainly does emphasize *aisthêsis* (sensation, sense perception). Rather, his ultimate interest as a rhetorical critic seems to fall on assessing and evaluating particular, imitable features of the rhetorical practices of certain writers for the effects that they have on audiences *now,* and thus for the desirability and usefulness that they may have for the rhetor *now.* With these general observations in mind, let us look at the essays and letters more closely.

On the Composition of Words

As already noted, from its opening line this text declares itself a birthday gift for seventeen-year-old Metilius Rufus, a young man who recently has begun his rhetorical studies: "And I, dear child, give to you this gift" (1). As Dionysius explicitly points out, the line is a quote from Homer (*Odyssey* 15.125), spoken by Helen to Telemachus at the end of his visit to Sparta as she presents him with a robe for his future bride and sends him on his way. The text, then, like the robe, is a farewell gift. Thus Dionysius not only gives the text an elegant literary opening but also connects immediately with the young man's grammatical training and looks forward to his journey on the long road to rhetoric and beyond that to adult responsibilities and, probably, a political career.[40] But Rufus of course is not the only intended audience. As Dionysius goes on, he points out that his gift is useful for everything in life that requires speech, but is most useful for "all who practice civic discourse" (*logos politikos*), especially "for you young men [*meirakia*] just now taking up the study" of it (1). So here the text presents itself as what I have called a "Proclus' bookcase" item—a supplement to, hornbook for, or memorandum of a course of study—and the audience appears as "you young men." Notably, Dionysius' presentation of the book as a parting gift figures it as a summation of a course already completed.

The text's closing, similarly, is an exhortation to Rufus and the student addressee to "keep [this book] constantly at hand, like any other really valuable thing, and train [*sunaskein*] yourself in daily exercises [*gumnasiai*]; for the precepts contained in handbooks [*technai*] cannot by themselves make brilliant advocates [*deinoi agônistai*] of those who hope to have such a career without practice [*meletê*] and exercise" (*gumnasia;* 26). One hears echoes of the *Rhetoric to Alexander's* exhortations, including the exhortation not to let the text slip abroad (lest the "Parian sophists" plagiarize it), and those of the *Rhetoric to Herennius,* urging Herennius to use the text as a supplement to his oral instruction and to keep up his regimen of exercise when the teacher cannot be with him. These are commonplaces of the Hellenistic *technê* tradition. The references to *gumnasiai* and *meletai* suggest that the addressee is or has been doing progymnasmata and may be moving to declamation. Again, this suggests that "Rufus" may already have completed the course of study that the book encapsulates. In sum, the book presents itself as a valuable keepsake, a review guide and supplement to the training process, a literary object to be kept in one's private library; the addressee, a beginning rhetoric student, is to keep it close by and be diligent about his exercises.

The opening salutations are followed by the introductory lesson already discussed, in which Dionysius parses rhetorical study into the *pragmatikos topos* and *lektikos topos,* focuses on the latter as most suitable for *meirakia,* and declares, "I offer you a song [*sumballomai soi melos*] on the composition of words" (*peri suntheseôs onomatôn; 1*). He then immediately remarks that "this subject occurred to few of the ancient writers of handbooks [*technai*] on rhetoric or dialectic, and noone up to the present day has carried out a detailed or even an adequate study of it, as I believe" (1), an interesting remark, considering the earlier and similar treatment of composition in Cicero's *Orator,* which surely is derived from Hellenistic sources but is less exhaustive than Dionysius' treatment. Dionysius then reverts to his address to Rufus, promising to write another book on the "selection" of words (the other part of the *lektikos topos,* concerned with diction and figures of speech). But the remark that no one yet has written an adequate *technê* on "composition" suggests that Dionysius also intends *On Composition* as a *technê* for an audience of rhetoricians, for whom the text would be both a teaching resource and a contribution to professional lore concerning "the things that can be taught," as Isocrates puts it. The text is thus a *technê* with a layered audience and layered purposes: Rufus, the ostensible addressee, and "young men" like him, for whom the text is a "Proclus' bookcase" item and a literary keepsake, and beyond them an audience of rhetoricians, "Procluses," for whom the text models a course of instruction that claims to supercede all previous approaches.

Dionysius completes his introduction by laying out the headings to be covered: what composition is, its effect, its aims and how it achieves them, its varieties and the *charaktêr* of each, and which are the most effective. "And besides these things" (*kai eti pros toutois*) he adds "poetic" rhythm in prose—a sort of ultimate compositional *charaktêr*—and, again, its nature, effects, and methods (1). This is the course of instruction, the syllabus.

The definition of composition is dealt with fairly quickly, again in the manner of an introductory lecture laying down basic axioms: "Composition is, as the name [*sunthesis,* "placing together"] makes clear, a sort of placing [*thesis*] beside each other of the parts of speech [*ta tou logou moria*], or what some call the elements of diction [*stoicheia tês lexeôs*]" (2). This is followed by a brief discursus on the "parts of speech" (and their number) recognized by various philosophers and grammarians: Aristotle, for example, thought there were three (nouns, verbs, and conjunctions); the Stoics thought there were four; others have theorized five, six, seven, and so on. This quick review serves mainly to show that there is no consensus and that "a discourse on these matters would not be short" (2); so the subject is dismissed. Whatever the parts of speech and their number may be, the important precept is that they combine to form "what are called *kôla*" (clauses, phrases), and clauses/phrases combine to form "what are called *periodoi*" (periods, sentences; 2). Evidently there is no need to precisely define these things or to debate competing definitions. A native speaker of Greek intuitively knows, "feels," *kôla* and *periodoi* as the main constituents of intelligible speech. One intuitively recognizes and produces these smaller and larger units bounded by pauses and marked by intonation, whether or not one can explain the syntactical intuition; it is a matter of know it when you hear it. (Thus things recognized as *kôla* may not always match our modern notion of "clause," which is a logical rather than a stylistic or compositional entity.) Dionysius' discussion in this segment is a model of good pedagogy, indeed, good lecturing. He keeps the student's attention focused on essential concepts while acknowledging but passing over theoretical complications—things that may be interesting in themselves as a matter of knowledge but that contribute little to the student's ability to develop skill in the *sunthesis* of words in well-formed *kôla* and *periodoi*. (Cicero's Antonius would approve.)

The next key point—moving to the second item in the syllabus (and a second short lecture?)—is that, though composition is the second part of the *lektikos topos* and "naturally" or logically follows the first, nevertheless it is more powerful in effect and more important (2). This assertion is illustrated with a number of comparisons to other arts, such as building, carpentry, and embroidery, in which the synthesis (composition, arrangement) of materials is more crucial to the effect than the materials themselves. A well-made chair, for example, is more impressive than the pile of materials it originally was made from, and more impressive too than a badly made chair composed of the same materials. The analogy appeals to the student's experiential common sense, but precisely how it applies to prose style may at this point not be clear to the beginner, so Dionysius says he will now give "proofs" (*pisteis;* 2). The first proof is a general observation that both poets and prose writers have chosen elegant words and striking metaphors to express their ideas but have spoiled the effect by combining them badly, that is, in clumsy or reader-unfriendly constructions. Examples are not given; this is something that the student is expected to recognize in his own experience as a reader.

The second proof is a practical demonstration meant to show "by what things [*ex hôn*] I was persuaded that composition is stronger [*kreitton*] and more important [*teleioteron*] than selection" (3). This takes the form of an examination of two sample passages: one from Homer (Odysseus in disguise breakfasting in the swineherd's hut, *Odyssey* 16.1–16) and one from Herodotus (the Gyges story, 1.8–10).[41] The passages are presented verbatim in the text: If we think of the text as a script for a lecture, or a representation or recording of one, they are *read out* with proper delivery and then discussed, as Aelius Theon specifies. The initial point of each sample passage, once it has been heard, is that "*everyone would testify*" on the basis of *aisthêsis* that it has persuasive charm and power, beauty and dignity (3). The student thus is asked, and expected, to *feel* the charm and power of Homer's and Herodotus' language. This directly felt effect is the starting point for instruction. But as Dionysius points out, in these passages the effect comes neither from the subject matter nor the choice of words. In Homer's case the subject matter is mundane, and in Herodotus' case it is sordid; and both use plain, ordinary diction. The point of course is that the felt charm and power of these passages come almost entirely from the rhythmic composition of the words. In Homer's case in particular, it is clear that "breaking up the meter will make these same lines appear to be ordinary and unworthy of emulation" (3); without the meter they become dull prose, discussing a low subject in forgettable language.

Thus far the student chiefly has been asked to critically reflect on passages that he probably has read before, in his grammatical training. This looks like a classroom activity, though the student could continue it on his own by reading and reflecting on other passages in the same way. The activity is mostly observational. The next proof looks more like a writing exercise. As Dionysius says, "So that one may perceive [*aisthêtai*] much more clearly how much power the faculty [*dunamis*] of composition has, in both verse and prose, I will take some passages [*lexeis*] that are considered good, and, by transposing [*metatheis*] their arrangements [*harmoniai*], I will make both the verse and the prose look different" (4).

This is, of course, the method of *metathesis,* "transposition," which modern commentators have recognized as a key technique in Dionysius' criticism. Casper de Jonge, who provides an overview of the commentary and makes a good case that Dionysius' handling of *metathesis* is more sophisticated than he generally has gotten credit for, observes that it is a kind of "language experiment intended to demonstrate the merits and defects, or more generally the particularities of a text," and that it is a widely used technique among Hellenistic grammarians.[42] We find it in use, as de Jonge points out, as early as Plato's *Phaedrus* (264d), where Socrates rearranges the lines of the "Midas epigram" to show that it makes no difference what order they are put in, and that the poem is therefore badly composed. *Metathesis* in the more general sense of "change" may also be applied to any rewriting of a text that changes the words, uses different figures of speech, and so on. *Metathesis* is therefore a flexible critical probe that can be used to bring out the subtle qualities of a text and its felt effects by seeing what difference transposition or rewriting makes.

That may be true—and certainly may be true of the Hellenistic *kritikoi* (grammarians) that Dionysius undoubtedly drew from—but it seems to assume that the goal of criticism is aesthetic appreciation. Dionysius does assume *aisthêsis,* "sense perception," as the natural *starting point* for rhetorical criticism and instruction, but the goal is instruction. *Metathesis* is a tool of pedagogy.[43] This is certainly the case in *Phaedrus,* for Socrates is not carrying out a bit of literary-critical research but is demonstrating to Phaedrus the importance of arrangement, or a certain kind of arrangement, for effective speech. Likewise, in *On Composition* Dionysius introduces *metathesis* as a form of exercise that will demonstrate to the student the power of composition and reveal its effects. As Dionysius shows, by rearranging the words in a series of passages from Homer, "While the choice of words remains unchanged, and only the arrangement of words is changed, the meters and rhythms change, and with them the figures [*schêmata*], the complexion, the character, the feeling, and the whole dignity of the poem" (4).

He then does the same with prose, showing that by merely rearranging the words and *kôla* of the opening passage of Herodotus' narrative he can change its tone from "leisurely and explanatory" to "direct and argumentative" (4). Other changes produce other effects. One "scheme of composition" (*schêma tou suntheseôs*), for example, is "Hegesiastic, affected, cheap, and limp-wristed," even though the words themselves are all the same. Whatever one thinks of Dionysius' judgments in this segment, the key points are, first, that he is presenting the student with a basic exercise that can be "tried at home"—that is, by playing with passages, rearranging them to see what differences the different arrangements make—and second, that he is not at this point imposing on the student a detailed stylistic criticism but only appealing to the general impression (the *aisthêsis*) that rearrangement *does* make a noticeable, felt difference, even if one cannot always clearly describe what the difference is or explain what causes it. As Dionysius later asserts, even the most uneducated audiences "naturally" feel and respond to the differences between rhythms, though they cannot explain it if asked: "Why so? Because the latter is a matter of knowledge [*epistêmê*], which not all share, but the former is a matter of feeling [*pathos*], which nature has given to everyone" (11).

Dionysius' opening exercise in *metathesis* is not unlike Erasmus' famous demonstration of 150 different ways to rewrite the sentence "Your letter pleased me very much" in *De Copia* (1.33); there is no close analysis of the different stylistic textures (moods, tones) that the different rewritings produce, but only a few brief comments that ask the student to observe that the changes do indeed make differences in form and feeling, from the businesslike to the elegant, the prosaic to the poetic, and the sublime to the ridiculous. Erasmus' demonstration, however, is something of a free-for-all tour de force that involves not only re-arrangement but also changes in diction and figuration—that is, all aspects of the *lektikos topos*. It performs a summative role in Erasmus' discussion, showing how the stylistic elements discussed in the preceding thirty-two chapters can be applied and combined. Dionysius more modestly intends to establish in the student's mind the specific principle that the composition of words in different rhythmic and syntactical constructions, with no change to the words themselves, makes a great difference to the effect they produce; and this principle is established through an appeal to the student's direct sensory experience, or "feeling." One can easily imagine that Dionysius ended his lecture, at this point, by assigning some exercises in *metathesis* for the "afternoon work," and that, like Erasmus, the student might have had some fun with it, producing rewrites that varied from the solemn and dignified to Hegesiastic frippery.[44]

Having taught this basic point concerning the impact of composition, Dionysius begins to turn toward the third item—the means by which composition accomplishes its effects. Here the discussion will increase its investment in technical *minutiae* dramatically. But first, he remains in a sort of holding pattern while the established lesson is amplified and reinforced. He begins with a summary reassertion of it, comparing composition to Athena transforming Odysseus to make him look now like an old beggar, now like a handsome young man, and so on (4). Then he turns to the tale of his failure to find anything useful in the grammarians' and philosophers' accounts of the "rules" of logical or natural word order (4–5) discussed earlier. Dionysius' account, long enough to be a short lecture in itself, resembles the earlier discursus on theories of the "parts of speech," and Dionysius' presentation of it as a serio-comic narrative of his futile search suggests a student audience. The length at which the point is made, however, also suggests an audience of rhetoricians, and an intent to make an Antonius-like argument about the relevance of Hellenistic linguistic theory to rhetorical training. As with the earlier digression on parts of speech, the theory and its attendant disputes are marked as interesting enough, an intellectual way to occupy one's leisure, but not really helpful for the purpose of developing an effective prose style.

Dionysius then says he will "return to the starting hypothesis from which I digressed into those matters" (5)—a proposition that the celebrated "ancient poets, historians, philosophers, and rhetors . . . had an art [*technê*] and precepts [*theôrêmata*], by means of which they composed well" (5). This is a new "lecture." Dionysius lays down what the core precepts are: "It seems to me that compositional expertise [*hê sunthetikês epistêmê*] has three tasks [*erga*]. The first is to see what joined to what will naturally produce a noble [*kalê*] and pleasing [*hêdeia*] combination. The second is to judge [*gnônai*] how each of the things that are to be joined together should be configured [*schêmatisthen*] to make the combination seem better [*kreittona phainesthai*]. And the third is to judge whether any of the materials that have been put together should be modified—I mean, by subtraction [*aphairesis*], addition [*prosthêkê*], and alteration [*alloiôsis*]—and to work them up properly with regard to their intended use" (6).[45]

This framework follows from what has already been demonstrated to the student about composition's effectivity and the means of acquiring and developing "expertise." Again, the starting point is *aisthêsis*, one's experience as a reader or listener, closely followed by analysis. The student is, first, to note striking "combinations" that seem "noble" and aesthetically pleasing, and to observe what is joined to what. The second and third *erga* are writing activities. With a set of ideas/words in mind, one is to choose which way of ordering and combining them—in a phrase, clause, or sentence—is most euphonious and suitable to one's purpose, an activity that, for those composing in Greek, has many options and thus requires the student to experiment via *metathesis,* considering what ways the words can be arranged. Then, having chosen the best available combination, the student is to further consider how its components can be individually modified to improve or heighten the effect. (The word for "combining" here is *harmozein,* "join or fit together"; there is an implicit metaphor of "joinery," as in a craftsman closely fitting pieces of wood together.)

Both of these writing activities are illustrated, the former in rather general terms, but the latter in concrete detail at the level of metaplasms (subtraction, addition, and modification of letters or syllables in single words). For example, the combination *eis toúton ton agôna* (to this trial) can be altered to *eis toutonì ton agôna*, which does not change the essential meaning but sounds better and has more impact.[46] The circumflex (rising/falling) pitch accent in *agôna* remains on the long *ô,* but the addition of *i* to *touton* shifts the accent to the end of the word, breaks up the awkward, unaccented repetition of *ton-ton,* and subtly reconfigures the overall rhythmic shape and emphasis of the phrase (its *schêma*) as well as its "music" or tonality.[47] (There seems to be more emphasis on "this," *toutonì,* which in turn seems to invest "this trial" with greater dignity.) Other such examples are given, illustrating subtraction and modification, such as, for the latter, changing *luthêsetai* (he will be ransomed) to *lelusetai* (he will have been ransomed) for the sake of word joinery that is "more beautiful and more suitable to the purpose" (6). The point here is not the subtle, negligible shift in meaning from a future to a future perfect form of the verb, but improving the overall sound of the phrase it is part of. Dionysius then does the same with whole clauses—rearranging and modifying the *kôla* of sentences from Thucydides and Demosthenes—thereby demonstrating that what he has illustrated at the very minimal and easy-to-observe level of metaplasms applies as well to larger and more complex syntactical units (7). For the most part, still, he does not explain the causes of the different effects these changes produce but simply notes that they produce them. His purpose still is to lay down basic principles, here regarding in particular the second and third *erga* of compositional expertise, the joining and modification of elements for optimum effect, and to have the student exercise with them and observe the effects.

This demonstration with its associated exercises leads—in what looks like the opening of another short "lecture"—to the question, "Such is the theory [*theôria*] concerning the fitting together of clauses; but what about their configuration [*schêmatismon*]?" (8). This produces yet another brief digression on grammatical theory, this time concerning the different types of utterances, such as statement, question, prayer, command, dilemma, supposition, and so on, and the various forms of diction in which they might be cast, leading once again to the conclusions that "long is the discourse and deep is the study concerning these things," that the various possible forms of clauses and diction are virtually infinite in number, and that it is enough simply to note this infinite variability (8). This is a principle that a student who has been doing *metathesis* exercises would easily find persuasive at this point. So the topic of rules for clause configuration is dismissed in favor of a discussion of methods for the lengthening or shortening of clauses, that is, the addition or subtraction of material (9). Presumably this discussion too would be accompanied by exercises, for which it provides a model: the "making long things short and short things long" attributed originally to Isocrates.[48]

Dionysius now turns to the third heading of his "syllabus"—the aims of composition and how they are achieved—and thus to the technical heart of the subject: "It seems to me that there are two things that those who compose both poetry and prose should aim at: pleasure [*hêdonê*] and nobility" (*to kalon,* literally "the beautiful and good"), because "the sense of hearing (*akoê*) craves them" and is satisfied by them (10).[49] That is, these are things that the human psyche naturally responds to, educated or uneducated, and that give style its grace and power. Both of these qualities are composed of other elements, of which "the most important and effective" (*ta kuriôtata kai ta kratista*) are "melody, rhythm, and variation, and appropriateness with all three" (11). Further, pleasure and nobility have subsidiary qualities:

Pleasure (*hêdonê*)	Nobility (*to kalon*)
Freshness (*hôra*)	Magnificence/impressiveness (*megaloprepeia*)
Grace (*charis*)	Gravity (*to baros*)
Euphony (*eustomia*)	Solemnity (*semnologia*)
Sweetness (*glukutês*)	Dignity (*axiôma*)
Persuasiveness (*to pithanon*)	Age (*pinos*)

Hôra here broadly signifies timeliness, seasonability, the "bloom" of a season or of youth, and generally "beauty" in the sense of briefly blooming liveliness, flourish, elegance, freshness. Along with grace, euphony, sweetness, and persuasiveness, it contributes to a style that is aesthetically pleasant and attractive.[50] *Pinos,* which literally means "dirt," signifies the patina of age on an old statue or, by extension, the weathered face, full of character, of a respected elder or a senior politician. The point is that a style with a patina of "age"—a slightly old-fashioned, slightly battered finish—is consistent with such qualities as dignity, solemnity, gravity, and impressiveness, and with them is conducive to an overall impression of nobility. The best style will mix both pleasure and nobility, achieving both through the appropriate melodies, rhythms, and variations.

This discussion in some ways seems to prefigure Hermogenes' *On Types of Style,* with its breakdown of types and subtypes—such as "grandeur" with its subtypes of solemnity, asperity, vehemence, and so on—and the resolution of each into its technical constituents.[51] Dionysius, however, and again, is focused strictly on composition, and seems at this point less interested in classifying types and subtypes and systematically describing their technical elements. His list of qualities contributing to pleasure and nobility is presented as merely illustrative. This difference is perhaps further evidence that Dionysius' *On Composition* and Hermogenes' *On Types* have in mind students at different levels: Dionysius beginners, Hermogenes the advanced.

Next comes a discussion (another short lecture?) on "melody" in spoken language, how it is constituted in Greek by rising and falling pitch accents and the musical interval between them, which Dionysius estimates to be approximately a fifth, and how "melody" in speech differs from that in music. In music the "natural" pitch accents of words can be modified to suit the melody. As Dionysius points out, in the lyric sung by Electra to the Chorus in Euripides' *Orestes,* the "words *síga síga leukón* [silent, silent, lightly (step)] are sung on one note" although each *síga* "naturally" contains a rising and falling tone, and *leukón* a rising tone on its final syllable (11). In speech the reverse is true. The "melody" of speech depends on the "natural" pitch accents of the words and how the words are arranged; arrangement determines melody. To comprehend this explanation the student must already know something about pitch accent and music—for example, what are the musical intervals constituting a "fifth" and how the songs and choruses in *Orestes* are supposed to be sung—which he would have learned in his elementary education. What is new to the student, probably, is the notion that speech has melody; the transfer of musical terminology to speech, with awareness of the differences in application; and the connection of all this to composition. Dionysius then does the same with rhythm: Words in Greek are "naturally" composed of long and short syllables, depending on the length of vowels, consonant combinations, and so on, but in song these values can be altered to suit the rhythm. In speech the "natural" values must be maintained, so that the rhythm of long and short syllables arises from the arrangement of the words. All this discussion of melody and rhythm leads to the conclusion that "a civic style [*lexis politikê*] can by its composition please [*hêdunousa*] the listener through the melody of its tones, its measured rhythms, its variegated changes, and its appropriateness to the subject" (11).

My concern is less with the specifics of Dionysius' account of composition in Greek than with his general pedagogical approach. Suffice it to say that, up to this point, and beyond, the student presumably is applying Dionysius' lessons to the three tasks (*erga*) of "compositional expertise" in his reading and writing exercises, especially to exercises in *metathesis,* as he writes and rewrites bits of prose, rearranging, altering, adding and subtracting, and observing the differences each rewriting makes to the melody, rhythm, variation, appropriateness, and general impression of the language—whether it is aptly "pleasant" and "noble," attractive and impressive, charming and dignified. Meanwhile, the lessons continue. Dionysius argues that the aesthetic effects produced by composition reside in the sounds of syllables and "letters" (phonemes), which in different combinations can sound harsh or smooth, slow or quick, resonant or thin, pleasant or unpleasant, and so on. One should choose words that are "melodic, rhythmic, and euphonious," or mix such words with less attractive ones when those are unavoidable (12), and the same holds true for words and sounds conducive to nobility (13).

From here, then, begins a long lesson (at least one lecture) on the letters of the Greek alphabet, their specific sound qualities, and how they are to be pronounced (14). For example, the letters τ (*t*), θ (*th*), and δ (*d*) are all pronounced "with the tongue pressed against the top part of the mouth near the upper front teeth, and the breath puffed out and provided an exit downward around the teeth." This discussion, which provides some of our best information about the ancient pronunciation of classical Greek, may be motivated by the fact that Dionysius is addressing Romans, who may have a decent reading knowledge of Greek from their basic education but do not pronounce it especially well and thus are inattentive to the fine-grained texture of how it sounds. However, it also seems likely that Dionysius' purpose is, even with those with good or native-Greek pronunciation, to get past the elementary knowledge of "the sounds of the alphabet," a subject for young children, and to focus attention on the sheer physicality of the elemental sounds of which language is composed and their relation to the "natural" and indeed bodily responses of audiences to the phonetic textures of sung or spoken words: the open-mouthed resonance of a broad *a,* the smoothness of a liquid consonant, the harshness of a double consonant such as ξ (*ks*) and ζ (*zd*), and so on. This long discussion of letters leads to an even longer discussion (15–16, which looks like two lectures) on the *syllables* they compose, their different relative lengths, their specific phonetic qualities, and the ways they can be "woven" together in rhythmic, melodic sequences to render different "feelings" (*pathê;* 15). As Dionysius summarily puts it, "What is the main theme [*kephalaion*] of this argument of mine? That the power [*dunamis*] of the syllables arises from the weaving together of the letters, and the multiform nature of the words arises from the composition [*sunthesis*] of the syllables" (16).

This progression from letters to the syllables they compose, and from syllables to words, again matches the sequence of elementary literacy training.[52] Once more, Dionysius' intent appears to be not simply to revisit that material but to refocus attention closely on specific sound textures and the effects they produce while reinvoking a familiar and already deeply ingrained educational framework. The lecture in these sections is filled out with examples, all drawn from Homer, illustrating the point that poets select and combine words with letters and syllables whose phonetic textures reinforce the mood of what is being said: pleasant-sounding words with open vowels and smooth consonants for pleasant things, and harsh-sounding words (with lots of ξ [*ks*] and ζ [*zd*], and the like) for harsh, austere, or unpleasant things, such as the clashing sounds of battle. (This point about harsh words does not contradict what has previously been said about composing with melodically and rhythmically pleasant and noble words and "mixing" them with unavoidably ugly words; one can produce an effect of austere nobility with harshly clashing sounds appropriately used.)

Finally, in addition to the examples he presents, says Dionysius, "There are many others that you will find when collecting for yourself" (16).[53] The student, as before, is presumed to be doing "homework" in the first *ergon* of compositional expertise—observing the notable effects *he feels* in particular passages in his reading, "collecting" or copying those passages, and studying how the particular phonetic textures of the words contribute to those effects—while also doing exercises in the second and third *erga* with *metathesis*.

Having now presented the means of producing pleasant and noble "melody" (from the composition of phonetic textures and rising and falling pitch in sung and spoken language) Dionysius turns again to rhythm, greatly expanding the topic with a detailed technical discussion of the nature of poetic meter, prose rhythm, and the relationship and differences between them (17–18). The starting premise is that the words in spoken prose retain their "natural" rhythm (the alternation of long and short syllables) and that all words longer than a monosyllable fall into distinct types of rhythmic form, and these are the prose equivalents of feet in poetic meter. A disyllabic word, for example, may take one of four metrical forms:

Two shorts	˘ ˘	Pyrrhic (or hegemon)
Two longs	— —	Spondee
A short and a long	˘ —	Iambus
A long and a short	— ˘	Trochee

The same is true for trisyllabic words, which admit several more types of metrical form (such as the dactyl,— ˘ ˘, a long and two shorts), and so on. In all, says Dionysius, there are twelve basic rhythms arising from the metrical forms, or feet, that words naturally can take, and these compose the *meter* of a *line of verse,* or the *rhythm* of a *kôlon* in prose. The point is not that prose *kôla* are composed "in" meter, like lines of verse—they aren't and shouldn't be—but that spoken prose *contains* meter naturally and by composition can arrange the metrical forms of its words in flexible and varied rhythmic sequences. It is possible, for example, to construct a phrase or clause in predominantly "pyrrhic" rhythm by using predominantly disyllabic words with short syllables.[54] A pyrrhic rhythm, says Dionysius, can be neither impressive nor solemn, whereas dactylic rhythms are conducive to nobility and solemnity. Prose composition generally should aim at such effects as impressiveness, solemnity, high-mindedness, dignity, grandeur, nobility, and the like (18). These *theôrêmata* are then illustrated by analyses of noble and solemn rhythms in Thucydides, Plato, and Demosthenes. The absence of such qualities is illustrated with a long historical passage describing Alexander's sack and massacre of Gaza from the hapless Hegesias of Magnesia, who is said to be "foremost, middlemost, and last" in the writing of rhythmically clueless, "weak, disjointed, deformed and shapeless" prose (18); Hegesias' poor prose is then compared to the solemn dignity of a seventeen-line passage from Homer's *Iliad* describing Achilles' desecration of Hector's corpse.[55]

Dionysius does provide some rhythmic/metrical analysis of the passages in question, but not a highly detailed analysis. The student is expected initially to feel without explanation the solemnity, nobility, impressiveness, or lack thereof, of each passage's rhythm, while Dionysius' comments illustrate how metrical analysis can be used to parse the rhythm, explicate the causes of that feeling, and guide the student's efforts at imitation so that the deeper structure of the rhythm can be imitated and acquired without superficially copying the language or phraseology of the original. Again, this seems to model what the student should be doing in his own activities of collecting impressive passages, studying them, and doing exercises.

Having now discussed at some length melody and rhythm in prose, Dionysius works fairly quickly (in two lectures?) through the two remaining topics of his discussion of "the aims of composition and how it attains them": variation and appropriateness (19–20). The point of variation is that poetry, constrained by the repetition of melody and meter (from strophe to strophe, or line to line), has a limited capacity for variation, whereas prose has great freedom—as shown by the examples of Herodotus, Plato, and Demosthenes, and the counterexample of Isocrates and his followers, who used insufficient variety in their rhythms. The former are to be imitated on this point, the latter not. No passages are examined; the examples are simply mentioned, and the student is to observe their variegated rhythms or lack thereof for himself.

Appropriateness, which Dionysius introduces as too large a subject to be fully dealt with in this book, is discussed at slightly greater length, with two main points. The first, which is simply declared and not demonstrated—because it does not need to be and because the exemplification would be endless—is that composition should produce melodies and rhythms that properly reflect the speaker's state of mind; angry people and cheerful people, for example, should speak in different rhythms and melodies with different composition. The second point, which reflects the earlier discussion of melody reflecting subject matter, is discussed at greater length and given more illustration. "The good poet or rhetor" should compose in rhythms that reflect or "echo" the things described. When describing Sisyphus straining to roll his rock uphill, for example, the rhythm, and the melody, should sound labored, as in Homer (*Odyssey* 11.593–596).[56]

There follows a partly mutilated transitional passage (interrupted by a lacuna) which caps the long (multilecture) discussion of "aims and methods" and points forward to the two remaining topics that Dionysius originally set up in his "syllabus"—the different kinds of composition, and "what makes prose seem like a poem while remaining in the form of prose, and what makes poetic style resemble prose while maintaining the dignity of poetry" (20). This passage, however, feels much like a conclusion, as if the basic course has been completed and what follows is a more advanced supplement. This is apparent in two ways. First, Dionysius summarily declares, "Of the things that should be aimed at by those intending to create a composition [*sunthesis*] that is pleasing and noble in both poetry and prose, those that I have discussed in my opinion are the most important and effective," and adds that there are other "things" that he could not include in the present treatise but will introduce "in our daily exercises" (*en tais kath' hêmeran gumnasiais*) with examples from poets, historians, and orators. This gesture matches that made by Pseudo-Dionysius in the final lines of his lecture *On Mistakes Made in Declamation:* "These are the most obvious things. A greater number have been passed over, which our discussions will point out."[57] Interestingly, Dionysius' use of this gesture not only suggests that the main topics have now been covered but also clearly characterizes his "lecturing" as a prelude to daily schoolroom exercise and foregrounds the nature of *On Composition* as a *technê*.

The second way in which the "concluding" nature of this passage is apparent is Dionysius' forecast of the remainder of the book: "Now, when I have added [*prostheis*] the remaining matters that I promised, and that are not at all less necessary to discuss, I will bring my discourse [*logos*] to an end" (20). This gesture performs the double function of asserting, on one hand, the importance of the "remaining" matters that were promised, and, on the other hand, figuring them as a sort of supplemental ("prosthetic") digression before the conclusion of the course of study. They are important parts of the additional matters to be addressed "in our daily exercises." In short, this transitional passage figures the basic course as functionally complete at this point; what follows is a supplemental short course in some more-advanced matters.

So, then, Dionysius discusses the types of composition (21–24) and prose that resembles lyric verse and lyric verse that resembles prose (25–26). These discussions are perhaps the most interesting parts of *On Composition,* but I do not intend to discuss them in detail here. Suffice it to say that, in the first discussion, Dionysius presents an account of three basic compositional types—the austere (*austêra*), the polished (*glaphura*), and the well-blended (*eukraton*)—which appears to be a more developed version of his earlier account of nobility and pleasure in prose melody and rhythm. (The polished is the pleasant, the charming; the austere is the noble, the dignified.) These types also appear, superficially, to be a reinterpretation of the then-traditional Theophrastean notion of grand, plain, and middle styles; however, the "polished" type of composition seems more akin to the middle style, and in general the alignment with the Theophrastean triad is problematic. What Dionysius presents in fact seems more akin to the sort of analysis that appears in Hermogenes' *On Types of Style,* and probably anticipates it. For example, just as Hermogenes makes the ultimate style (*deinotês,* "forcefulness," the supremely skillful style) arise from the apt mixing of all the other types of style, Dionysius makes "well-blended" composition arise from the mixture of the austere and polished types and declares it the best and most effective kind. Each of Dionysius' compositional types is illustrated with examples from the poets, history writers (especially Thucydides), and orators (especially Demosthenes) and analyzed in greater detail than in the earlier lectures, though the terms of analysis remain essentially the same (phonetic sound textures and melody; metrical forms and rhythm). Each of these discussions is long and detailed enough to be conceived as a short lecture that would be followed by more work in "daily exercises."

Much the same is true in the discussion of poetic prose and proselike poetry: Dionysius expands his earlier discussion of metrical forms and rhythms with a more in-depth analysis of examples, particularly of Demosthenes, whose rhythms are shown to incorporate metrical forms with such frequency and skill that it could not, as Dionysius maintains, be accidental. Thus the most powerful kind of composition in civic discourse, which is that of Demosthenes, is shown to deliberately deploy all possible rhythmic forms with consummate adroitness and effect. (This is "well-blended" rhythm.) Likewise, the most effective kind of poetry is that which approximates the rhythmic variability of prose by composing in *kôla* that cut across the boundaries of the metered line: the poem maintains its metrical and strophic form, while its sentences operate according to the principles of prose rhythm. (The worst poetry, by implication, is doggerel in which the rhythm is always the same as the meter.) In keeping with its rhetorical character as a "digression" before the conclusion, this discussion also includes the "objection" from "certain people" who lack education and who practice "the vulgar sort of rhetoric without art or method" and are incredulous that Demosthenes could have composed his words with such elaborate care (25), to which Dionysius replies with several arguments, including anecdotes about the care with which Plato and Isocrates composed, and the comparison to learning grammar and its internalization as a cultivated habitude, which I already have discussed.

While these "supplemental digressions" carry into deeper detail the principles discussed in the more "basic" part of *On Composition,* Dionysius also emphasizes that he still is discussing his examples in more or less summary ways. As he says at the start of his discussion of austere, polished, and well-blended composition, "At this point the subject calls for many examples taken from each of the authors mentioned ... but then this composition would seem excessively long, and more scholastic [*scholikon*] than preceptive" (*parangelmatikon;* 21). He thus emphasizes the status of the text as a *technê* in the form of a literary representation of a course of study, as opposed to a scholastic treatise such as might be produced in the philosophical schools or by Alexandrian scholarship. Such a text would aim at exhaustive demonstration of its theoretical claims. This does not mean that he has composed a "merely" pedagogical treatise or that he is Norden's "dumb schoolmaster" who can only crib from scholastic treatises and cannot equal or produce them. As Dionysius has made clear at several points, he has consulted the available scholastic literature and found it not especially useful for the purpose of cultivating stylistic skill in rhetorical beginners such as Metilius Rufus. Instead he has offered an analysis, apparently structured as a sequence of short lectures meant to be accompanied by daily exercises, designed to give the student an apparatus by which he can sharpen his perception of the literature that impresses him—the examples by poets, historians, philosophers, orators he has been collecting—and acquire its *charaktêr* through "patient study and laborious exercise," so that it becomes internalized as habitude, as part of his "intuitive" rhetorical competence, his *dunamis,* and can be deployed in apt, "well-blended" ways in performances of his own. *On Composition* presents Dionysius as a brilliant enough teacher that one can grasp why Aelius Theon would call him "great."

The Ancient Orators: Lysias, Isocrates, and Isaeus

The introduction and the "essays" on Lysias, Isocrates, and Isaeus are what remains of this text, which originally was to include Demosthenes, Hyperides, Aeschines, and a second volume on the historians "if there is time" (*Ancient* 4). Dionysius' *On the Style of Demosthenes* and *On Thucydides* are possibly part of this project, but most likely not in their present form. I already have noted how the

Lysias embodies the general paradigm for the others—examination of the *rhêtôr* in an "Isocratean" manner according to the *lektikos topos* first and the *pragmatikos topos* second, with attention to which features to imitate and acquire, and which to avoid—but here there is more to say.

First, there is the question of what sort of document these texts are, who they are intended for, and how they are meant to be used. The introductory piece addresses itself to "my most distinguished Ammaeus" (*ô kratiste Ammaie*), to whom Dionysius addresses also the *Demosthenes* and two letters. Ammaeus' precise identity is unknown,[58] but the epithet *kratiste* suggests a person of high rank, perhaps a holder of a political post, and thus possibly a literary patron.[59] Near the end of his introduction Dionysius remarks that "what one should take from each orator, and what one should avoid, are excellent and necessary precepts [*kala theôrêmata kai anankaia*] for those who study political philosophy" (4). "Study" here is *askeô,* "exercise, practice, train," as in *askêsis,* which figures both Ammaeus and the intended audience as either those at the more advanced level of rhetorical study—people of some maturity and experience for whom the study and practice of the *pragmatikos topos* is appropriate—or those already actively engaged in political affairs, for whom "political philosophy" is a discipline (*askêsis*) that consists of doing rhetoric in practical situations and who retain a cultured interest rhetorical and literary matters. Elsewhere, Dionysius addresses his letters "to my dearest Ammaeus" (*Ammaiôi tôi philtatôi*), which says little about rank but does suggest a relationship between intellectual (if not social) equals.

None of the three surviving "essays," however, addresses itself explicitly to Ammaeus. In the *Lysias,* Dionysius says, "Perhaps it is not necessary to say *to those who know* [*pros eidotas*] that Lysias' style is persuasive and convincing, and seems very natural and retains all the qualities of naturalness—for that already is common knowledge, and there is no one who does not agree, having learned both from experience and from instruction [*kai peirai kai akoêi*] that Lysias is the most persuasive of all orators" (10; emphasis added).

Here the audience is figured as persons already familiar with the canonic orators, and with the usual lessons taught about Lysias, namely, the naturalness and persuasiveness of his style, the things that "everybody" who has had a rhetorical education knows. The phrase "experience and instruction" also indicates rhetorical training: the student's direct experience (*peira*) of Lysianic eloquence, which can include both reading and "experimenting" with it through *metathesis* and other exercises and his "hearing" (*akoê*) of the rhetorician's commentary. Speaking of Lysias' handling of narrative, Dionysius says, "This is the part [of an oration] that I would advise everyone to practice [*askein*] when doing exercises [*poioumenos tas gumnasias*] in the Lysianic examples" (18). This can be understood as an address to those who will be doing the recommended exercises, whether young students or mature practitioners who wish to continue honing their skills, but it also can be understood as an address to rhetoricians supervising their students' exercises and who know what "the Lysianic examples" are.[60] A little further on, as Dionysius is summing up "the Lysianic character" (*ho Lusiou charaktêr*), he declares, "If anyone has formed a different judgment of these things, let him say so" (20). This suggests an audience with some expertise and definite opinions concerning the stylistic and argumentational characteristics of Lysias. Further, Dionysius follows this remark with a full-length reading of and commentary on Lysias' oration *Against Diogeiton,* after which he concludes the essay with, "But [this is] enough examples already, if we are to discuss the rest of the orators in the same fashion" (34). This suggests a somewhat more "scholastic" kind of treatise than a "preceptive" one, insofar as the motive seems to be an ampler though still not exhaustive demonstration of a critical point about Lysias. Within the text, then, Dionysius seems to address an audience of mature persons who already have completed the basic rhetorical education—whether active politicians/rhetors or rhetoricians—on the question of what aspects of the canonic rhetors should be studied, exercised in, and acquired.

Oddly, though, each essay begins with a short biographical note on each orator: "Lysias was the son of Cephalus, who was of Syracusan ancestry . . ."; "Isocrates was an Athenian, born in the eighty-sixth Olympiad when Lysimachus was Archon at Athens . . ."; "Isaeus was the teacher of Demosthenes and became famous mostly for that reason." Who among "those who know" the lore of rhetoric needs to be told these things? Biographies of the major fourth-century Athenian orators had been available for centuries. Perhaps it is merely conventional, but these openings that rehearse the sorts of things that most but not all educated grownups might recall from school also suggest something like a public lecture.[61] All three essays are, in fact, approximately the length of a one-hour speech: *Lysias* takes roughly seventy-five minutes to read aloud; *Isocrates,* sixty-five; and *Isaeus,* fifty-five. These lengths might be compared with the two lectures falsely attributed to Dionysius—*On Mistakes Made in Declamation* and *On the Assessment of Speeches*—which more clearly are schoolroom lectures. The two are nearly the same length, averaging roughly twenty-eight minutes each for delivery.[62] The discourses of *On the Ancient Orators,* at roughly double that length, seem longish for the schoolroom, or at least a schoolroom of beginners where the emphasis is on getting to the exercises, but quite suitable for an audience of "those who know" in an *ôdeion* or *theatron*. Their length is comparable to the text of Aelius Aristides' Sicilian Orations, which certainly are meant for "concert" performance and take approximately forty-five minutes to deliver, not including the time for the informal preliminary talk or *lalia* that conventionally preceded the declamation proper.

Moreover, all three discourses in *On the Ancient Orators* make references to "the time." Dionysius ends the *Isocrates,* for example, by declaring that he could present more examples of the rhetor's *charaktêr,* "but perhaps I must keep an eye on the time" (*anangkê de isôs stochazesthai chronou;* 20). One wonders if this remark is an indirect acknowledgment that he ran a bit long in the preceding lecture on Lysias. Nearly the same gesture, however, appears there too: many more things could be discussed, "but, keeping an eye on the time [*stochazomenos chronou*], I will omit them" (*Lysias* 10). Midway through the *Isaeus,* he mentions that there are many more examples of Isaeus' handling of narrative that he could discuss, "but I do not have time [*chronos*] to discuss all of them" (15).

Further, Dionysius tends to refer to his text as a *logos,* a "speech," rather than a written "composition" (for example, *sungramma, suntaxis*), as at the end of *Isaeus:* "I shall make a new start to my *logos,* and speak [*legôn*] of Demosthenes, Hyperides, and Aeschines" (20). He does, however, also speak of writing his *logos:* "If I had decided to write [*graphein*] about all [the notable ancient orators], my *logos* would have become incoherent" (*Isaeus* 20). In short, the essays of *On the Ancient Orators* present themselves as the written/published text of a series of probably public lectures, with a particular argument to make, composed for a mixed audience of educated grownups interested in rhetorical-critical issues: active practitioners, rhetoricians, advanced students, cultured persons generally, and the curious.

Finally, the essays of *On the Ancient Orators* display the features of good lecturing style that Malcolm Heath remarks in the two lectures falsely attributed to Dionysius: an opening statement of the "organizing framework," "reinforcement by repetition," "sign-posting" and "summary" for each point, clear transitions, and a recapitulation at the end.[63] In Dionysius' *Isaeus,* for example, there is the opening biographical note, which in this case is very short (1); an announcement that Dionysius will discuss the *charaktêr* of Isaeus' oratory, followed by the observation that he modeled his speech on that of Lyias (2), an assertion that the two are nevertheless distinguishable in both style (*hêrmeneia,* "expression") and subject matter (*pragmata*), and a declaration that Dionysius will give his views on both heads, starting with style (*lexis*) because this is the point of greatest similarity (2). This is followed by a comparison of the two orators' stylistic traits, arguing that Lysias is more natural and Isaeus more elaborate in ways that anticipate Demosthenes but that also can make him seem tricky and insincere (3–4). This point is illustrated with a reading and discussion of several proemia by Isaeus and Lysias—a discussion fortified by the use of *metathesis* to bring out the differences made by the two orators' stylistic choices (5–11); the point is then reemphasized with another collection of passages to be compared (12–13) and then restated as a conclusion: "What need is there to prolong this with more examples? One will find many instances in which the speeches of Isaeus differ from the style of Lysias in both composition [*sunthesis*] and figuration [*schêmatismos*], while resembling the brilliance [*deinotês*] of Demosthenes" (13).

The next major segment is then introduced by hearkening back to the original outline: "I will say, too, concerning his subject matter, that he is more clever [*deinoteros*] than Lysias in the arrangement [*oikonomia*] of both the whole speech and of its parts, and he does nothing without the artistry [*technê*] that Demosthenes later used" (14). Dionysius remarks that "there is no space" to give examples of everything (14) but discusses Isaeus' distinctive handling of the parts of the oration in general terms (14–15). He then summarizes his opinions on this matter, remarks on Isaeus's differences from Lysias, and declares, "If I must give examples, lest anyone think me to speak without proof," he will now present a passage from the speech that Isaeus wrote for a certain Euphiletus in a case over citizenship rights (15–16). After sketching the *hupothesis* (case) of the speech (16), Dionysius reads out its proof section in full (17). Then, without making any comment on the passage, he concludes by summing up the central difference between the orators: "Lysias strives more for sincerity [*alêtheia*, "truthfulness"], Isaeus for artistry [*technê*]; the former aims to be graceful [*charieis*], the latter to be forceful" (*deinos;* 18). As Heath remarks of Pseudo-Dionysius, Dionysius lays out his heads, develops them methodically, provides redundant exemplification, summarizes and reiterates his points, clearly signposts the stages of his discussion, and tidily sums up.

The essays of *On the Ancient Orators*, then, present themselves as the published text of a set of *logoi* that probably were delivered as public lectures for an educated audience. Possibly they were lectures for an advanced course in rhetoric, or, as with *On Composition*, a literary representation of such a course, but the length of each *logos*—longer than a schoolroom lecture, shorter than a *technê,* but suitable for performance in a *theatron*—suggests otherwise. Since only the first three *logoi* have survived, one can only speculate about what overall *logos* the complete set of six was meant to constitute—the *logos* that Dionysius says he must defend from becoming incoherent. The surviving three form a sort of progression from the pleasant, clear, charming, and practical style of Lysias, to the ornate, dignified, and rather poetic style of Isocrates, to, in Isaeus, something of a "well-blended" style that absorbs the other two and anticipates Demosthenes. Dionysius suggests as much, at the end of *Isaeus,* in his explanation of his choice of these three rhetors for discussion (19–20). The next three *logoi* on Demosthenes, Hyperides, and Aeschines may have been meant to constitute a similarly "triangular," next-generation progression from the perfectly "blended" and "forceful" style of Demosthenes, to the contrasting (more polished, less forceful?) style of Hyperides, and, with Aeschines, to another synthesis (of the Demosthenic and Hyperidean *charaktêres*) that sets the course for the "Rhodian" school of rhetoric in the Hellenistic age. Possibly the second triad embodied a "decline" from Demosthenes to Aeschines, and figured Aeschines' school as the source of Asianism.

Or perhaps the overall *logos* of *On the Ancient Orators* was simply an argument for the canonic status of the chosen six, who between them embodied all the fundamental *charaktêres* that a student of philosophical rhetoric, or an educated grownup looking to hone his skills, should study, imitate, and acquire. As R. M. Smith has argued,[64] the standard canon of the Ten Attic Orators probably had been worked out by Alexandrian scholars in or before the first century B.C.E. The earliest attested mention of the Ten is the title of the now-lost treatise *On the Styles of the Ten Orators* by Dionysius' contemporary, Caecilius of Caleacte.[65] But this was a grammarian's or philologist's canon and was not necessarily authoritative for rhetoricians. Quintilian, for example, refers to the Ten but makes his own list of recommendations for study and imitation (*Institutio* 10.1.76).[66] Dionysius does seem motivated—as in his catty remarks about Plato's *Menexenus* and his dismissal of scholastic treatises on sentence structure—to sometimes tweak the philosophers and the Alexandrian philologists. Thus in *Lysias* he delivers a short digression on Theophrastus: "One indeed may wonder whatever has happened to Theophrastus, when he considers [Lysias] to strive for vulgar and over-elaborate speech, and to chase after poetical rather than truthful expression!" (14).

This is followed up with presentation of the full passage in which Theophrastus makes this judgment, followed in turn by the observation that the speech Theophrastus is criticizing is not, and obviously could not be, a speech by Lysias. So Theophrastus, the mighty theorist of style, is shown to be too obtuse to differentiate the genuine and nongenuine speeches attributed to the great *rhêtôr*. Theophrastus' *aisthêsis* has been buried under schoolish pedantry. Likewise, in the closing sections of *Isaeus,* Dionysius mentions the many other fifth- to fourth-century orators "that everybody knows" that he might have discussed beyond his chosen six—from Gorgias and Antiphon to Polycrates, Zoilus, and the students of Isocrates—and explains why, for the purposes of his argument, they are extraneous (19–20). They all are interesting as literary figures, and thus the grammarians have preserved, edited, catalogued, and commented on their works, but for the rhetorician's purposes some critical distinctions can and should be made. All their imitation-worthy virtues can be had, in better form, from Dionysius' six. A discussion that tried to comment on all the orators whose writings have been preserved would "degenerate into pointlessness" (*kenotêtas exepipte;* 20). Dionysius, in short, may have intended his six lectures to make a case for a more focused rhetorician's canon of the "ancient [Attic] orators" most essential for study and imitation *now,* especially in light of the first century B.C.E.'s preoccupations with Atticism and Asianism.

Demosthenes, Thucydides

Both of these pieces seem too long to be lectures. The fifty-eight sections of *On the Style of Demosthenes* occupy 108 Loeb pages and would take about three and a half hours to deliver, and the surviving text is incomplete. The fifty-five sections of *On Thucydides* occupy 85 Loeb pages and would require approximately three hours. And that text is incomplete too. The twenty-six sections of *On Composition,* by comparison, occupy 115 pages and would take nearly four hours to read aloud, should one choose to do so, though the text seems fairly clearly to have been intended as a "Proclus' bookcase" item, that is, as a *technê* for private reading. And what are most likely the public lectures of *On the Ancient Orators* seem designed to last for about an hour. None of this, of course, absolutely rules out an oral recitation of either the *Demosthenes* or the *Thucydides,* especially if one considers that the initial "publication" of a literary work in antiquity—such as a declamation, poem, panegyric, or the like—generally took the form of an oral performance in either a public *theatron* or a private recitation for a select audience (such as we see portrayed in Isocrates' *Panathenaicus*), followed by revision, copying, and distribution or sale of the polished written text.[67] But in this case such performance seems unlikely.

The *Demosthenes*' introduction is missing—the surviving text begins in the middle of a discussion of Gorgias—but it is addressed to the same Ammaeus as *On the Ancient Orators,* though here Ammaeus is addressed within the text itself (*Demosthenes* 49, 58). At one point Dionysius says he will refrain from presenting sample passages to support his claim about the mixture and variety of styles in Demosthenes, "for it would make my composition [*suntaxis*] very long, and I fear that it may go from the essayistic [*ek tôn hupomnêmatikôn*] to the scholastic" (*eis tous scholikous;* 46). Here *suntaxis,* "composition," signifies a written text; *hupomnêma* signifies an "essay" in the sense of "notes" or "commentary" composed as a "memorandum," "reminder," "summary," or "brief";[68] and a *scholikos* or "scholastic" piece of writing signifies a more formal and more exhaustive treatise, perhaps the sort of encyclopedic pedantry that *On the Ancient Orators* avoids or the exemplification typical of a *technê.* In the *Thucydides* Dionysius likewise refers to his treatise *On Imitation* as a *hupomnêma,* making the point that it deals in summary fashion with the various authors that should be imitated (1). Further, at one point in the *Demosthenes* the audience is named explicitly as "the readers" (*hoi anaginôskontes;* 40). And Dionysius closes with "This is what I have, my most distinguished Ammaeus, to write [*graphein*] to you about the style of Demosthenes" (58). In *On the Style of Demosthenes,* then, Dionysius is addressing himself to social and intellectual equals—Ammaeus and readers like him—on a topic of rhetorical-critical interest, in a written text that is probably meant for private reading and that aims to retain the "essayistic" informality, but also the "summary" clarity, of a *hupomnêma.*

The *Thucydides* is addressed to Quintus Aelius Tubero, a fellow historian whom Dionysius approvingly cites in his *Roman Antiquities* (1.80.1), and the son of another Aelius Tubero, also a historian, who was a boyhood friend of Cicero.[69] Tubero is addressed simply in the vocative (*ô Kointe Ailie Touberôn;* 1), without epithets, which may suggest a close relationship, though it does not preclude his being a literary patron. Dionysius presents what he has written as a response to a request from his friend. He has discussed Thucydides briefly and summarily in *On Imitation*, but Tubero would like a more detailed explanation (*dêlôsis):* "You wished me to compose [*suntaxasthai*] a separate text [*idian graphên*] on Thucydides, including everything that needs discussion" (*hapanta ta deomena logôn;* 1). Here the text explicitly is presented as a piece of writing (*graphê*) composed for a historian, and other historians, with an interest in the rhetoric of Thucydides, something more detailed than a *hupomnêma* but still more intimate and informal than a "scholastic" treatise or a *technê*. The situation, then, is similar to the *Demosthenes*.

Dionysius mentions that he has interrupted his writing of the *Demosthenes* to do the *Thucydides* (1). The *Demosthenes,* in turn, seems to intersect with *On Composition,* which generally is presumed to be an earlier text: some of the same material appears in the later parts of the *Demosthenes* (35–41), though it is treated somewhat differently, and Dionysius refers the reader to *On Composition* for fuller treatment of matters that he has treated summarily (49). Did *On Composition* also interrupt the *Demosthenes?* Whatever the case may be, the *Demosthenes* and the *Thucydides* both present themselves as works of rhetorical criticism intended for the educated audiences that Ammaeus and Tubero represent, framed in the more accessible, "hypomnemic" form of an "essay" meant for private reading.

The interruption in the *Demosthenes* is noticeable. The first surviving part of the text (1–34) shows signs of having been derived from one of the lectures in *On the Ancient Orators.* Here the text names itself as a *logos* (8), makes gestures toward the time (14), and uses locutions that suggest speech—for example, "as I said [*eirêkôs*] at the beginning," and so on (16)—which feel like traces from a lecture text, whereas the reference to "the readers" and the locutions that suggest textuality occur mainly though not exclusively in the latter part (while "speech" locutions disappear). Further, there is a shift in terminology.

As I have noted, the extant text begins in the middle of a discussion of Gorgias. Then there is a lacuna, after which the text resumes with an excerpt from Thucydides: Dionysius says this illustrates "the set-apart, striking, elaborate style, filled with every supplemental embellishment" (*epithetos kosmos;* 1). So Dionysius appears to be giving a short historical account of the evolution of the highly figured or "grand" style from the earlier sophists such as Gorgias to Thucydides. He next takes up "the other style" (*hê hetera lexis*), which is "plain and simple, and seems in its construction and force to resemble common speech" (2). Again there is a short history. The plain style was employed by many history writers, philosophers from the fifth-century natural philosophers to "the whole Socratic school except Plato," and orators, especially political and judicial speakers, but it was perfected by Lysias. So Thucydides and Lysias represent the historical culmination of the grand (or elaborate) and plain styles, and the relation between those styles is said to resemble that between the high and low notes in a musical scale. One startles the mind, creates tension and strain, and induces strong emotion (*pathos*); the other relaxes the mind, gives pleasure, and induces moral character (*êthos*, that is, the milder, more ethical attitudes; 2).[70]

Dionysius then turns to the third and, in his view, best kind of style, which he describes as "mixed and composed" (*miktê kai sunthetos*) from the other two (3). Again there is an account of its historical evolution, from Thrasymachus of Calchedon, Gorgias's contemporary, to Isocrates, Plato, and finally Demosthenes, who perfects it. The elaborate style appeals to sophisticated, elite audiences, such as the readers of Thucydides, but is offputting and difficult for common people, and the plain style appeals to common citizens but alienates the elite; but the masters of the "mixed" style and especially Demosthenes succeed in appealing to both kinds of audience (15). The argument is briefly stated but illustrated at length with substantial passages that are read out, commented on, and compared, showing that Isocrates is deficient on the plain side, and Plato on the elaborate side, while Demosthenes excels them both (3–33). This "historical" and comparative procedure has the feel of a public lecture, though it seems considerably expanded. So do such remarks such as, at the start of the discussion of Isocrates, "As for the style of Isocrates, who acquired among the Greeks a great name for wisdom, and contended neither in private nor public trials but composed many fine writings [*graphai*] in every type of discourse, I have explained at length before [*proteron*] what character it seems to me to have" (4). For what sort of audience is that little biographical "parenthesis" on Isocrates intended? Why is it necessary to say that Isocrates won a reputation "among the Greeks"? Dionysius here seems to be addressing not only an audience of specialists, but also a more general sort of educated audience, a Greek-speaking Roman audience, such as one might find at a public lecture.

While many passages are read out, examined, and compared, the examination is mostly impressionistic and supported by little technical analysis, as in the earlier parts of *On Composition*, though Dionysius is not addressing young *meirakia*. He does sometimes engage in *metathesis*, rewriting sample passages to illustrate his point about their effect. But rather than using *aisthêsis* as the starting point for what will become an analytical lesson, Dionysius tends here to use it as a final appeal:

Anyone who wishes may consider whether my judgments of Demosthenes are proper, by making an examination of examples. (9)

Anyone who wishes may consider whether I have reasoned correctly about these matters and whether Isocrates is deficient in these [stylistic] virtues, by making an examination of the passages I have just set forth. (19)

Each person must learn this not by reason [*logos*], but come to know it from his own feelings [*pathê*]; for by nonrational sensation [*aisthêsis*] all things unpleasant and pleasant are judged, and for that none need instruction or persuasion. (24)

There is no one who would not agree, even if he had only moderate perception [*aisthêsis*] concerning rhetoric [*logoi*], and was not a perverse and quarrelsome person, that the passages I have just set forth are as different as the armaments used in war and in ceremonial parades. (32)

And so on. Dionysius may, on one hand, be assuming a grownup audience that already has had a rhetorical education and has at least a moderately developed sensitivity to qualities of style, and has no need to rehearse *On Composition*'s lessons about the phonetic and aesthetic qualities of letters, syllables, rhythms, and so on. That audience can, conceivably, engage in a more technical analysis when "examining examples" for themselves. On the other hand, Dionysius seems also to be reflecting the experienced rhetor's knowledge, as voiced by Cicero's Antonius, that audiences do not need a detailed technical analysis, or a theory, to tell them whether a passage has grace and dignity, or is offputtingly contrived, or has some other quality, or how they ought to respond; they just feel it by nonrational *aisthêsis,* which is the bedrock standard of judgment. Either way, technical analysis and theory cannot overrule *aisthêsis* but can only try to elucidate it.

So in the first surviving part of the *Demosthenes,* there is a historical and comparative argument, grounded in appeals to *aisthêsis,* that the "mixed" style is the best and that it reaches its highest point of evolution in Demosthenes. This argument comes to an end in section 32, and is summarized in section 33, with some additional reflections in section 34. This material feels like a conclusion. Notably, at the end of 32, Dionysius says, "I wish to sum up [*sullogisasthai*] what I have said [*ta eirêmena*] from the beginning, and to show that *I have done all that I promised* at the start of my consideration [*theôria*] of the domain of style [*ho lektikos topos*]" (32; emphasis added).

This remark clearly characterizes Dionysius' treatment of Demosthenes' style as complete at this point. (It also suggests that there may have been a discussion of Demosthenes' handling of the *pragmatikos topos,* the "domain of subject matter," before the discussion of the *lektikos topos,* as in the *Thucydides.*) The lecture material that Dionysius has reworked is finished. But after summing up, he sets out again: "Well then, now that I have spoken [*eirêmenôn*] of those things, next I will also speak about the composition of words [*peri tês suntheseôs onomatôn*] that Demosthenes employs" (35). What follows is in essence a reworking of material from *On Composition*—the title of which Dionysius' remark repeats verbatim—but in a more "popular" form. Again the minutiae of phonetics, syllable lengths and textures, and rhythm and melody are eschewed, in favor of appeals to *aisthêsis* and the presentation and discussion of substantial passages, with the focus on Demosthenes.

The language of "three styles" used in the first part of the *Demosthenes* now gives way to *On Composition*'s terminology of three kinds of composition. As Dionysius says, "There are three principal types [*charaktêres*] of excellent composition" (37): the "austere and oldfashioned" (*austêros kai philarchaios*) kind, which aims "not at elegance (*to kompson*) but at solemnity" (*to semnon;* 38); the "polished and theatrical" (*glaphuros kai theatrikos*) kind, which "prefers elegance (*to kompson*) to solemnity" (*to semnon;* 40); and the "mixed" (*miktos*) kind, which varies depending on the purposes and capacities of those who attempt it, like painters choosing and mixing colors from a palette (41). The great representatives of the "austere" kind are Aeschylus and Pindar among the poets and Thucydides among the historians and prose writers in general; those of the "polished" kind are Hesiod, Sappho, and Anacreon among the poets and Isocrates "and his followers" (40) among the prose writers and orators; and those of the "mixed" kind are Homer among the poets, Herodotus among the historians, and Demosthenes among the orators. These citations of authors in different categories reflect the lists of models in *On Imitation* and suggest that one of Dionysius' motives is to canonize Demosthenes as the orator most worthy to be studied and imitated.

Obviously Dionysius is working again with a three-part typology, as in the first part of the *Demosthenes,* but the categories have shifted. Elaborate and plain, for example, are not the same as austere and polished, despite some overlap. Thucydides remains the representative prose writer for both elaborate and austere, but in the new compositional typology he is paired off not with Lysias (plain) but Isocrates (polished); indeed, there seems to be no "plain" category at all. And Isocrates no longer represents the "mixed" kind (as in the former typology, where he is a precursor to Demosthenes) but one of the extremes from which the Demosthenic mix is compounded. These shifts might be explained by the fact that Dionysius is now talking about "composition" (*sunthesis*) specifically rather than "style" (*lexis*) in general—*sunthesis* is an aspect of *lexis*—but there seems to be a more fundamental retrenchment going on.[71] The plain-elaborate-mixed typology of the first part seems more akin to, and probably is derived from, the older Theophrastian typology of plain-grand-middle styles (which the *Rhetoric to Herennius,* Cicero, and Quintilian repeat). That typology might be described as fundamentally *quantitative,* insofar as the three types represent degrees of figuration, or degrees of departure from "common speech"; the grand style is heavily figured, the plain not, and the middle moderately. These types do have certain effects—the elaborate, for example, impresses and induces emotion, and the plain relaxes and induces the milder "ethical" moods—but the theoretical description is grounded in quantity of figuration. Dionysius' typology for composition, in contrast, is *qualitative,* insofar as each type has a certain "feel" that is perceptible to *aisthêsis* and is grounded not in degree of figuration but in specific arrangements of language (phonetic textures, rhythms, melodies, and so forth).[72] This seems to be a definite shift away from the Theophrastian account of stylistic types and toward the later Hermogenean account, for which, again, it appears to be a precursor. Through his account of composition Dionysius has developed a model for stylistic analysis that is much more subtle and sophisticated than the approach he has inherited from his Hellenistic predecessors. (Perhaps that is why Aelius Theon thinks him "great.")

At sections 44–46, Dionysius sums up his argument on Demosthenes as the best embodiment of the "mixed" and best kind of composition and digresses briefly on the "standards" (*kanones*) by which Demosthenes decided what *charaktêr* of style to use when. The argument is that Demosthenes was initially "taught" (*didachtheis*) "by nature and experience" (*phusei kai peirai*) and "learned well" (*katamathein*) that different occasions and genres, and even the different parts of a single speech, require different types of style (44, 45–46). The next major topic is "what precepts [*theôrêmata*] and what sort of exercise [*askêsis*]" led Demosthenes to master "mixed" composition (*harmonia; 47*). This leads to a discussion of how Demosthenes learned through observation and experience that *harmonia* in both prose and poetry should have both "pleasantness" (*hêdonê*) and "nobility" (*to kalon*), and that these are composed of the same elements (melody, rhythm, variety, and propriety), so that he became more attentive to them in the arrangement of his words (47–50).

Dionysius then refers Ammaeus and "anyone who wants" a fuller treatment of these matters to "my notes [*hupomnêmatismoi*] on the composition of words" (50) and drops the subject. His intention thus appears to be not an exposition of the principles of composition themselves but an argument that Demosthenes discovered them through his own *aisthêsis* and made them part of his rhetorical *dunamis* through study and exercise. Thus the Demosthenic rhetorical *dunamis,* while grounded in his "nature" (*phusis*) and its capacities for *aisthêsis,* is also a *dunamis artistically produced* or cultivated through the regime (*askêsis*) of studious attention to and practice with what *aisthêsis* discloses. The Demosthenic *dunamis,* then, is an artistic construct, and as such can be acquired, or approximated, by anyone with the necessary *phusis* and *aisthesis,* and a sufficient capacity for discipline. (The traditional story of Demosthenes' self-cultivation and overcoming of deficiencies through training clearly lends persuasiveness to such an argument.) It is hardly the case that, as Stephen Usher suggests, the *Demosthenes* demonstrates that "admiration and aesthetic pleasure are all that [the student of Demosthenes] may allow himself";[73] the case, rather, is just the opposite. Dionysius shows that one can learn to compose discourse Demosthenically, though it is not a simpleminded matter of following some rules or aping the great orator's quirks, as in a caricature.

What follows from this argument are recommendations on how to form an accurate understanding of, and an ability to recognize, Demosthenes' rhythmic and melodious composition—that is, by exercising and training one's *aisthêsis* through the study of examples—accompanied by the argument that no one can truly grasp the nature of such composition merely by learning a few technical precepts (50). This is followed by Dionysius' responses to the objections from skeptics who cannot believe that Demosthenes could have composed his words with such minute attention to detail (51–52). The refutation includes the comparison to grammatical training and the way that principles become, with lengthy practice, internalized habits that no longer need conscious attention (52). Dionysius then turns to a discussion of delivery (53–57), which partly rehearses the earlier argument (22) that Demosthenes' carefully composed style makes clear what sort of delivery it requires (53–54) and adds the further observation that it is impossible for a person with the psyche of an "unreasoning animal" or with the "inert nature of a stone, without perception (*anaisthêtos*), immobile, without feeling," to "perform [*propheresthai*] the style [*lexis*] of Demosthenes" (54). Dionysius next presents some passages and comments on their proper delivery (55–58) and then concludes (58).

In the end, Dionysius' treatment of Demosthenes bears a curious resemblance to Dio Chrysostom's *On Training in Speech* (*Discourse* 18.18–19), discussed in the previous chapter. They differ in that Dio is prescribing a short road to rhetoric for a wealthy man who wants to enter politics and Dionysius clearly is a long-roader. But both converge on the practice of reading aloud—oral interpretation or "delivery"—as an essential, perhaps *the* essential practice for developing one's rhetorical *dunamis.* As Dio suggests, the short-roader might dispense with virtually everything but that, along with some ex tempore speaking practice. Dionysius, similarly, is addressing an audience not exclusively composed of specialists and making a twofold argument. First, Demosthenes is the best of all orators for study and imitation, and second, the best and most necessary approach to study/imitation is to cultivate one's *aisthêsis* through reading Demosthenes aloud, with understanding and with proper delivery, and internalizing the key elements of the Demosthenic *charaktêr* as a set of habituated practices.

These habituated practices constitute an "artistically" developed rhetorical *dunamis*. This process can be supplemented and aided by a limited number of technical precepts, and if the audience wishes they can go deeper into the technical details by reading *On the Composition of Words*.

On Thucydides can be discussed more briefly. Dionysius is very clear about his purposes. As he says to Tubero and the rest of his readers, "I ask of you and of other scholars [*philologoi*] who may encounter this writing [*graphê*] to observe my intention in choosing this theme [*hupothesis*]: it is a clarification [*dêlôsis*] of [Thucydides'] *charaktêr*, embracing all of its attributes that need discussion, with the aim of assisting those who may wish to imitate him" (25).

Accordingly, the text discusses Thucydides' handling of both the *pragmatikos topos* and the *lektikos topos*, with an eye to which characteristics should be imitated by those intending to write history and which characteristics should be avoided. Thus Dionysius, in the passage above, presents a sort of apology for his often-censorious treatment of the great historian. (As he says in his introduction, he has never before written anything "in which I attack someone," except for his treatise *On Behalf of Political Philosophy;* 2.) After an overview of the historians before Thucydides, and especially of Herodotus, Dionysius briefly notes Thucydides' virtues—chiefly his truthfulness and his painstaking research—then proceeds to criticism of the *pragmatikos topos* (9–20). Dionysius faults Thucydides for dividing the narrative by seasons rather than narrating each action from beginning to end, as Isocrates recommends; for sometimes making poor choices about where to begin and end and what to include or omit; and for similar inconsistencies in his treatments of speeches and dialogues. The result in every case is that the narrative is rendered less comprehensible. Dionysius makes the pointed remark that no one since Thucydides has chosen to follow the Thucydidean model of historical narration, and for good reason (9).

Almost all of the rest of the treatise is taken up with Thucydides' style (21–49): in general (21–24), in his narrative passages (25–33), and in speeches (34–49). The rest (50–55) digresses into a consideration of Thucydides as a model for practical oratory. The general argument is that Thucydides developed an "elaborate" style far removed from common speech, that the more elaborate and convoluted it becomes the more obscure it is, and that his best passages—the ones that other historians should imitate—are those in which he hews closer to common speech and is more accessible, that is, when he achieves something like an Isocratean or Demosthenic "mixed" style. Likewise it is in those passages that Thucydides might provide usable (imitatable) models for the practical orator, but, as Dionysius maintains, Demosthenes is in every way preferable for that.

In its goals and general procedures, then, *On Thucydides* resembles, as does the first half of the *Demosthenes* for its own and different reasons, an expanded version of a "lecture" from *On the Ancient Orators,* or, rather, its proposed companion series on historians, though there are no locutions that suggest a speech, such as gestures at the time, and the text consistently refers to itself as a piece of writing. We do not know which historians Dionysius meant to include in his treatise "on the ancient historians," but to judge from *On Thucydides,* the plan of the *Ancient Orators,* and the fragments of *On Imitation,* Thucydides probably would have represented an extreme—opposed to the simpler narratives of earlier historians, or to Herodotus and Xenophon—that is brought into balance by such later historians as Theopompus, who might be said to provide the "modern" historian with better rhetorical models. In his *Letter to Gnaeus Pompeius,* Dionysius mentions his treatment of historians in *On Imitation* and says that those most worth imitating are Herodotus, Thucydides, Xenophon, Philistius, and Theopompus (3). At the outset of his *Roman Antiquities* he cites Theopompus and Anaximenes. (Philistius and Anaximenes are, with Theopompus, figures of the fourth century B.C.E. Philistius wrote about the Peloponnesian War, and Anaximenes, like Theopompus, wrote about Philip and Alexander.)

In Dionysius' treatment of style there is one "new" feature worthy of note. When he introduces the basic framework of the *lektikos topos,* he raises the notion that the "virtues" (*aretai*) of style are divided into the "necessary" (*anankaiai*), which are obligatory in every discourse, and the "supplemental" (*epithetoi*), which depend for their effect on the presence of the former (22). The "necessary" virtues are purity, clarity, and conciseness; the "supplementary" virtues include

Sublimity (or elevation)	*Hupsos*
Elegance	*Kallirêmosunê*
Solemnity	*Semnologia*
Magnificence	*Megaloprepeia*
Tension	*Tonos*
Weightiness	*Baros*

In addition to these there are "emotion rousing the mind" (*pathos diegeiron ton noun*) and a "robust, combative spirit" (*errômenon kai enagônion pneuma;* 23). Dionysius refers to this scheme as something that "many have spoken of before" (22). As Stephen Usher points out, however, this is the earliest surviving "explicit reference" to it in ancient literature, though there are some "indirect references" in Cicero.[74] Evidently it is a partition of the older Theophrastian notion of the "four virtues" of style—purity, clarity, ornament, appropriateness—with purity-clarity becoming the "necessary" virtues, ornament giving rise to the "supplemental" virtues and appropriateness governing all. Since Dionysius says that "many" have mentioned this scheme before, and Cicero was aware of it, it seems to be an innovation of the later Hellenistic period. It also seems to be the basis from which Dionysius develops his account of "composition" (*sunthêsis*) producing different "characters" or types of style, in which there is no distinction between "plain" and "figured" but only different configurations with different qualities. (In Hermogenes' *On Types of Style,* for example, "clarity" and "sincerity" are *styles* with distinct configurations.) These developments thus seem to be the basis for not only such later work as Hermogenes but also "Longinus'" *On the Sublime (Peri Hupsous),* which presents itself as a response to a work on sublimity by Dionysius' associate Caecilius of Caleacte. In *On Thucydides,* however, this notion of virtues has only the function of providing the conceptual frame for Dionysius's criticism; in Thucydides the "supplemental" virtues are highly developed, sometimes impressively, and sometimes to the point of excess, thereby undermining the "necessary" virtues and producing mere obscurity.

But *On Thucydides,* like *On the Style of Demosthenes,* is neither a *technê* nor a work of scholastic theory. Rather, both are extended "hypomnemic" essays, possibly expanded versions of public lectures, produced for an educated readership on the questions of the particular *charaktêr* of each writer's discourse, which features of each to imitate and acquire, and how to do that. There is some discussion of principles, and there are large slabs of illustrative passages that the reader is to examine for himself, as well as any that he may collect. In every case the test and starting point is *aisthêsis,* "perception," arising from *phusis,* bodily nature, supplemented by the studious attention made possible by *technê* (explaining what can and needs to be explained), and followed by assiduous practice in oral interpretation, imitation, and original composition, over a long period of time, until the particular features become habituated second nature, components of one's rhetorical *dunamis,* one's artistically crafted competence.

Dinarchus and the Letters

These texts mainly have the character of brief scholarly notes. *On Dinarchus* is concerned with the problem of discriminating the genuine from the spurious speeches attributed to Dinarchus, the last of the canonic Ten Attic Orators. As Dionysius notes, "Neither Callimachus nor the grammarians of Pergamon have written about him," and even the first century B.C.E. scholar Demetrius of Magnesia has nothing but generalities to say (1).[75] The result has been no clarity about which of the more than one hundred speeches attributed to Dinarchus are genuine, or about how to make that discrimination. The problem is that, unlike Lysias, Isocrates, or Demosthenes, Dinarchus has no distinct style of his own: he is not a stylistic originator but an imitator and polisher.

Dionysius' solution is to note two kinds of imitation: one is "natural" (*phusikos*) and is acquired by "thorough instruction and familiarity" (*katêchêsis kai suntrophia*)—the disciplining of *aisthêsis* and habit through guided experience and practice that he everywhere talks about—while the other is acquired "from the precepts of the art" (*ek tôn tês technês parangelmatôn;* 7). The second, a superficial matter of following rules, even if it reaches the "height of imitation" (*akron mimêseôs*), inevitably has an air of unnatural contrivance (7). This, it appears, is the case with Dinarchus, who is the best of the artificial imitators of Demosthenes (8). (The best "natural" imitator, by contrast, would not be a pale copy of Demosthenes, or a copy at all, but would have internalized and synthesized the Demosthenic qualities as part of his own *dunamis,* and hence would speak with an original voice.) The problem of identifying Dinarchus' genuine speeches thus becomes a matter of recognizing high-quality pseudo-Demosthenics that fall just short of naturalness, as well as recognizing which belong to the historical period of Dinarchus's activity. The rest of the *Dinarchus* (10–13) sorts the Dinarchan catalogue, as Dionysius knows it, into genuine and spurious speeches, with brief explanations of the reasons for each rejection. At one point Dionysius mentions that one genuine Dinarchan speech, a criminal prosecution *Against Theocrines,* is classed by Callimachus as a work of Demosthenes. This suggests the high level of Dinarchus's artificial imitation, and as with Theophrastus in *Lysias* 14, it enables Dionysius to tweak the famous Callimachus and Alexandrian and Pergamene scholarship in general.

The three extant letters—*First Letter to Ammaeus, To Gnaeus Pompeius,* and *Second Letter to Ammaeus*—are a miscellany. The *First Ammaeus,* which I have discussed before, may be a sort of *jeu d'esprit.* It responds to a statement from Ammaeus that a Peripatetic philosopher has claimed that Demosthenes learned the rules of eloquence from Aristotle's *Rhetoric* and applied them in his speeches (1). Considering Dionysius' approach to rhetorical education, the whole idea is patently absurd. Nobody becomes an excellent rhetor in that way, no matter whose *technê* they might have read. But rather than take that approach, Dionysius simply remarks that he doesn't want it thought that "all the precepts of rhetoric" are encompassed in Peripatetic philosophy, or that the earlier sophists and Isocrates contributed nothing, and he undertakes to prove that the story about Aristotle and Demosthenes is false (2–3). Thus he concedes the Peripatetic's foolish premise (that eloquence is a matter of following rules) and demonstrates instead that, even if that premise were true, the historical claim itself is false. What follows has something of the character of a judicial speech (at the conjectural stasis), with Dionysius producing "testimony" from biographers and historians and invoking "evidence" from Aristotle's and Demosthenes' writings and from historical records such as archon lists to show that the *Rhetoric* was a product of Aristotle's late career (7–9), and that before he wrote it Demosthenes already had delivered all of his most important speeches but *On the Crown* (10–12). The conclusion is not only that Aristotle was not the source from which Demosthenes developed his eloquence, but, rather, the reverse: "Aristotle wrote the *Rhetoric* with reference to the works of Demosthenes and other orators" (12).[76] As Cicero's Crassus might say, and as Dionysius suggests both here and in virtually all of his writings, eloquence is not a consequence of art, but art of eloquence.

The *Second Letter to Ammaeus* is a sort of addendum to the *Thucydides*. As Dionysius remarks, "I thought I had sufficiently clarified the *charaktêr* of Thucydides . . . first, in the notes [*hupomnêmatismoi*] *On the Ancient Orators* that I drew up and dedicated to your name [*pros to son onoma*], and a little while ago in the text [*graphê*] addressed to Aelius Tubero [*proseipon ton Ailion Touberôna*] on Thucydides himself" (1). Ammaeus, however, thinks those writings not precise enough, because Dionysius gives a summary list of all of Thucydides' distinctive characteristics (*idiômata*) and only afterward furnishes proofs (*pisteis*) or demonstration; instead he should follow each statement with illustration, in the manner of "those who produce *technai* and introductions to speeches" (*hoi tas technas kai tas eisagôgas tôn logôn pragmateuomenoi*). Dionysius dutifully replies that, "wishing for nothing to be left out," he has done as requested and has "adopted the didactic mode rather than the epideictic" (*to didaliskon schêma labôn anti tou epideiktikou; 1*). The rest of the letter consists of a re-presentation of the summary description followed by exemplification of each statement. Dionysius closes with, "You have, my dear Ammaeus, my statements individually confirmed by the usual treatment [*ek tês koinês pragmateias*], as you requested" (17).

While this letter says nothing new about Thucydides, it raises several suggestive points. First, it presents Ammaeus as possibly a literary patron, a person to whom texts can de dedicated and for whom texts can be produced on request. (As Stephen Usher observes, Dionysius seems to have little enthusiasm for his task in this letter but performs it anyway.)[77] It also shows that Ammaeus was a recipient of the *Thucydides*. (Perhaps, on seeing that it was addressed to Tubero, he wanted some addendum produced for himself.) Second, the letter indicates that Thucydides was discussed in *On the Ancient Orators*. No such discussion appears in the extant text, but Thucydides is discussed in *On the Style of Demosthenes* (10). These facts suggest a range of possibilities: the companion volume to *Ancient Orators* on the historians was produced, or the *Demosthenes* is derived from a "lecture" that once was collected in that text, or both the *Demosthenes* and the *Thucydides* are so derived. Third, Dionysius' opening and closing remarks indicate that he thinks of the *Demosthenes,* the *Thucydides,* and the *Ancient Orators* as discourses produced in the "epideictic" mode, in contrast to the "didactic" mode of *technai,* "introductions to speeches," and his own *On Composition*. Fourth, his closing remark shows that the "usual" or common (*koinê*) treatment in "didactic" texts consists of precept-plus-examples.

Finally, the *Letter to Gnaeus Pompeius* has two functions. First, it responds to Pompeius' dismay at Dionysius' criticism (*katêgoria,* "accusation") of Plato's limitations in the "elaborate" style, arguing that admiration of great writers should not prevent one from exercising critical judgment and that others have criticized Plato before. Dionysius then defends his point by quoting verbatim and discussing the passage in question "in the treatise [*pragmateia*] on the Attic orators" (1–2). The extract is sections 5–7 of the *Demosthenes,* suggesting that that text was developed from a "lecture" originally composed for *On the Ancient Orators.* The next and major part of the letter (3–6) responds to Pompeius' wish "to learn about Herodotus and Xenophon" and his wish "that I write about then" (3). Dionysius replies that he already has written about them, in *On Imitation,* and reproduces that work's discussion of historians, which is now the only surviving fragment of the text;[78] it summarily reviews the strengths and weaknesses of Herodotus, Thucydides, Xenophon, Philistus, and Theopompus as writers of history. Dionysius' reply suggests that Pompeius may also be a patron, but one less well read than Ammaeus or Tubero—though he seems devoted to Plato, if uncritically, and apparently has obtained a copy of Dionysius' essays on the Attic orators from a mutual friend (1). As Usher points out, this friend-of-a-friend transmission implies that Pompeius is "not one of Dionysius' closer associates."[79] Pompeius wants to "learn about" Herodotus and Xenophon, and Dionysius is providing him with a basic overview straight from his bookcase.

Aside from its brief treatments of the historians, and its passing mention of "my dear friend Caecilius"—Caecilius of Caleacte, author of the lost treatise on "sublimity" to which "Longinus'" *On the Sublime* responds—perhaps the most important part of this extract from *On Imitation* is its presentation of the main headings for criticism of history writing under the *pragmatikos topos* and the *lektikos topos*:

Pragmatikos topos	*Lektikos topos*
Nobility of the subject matter	Primary qualities
Choice of where to begin and end	Purity of idiom
Which events to include	Clarity
Arrangement of the material	Conciseness
Fairness of treatment	Ancillary qualities
Vividness	Mimesis of characters and emotions

Thus, for example, under the *pragmatikos topos* Herodotus is judged to have chosen a nobler subject than Thucydides, to have made better choices about beginning/ending and what to include, to have arranged his materials better, and to have treated things more fairly; under the *lektikos topos* Thucydides is in some respects superior (when he retains the primary virtues) and in others inferior (when he does not). And so on. Notably the virtue of "mimesis of characters and emotions" resonates with the Pseudo-Dionysian lecture *On Mistakes Made in Declamation,* and suggests that Dionysius is thinking of the historians' presentation of character and emotion *in speeches,* and is thinking of those speeches too as declamations. Which brings me, finally, to the *Roman Antiquities.*

History as Political Philosophy as Rhetoric: Declamation in the *Roman Antiquities* (*Rhômaikês Archaiologiai*)

In his study of Theopompus of Chios' historical writings, Michael Flower argues at some length the strained thesis that Theopompus was not a student of Isocrates, despite the ancient tradition that he was.[80] But it makes no difference for present purposes whether that thesis is true, or whether Flower makes a probable case. (He certainly makes an ingenious one.) The point I wish to note, instead, is that his fundamental intent is to deny that Theopompus' historiography was "corrupted" by the new fashion of "rhetorical history" (or panegyric or sophistic history) that supposedly emerged from the school of Isocrates in the fourth century B.C.E. and cast its "rhetorical cloud," to use Bonner's metaphor, or "shadow," to use Flower's, over history writing in the Hellenistic age.[81] Flower's argument, in essence, is that rhetorical historiography in the tradition of Isocrates is corrupt. Theopompus is not a student of Isocrates, however, so Theopompus' historiography is not corrupt, and he therefore can be taken seriously as a historian.

What is not questioned in that argument is the assumption, or prejudice, that rhetorical historiography is necessarily corrupt—or more concerned with rhetorical effect than with truth—and that any history written by a sophist in the tradition of Isocrates can be dismissed. This certainly has been the case with Dionysius' *Roman Antiquities.* As I already have noted, Dionysius' Loeb translator, Earnest Cary, considers the historical narrative to be spoiled by the desire to please the reader, and by the insertion of full-length speeches, usually several full-length speeches on opposing sides, in almost every important episode. Likewise Stephen Usher, Dionysius' other Loeb translator, in his study of Greek and Roman historians treats Dionysius as a minor figure and considers that, despite Dionysius' painstaking research, the "rhetorical spirit" of his narrative "destroys the historical perspective": "Like the public declamations," the *Roman Antiquities* has been designed "to make the maximum emotional impact on a listening public" through the insertion of vivid descriptions, amplifications, and many speeches to heighten the drama. Thus Dionysius invents speeches for scenes from archaic legends, such as the speech by Romulus (*Roman Antiquities* 2.3–11), that cannot make "any serious claim to authenticity." Further, Dionysius sometimes treats at great length episodes that Livy, whom Usher considers a genuine historian, treats very briefly. For example, Dionysius spreads the story of Coriolanus over forty-eight chapters (actually it is much longer than that, as it is interwoven with several other stories related to the evolution of the Tribunate), whereas Livy gives Coriolanus only half a chapter.[82] Apparently the reasoning is that the Coriolanus story deserves a brief treatment because Livy treats it so. Usher recognizes that Livy also invents speeches for ancient episodes just as Dionysius does, but that is somehow justified because Livy writes in Latin whereas Dionysius writes in Greek and bases the speeches on Greek models. That reasoning does not deserve even a critique.

As Emilio Gabba has observed, all such assessments have their roots in turn-of-the-twentieth-century German scholarship, particularly that of Eduard Schwartz, who dismissed Dionysius as a "small soul" blind to the great political and social issues of his day.[83] Schwartz assumed that great historiography could arise only from "moments of great political tension,"[84] as in Thucydides' history of the Peloponnesian War, and must deal with contemporary events, concentrate on the factual realities, and minimize rhetorical display. Schwartz, in essence, subjects historiography to a positivist standard that eschews "universalist" judgments, hews to a *wissenschaftlich* analysis of material particulars, seeks the truth of empirical fact, and favors a plain style that aims at accurate reportage and makes no concession to the reader, not even, presumably, a Lysianic grace. Thus Dionysius' *Roman Antiquities*, which attempts a comprehensive narrative of early Roman history from legendary times to the First Punic War, where the history of Polybius picks up, comes in for dismissal as an example of decadent "rhetorical historiography." It is a backward-looking piece of antiquarianism with nothing at stake but the celebration of conservative ideals and the tedious laying on of embellishments and ornaments as thick as the frosting on a birthday cake. A "true" history would concentrate on the great events of Dionysius' time—the fall of Ptolemaic Egypt to Roman power, the absorption of the Hellenistic world in the Roman Empire, the consolidation of imperial power—and it would, apparently, consist of narrative unadorned with speeches, vivid description, or other forms of rhetorical display. The true historian might, of course, include speeches, letters, and other documents if the authentic texts have been obtained, though generally these could be represented by brief reports of their essential contents.

As Gabba maintains, "Schwartz's point of departure entails a complete misunderstanding of Dionysius, which, given the prestige of the German historian, has been imposed in turn on a lengthy period of subsequent research," a fact that is evident in the repeated dismissal of the *Roman Antiquities* on the generally unexamined grounds that it is "rhetorical."[85] Gabba's much more sympathetic argument does not answer the charge of "rhetoricality" directly but claims that Dionysius' starting thesis—that the Romans had Greek origins and that the development of the Roman state was a continuing evolution of the aboriginal Greek identity—was not only more defensible than may appear to the modern mind but also was an astute political argument that responded precisely to the problem of the absorption of the Hellenistic world in the Roman

Empire. In effect Dionysius demonstrated to resistant Greeks that they and the Romans had a shared identity and that the Romans at their best embodied the classical Greek ideal and even had improved on it. To the Romans he demonstrated the centrality of classical Greek ideals to their own identity and helped to open the way to Greek participation in the governance of the Roman Empire, such as we see in the first and second centuries C.E., the age of the so-called Second Sophistic or Greek renaissance.[86] Moreover, as Gabba argues, Dionysius' historical argument was consistent with the "Atticism" of his rhetorical writings, and with them was part of a single educational and political project. In this way, then, Gabba refutes Schwartz's dismissal of Dionysius as a "small soul" out of touch with the exigent issues of his day and pursuing a backward-looking, decadent antiquarianism festooned with meretricious "rhetorical" embellishments.

I cannot possibly offer an analysis as comprehensive as Gabba's here, but I mean to explore a different if related question, namely, that the "rhetoricality" of the *Roman Antiquities* is central to its intention and is an essential part of Dionysius' rhetorical *paideia*. While I am persuaded by Gabba's treatment of Dionysius' argument concerning the Greekness of the Romans, in fact, Dionysius' actual, explicit presentation of that argument takes up little more than the first volume of a twenty-volume history. Of course, if one accepts the argument of book 1 and then makes it the starting premise for an interpretation of the remaining nineteen (or ten, in the surviving text), the remainder can be *understood* as narrating the working out of the Romans' aboriginal Greekness, and the development of the Roman state, through a series of episodes of crisis and resolution. But that view leaves unexplained the "rhetorical" dimension of the text, in particular the function of the speeches, which do indeed take up a considerable amount of space. I suggest that they are not there merely as entertainment for the reader, or because Dionysius has been so "corrupted" by rhetoric that he can't resist inserting them whether they are relevant or not. Rather, they are in large measure what his history is about. In essence, the *Roman Antiquities* can be understood as a declamation problem writ large, or a series of problems for which the historical narrative supplies the hypotheses.

As he is wrapping up his introductory remarks, Dionysius says:

> I give this work a form [*schêma*] unlike what is given to histories written only about wars, or to those that describe individual constitutions [*politeiai*] by themselves, or to those resembling the chronicles which the writers of the *Atthides* published, for these are monotonous and quickly become tiresome to the audience [*tois akouousin*]. It is instead a mixture of every kind [*idea*]— contestatory [*enagônios*], speculative [*theôrêtikê*], and narrative [*diêgêmatikê*]— so that it may be satisfactory for those who study civic discourse [*politikos*

logos], for those concerned with philosophical speculation [*philosophos theôria*], and for anyone who wants to spend some leisure time reading history. (1.8.3)

The first part of this statement could be read, à la Schwartz, as an expression of the "corrupt" desire to please the audience. God forbid that a work of history should be a good read. The real point, however, is that Dionysius is comparing himself to three kinds of historians: the writers of mere chronicles such as the *Atthides*,[87] those who have written celebratory histories of Philip's and Alexander's conquests or of other campaigns—the best of these writers perhaps would be Theopompus, and the worst Hegesias of Magnesia—and those who have written histories of constitutions. The first group embodies the kind of history that Aristotle in the *Poetics* (8, 1451b) describes as less philosophical than poetry because it deals in particulars rather than universals (*ta katholou,* "general truths"). It is these chroniclers of sheer particulars who most resemble Schwartz's historiographical ideal, though he would expect more analysis, and who also are the most tedious to read. In fact, the statement about tedium may be read as applying specifically to them. The historians of wars, if they are not also mere chroniclers of events, present a sort of contrast. The histories of Philip's and Alexander's campaigns, or of the wars of Hellenistic kings or the campaigns of Roman generals, generally were encomiastic accounts meant as popular propaganda and thus were highly embellished with vivid narratives and descriptions. While the chroniclers presented a bare record of events, the war historians praised and amplified the greatness of their heroes and their deeds. (Or, in Thucydides' case, blamed the moral degeneration of the Athenians in the Peloponnesian War.) Dionysius' history is comparable to both but strictly speaking, as he says, it is identifiable as neither.

The third group presents a more interesting comparison. The histories of constitutions "by themselves" might include things such as Cicero's *De Re Publica* or the Aristotelian *Constitution of Athens,* both of which narrate the evolution of a polity. While the *Constitution of Athens* may be considered, from a Peripatetic viewpoint, a critique of Athens' devolution into radical democracy, the *De re publica* is a defense of the republican constitution that Cicero struggled unsuccessfully to preserve: the wisest possible arrangement, worked out over centuries in response to specific circumstances and emergencies. A constitutional history like Cicero's may be thought an illustration of the Heraclitean maxim that "the community [*dêmos*] must fight for its law [*nomos*] as for its walls."[88] The community must work out the problems of its polity from within the existing *nomos*—"law" in the sense of its customary rules and practices, its particular "social contract," as well as its written laws—because its *nomos,* like its city walls, is what defends it from arbitrary violence, tyranny, or a descent into lawless chaos.[89] (In Cicero's day, the republican *nomos* was unraveling in a series of bloody civil wars and giving way to rule by military autocrat; by the time that Dionysius came of age the new, Augustan order had been established.)

Such historiographic models suggest a conception of history as philosophy in the Isocratean mode. All real polities are the product of a history. Rather than imagine an ideal polity created ex nihilo, deduced from first principles and imposed on an ahistorical blank slate—as in Aristotle's *Politics* or Plato's *Republic* or *Laws*—the Isocratean political philosopher undertakes something more like a Foucauldian "archaeology" of the present.[90] He considers how the laws (*nomoi*) and constitution (*politeia*) of a community have emerged historically and pragmatically from within the situated particulars of its experience: how the civil community has adapted, evolved, and succeeded or failed. The process through which the community and its *nomos* are created, sustained, adapted, and transformed *peacefully* is rhetoric, or what Isocrates calls *politikos logos,* civic or public discourse. Dionysius' *Roman Antiquities* (or *Archaiologiai*) may be considered as a history or "archaeology" of the rhetorical transformation of the early Roman state.

But Dionysius' history is not the same as histories of constitutions either. It is, he says, a "mixture of every kind" (*idea*) of discourse, and again he gives three examples: contestatory (*enagônios*), speculative (*theôrêtikê*), and narrative (*diêgêmatikê*). *Enagônios* can suggest the "contestatory" discourse of any kind of dispute or contest (*agôn*), including a trial, and points to the opposing speeches that take up so much of the *Roman Antiquities. Theôrêtikê* suggests the political-philosophical orientation of the work and points to Dionysius' reflections on the political wisdom, or lack thereof, of various actions and institutions, while *diêgêmatikê* recognizes that the text is in fact, too, a narrative of events. Each of these *ideai,* moreover, is associated with an intended audience: contestatory discourse, opposing speeches "for those who study" civic discourse, or rhetoric; speculative discourse "for those concerned with" political philosophy; and narrative for those who, like Cicero's Antonius, just enjoy reading history in their leisure time. These audiences, the first two in particular, tell us much about Dionysius' intentions beyond the simple aim of providing a good read for the casual reader, or even the complex aim of reconciling Greeks and Romans to each other.

Recall that, at the outset of *On Composition,* Dionysius argues that young men (*meirakia*) at the threshold of rhetoric should be directed first to the *lektikos topos,* the domain of style, since a "grasp of the subject matter belongs more to an already mature understanding, and to an age disciplined by grey hairs, augmented by much examination [*historia*] of speeches [*logoi*] and deeds [*erga*], and by much experience and suffering of one's own fortunes [*pathê*] and those of others." Recall, too, his statement late in the *Roman Antiquities* that the "lessons" conveyed by its representations of events "are a necessary and excellent thing for virtually all people, but especially for those who occupy themselves with philosophical speculation [*philosophos theôria*] and political affairs [*politikai praxeis*]." As Dionysius goes on to say, the latter group are pragmatists concerned with "fine deeds" as well as fine ideals. Learning the lessons of history enhances their practical judgment and enables them to better serve their cities with wise counsel in persuasive speech in situations where decisions must be made and action taken (11.1.1, 4). In these statements the practical political philosopher, the active politician, and the rhetor fuse. The *Roman Antiquities,* in short, is not only a work of literature but also an advanced course of study in the *pragmatikos topos,* providing an *historia* of "speeches and deeds" at various key moments in the evolution of the early Roman republic. It is meant to develop the "mature understanding" appropriate to "an age disciplined by grey hairs" and necessary for intelligent deliberation and good counsel.

The underlying "plot" of Dionysius' history is provided by the Isocratean myth of *logos:* Originally, primitive humanity lived in isolated, nomadic bands, subject to the violence of nature and each other, until an eloquent speaker, or speakers, appeared who could persuade them to form a civil community and submit to the authority of common laws and public institutions. Book 1 of the *Roman Antiquities* thus narrates the prehistoric migrations of Greek tribes into the Italian peninsula, leading to the Romulus-Remus story and the founding of Rome. The early Latin settlements are in essence Homeric (post-Troy) societies, ruled by warlord-kings and having no real law beyond the warlord's ability to enforce his control. The overarching theme of this narrative is violence. Consider, for example the foundation story: Amulias' usurpation of the kingship of the Latins, then settled in Alba Longa, from his brother Numitor; Amulias' rape of Numitor's daughter, the Vestal Ilia; Amulias' attempt to have her and her offspring put to death to ensure that Numitor will have no progeny; the abandonment of the infants Romulus and Remus in a basket near the Palatine hill; their being discovered and suckled by a she-wolf, and their survival; the killing of Amulias and the restoration of Numitor; violent disputes between Romulus and Remus and their fellow Latins; strife between Romulus and Remus and their followers, with constant discord and war; and finally the killing of Remus in battle and Romulus' founding of the first settlement on the Palatine hill with the by-now decimated survivors, which is the beginning of Rome (1.75–88). In all of book 1, though Dionysius reports councils and discussions, such as Amulias' accusation of Numitor for the rape of Ilia, he does not present a single speech.

At the outset of book 2, however, Romulus calls an assembly of his people and delivers a speech on the need to establish a government and civil institutions that will promote the civic virtues—self-control, lawfulness, harmoniousness—and thereby ensure the safety and the flourishing of the city (2.3–11).

Romulus thus is figured as the civilization-bringing first orator in the Isocratean myth of *logos*. The citizens then deliberate on what form of government they want, choose monarchy, and appoint Romulus as king; he divides the people into tribes and classes (patricians and plebeians) and assigns to each group its duties, supposedly on the model of Theseus at Athens (2.8.1–2). This, for Dionysius, is truly the founding event. From this moment, he argues, the Romans lived free of civil war for 630 years—he does not say, but he means the whole period up to the civil wars that ended the republic—because they established a practice of settling their disputes through debate, persuasion, negotiation, and compromise in public assemblies (2.11.2–3). The rest of the *Roman Antiquities,* then, is the record of this rhetorically constituted civil sphere as it copes with various disruptions and crises and thus evolves.

The disruptions and crises come from two main sources. The first is Rome's external enemies, war with whom is a constant threat. Outside the rhetorically constituted civil sphere of Rome, beyond the city's walls and its laws and institutions, there is only a state of Hobbesian universal war between the various settlements of Italy, in which the governing principle is force—conquer or be conquered—unless and until the Romans can persuade an adversary into an alliance or can subdue and absorb them. Thus in book 3, for example, the confrontation between Rome and Alba Longa, Rome's mother city, comes to the verge of war but ends in a peace conference between the two cities' kings, Tullus Hostilius and Mettius Fufetius. A merger is proposed, and there is an exchange of speeches on how the merger should be carried out and who should be the ruling partner (3.7–11). This exchange of speeches looks exactly like a declamation exercise, exploring the best arguments that can be made on either side in that particular set of circumstances. Mettius' crowning argument is that Alba Longa should rule because Rome has "corrupted" itself by admitting foreigners to citizenship, a practice frowned upon, Dionysius notes, in the Greek world; Tullus defends that practice as a principal reason for Rome's success, an argument with which Dionysius agrees. The debate ends in a draw, but they finally resolve the issue by holding a ritual combat, a sort of gladiator contest between three Albans and three Romans. The Roman hero Marcus Horatius prevails—he is the only man left standing—and Alba Longa submits to Roman rule. Later, however, Mettius betrays Tullus on the battlefield against another set of adversaries, Veii and Fidenae. Tullus then executes Mettius and has Alba Longa razed to the ground, but he transfers all the citizens to Rome and makes them Roman citizens.

The second and most dangerous source of crisis, however, is internal tensions that threaten civil strife. Rome cannot meet its almost-constant external challenges without maintaining internal concord and cooperation. Internal tensions arise mainly from the competing interests of patricians and plebeians and the concentration of power and wealth in the hands of the patricians. The root of this persistent trouble is the reorganization of voting in assemblies under king Servius Tullius in the sixth century B.C.E. (4.16–21). Tullius instituted voting by "centuries," that is, by military units, and gave one vote to each century regardless of its size. He further gave ninety-eight centuries, and votes, to the richest class of citizens and divided the remaining citizens into five more classes (ranked by wealth) with a total of ninety-five centuries between them. The sixth and lowest class, consisting of "the majority of the citizens, who were poor and for that reason exempt from military service and taxation" (4.20.5), counted as just one century and got one vote. This made for a total of 193 centuriate votes, with 97 required for an electoral majority.

As Dionysius describes it, the voting procedure was for the first class to cast their ninety-eight votes first; if they fell short of ninety-seven votes for the proposal in question, the second class (with twenty-two centuries) would be polled, and then the third (with twenty), and so on, until a ninety-seven-vote majority was obtained.[91] Most questions were settled on the first vote, if the patricians were unanimous, and few got past the fourth. The sixth class, which could cast its one vote only in the case of a tie after the first five rounds of voting, was almost never called. The obvious purpose of this reform was to prevent the poor majority from having much if any influence in the decisions of the assembly, to placate them by giving them a vote in principle only, and likewise to placate the ranks that occasionally did get to vote, but above all to ensure the dominance of patrician interests as long as they could maintain consensus. (The obtaining of which was the function of senate meetings.) In this way, as Dionysius observes, Tullius made the patricians "lords of the whole polity" (*pasês tês politeias kurioi*) and "excluded the poor from the commons" (*tous penêtas apelasas apo tôn koinôn;* 4.20.1). Dionysius claims that the Roman people did not notice the implications of this change when it was made, and that it later became a source of trouble.

The crises that emerge from these external and internal sources, and primarily the latter, produce the occasions for which Dionysius composes speeches on opposing sides. In book 4, for example, the story of Lucius Tarquinius the Younger (the last king of Rome) begins with his efforts to wrest the kingship from Servius Tullius (4.28–39). Claiming that he is the rightful heir (of Lucius Tarquinius the Elder, whom Tullius succeeded), Tarquinius calls an assembly of the senate and the people, at which he and Tullius state their claims to the kingship. Dionysius gives each a speech. Tarquinius argues fairly persuasively, at first glance, that the throne is his by right of inheritance from his father. Tullius obtained it in emergency conditions without the usual procedure—after the death of a king, the succession normally was decided by the senate and people, and confirmed by auguries—when Tarquinius was still a child. Since then, Tarquinius maintains, Tullius has illegally and unjustly kept the kingship, long past the date when it should have passed to himself. Tullius' reply, besides arguing that his rule has been beneficial to the Roman people, which was generally true, also makes this argument: "The Roman people [*ho dêmos ho Rhômaiôn*] called to the governance of state affairs [*hê archê epi ta pragmata*] not the heir of the father, but the one worthy of it. For they believed that property belongs to those who have acquired it, but the kingship to those who have bestowed it—and that property, when something happens to the owners, should pass to the natural or testamentary heirs, but the kingship, when those who have received it die, should return to those who gave it" (4.34.4). This is a striking, and fundamentally democratic, principle to be invoking in the political culture of Augustan Rome.

This episode ends with Tullius putting the kingship to a vote of the people, who confirm him as king. Tarquinius continues to scheme, however, and eventually he engineers the aged Tullius' murder and seizes the throne. He soon is at odds with and comes to despise both plebeians and patricians, and he becomes increasingly isolated and tyrannical (4.40–44). This is an example of a theme that recurs throughout the *Roman Antiquities:* the destructive effects of putting one's personal desires and ambitions above public responsibility and the covenants of the law, especially when one has unrestricted power.[92] Tarquinius governs the Romans by keeping them in a state of terrorized subjection. When he attempts to enlist the other Latin states in a campaign against the Sabines, at the council meeting he is opposed by one Turnus Herdonius from Corilla, who forcefully indicts Tarquinius' tyrannical reign and advises against alliance with such a ruler (4.45–46). Tarquinius' speech, which Dionysius reports rather than presents directly, does not reply to Turnus' arguments but attempts instead to destroy him personally, calling him a liar and a "demagogue" and accusing him of a treacherous plot (having planted false evidence in advance); Turnus is put to death (4.47–48). Tarquinius is the very portrait of a tyrant, and his speech the portrait of tyrannical discourse. (In presenting such discourse indirectly, Dionysius succeeds in portraying it while refusing to practice it.)

Eventually Tarquinius' arrogant excesses and the misdeeds of his son Sextus—culminating in the rape of Lucretia—exasperate the senate and the people. Under the leadership of Lucius Junius Brutus they drive him from power, abolish the monarchy, and establish the republican constitution as a modification of the old, replacing the kingship with annually elected consuls and effecting a compromise between rule by senate (patrician oligarchy) and democracy (the assembly of the people; 4.63–75). Brutus is given a long and stirring speech (4.77–83), which includes the line "One must choose between two things: either life with liberty, or death with honor" (4.82.4–5). However, Servius Tullius' rigged procedure of voting by centuries is retained.

Arguably the republican constitution retained an element of democracy, and at first it probably was perceived that way and seemed fair, despite its granting of nearly all decision-making power to the patrician class. After all, one might rationalize, when the senatorial rank could not produce a majority of centuriate votes for a proposal, the decision was passed downward to the plebeians, and if it ever happened that the first five ranks of centuries were deadlocked, then the poorest largest class was given the tie-breaking vote. And, one might further rationalize, shouldn't the richest citizens bear the greatest responsibility for the guidance and maintenance of the state? Nevertheless the practical effect was that plebeian concerns could virtually never get a hearing, or could be rejected out of hand by the patricians. Thus in books 5 and 6, as a result of the continual strife with Rome's surrounding neighbors and the repeated mobilizations of the citizens for war, the plebeian classes become increasingly impoverished and are driven into unsustainable debt to the increasingly rich patricians from whom they are compelled to borrow for basic sustenance. This makes them increasingly unwilling to perform their military service, which puts the state in jeopardy. This situation leads to a debate (5.64–69) concerning debt relief and the redistribution of public lands, most of which have been occupied illegally by patrician estates for generations. No decision is made, and the debate is postponed until after the current war. This use of war, and the rhetoric of national emergency, to defer discussion of debt relief becomes a repeating pattern with the patricians. Meanwhile, they institute the office of temporary dictator for periods of emergency (5.70–77). Dionysius describes this legislation as "deceiving the poor" and as contravening the legal protections of their liberty because it gave the senate sole power to appoint the dictator and gave the dictator absolute autocratic power (5.70.4–5). Thus the poor could be ordered into military service and deprived of any recourse.

The problems with this arrangement come to a head in book 6. With enemy armies repeatedly advancing on Rome (Volscians, Sabines, Auruncans), the plebeians are deeply unwilling to be mobilized. The patricians are faced with going into battle unsupported, against a numerically superior enemy. As the senate debates what to do, there is a rhetorical confrontation between the two consuls: the pro-plebeian Publius Servilius Priscus, who favors debt relief, and the resolutely pro-patrician and rhetorically capable Appius Claudius Sabinas, who staunchly opposes it and carries the day, thus exacerbating the crisis (6.23–27). Servilius, however, persuades the people to mobilize by promising that there will be debt relief once the war is concluded and wins a great victory; but afterward the senate refuses to enact the promise (6.28–34). This also becomes a repeating pattern, which produces recurring and escalating crises, and recurring exchanges of speeches.

In one of the senate debates over this issue, one Titus Larcius makes a pro-plebeian speech (6.35–36) that includes the arguments that "We live apart and have two cities: one ruled by poverty and necessity, the other by surfeit and arro-gance" (*hubris;* 6.36.1) and that the public good should be put above private considerations. This appeal to compassion, basic justice, and civic responsibility is opposed by Appius, who speaks impressively and again sways the senate (6.36–39). They appoint a dictator to enforce the decree to mobilize, Manius Valerius, but Valerius has plebeian sympathies and persuades the people to mobilize by once again promising debt relief after the current war (6.41–42). And once again the senate reneges. Valerius then makes an angry speech to the assembly of the people about the betrayal, accusing the senate of preferring not what serves the long-term interests of the state but only what serves their short-term private greed (6.43.3).

The people, now almost in open revolt, in essence go on strike. They physi-cally remove themselves from the city and camp outside the walls, refuse all forms of cooperation or negotiation, and insist that the senate knows what it should do. In the senate's debate a respected elder, Menenius Agrippa, makes a long pro-plebeian speech (6.49–56) that argues from the headings of advantage, possibility, feasibility, justice, and compassion that the senate should put aside its sense of legal principle (that is, all decent men must repay debts according to the contract) and should grant the plebeians debt relief since their position has become unen-durable. This speech persuades the older, that is, pragmatically wiser, senators. Appius then makes an even longer and in truth highly impressive speech in reply (6.59–64), arguing from the headings of justice, honor, and expediency that debts must be paid and laws and contracts observed, and that making concessions to the demands of shiftless, improvident plebeians will lead to democracy, which is the worst of all forms of government. Interestingly, he cites the democratic revo-lution at Syracuse, the supposed origin of rhetoric, in the fifth century B.C.E. as his chief example of decline into mob misrule (6.62.1–2). Appius persuades the younger senators—those with less mature political judgment and a hotheaded attachment to their sense of aristocratic honor and entitlement—and there is a tumult in the senate, full of shouting and threats.

Unable to decide anything, they call a joint meeting of the senate and assem-bly, at which the now-chastened senate, faced with popular rage, moderates its position. Menenius Agrippa also succeeds in moderating the plebeians' rage (with his famous "organs of the body" metaphor for the social classes compris-ing the state), and in the end the plebeians propose creating the institution of the Tribunes of the People and the Aediles to represent plebeian interests.[93] The motion carries (6.65–90).

I have reviewed this long episode—in itself only half of a yet-longer story about the Tribunate, as Dionysius says (7.65–66)—in order to make the following observations. First, it seems unlikely that Dionysius has told this lengthy story with its repeating patterns and many speeches simply to add drama to what might otherwise be told in a few paragraphs or pages. Rather, one purpose seems to be to show precisely the evolution of a major political institution out of a specific discourse recurring in specific but evolving circumstances. The Tribunate does not happen all at once, or through a single wise speech, or by deduction from first principles, but through a series of materially situated speech acts whose cumulative effect eventually tips the balance and occasions a major shift in both senatorial and popular consensus and in civil institutions. Imagine presenting an account of the civil rights movement in the United States by mentioning only the legislation enacted in the 1960s or by reducing the whole story to the *Brown v. Board of Education* decision and Martin Luther King Jr.'s "I Have A Dream" speech, without considering how the political consensus developed and shifted over a series of dozens, hundreds, or, in truth, thousands of acts and discursive exchanges over a period of decades. Dionysius' history can be seen as an effort to depict how the rhetorical, persuasive process that produced the Tribunate developed over time.

Second, by presenting the story as a series of occasions for debate which can be treated as declamation problems (with shifting *kairoi*), Dionysius is able to construct the strongest available arguments on opposing sides as a means of "philosophically" exploring the political issues within their contexts, and at the same time teach some rhetorical and practical political lessons to his audience of would-be and active rhetors engaged in public affairs or imperial administration. The lesson is complex. On one hand, it pits arguments proceeding from what Dionysius calls *dêmotikos*, "popular," perspectives against "aristocratic," that is, senatorial, patrician, and oligarchic, perspectives and generally makes both sides seem rational and persuasive when considered on their own terms. Indeed, as I have suggested, the pro-patrician speeches of Appius frequently operate as a combined defense of high principle and practical advantage to the state, and generally come across as the most impressive. In fact, they reasonably could be judged on technical grounds the *best speeches* in their exchanges, and they very probably would appeal to Dionysius' upper-class readers as the most persuasive or the most "noble" and high-minded. On the other hand, these excellent and apparently persuasive speeches generally have the effect of winning the immediate argument in the senate but of exacerbating the tension and strife that occasioned the debate in the first place; they solve nothing, and actually make things worse, as matters of practical policy.

So the rhetorical lesson is, in part, the old sophistic truism that the worse argument can defeat the better, if "worse" and "better" refer to practical political wisdom. The lesson also is a study of aristocratic/oligarchic and *dêmotikos* ideologies in performance. The point in presenting these ideologies, it would seem, is not simply to demonstrate their potential for internal consistency and logicality, or their capacity for being forcefully and cogently presented, but to highlight the problem of their engagement. That problem necessitates the old sophistic skill of fully representing and entertaining the "arguments on both sides" and "making the weaker stronger" in order to more fully understand the issue and thus arrive at the best available decision—the one skill neither Appius nor the more demagogic plebeians has but that the more moderate patricians, such as Valerius or Menenius Agrippa, do have, and that Dionysius himself is putting richly on display.

From this rhetorical lesson arises the practical political-philosophical lesson: Effective government, or a successful civil society, must as a matter both of justice and of practical policy make concessions to plebeian interests; the alternative is for the state eventually to be torn apart by civil strife. One of Dionysius' recurring points is his admiration for the early Romans' ability to eventually effectively deliberate and to arrive at the proper "demotic" concessions and do the right thing, even in highly charged, difficult circumstances that easily could have produced civil war. Alongside this admiration one should also put his occasionally repeated observation that the Romans "today" are nothing like their archaic ancestors (see, for example, 10.17.6). This, again, is a remarkable and significant point to argue, even if obliquely, in Augustan Rome.

This lesson is expanded in the sequels to this episode: the long and tragic Coriolanus story (6.92–8.62) and the shorter, tragi-farcical story of Appius' son Appius, who also became a consul (9.42–54). The main focus of the Coriolanus story is not the events portrayed in Shakespeare's tragedy but Coriolanus' role in a dispute over grain distribution. The plebeians are threatened with famine, and the patricians, who control the grain supply, are accused by the Tribunes of the People of mismanagement, of manipulating the supply to maximize prices. Coriolanus in a long speech to the senate (7.21–24) argues not only the recurrent aristocratic/patrician position of making no concessions to plebeian demands for wealth redistribution, or the freeing up of the grain supply—the patricians have a right to control their own property—but he also takes the frankly vindictive position that grain should be kept scarce and expensive in order to "punish" the plebeians and the Tribunes for insubordination.

This speech produces a tumult in the senate, the Tribunes attempt to arrest Coriolanus, some senators prevent it, there are blows, and the Tribunes call an assembly and indict Coriolanus (7.25–27). The current consul, Minucius, makes a conciliatory speech, which calms things down, but the more "demagogic" of the Tribunes still want Coriolanus to explain or apologize for his speech (7.28–34). Coriolanus, who is incapable of "humbling" himself in public, makes an arrogant, in-your-face speech to the assembly (7.34), thereby producing a new tumult in which the Tribunes condemn him to death on the spot, with the threat of serious violence spinning out of control. Finally the senate agrees to reduce grain prices and yield up Coriolanus, later, for a proper trial (7.35–39). In an effort to persuade him to stand trial, one of Tribunes, Decius, makes the arguments that all should be equal before the law and that Coriolanus should make himself more *dēmôtikos:* "To suffer no injustice, and to receive the justice befitting whatever wrong one may have suffered, we hold to be rights possessed equally and in common by all citizens. . . . Drag yourself down, wretched man, from that overbearing, tyrannical haughtiness to an attitude more populist [*epi to dēmôtikôteron*], and make yourself at last like other people" (7.41.5–6, 7.45.4).

This would seem to be the heart of Dionysius' political-philosophical lesson in the *Roman Antiquities.* The tragedy of Coriolanus, the old-fashioned hero, the man of unbending will, is that he cannot learn it, as Dionysius explicitly remarks (8.60–61). He is put on trial, convicted, and banished. He then goes over to Rome's enemies to get revenge and eventually comes to an ignominius end— he is stoned to death by the Volscians, the victim of political intrigue and his own overbearing behavior (7.57–8.59).

My overview of the *Roman Antiquities* must now break off here, necessarily incomplete. I hope, at least, to have demonstrated that it is not only, as Emilio Gabba would contend, a credible and significant work of history for its time but also a significant work of rhetorical and practical political philosophy for its intended audience(s) of students and practitioners of rhetoric in civic affairs in the Augustan age. Dionysius' history makes a case for the virtues of the ancient Roman-republican constitution—with its manifest but resolvable imperfections—and for the ancient Romans who developed it by generally rhetorical means, even in situations that had come close to civil war. As Dionysius puts it, while summing up his reflections on the Tribunate, "Discussing what was fair and just, they resolved their quarrels by persuasion and speech, and allowed no irreparable or unholy deed to be done against each other" (7.66.4–5). One might add, for the most part.

It should be noted too that Dionysius implicitly shows something else as well: that this process generally worked out when consensus broke down in the senate and when the patricians lacked the unity to control deliberation and decision on contentious issues. There had to be patricians willing to break the old consensus and voice *dēmotikos* positions, even if only—or especially—in view of practical considerations as well as a sense of justice. There had to be, too, a mechanism of making the ruling order answerable to the people, such as the Tribunes, even if the Tribunes sometimes abused their office or exercised their power irresponsibly. In short, political wisdom and the successful evolution of the Roman state required the disruption of consensus, the play of opposing arguments, people capable of making those arguments effectively, and people capable of hearing them intelligently, in difficult as well as easy times.[94]

Dionysius finds this rhetorical and political virtue in the ancient Romans, and the early republic, more than in the "moderns," and he presents a large gallery of rhetors and speeches, an extended theater of declamation, to be considered for critique and imitation.

On Rhetorical Scholarship

If, then, we can take Dionysius of Halicarnassus as an example of what it may mean to do rhetorical criticism or rhetorical scholarship per se, and as a potential paradigm for what we might call "rhetorical studies" now, what have we come to?

Dionysius certainly lives in a world that is in many ways different from the postmodern world of late capitalist/industrialist societies—as, for example, Fredric Jameson, Jean-François Lyotard, and others have described it[95]—and different too from the modern North American research university, though it is a world no less shot through with "rhetoricality." And in truth it is a world to which the *idea* of rhetoric is far more central than our own; a world in which no one who lacks an at least adequate rhetorical training can be recognized as "well educated"; a world in which rhetorical ability is understood as fundamental to intelligent practical thought, speech, and action, especially in civic affairs; a world in which rhetoric is central to literary culture and public discourse in general. In the major Greek cities of Dionysius' world there were, of course, municipally subsidized teachers of grammar and rhetoric provided with salaries and teaching spaces, and these small collections of colleagues might very loosely be described as "colleges," but only by approximate analogy or metaphor. By far the greater number of rhetoric teachers and schools in antiquity were small, private, unsubsidized affairs not unlike today's "consultants" who do short seminars on business writing or "how to do an effective presentation" for corporate clients (though such training is far more marginal to modern culture than rhetoric was to the ancient world, and the training that such consultants offer is clearly of the short-road and five-rules-for-success variety). The rhetoric student from Hibeh, whose declamation was examined in chapter 4, probably was taking his lessons from a private teacher, possibly in a small *phrontistêrion,* a private institute or school that met in a rented space or in the rhetorician's house.[96] Dionysius himself appears to have been a private teacher, too, giving rhetorical instruction and training to individual clients such as young Metilius Rufus, who one day would be proconsul of Achaea and whose father probably was an important man.[97]

In Dionysius' world the rhetorician is fundamentally, first and foremost a *teacher.* The municipal schools of rhetoric and the private *phrontistêria* were not research institutes but places for an *askêsis,* a training regimen. "Rhetoric" might be an object of theoretical speculation or "scientific" study in the philosophical

schools, and philosophical *theôria* might be of interest to the rhetorician. Dionysius clearly is familiar with, and in conversation with, the work of the philosophical schools and Alexandrian literary scholarship so far as they bear on the work
of the rhetorician. But in the rhetorician's practice, "rhetoric" itself was neither
a theory or "metaphysics" of discourse nor a systematic art or set of rules for
producing a few types of speeches, but an art of producing speakers, writers,
and thinkers by means of a "gymnastic" process of "patient study" and "laborious exercise." The goal of that process was to cultivate the student's rhetorical
dunamis, a complex construct of habituated practices that ultimately became, as
Dionysius puts it, a "nonrational" capacity for quick apprehension and improvisational invention that would operate as second nature and eventually would
far exceed the precepts of the *technai.* The precepts were an apparatus for that
process; they put names to what the student was experiencing and explained
what usefully could be explained at a given stage in the student's development.
Much of what the philosophers had to say was unnecessary to that work, even
if true. But the effect of the training was greater than the sum of its parts.
Ultimately, as Cicero's speakers say, the successful student would outgrow the
technai, necessary as they once were, as he left the sweet garden of the school,
continued to develop his *dunamis* through years of practical experience, and
matured into his own, distinctive, rhetorical *charaktêr.*

Dionysius' work as a rhetorical critic and scholar is organized around that
primary, pedagogical function. As such, it presents three recognizable paradigms
for modern academic work in rhetorical studies. First, *the production of technai,* or
"textbooks." As I have stated, in the ancient paradigm the *technê* typically is not
a work of theory in the philosophical or *wissenschaftlich* sense but is either a sort
of resource manual for the teacher or a "Proclus' bookcase" item that a student
may consult for review or use to supplement the rhetorician's teaching, and it
generally is not a primary course material. It is, in essence, a collection of the
things that usefully can be said to students doing exercises. Indeed, most students
probably never consulted or owned a *technê,* unless they themselves intended to
become a rhetorician, or like Cicero or Dionysius' addressees took a cultured
interest, either professional or amateur, in the technicalities of rhetoric. Dionysius' *On the Composition of Words* seems fairly clearly to be a memorandum
(*hupomnêma*) of a course of instruction, but in the course itself the student is
mainly studying examples, hearing the teacher's commentary, and doing "composition" (*sunthesis*) exercises. Considering Dionysius and the ancient *technai,*
then, one might argue that a primary form of publication for the rhetorical
scholar is the textbook, the *technê.* One might consider what a "Dionysian" view
of modern textbooks would be: some unnecessarily theoretical, some too formulaic in giving "rules" and recipes for a few discourse genres, some a usable
resource, and so on. I leave those judgments to the reader. But I think they

would be matters not of theoretical correctness but of, pragmatically, what *dunamis* one wants rhetorical training to cultivate, and how effectively a given text or pedagogy helps to cultivate it.[98]

The second paradigm is *rhetorical criticism*. In the early days of rhetoric's revival as a discipline, early in the twentieth century, Herbert Wichelns looked to literary criticism as a model for "the literary criticism of oratory," which would be distinguished primarily by its object of study (oratory) and by the considerations peculiar to its object: the oration's, or practical orations's, embeddedness in a specific historical situation and its persuasive function.[99] For the modern discipline this was, and largely still is, the rhetorical scholar's primary form of work. Its best contemporary conceptualization arguably is Steven Mailloux's notion of "rhetorical hermeneutics," or what he has more recently called "reception histories," an approach that originated from reader-response criticism, as well as the critical-theoretical issues it generated, and developed into the analysis of the persuasive effects of textual "trope and argument" on audiences in and across particular cultural-historical situations.[100] Mailloux's approach has considerable advantages, such as taking not only "oratory" as its object of study but *persuasive effect* in any and every kind of discourse. Rhetorical hermeneutics thus provides a propaideutic bridge between grammatical and rhetorical study —framing literary analysis and explication in rhetorical terms—and provides also a method for continuing and more advanced rhetorical studies. However, if such a rhetorical criticism remains focused only on the explication of particular discursive events in their historical contexts, we are brought back to the problem of making rhetoric a hermeneutic of the rhetorical. It becomes in essence, a grammatical analysis of the rhetorical, or a mode of literary or cultural study, with the consequence that rhetoric never quite emerges as a distinct disciplinary entity but remains an interdiscipline available to scholarly work in a variety of disciplines.[101] If one does cultural studies with a rhetorical approach, one still is, primarily, doing cultural studies.

Perhaps, of course, rhetoric *should* be an interdiscipline that operates across disciplinary boundaries, Proteus-like, without ever assuming a shape of its own or ever being wrestled down to a fixed position. But if we consider Dionysius as a possible paradigm for rhetorical criticism per se, the distinctive feature is his orientation toward pedagogy. The function of rhetorical criticism per se is to identify and evaluate discursive practices, or particular features of discursive practices, or the practices of particular rhetors, as desirable, or not, for rhetorical practice *now* and thus as suitable objects for study and imitation or avoidance. Such criticism thus includes a hermeneutic of the rhetorical effects of particular discursive practices, as with Mailloux, but it is committed to more than that, for it never completely loses sight of the pedagogical intent to cultivate rhetorical competence in students at all levels and in grownups grayed by experience. This requires acts of critical judgment—of deciding whether a particular discursive act is "good," and of deciding in turn what "good" means when making such decisions—which themselves will be rhetorical acts requiring argumentation and analysis focused explicitly on the functions and methods of discursive transactions, and on the grounds by which we judge them, such as utility, justice, ethics, and so on. In short, what Bonner and others have viewed as Dionysius' failure to produce modern literary criticism should in fact be viewed as his distinctive virtue, and as a potential paradigm for the disciplinary practice of rhetoric per se.

The third paradigm is *the writing of history.* For reasons that, as far as I know, have never really been examined or explained, history writing seems to have been a distinctive literary practice of sophists from the later fourth century B.C.E. onward—that is, the rhetorical or panegyric histories whose ancient popularity modern critics have mostly failed to understand. Even the unfortunate Hegesias of Magnesia was well published and widely read, so much so that Dionysius needed to stamp him down and castigate his prose as piffle. Probably some account should be taken of the different purposes and audiences these histories serve, and their differences from what we more conventionally recognize as "history." For example, one might argue that the panegyric histories were to "regular" history and chronicle what, in our time, the "new journalism" has been to conventional journalism. Should we think of panegyric histories as historical novels, or as a literary counterpart to the Greek novel, which in Dionysius' time was just beginning to be popular?[102]

Looking specifically at Dionysius, however, it seems clear that historiography is with him an extended means of doing both rhetorical criticism and practical political philosophy, as part of the advanced education of the rhetor. Like Cicero, he presents an account of the Roman-republican constitution's evolution as a way of arguing for its wisdom, and to make a case for balancing the power of patrician or imperial elites with at least some representation of *dêmotikos* interests. Like Aristides in the Sicilian Orations, and many other Greek declaimers, he presents a gallery of declamations with opposing speeches set in particular situations as a means of reflecting more generally on the wisdom and effectivity of different discursive practices and ways of deliberation. The analysis, in short, is *performative.* If taken as a paradigm for modern rhetorical scholarship, it points to histories of rhetorical practices or of particular rhetorical events insofar as the treatment addresses, either explicitly or implicitly, issues in contemporary rhetorical practice and pedagogy. A rhetorical history that became wholly and only an explication of a particular event would no longer be doing "rhetoric per se," but history with a rhetorical methodology.

Finally, Dionysius also presents some paradigms that are less familiar or less consistent with "scholarly" performance in the modern research university, including the address to a popular if cultured audience, as in his "lectures"; or the skilled performance of the art he teaches, as in the "literary" achievement of the *Roman Antiquities* or the declamations it contains. Rhetoricians working in such a paradigm today would address themselves not only to fellow rhetoricians in scholarly monographs but to a wider public sphere. Perhaps the modern rhetorician should present his or her rhetorical criticism or rhetorical history in the form of a "new journalistic" narrative, or a historical novel, or a documentary film or video, or a blog or other digitally mediated text. (Without forgetting to include reflection on the contemporary value of the practices performed and/or examined.) Perhaps the modern rhetorician should, at least, write well, or eloquently, and as Isocrates long ago suggested should himself or herself be a model for his or her students' emulation.

In these different and overlapping ways, then, rhetorical criticism and scholarship might remain identifiably rhetorical in some meaningful sense and at the same time may be relevant to, or part of, an effective and desirable pedagogy. That, it seems to me, is the view from Halicarnassus.

Epilogue
William Dean Howells and the Sophist's Shoes

I'm resigning from the Kenneth Burke Society. No-one
will disagree with me.

*Kenneth Burke, at the Conference on College Composition
and Communication (1989)*

Additional Reflections, or Epiphonemas

As I said in the prologue, this book is a sequence of extended, overlapping essays
that do not necessarily have to be read in the order presented (with the exception of chapters 2–3). As such they do not quite constitute what Kenneth Burke
would call a syllogistic progression,[1] though there are reiterated themes and a
general stance that has, I hope, held things together. In this epilogue, then, my
"conclusion" takes the form not so much of a conclusion as of additional reflections, or epiphonemas, as well as two chreias.

But first, perhaps, I should summarize a little. In this book I have taken the
general position that what makes rhetoric rhetoric is its teaching tradition, its
function as an "art of producing rhetors." Without that tradition it ceases to be
an independent entity distinct from "grammar" (philology and hermeneutics),
philosophy (theory), or the social-scientific versions of those things (linguistics,
political science, and so forth). Instead it becomes a version of grammar or philosophy or social science devoted to rhetorical objects of study, which turn out,
in a world saturated by "rhetoricality," to be virtually anything having anything
to do with language and human behavior.[2] At which point rhetoric risks becoming nothing in particular, without a subject matter, purpose, methodology,
or body of knowledge of its own. Or it fails to emerge as a discipline in its own
right and subsists as an interdiscipline or subdiscipline or subtopic of something
else, which of course is very much the story of rhetorical studies in the university today.[3] What makes rhetoric distinctly rhetoric, again, is its teaching tradition. That central project provides the reference point, the application, for
rhetoric's other, more scholarly projects in history, criticism, and theory.

In taking this general position I have sided with Cicero's Antonius in *De oratore*. As he argues, the "genuine teachers of this art" are not the philosophers and grammarians who may study rhetoric—Plato, Aristotle, and their successors, as worthy of (some) attention as they are—but the teachers in the *technê* tradition. This is the tradition of the rhetoricians' "little books" and the pedagogy they supported, which the Academic Charmadas dismissed as having nothing to say about politics or ethics, indeed, nothing but a bagful of precepts for the handling of introductions and the like, or a body of lore concerning pedagogy. The rhetoricians' "little books" present not a systematic account of rhetoric's nature and its principles, not a "metaphysics" of rhetoric but an aggregate collection of things-to-say-to-students that have worked, arranged under a set of headings— such as Isocrates' "domains" of style and subject matter, the *lekitkos topos* and the *pragmatikos topos*—and meant to support a *system of exercises* from the progymnasmata to declamation.[4] This is the tradition, too, that modern scholarship has tended to characterize as "pedestrian" in comparison with the philosophizing-on-rhetoric of the Peripatos, Academy, and other schools.[5]

And yet, that supposedly pedestrian tradition really is the main tradition, from at least the fourth century B.C.E. to late antiquity. It is, in Cicero's metaphor, the main "stream," the great river, that flowed from Isocrates and his school and through all subsequent rhetoricians. I have tried to show that Cicero had it mostly right, that while it cannot be proved to a certainty, nevertheless it is likely that Isocrates wrote, or at least transmitted, a *technê;* that the *technê* of Isocrates was disseminated through his students to subsequent generations of rhetoricians, that it was the ancestor of, and prefigured, the *technai* that survive today, and that it was rendered obsolete and replaced by later iterations, especially the rhetoric of Hermagoras, so that it eventually disappeared, as did the rhetoric of Hermagoras in its turn. An implication of that argument is that the conventionally presumed division between the philosophical rhetoric of Isocrates and the technical rhetoric of the handbooks probably is illusory.[6] Isocratean and technical rhetoric are one and the same.

What makes this ostensibly technical training also philosophical in Isocrates' terms is partly the literary education that it presupposes, builds on, and continues: readings in the canonic poets, historians, philosophers, and orators, in which the student performs, explicates, critiques and imitates the writers studied. Through performance the student develops the *aisthêsis* that Dionysius of Halicarnassus regards as the foundation, starting point, and ultimate criterion for rhetorical analysis, and that Cicero's Crassus regards as the source of the experiential knowledge that enables the student to understand what the precepts of rhetoric "refer to." Indeed, as Isocrates suggests, the talented student will take the impress of the authors and texts that he or she has read/performed and will reflect their influence in his or her speech even before the art embodied in them has been explicitly taught or understood. At the same time, however, through explication/critique (interpretive and critical discussion of what has been read/ performed), the student will begin to develop the conceptual frameworks that later will inform study and performance in the rhetorical curriculum itself. These include not only grammatical and rhetorical concepts but also the ideas, the grand themes, and the famous lines of what Isocrates calls the "celebrated" authors—culturally authoritative ideas that can be invoked as commonplaces, elaborated, and made the basis of flights of eloquence. These conceptual frameworks include, as well, standards for judging what to imitate and what to avoid.

But the truly philosophical dimension of the rhetorical *paideia* lies, first, in the progymnasmatic restatement, elaboration, contradiction, and disputation of general beliefs, as in, to give a short list, the maxim/chreia, encomium, commonplace, or thesis exercises. Likewise exercise in fable and narrative rehearses the student not only in the means of storytelling and factual narration but also in the resources for arguing and assessing a story's probability, truth value, and quality—whether it is noble, beneficial, just, aesthetically pleasing, and so on. Such exercises, one might argue, are not only training in the elementary "forms" from which complex discourses are composed but also training in what might be called "popular philosophy," the engagement with communally shared belief, as distinct from the more austere and abstruse researches of the philosophic schools.[7] Ultimately, the *philosophia* of rhetoric lies in the pursuit of practical wisdom in declamation, through the process of inventing and forcefully presenting arguments "on both sides" of a specific case. The philosophical aspect of Isocratean/technical rhetoric lies not in the narration of a political, ethical, or other doctrine, but in the provision of resources for arguing a question of belief or action in different ways, especially in practical situations where a decision must be made, the choice is not obvious, and counsel must be taken. So it is not true, as Charmadas said, that the writers of "little books" titled *Rhetoric* had nothing to say about politics, ethics, and the like. Within the school of rhetoric, in the process of exercise, such things were constantly and perennially discussed.

One might object that my Antonian image of the "genuine teacher" of rhetoric, or of rhetoric as a teaching discipline, is hopelessly unrealistic and unsustainable in the modern, *wissenschaftlich* "research" university, where teaching typically gets plenty of lip service but little substantial respect.[8] One cannot found a modern academic discipline on the activities of master craftsmen (rhetors, writers) training apprentices to be rhetors, as effective and socially beneficial as that might be. The tenure line professor is supposed to be a scholar, a researcher, who like the scientist generates new knowledge in his or her field of specialty. The physicist smashes atoms and identifies the ultimate particles and forces of which the universe is composed; the theorist of discourse deconstructs the deep webs of signification and the discursive forces that construct our very being. Every rhetorician who holds the title of professor, like every professor in the humanities, has been trained to be a "doctor of philosophy," in essence a grammarian/philosopher, an explicator/critic/theorist. And so, in one sense, *no one is a genuine rhetorician* in Antonius' terms, or no one can be as long as they persist in what Kenneth Burke would call their "trained incapacity," their "occupational psychosis" as a professional humanistic scholar in the modern "research university."[9] And if that is true, then the constitution of the modern university and the dominant construction of academic disciplinarity would have to change before the "genuine" art of rhetoric could reemerge as an authentic discipline. I can't just resolve to do things differently tomorrow.

Or so that argument goes. It begins to sound like Jacques Derrida's conversation with Giovanna Borradori on the ineffable meaning of 9/11 and the problem of terrorism, with its paralyzing results.[10] Obviously the argument does not apply as much to rhetoricians teaching in four-year colleges where "research productivity" receives less emphasis and teaching is the primary enterprise. Further, speaking even of research universities, one might retort that it would be strange if a school of art produced no artists, a school of music no musicians, a school of broadcast journalism no broadcast journalists, a school of engineering no engineers, a school of medicine no physicians—and so on—but only explicators/critics/theorists of those things. Rhetoric is an art of cultivating a productive, performative capacity. The rhetorician fundamentally and distinctively is a trainer of rhetors. However, the ancient example of Dionysius of Halicarnassus suggests how the "genuine rhetorician" may also be a scholar, critic, and historian. Rhetorical criticism and histories like that of Dionysius rest on scholarship, including archival work, and are the rhetorician's ways of doing contextualized pragmatic theory. The rhetorician-scholar is a critic/historian/theorist of how it was done, what should be imitated/acquired and what should be avoided, and how it can be acquired. What we do in our scholarship ultimately should have some relevance to rhetoric's distinctive point of application in the schoolroom.[11] Rhetorical scholarship that made no consequential difference to what rhetors/writers do, or to how rhetors/writers are trained, would have little point. Perhaps that is obvious. Yet it is easy to forget.

On a Passing Remark by William Dean Howells

I remember that roughly forty years ago, around 1970, when I was young and an English major, one of my reading assignments was an essay titled "Novel-Writing and Novel-Reading" by William Dean Howells, the "dean of American letters" at the end of the nineteenth century. That essay, originally a public lecture delivered somewhere in the American Midwest in 1899, when Howells was sixty-two years old, was a manifesto for realist fiction, upholstered with genteel turn-of-the-century talk about truth, beauty, art, and the sins of romanticism. The manifesto made little impression on me then, nor did the classroom discussion of it, which I cannot remember at all. Nothing has stayed with me but the title and a couple of lines near the beginning: "The reader who is not an author considers what the book is; the author who is a reader, considers, will he, nill he, how the book has been done."[12] Along with this goes some other stuff, as I reread the essay now, about the "chasmal difference between the author and the reader, which Goethe says can never be bridged," and a reflection that "others" who are not authors "may learn to enjoy, to reason and to infer," about a work of literature, but only a fellow writer can truly appreciate and have insight into the writer's craft.

I recall this snippet for two main reasons. First, because it *has* stayed with me, though I generally misremember the actual words. I suspect that it spoke to my interests as a young would-be writer surrounded by a late-sixties literary-studies curriculum that still was heavily New Critical and that had much to say about things such as "existentialism in Walt Whitman's poetry" or "the symbolism of whiteness in *Moby-Dick*"—or the formal thematic structure of John Donne's "Good Friday, Riding Westward," which was not the actual, perceivable structure of the poem but a "deep" structure that had gone unnoticed for centuries and only analysis could reveal. Such criticism generally did little or nothing for me as a writer. Second, in Howells' remark I hear a lingering echo of the classical rhetorical curriculum, which in 1899 was at low ebb in Western European and American education. Whether Howells was channeling something from his limited formal education, or from some source in his voracious reading, his personal experience, or some other source, I leave to others to decide. But I suspect it was his own experience of the divide that writers regularly feel, even today, when confronted with academic literary criticism and high theory.[13]

In essence, Howells voices the fundamental distinction in the classical curriculum between grammatical and rhetorical approaches to literature, or to discursive art in general, that is, the approaches of *grammatikê,* the "art of letters," and of *rhêtorikê,* the "art of the speaker" or of fashioning a speaker (or writer). In the grammatical curriculum, one asks "what the (text) is"—a poem? a political pamphlet? an example of romanticism or realism? fine art or lowbrow kitsch? an instance of truth and beauty?—and one may "reason and infer" about what it means, implies, argues, signifies, suggests, represents, reflects, and so forth, with the goal of producing a defensible reading or analysis, or an aesthetic or moral judgment. One can say things such as, "According to the Neoplatonists, the *Odyssey* is an allegory of the soul's journey of return to unity with the One" or "Let me tell you about the poststructuralism of Don DeLillo's *White Noise*" or "See how these eighteenth-century artworks embody the ideology of colonialism." In the rhetorical curriculum, by contrast, one asks, "How was it done?" Or more to the point, "How can I do that?" It casts the practitioner in the role of rhetor and/or rhetorician—as either a performer or would-be performer of discourse who wants to acquire the capacity (*dunamis*) of an admired model or a master performer who trains performers and does so not through the narration of a theory but through the supervision of a training regimen that includes the critical study and imitation of exemplars, progymnasmata in the basic "forms" of eloquence and argument, and advanced exercise in declamation, requiring the composition of complex discourse for imaginary cases that admit strong arguments on both sides.

Both the rhetorical and grammatical perspectives depend on each other, at least in principle. One cannot take a rhetorical perspective without at least a basic, grammatical understanding of a text—although advanced grammatical readings, like the Neoplatonic reading of Homer, or Jacques Derrida's reading of Plato's *Phaedrus,* often go far beyond what a rhetor needs to know—and the grammatical perspective, with an eye to rhetoric, can frame itself as "rhetorical hermeneutics" and can stage rhetorical performances in the form of interpretive debates.[14] But there is, nonetheless, a fundamental distinction between the two, as Howells recognizes from his writerly perspective.

Howells' remark, moreover, recalls to mind the seldom-noted but real resemblance of the classical rhetorical *paideia* to certain aspects of modern "creative writing" instruction.[15] That should be put the other way around: creative writing bears a surprising resemblance to the classical rhetorical *paideia,* at least in certain respects. The similarities include, first of all, a master/apprentice model of instruction. The teacher of creative writing always is a proven, published performer of the species of discursive art in question, whether it be short or long fiction, poetry, drama, or literary nonfiction. As with Isocrates, too, the student in this arrangement is assumed to have the requisite modicum of talent, preparation, and desire. There is no such thing as "remedial" creative writing or a creative writing requirement in any collegiate curriculum that I know of. Further, both ancient rhetoric and modern creative writing feature a pedagogy centered on the study of models or the particular elements of *technê* that they embody, large amounts of exercise/performance, and the workshopping of drafts in progress. Notably, many creative writing textbooks consist primarily of exercises or creative games that often look like progymnasmata—that is, they focus on component skills or forms, or what Isocrates would call the basic *ideai* from which "all discourses," or at least the main types of literary discourse are composed—while a smaller number of exercises resemble declamation, insofar as they ask the student to compose for imaginary situations.[16] Moreover, the ethos of creative writing tends to be resistant to the high-theoretical preoccupations of academic literary criticism, regarding them as wafty readerly philosophizing with little or no practical utility for the writer. Derrida's reading of the *Phaedrus* is a brilliant tour de force with no use at all for someone who wants to write a literary dialogue. This attitude is particularly noticeable, for example, in Francine Prose's 2007 *Reading Like a Writer,* which at several points takes a stance rather like that of Dionysius of Halicarnassus on the uselessness of some aspects of Alexandrine grammatical theory to the teaching of style.

Contemporary creative writing resembles ancient rhetoric, or rhetoric in its early development, in another way too. As a quick survey of creative writing handbooks makes evident, there is nothing like the ordered sequence of the classical progymnasmata, or anything like the classical distinction between progymnasmata and declamation—no standardized curriculum. Nor is there a consistent *technê* from handbook to handbook, though there is a small core of shared technical terms. Each handbook takes an approach that is idiosyncratic to a certain degree. In this respect, then, creative writing resembles rhetoric before Isocrates in that it is somewhat a hodgepodge of *technai* that have not settled into a stable canonic form. Interestingly, there have been some recent voices within the creative writing community calling for a new or revised model of disciplinarity based on rhetoric.[17]

The points of resemblance between rhetoric and creative writing are seldom noted, probably because of the near-complete isolation of creative writing and rhetoric/writing programs from each other in most colleges and universities, although they both teach writing and could easily form the basis of an independent discipline, one that would stand to English as ancient *rhetorikê* stood to *grammatikê.* The sad contemporary state of affairs is based mainly on ideological assumptions on both sides about "aesthetic" versus "practical" kinds of discourse, and on the inertias of institutional history. The creative writers and the rhetoricians in the modern *wissenschaftlich* university belong to different, demarcated fields with different modes of professionalization and different career trajectories. Something similar can be said, of course, about the institutional separation between rhetoric/writing and communication/speech programs, which also have a natural affinity and indeed are fragments of the "genuine" discipline of rhetoric but often are housed in different *colleges* on the same campus. It is all the result of history, not intelligent design.

It would be too much, in sum, to suggest a complete identification of creative writing as it now stands and classical rhetorical instruction. There are some obvious differences, beside those I have already mentioned. One is the modern idea of "creativity" itself, defined in terms of generally romantic notions of intuition and distinguished from the supposedly repressive forces of rationality, rules, and *technê.* Another, and a big one, is ancient rhetoric's civic orientation—especially the civic theater of declamation and its evocation of an imagined democratic polity—which contrasts with creative writing's tendency to privilege private, individual experience: the life and problems of the *idiotês,* the individual person, the "nobody," in contrast to the *politês,* the active citizen performing on the public stage, in the realm of contestation as an embodiment and agent of the communal *êthos.* The creative writer typically tells the *idiotês'* tale; the rhetor *is* the *politês.* But their training regimens are notably comparable in certain ways.

Ancient rhetoric interestingly compares, as well, with modern rhetoric/ writing instruction, the fragment of rhetoric with which I am most familiar. As I have noted occasionally in the preceding chapters, a number of things are strikingly familiar, in particular the conception of the schoolroom as a "speech workshop," the primacy of exercise and group discussion, the process of commentary and revision of evolving drafts, small working groups, and individualized attention from the teacher. Further, the kinds of errors that ancient students seem to have made in their declamations, and what seems to have been the typical length of their compositions, also seem familiar. So do patterns of teacherly response to student error, where we can see them. Some things, it seems, have never changed.

But there are some notable contrasts, too. For example, the progymnasmata bear some resemblance to the now-anathematized "modes" of composition featured in the so-called current-traditional rhetoric that dominated writing, and to some degree speech, instruction from the late nineteenth century to the 1960s—that is, forms such as narration, description, definition, comparison, exposition, argument, persuasion, and so on.[18] The modes are sometimes identified with topics of invention or methods of amplification, but they really make more sense as progymnasmata, insofar as the purpose would be to learn to manipulate, expand/contract, elaborate, contradict, and dispute a story or some idea. And to function like the classical progymnasmata, each mode would need to be furnished with the headings appropriate to it, as well as prescriptions for organization and style, and explicitly treated as an elemental rhetorical form that is to be combined with others in complex real-world discourse. In current-traditional rhetoric, however, the modes typically were reified as types of essays and treated as empty forms that a student had to fill up with "content," usually drawn from his or her experience. Further, the game-playing aspect of the progymnasmata—suasion and profusion—was replaced by an ethic of sincere, clear reportage.

Some recent voices in rhetoric/writing studies have argued for returning to the progymnasmata, or a modernized version of them, as a way of reintroducing *technê* to the "writing process" pedagogy that has dominated since the late 1960s.[19] Frank D'Angelo, for example, has published a first-year composition textbook based closely on the classical progymnasmata, and A. P. Church and Anders Sigrell describe experimental programs based on the progymnasmata for "transitional and developmental" writing students at universities in Texas and Sweden.[20] Perhaps most interesting, James Selby has developed a writing curriculum based on Aphthonius' progymnasmata for the fourth through ninth grades at a private academy in Kansas and claims measurable improvement in student performance.[21] Selby's example suggests, too, the propriety of the progymnasmata to lower-level, precollegiate education—which is in line with its ancient use—followed by declamation at the college level.

The ancient example of schoolroom exercise in declamation, as well as the progymasmata, may make a case for the pedagogical value, too, of the *fictionality* and *gameplay* aspect of *civic theater* in imaginary scenes, cases, characters, as we see it in ancient rhetorical education. As I have argued, and seen in my own experience, this ludic fictionality encourages profuse imaginative invention, argumentational play, and engagement with the deeper principles at stake—the rules of evidence, the criteria of judgment—and encourages as well the capacity to enter into alternative perspectives while inventing arguments *in utramque partem*.[22] That fictionality challenges contemporary rhetoric's split emphases, depending on one's camp, on earnest argument on "real" contemporary issues or on sincere personal self-expression in reflective essays, or on both together. The basis for that argument is laid out in chapter 4 and need not be repeated here. All I will insist upon, in closing, is that ancient rhetorical education remains useful as an object of contemplation for rhetoric in its modern form.

It is worth remembering that ancient rhetorical education in the mainstream from the fourth century B.C.E. to late antiquity—and beyond—retained the basic pedagogical form that Isocrates seems to have established: reading/performance of exemplar texts, rhetorical-critical studies, progymnasmata, and declamation. Those centuries of persistence and stability cannot be explained by portraying generation on generation of rhetoricians as "dumb schoolmasters" too dull to innovate, or by portraying the ancient rhetorical *paideia* as a punishingly tedious regimen of mindless exercise.[23] Nicolaus Mesarites' and Gregory Antiochus' descriptions of the school as a sort of paradise where the voices of children reciting their lessons and doing elementary exercises sound like angel choirs and young men dispute like sparrows around a fountain, or Lucian's and Michael Psellos' portrayals of the effect of their schooling as intellectual and spiritual liberation, suggest quite otherwise. The better argument is that the ancient pedagogy, organized around the fictive "theater" of progymnasmata and declamation, remained in place, in a homeostatic stability-in-variation, *because it was effective* and *because it was enjoyable*.

Ancient rhetorical education appealed to the desires that brought the motivated student to it and that persist today: the desire expressed by Isocrates' students to say admirable things; or Plato's Phaedrus' remark that he would rather be eloquent like Lysias than rich; or Plato's Hippocrates' wish to learn to speak "awesomely" like Protagoras; or young Lucian's dream of being "lifted up on high" in Lady Paideia's chariot and "surveying cities and nations and peoples from the very east to the very west, and like Triptolemus sowing something broadcast over the earth"; or young Michael Psellos' dream in the eleventh century of rhetoric as a realm of reasoned deliberation, law, and freedom from violence and coercion. Rhetoric, as a *paideia,* was a "sweet garden" where the young could experience and enact such things *as theater, as game,* and in so doing could cultivate their *dunamis* for wise and eloquent speech, thought, and writing in practical situations as well as develop an attachment to a dream paradigm of democratic civic life that would not be realistically possible again until the modern era, but that nevertheless could mitigate the autocratic politics of the Roman Empire.[24]

Things are not so different now, in some respects. I recently had an office conference with a student in a "Principles of Rhetoric" course that I was teaching (the gateway course to the undergraduate major in rhetoric and writing at the University of Texas). She had come, as required by the assignment, to talk about the topic for her term paper project. She wanted to do an analysis of an online issue of the *Onion,* a news parody and social/political satire magazine— an excellent example of the rhetoric of comedy/satire. Trotting out my lame professorial student conference gambits, I asked what had gotten her interested in that topic. "I want to write like that," she said.

The Sophist's Shoes

In a famous passage near the end of his *Sophistical Refutations* (34, 183b–184a), Aristotle ridicules Gorgias and other sophists for teaching by giving their students speeches to be learned by heart (as well as, I strongly suspect, parts of speeches, sample arguments, and so forth). Aristotle does not say so, but it seems likely that he also is thinking of Isocrates, who presented his students with model *logoi* that he himself had written. It is, says Aristotle, as if one tried to teach shoemaking by handing out examples of shoes.

The remark is witty, but one might ask, should one instead hand out systematic treatises on the theory of shoemaking, or the theory of shoes, or ingenious critiques of shoes, *without* showing the students any shoes? ("The shoe is a sort of extension of the foot, and thus its principles arise from the foot's mechanics and biology. Let us, then, first consider the nature of the foot. What is a foot? We must interrogate this notion . . .") Would one then ask one's students, who have not yet examined an actual shoe, to "be creative" and "invent" shoes that correspond to "the idea of shoes" in the theory one has taught them? Or would they simply turn to critiquing shoes according to the terms of the theory, or to discussing shoe theory, without actually making any shoes? (Which seems most probable.)

Instead, wouldn't one look at and discuss some example shoes, in particular the kinds the students want to make, and especially shoes that are acknowledged to be wonderful—perhaps comparing them with other shoes acknowledged to be bad—and set the beginning students to elementary exercises, such as cutting leather into the requisite parts, and model and explain all that can be modeled and explained at each stage along the way?

I suppose the analogy is bad to start with, and misleading. Speeches and written works are not shoes and are not exactly made in the way that shoes are made. And the memorizing of exemplars was a preliminary stage of sophistic rhetorical instruction, not the end of it. The students were memorizing speeches to perform them, and performing them to learn to inhabit them, *and to be inhabited by them,* on the way to acquiring a feel for discursive art—what it feels like to be Demosthenes, or Lysias, or Thucydides speaking—so that the technical precepts of the art, when they were discussed, would have something *that the student had experienced and was intimately familiar with* to elucidate and would thus be meaningful. And from there began, when rhetoric had taken on its distinctive form, a graded sequence of exercises in the progymnasmata and declamation that went on for years, accompanied by continued rhetorical-critical studies of exemplars, to be read with writerly attention, and all meant to train the student to be a rhetor and practical philosopher in the theater of civic life. So Aristotle was, I think, mistaken on that point about shoes.

NOTES

Prologue

1. With the cry-in-the-wilderness exceptions of McCloskey 1985/1998 and Billig 1987.

2. This is the explicit mode, for example, of Brooks Jackson and Kathleen Hall Jamieson's 2007 *unSpun*.

3. Walker 1998, 2003, 2006a, 2006b. See also Fleming 1998, 1999; and Graff and Leff 2005, who take a similar position.

4. Bender and Wellbery 1990.

5. For example: Struever 2009—an admirable book—considers rhetoric in the classical to modern traditions as a pragmatist mode of inquiry, particularly into civil questions, in the modality of "possibility" (in contrast to philosophy, whose modality is "necessity"); this is "rhetoric" in definition 1 and/or 2, as the object of study. What Struever *does* is theorize the nature of rhetoric, as she defines it, and its manifestations from early modernity to our own times; this is "rhetoric" in definition 3. But it can be said that, disciplinarily, what she does is not *primarily* rhetoric but "rhetorical studies" as a subfield of something else (for example, the history of ideas or the theory of knowledge).

6. Marrou 1956; Clark 1957. See also Bonner 1949, 1977.

7. See Kennedy 1963, 1969, 1972, 1980 (and 1999), 1983, 1991 (and 2007), 1994.

8. Cribiore 2001, 2007a; Too 2001; Hawhee 2004; and Heath 1995, 2004. See also Gleason 1995; Browning 1997; Too 1995, Too and Livingstone 1998, and Too 2008; Murphy 1990; Gunderson 2003; Poulakos and Depew 2004; and Morgan 1998, 2007. Woods 2010, a study of classroom uses of Geoffrey of Vinsauf's *Poetria Nova,* is outside the historical boundaries of this book but relevant to its purposes. See also Kraus 2009 and Camargo 2009.

Translations of documents heretofore inaccessible to nonclassicists include Russell and Wilson 1981; Russell 1996; Kaster 1995; Dilts and Kennedy 1997; Kennedy 2003, 2005; Gibson 2008; and Penella 2009. The appendix of Cribiore 2007a is a translation of the (previously untranslated) letters of Libanius related to the business of his school, organized into "dossiers" for individual students.

9. For example, Corbett 1998; Connors, Ede, and Lunsford 1984; Murphy 1990; Crowley and Hawhee 2008; Horner and Leff 1995; Fleming 1998, 1999, 2003; D'Angelo 1999; Petraglia and Bahri 2003; Axer 2003; Graff and Leff 2005; and Desmet 2006.

10. Apuleius of Madaura's second-century C.E. treatise on logic is titled *Peri Hermêneias* (On Interpretation); likewise the treatise on logic attributed to Augustine is clearly intended for textual interpretation (particularly of metaphor and other tropes),

and in *De doctrina Christiana* logic is explicitly treated as an aid to the interpretation of scripture.

11. See "Lexicon Rhetoricae" in Burke 1968a.

12. Two full-length monographs on Dionysius have recently been published—see Gabba 1991 and de Jonge 2008—but neither considers him primarily as a rhetorician and neither considers the whole Dionysian corpus. Gabba focuses on Dionysius' history of Rome and mostly ignores the critical writings, and de Jonge focuses on Dionysius' linguistic theories and their relation to Hellenistic developments in grammar.

13. Walt Whitman, *Song of Myself* sec. 51, lines 1324–26.

14. In this I am following Anderson 1993.

Chapter 1: Cicero's Antonius

1. See, for example, Kennedy 1994, 141–42; May and Wisse 2001, 26–39; Wisse 2002a, 2002b; Fantham 2004, chap. 7.

2. My translation here is partly based on those of Sutton and Rackham 1942, and May and Wisse 2001.

3. Antonius's apparent reference to the *Rhetoric,* if it is not a deliberate anachronism by Cicero, suggests that it (or the books composing it) was in circulation well before 91 B.C.E., whereas the usual assumption has been that the *Rhetoric* was out of circulation and unpublished from the death of Theophrastus (c. 285 B.C.E.) until Tyrannio and Andronicus issued their edition of the Aristotelian corpus in 83 B.C.E.. See, however, Barnes 1997, who argues that copies of the *Rhetoric* (and Aristotle's other "esoteric" works) were continuously available through the Hellenistic period, in some form, though little read. See also Fantham 2004, 164, who finds Barnes persuasive. For the standard history of the text, see Brandes 1989 and Kennedy 1991, 305–9.

4. Behind this idea lies the point, in Plato's *Phaedrus* (268a–269c), that the contents of the sophists' rhetoric manuals are "preliminaries" (*ta pro*) of the genuine art—techniques it can deploy—but not the art itself.

5. On enthymeme and syllogism, see also *Posterior Analytics* 1.1 71a, and *Topics* 8.14 164a.

6. On the problematic history of this notion, see Green 1990.

7. Borradori 2003, 85–86.

8. Borradori 2003, 118, 120–21, 130.

9. Borradori 2003, 106.

10. A similar criticism may be made of the "pragma-dialectical" approach to argumentation in Van Eemeren and Grootendorst 1992, 2004.

11. The disparaging remarks are mainly found in *Rhetoric* 1.1, for example, 1.1.3–4, 1.1.12.

12. For Isocrates, see, for example, *Against the Sophists* 15. Concerning Protagoras and Antiphon, see Gagarin 2002, chap. 5.

13. For an exploration of the possible meaning(s) of *endechomenon,* see Montefusco 2002.

14. On this point, see Neel 1994 (especially chaps. 2 and 4), which argues this case at length.

15. See Brandes 1989; Kennedy 1991, 299–305; and McAdon 2004, 2006a. For the contrarian argument that the text as we have it (more or less) was available through the whole Hellenistic period, see note 4, above, and Barnes 1997.

16. On the internal inconsistencies of the *Rhetoric,* its tensions with the rest of Aristotle's thought, and the remarkably incommensurate interpretations and uses of the *Rhetoric* in recent scholarship, see Leff 1993; the essays collected in Rorty 1996; Poster 1997; and Walker 2000b. Neel 1994 argues that the *Rhetoric* is "a failed attempt to cobble together a new art by extracting various components of already existing arts" (43); likewise Barnes (1995b) argues that the *Rhetoric* is a "muddled" collection of materials "botched" together from various other arts (262–64).

17. See Haskins 2004a, 23–30.

18. On this point, again, see Neel 1994, 73, 143.

19. On the institutions of Athenian government in the fourth century B.C.E., see Hansen 1991.

20. In *Politics* 7.9, Aristotle justifies his ideal oligarchic system based on social caste by appeal to supposedly longstanding practices in Egypt, Crete, and Italy.

21. As Poster 1997 argues, Aristotle views rhetoric as "an unfortunate necessity" that "a proper political science" would make "unnecessary" (244).

22. On this point, again, see Barnes 1997.

23. On the *Rhetoric* as proceeding from *endoxa* (generally accepted premises) rather than from actual examples, see Poster 1997, 237; Haskins 2004a, 60; and Trevett 1996, 371.

24. Barnes 1997, 54–57. On Cicero's knowledge of Aristotelian or Peripatetic doctrines, see also Fortenbaugh and Steinmetz 1989, Fortenbaugh 2005.

25. This is "pre-Aristotelian" in the sense that it is generally believed to have been composed c. 390 B.C.E. and Aristotle was born in 384–83.

26. As Barnes 1997, 45, observes, it seems that Aristotle was never widely read in antiquity.

27. Hubbell 1949.

28. On Hermogenes, see Heath 1995.

29. *Brutus* 306–7, 315–16; *De oratore* 3.110; see also Fantham 2004, 93–96.

30. Gaines 2002, 466–75, makes a strong case for New Academic origin, though he also notes that at least some features of the *Topica* "might be expected in any pair of rhetorical works from the late Hellenistic period" (475).

31. Spengel 1853–56, 2: 12.120–28; Patillon and Bolognesi 1997, 11.82–94; Kennedy 2003, 11.55–61.

32. Kennedy 2003, 1; Patillon and Bolognesi 1997, vii–xvi. For the *Suda* entry, see Adler 1928–38, Θ 206. See also *Suda On Line* (Finkel et al. 2001). The *Suda* is a tenth-century Byzantine encyclopedia.

33. Kennedy 2003, 1, 55, 67. The mention of "the great Dionysius" occurs in the part of the text transmitted in Armenian and translated into French by Patillon and Bolognesi 1997, 13.106.27–28; the mention of Theodoros occurs in the preserved (and incomplete) Greek text of Spengel 1854 (12.120.19).

34. Spengel 1853–56, 2: 1.61.29–30; Patillon and Bolognesi 1997, 1.4, xcviii n. 198; Kennedy 2003, 1.5 n. 17.

35. See Dionysius, *On the Ancient Orators* 1.

36. Spengel 1853–56, 2: 1.59.15–16.

37. Spengel 1853–56, 2: 1.59.18–20. Kennedy (2003, 3) translates this as "to the exercises as described by others," but the verbatim phrase is *tois êdê paradedomenois gumnasmasin,* "to the already transmitted exercises."

38. Spengel 1853–56, 2: 1.60.1–2.

39. Spengel 1853–56, 2: 12.120; Patillon and Bolognesi 1997, 11.83; Kennedy 2003, 11.55.

40. The main difference is that Quintilian has a single category, "narrative," which in the surviving progymnasmata texts (including Theon) is subdivided into fable, narrative, and anecdote. See Reinhardt and Winterbottom 2006, xxx–xxxiv, which argues that Quintilian's treatment is based on Theon "or something much like Theon's book" (xxxiv).

41. See Russell 1983.

42. *Rhetoric to Alexander* 28.1436a. For a discussion of the evolution of the progymnasmata, see Kennedy 1994, 202–8.

43. Relying on the texts of Spengel 1853–56, 2: 12.120–28; Patillon and Bolognesi 1997, 11.82–94; and Kennedy 2003, 11.55–61.

44. Spengel 1853–56, 2: 12.120–21; Patillon and Bolognesi 1997, 11.83; and Kennedy 2003, 11.55–56.

45. For Theon's treatment of the "commonplace" (*topos*) exercise, see Spengel 1853–56, 2: 7.106–9; Patillon and Bolognesi 1997, 6.62–66; Kennedy 2003, 6.42–45.

46. Spengel 1853–56, 2: 7.106; Patillon and Bolognesi 1997, 6.62; Kennedy 2003, 6.43.

47. See Perelman and Olbrechts-Tyteca 1969, 63–184; Perelman 1982, 21–40.

48. Diogenes Laertius, *Lives of the Philosophers* 11.8.51–53.

49. See the fragments of *Truth* and *Concord* in Sprague 1972, 212–33 (a re-collation and translation of the fragments collected in Diels-Kranz 1951–54) and the discussion of them in Gagarin 2002, chap. 3–4, and 183–94.

50. On Isocrates' use of the term *ideai* in this and in other passages, see Gaines 1990, Sullivan 2001, and my discussion of Isocrates in chapters 2 and 3 of this volume.

51. Gaines 1990, 169.

52. *Rhetoric* 1.1.3 1354a; 1.1.11 1355a: "The methods of proof alone are within the art, and other things are supplementary, yet they [the writers of rhetorical handbooks] say nothing about enthymemes, which are the substance of proof . . . proof is a sort of demonstration."

53. On the notion of enthymeme, see Conley 1984 and Walker 2000a, 168–84.

54. *Rhetoric to Alexander* 2.1423a. On the dating of the *Rhetoric to Alexander,* see Kennedy 1994, 47–48. On the resemblance to Isocrates, see Chiron (ed. and trans.) 2002, cxlvii.

55. On the Romans' schizophrenic attitudes toward Greek intellectual culture—so that one could dismiss it as foolish, but also invoke it in order to impress—see Wisse 2002a, 334–41.

56. Fortenbaugh 2003, 273–75. As Fortenbaugh (2005) argues, Cicero's very imperfect knowledge of Peripatetic rhetorical doctrine seems mainly to come from secondary

sources (or his Greek teachers), not from any detailed knowledge of Aristotle's and Theophrastus' writings.

57. I discuss this point in Walker 2000a, 290–302. See Lamberton 1986; Lamberton and Keaney 1992; Lamberton 1992a, 1992b; Long 1992; Irvine 1994, 34–38. See also Keaney and Lamberton's 1996 translation of (and introduction to) the anonymous, Pseudo-Plutarchan *Essay on the Life and Poetry of Homer.*

58. This view is generally asserted, moreover, as part of a refutation of Stoicism. For an extended discussion, see Brittain 2001, especially chap. 4.

59. It may also mean, of course, that Cicero is in some way imitating Aristotle's literary dialogues, especially the *Gryllus,* as is often suggested. But since none of those dialogues survive, the point is impossible to demonstrate. Indeed, *De oratore* sometimes is invoked, tautologically, as evidence for what Aristotle's dialogues were like. The explicit model invoked at the outset of *De oratore* is Plato's *Phaedrus.* "The Aristotelian manner" seems to mean no more than holding a discussion.

60. Wisse 2002a, 341–54.

61. *Letters to and from Quintus* 3.3.4. For discussion, see Clarke 1951, 163.

62. See *Rhetoric to Herennius* 1.8.12–13, 2.30.47–2.31.50, 4.49.63–4.53.66.

63. Translation of 5.5 from Kaster 1995; I have modified Kaster's translation of 25.4 (*quod genus* θέσεις *et* ἀνασκευάς *et* κατασκευάς *Graeci vocant*) to render more literally Suetonius' use of the Greek terms.

64. Fantham 2004, 172–77.

65. May and Wisse 2001, 32.

66. Perelman and Olbrechts-Tyteca 1969, 140 and passim.

67. This work is nicely summed up in Hartwell 1985.

68. The other reasons would include the fact that it says nothing about how the "sound pattern of English" is physically articulated, which a learner of the language would need to know.

69. These are Cnaeus Laelius Sapiens, consul in 140 B.C.E., and Publius Scipio Aemilianus Africanus the Younger, conqueror of Carthage and Numantia, both of whom were admirers of Greek learning; May and Wisse 2001, 347, 357.

70. This statement echos Plato's *Gorgias* 456b–c, where it is put in the mouth of Gorgias; but, as Schiappa 1991 suggests, the real "target" of the *Gorgias* may well have been Isocrates (45). If that is correct, Crassus' line of argument here may be Isocratean also.

71. The image of philosophers addressing a "large crowd of men" (*magna hominum frequentia*) from their "chair in the school" (*in schola assedessent,* literally "having taken their seat in the school") and inviting anyone in the crowd to propose a question makes more sense when it is understood that the "school" is located in a gymnasium, as the Peripatos and Academy were. In Cicero's day, the philosopher's inviting anyone in the crowd to propose a question for him to discourse on would have been a sort of carnival sideshow trick to get the crowd's attention. The crassness of the philosophic schools in marketing themselves is satirized, in the second century C.E., in Lucian's *Philosophers for Sale.* On the gymnasium setting, see Hawhee 2004, chap. 5.

72. As Cribiore 2001 (chap. 8) and many others have noted, only a very small percentage of the population proceeded to (and completed) this stage of ancient education.

73. Enos 1988.

74. At *Antidosis* 46, Isocrates describes the nobler form of discourse that he teaches and practices as *Hellinikous kai politikous kai panêgurikous,* "Hellenic and civic and panegyric," as opposed to *logous peri tôn idiôn sumbolaiôn,* "speeches concerning private business" delivered in law courts. Such later writers as Dionysius of Halicarnassus call such "Hellenic and civic and panegyric" discourses as *On the Peace* "advisory" or "deliberative" (*sumbouleutikon*).

75. May and Wisse 2001, 29–30.

76. Compare Isocrates at *Against the Sophists* 17, where the language is similar: achieving excellence in discourse "requires much diligence [*epimeleias*], and is the work of a vigorous [*andrikês,* 'manly'] and resourceful [*doxastikês,* 'idea-full'] mind," supplemented by intensive training and a teacher who can explain what needs explaining and provide good models for imitation. (Note that *epimeleias,* "attention or care paid to something, attentive pursuit, effort, diligence," is cognate with *meletê,* "careful attention, practice, exercise," the Greek term for declamation.)

77. This reading is admittedly conjectural. The manuscripts generally read *magister istorum omnium,* which, as A. S. Wilkins notes in his 1892 Oxford edition, "can hardly be defended," since *istorum,* "these," cannot "fairly be taken to refer to the writers mentioned just below" (274) and yields the nonsensical construction "the teacher of all *these* [genitive plural], from *whose* [genitive singular] school . . . nothing but *eminent men* [nominative plural] came forth." Thus the manuscript reading appears to be corrupt. Various emendations for *istorum* have been proposed: *historicorum* (of historians), *iste oratorum* (this [teacher] of orators), *historicum et oratorum* (of historians and orators), *disertorum* (of speakers), *rhetorum* (of rhetors; Wilkins 1902; Kumaniecki 1969). I follow Sutton and Rackham's Loeb edition (1942) in preferring *rhetorum* as the most probable in the context. In Latin the borrowed Greek term *rhetor* signifies a "rhetorician," a teacher of rhetoric, whereas the native term *orator* signifies an "orator," a "speaker." (In later Greek this Latin usage is absorbed, so that the Greek term *rhêtôr* eventually comes to mean both an "orator" and a "rhetorician.") In short, Isocrates is invoked as a master-teacher of rhetoric "from whose school" eminent writers, politicians, and rhetoricians emerged and who is, as Cicero says in *De inventione* (2.6–9), the fountainhead of the sophistic rhetorical tradition in the Hellenistic age; in this sense he is "the teacher of all rhetoricians."

78. See Heath 1995 and the Elder Seneca's discussions of the "division" of the stasis in various declamation problems, in *Controversiae.*

79. This has a certain resemblance to Quintilian's recommendation (*Institutio oratoria* 1.27), at a much more elementary level, for teaching children to write the letters of the alphabet by means of stencils that guide them to correctly form the strokes: once the child has gotten the idea, the stencils can be discarded.

80. Hubbell 1913, 41–53.

81. This is the same division we find in such later sophistic treatises as *On Types of Style* by Hermogenes and *On the Sublime* by "Longinus," where the discussion divides into the characteristic "thoughts" of a given stylistic type (sublimity, solemnity, asperity, and so forth) and the characteristic diction, figures, and rhythms through which it is expressed. On the idea that the *pragmatikos/lektikos* division is basically Isocratean, see Hubbell 1913, 1–15.

82. *Oikonomia* is really better translated as "management," but I have retained the usual rendering, "arrangement."

83. The basic conceptual divisions are laid out chiefly at *Demosthenes* 51, *On the Composition of Words* 1, and *Lysias* 16, though they crop up, sometimes with different names, through all of Dionysius' essays. See Roberts 1901 (9n1), whose analysis of Dionysius' essays provides the further subdivisions of diction into "proper usage" and "figuration," and of "preparation" into "judgment" (*krisis,* or the selection of which arguments to use). See also Pritchett 1975, who adds further subdivisions (xxxvi; citing Kremer 1907). Moreover, memory may be attached to the *pragmatikos topos,* and delivery may be attached to the *lektikos topos*—as we find in *De oratore.* It should be noted that Dionysius nowhere applies all these divisions in any given essay and, aside from the most basic division of "thought" and "expression," nowhere applies them systematically.

84. I have preserved here the usual translations—"tongue and mind" and "to think and to speak"—though *cordis* (mind) could also be rendered as "heart," and *sapere* (to think) as "to be wise."

85. See Bornecque 1902, 172, 192; Anderson 1993, 18–19; and Walker 2000a, 67–68, 338n39.

86. On which, see Sloane 1997.

87. This tactic is discussed explicitly in the Hermogenic *On Invention* 3.3 (*Peri Biaiou*) as a method of "forcible" refutation or reply to an opponent, but the general idea is hardly unique to that text.

88. See Hubbell 1913, 41.

89. See Mailloux 1995b; Schiappa 1995

90. See Augustine, *Confessions* 3.4.

91. For example, Gaines 2002. The Loeb translator, H. Rackham, rather profusely (and I think inaccurately) renders and "glosses" this line as "all the departments of oratory, that is those which have sprung from our famous school, the Middle Academy." That is a lot to squeeze from *omnes oratoriae partitiones, quae quidem e media illa nostra Academia effloruerunt.* (*E media* should be translated as "from within" or "within"; the reading *e media Academica,* "from the Middle Academy," is impossible since Cicero would have referred to the Academy of Philo as the "New" Academy.)

Chapter 2: On the *Technê* of Isocrates (I)

1. Kennedy 1991, 5–6, 299–305; 2007, 4–5, 306–11; Brandes 1989; McAdon 2006b.

2. Wilson 1994, 244, renders *tou andros epigraphomenên tôi onomati* as "attributed to him," which is a possible reading of *epigraphomenên* and suggests that Photius has only seen statements that attribute such a book to Isocrates; however, *tou andros tôi onomati,* "[with] the name of the man," does seem to suggest something more like a book "titled" (*epigraphomenên*) *The Rhetoric of Isocrates.* On Photius's library and the libraries of ninth–tenth century Constantinople, see Staikos 2004, 3:221–41.

3. Zosimus' locution, "when he was surveying rhetorical handbooks" (*sunagagôn technas rhetorikas*), is clearly an echo of the title of Aristotle's *Sunagôgê Technôn.* The author of this "Life of Isocrates" is not actually known but was identified by Dindorf 1852 as Zosimus of Ascalon.

4. See also Kennedy 1991, 11, 33–34, 293–94; and Radermacher 1951.

5. For a modern parallel, see the discussion of the *Harbrace College Handbook* in Connors 1997, chap. 2.

6. Barwick 1963, 54, 59–60. The *testimonia* and fragments of a possible Isocratean *technê* are gathered in Spengel 1828 and Radermacher 1951 (both of which are compilations of the remnants of pre-Aristotelian Greek rhetoric); see also Mandilaras 2003, 3:239–41.

7. But see Heath 1999.

8. Gagarin 2002 makes a similar argument regarding the three Antiphons that modern scholarship has posited (mistakenly) as the authors of the various Antiphontic writings. As Gagarin points out, contemporary sources, aware of the separate identities of the supposed three Antiphons, would have named them in ways that distinguished them, but none do.

9. Adler 1928–38, I 653; see also Θ 138. On the Internet, see Finkel et al. 2001. Speusippus's *Letter* to Philip of Macedon identifies this younger Isocrates as Isocrates' "Pontic student" and as his chosen successor; see Flower 1997, 53–54; and Natoli 2004.

10. Barwick 1963, 46–47.

11. Pseudo-Plutarch, *Life of Isocrates* 838f; Speusippus *Letter*, 4, 10; on Speusippus' letter, see Natoli 2004. This *Life of Isocrates,* and the *Isaeus* and *Lysias* discussed below, are part of the Pseudo-Plutarchan *Lives of the Ten Orators* preserved in Plutarch's *Moralia.*

12. Cole 1991, chap. 5.

13. As noted in chapter 1, Papillon 1995, 150–51, persuasively interprets *tetagmenai technai* as "rigid handbooks" or prescriptive "arts" consisting of rigid rules. Concerning the notion of *poiêtikon pragma,* see Bons 1997 and Vallozza 2003.

14. Schiappa 1991, 45; Hackforth 1952, 143; Howland 1937.

15. Recently, for example, Too 1995, 235–39.

16. Plato's *Phaedrus* is generally thought to have been written circa 370–65 B.C.E.; the *Panegyricus* was written in 380—at least a decade earlier. See Hackforth 1952, 3–7; Panagiotou 1975; and Nehamas and Woodruff 1995, xiii.

17. See Mandilaras 2003, 3:239, item 2; Syrianus and Siceliotes are probably drawing on Pseudo-Plutarch.

18. Natoli 2004, 106–7.

19. Natoli 2004, 19–31, argues that the letter should be dated to 343–41 B.C. At any rate it could not be later than 339.

20. In the first of these two quotations, the preserved text of which is corrupt and unintelligible, I am following the proposed emendation of Radermacher 1951, 156 (testimony 15), but my argument here chiefly rests on the second quotation. On Speusippus' letter, see Natoli 2004 and Flower 1997, 53–54.

21. Further, the expression "by praise of ancestors," *ek tês eulogias tôn progonôn* (literally *"from* the praise of ancestors") has the distinct ring of a technical term denoting a topic or "heading" of invention, such as we find in the Greek manuals of later antiquity.

22. Radermacher 1951, 160 (testimony 28); from Walz 1832–36, 7:930.

23. For a useful discussion of the earliest sophistic *technai,* see Kennedy 1959; 2007, 293–306 (which revises the 1959 account). For a recent reexamination of the *technê* tradition, see also Celentano 2003.

24. Kennedy 1994, 34–35.

25. This is, more or less, the argument of Cahn (1989) regarding Isocrates' supposed refusal to provide a *technê*.

26. Translated in Rackham 1957.

27. Kennedy (1994, 49–51) regards it as an example of the more "pedestrian" handbooks circulating in the period, but Chiron (ed. and trans.) 2002, cxlvi–cxlvii argues that the author was probably a follower of Isocrates.

28. Plato does not include the strong man's side of the argument, but in most versions the strong man argues that it is improbable that he would have done it because he knows that everyone would suspect him (that is, that knowledge would have deterred him).

29. Grenfell and Hunt 1898, 3:26–31.

30. Too 1995, chap. 5 offers perhaps the best recent articulation of this position.

31. Roochnik 1996, 283–88; Schiappa 1991, 40–49.

32. Roochnik 1996, chap. 1, and appendix 4.

33. On the dating of the *Gorgias* and *Phaedrus,* see Cooper 1997, xii–xviii; Howland 1991; Hamilton and Emlyn-Jones 2004, xi–xii; and note 17 above. *Antidosis* was produced in the 350s.

34. See Hawhee 2004; and Cribiore 2001.

35. *Peri Mimêseôs (On Imitation)* fr. 1, in Usener-Radermacher 1965, 2:197, 198–200. See the discussion of "Dionysius on Rhetoric" in chapter 5.

36. Compare, in Aristotle's definition of rhetoric, "observing *in each case (peri hekaston)* the possibly persuasive" (*Rhetoric* 1.2.1).

37. On Isocrates' teaching methods, see Johnson 1959, which stresses "group discussion" as probably the most original and distinctive component of Isocrates' methods; however, Johnson seems not to recognize the "two-stage" process discussed below. On ancient classroom practices see also Cribiore 2001, chap. 5.

38. See Theon, *Progymnasmata* chaps. 1–2 and 13–17, in Kennedy 2003.

39. See chapter 1 in "The Crassian Position."

40. On the enthymeme as a stylistic device, see Conley 1984; and Walker 2000a, 168–84.

41. Further, as Schenkeveld 1992 and Too 1995, 236 suggest, the verb *akouein* can also mean "to read," in the sense of "listening to" a text that oneself reads aloud or hears someone else read.

42. On Libanius' school, see Cribiore 2007a. Cribiore 2001 also observes that Libanius uses the term *koruphaios,* "chorus-leader," for an older student "who represented his classmates and could even do some teaching when the teacher was sick" (43).

43. Too 2008, 15.

44. Cribiore 2007a, 151. Libanius' own declamations, of which a large number survive (see Russell 1996), would have been presented in school and thus were not "summer reading." For an extensive selection and translation of Libanius' letters to (and about) his students, see Cribiore 2007a, 233–321.

45. Cribiore 2001 and 2007a, on which the following discussion is based.

46. There were, however, as Cribiore shows (2007a, chaps. 3, 4, 7), application procedures (letters and such), an initial "diagnostic" interview for the entering student,

and—for students who had completed their studies (whether brief or long)—letters of recommendation for jobs.

47. Cribiore 2001, 43. The term "symmory" normally signified a taxation class. On the size of Libanius' school, see Cribiore 2007a, 95–99.

48. As did Isocrates' student, Ephorus, according to the biographies (Pseudo-Plutarch, *Life of Isocrates* 839a).

49. The story appears in Zosimus' *Life of Isocrates* (Mandilaras 2003, 214).

50. On the size of Isocrates' school, see Johnson 1957.

51. Cribiore 2001, 144.

52. Grenfell and Hunt 1898, 17:106–9; Cribiore 2001, 144. A photograph of this papyrus can be viewed online at *POxy: Oxyrhynchus Online* (http://www.papyrology .ox.ac.uk/POxy/ (accessed January 2010).

53. Grenfell and Hunt 1898, 17:107. In a finished piece of writing, all lines would be completely filled, with no breaks at all (between words, sentences, paragraphs, and so forth). A *paragraphos* was literally a mark (*graphos*) "beside" (*para*) the text.

54. In the original papyrus, ΦΙΛΙΠ~ΕΣΤΙΔΗΤΑΓΕΜΟΙ. After *Philip. esti*, "Philip. is," the rest may be parsed as *dê ta g' emoi*, "[is] then the subject-matter for me," or *dêta g' emoi*, "[is] indeed (certainly, really) for me."

55. As determined by *Thesaurus Linguae Graecae* search.

56. In the original, ΡΙΚΕΦΑΛΑΙωΝ.

57. A translation of the Pseudo-Hermogenic *On Invention* is available in Kennedy 2005; the Greek text is in Rabe 1913. A complete translation of the Hermogenic corpus (in French) is available in Patillon 1997.

58. This would be the stasis of *metalêpsis*, usually translated as "objection" or "transference," in which one argues for the dismissal of the case. An alternative reading of *ê exeinai hup-* may be "or to go outside the hypothesis," that is, with some sort of digression.

59. The neatness of his writing also suggests a person at a relatively advanced level of literacy. See, for example, the clumsy scrawling of less advanced students in Cribiore 2001. One might conjecture that our note taker is at an "intermediate" stage of declamation exercise, since the matters under discussion seem to come from the "intermediate" Hermogenic treatise *On Invention* or something like it.

60. Cribiore 2001, 187.

61. See also Quintilian's discussion of lecturing and the assignment of declamation exercises, 2.5–6.

62. Translated in Cribiore 2007a, 237 (letter 287 in Foerster 1903–27); see also Cribiore 2001, 43, 49; 2007, 155.

63. In Foerster 1903–27; see also Martin and Petit 1979, with French translation.

64. Elsewhere, however, Libanius says the teacher's formal duties end at midday (*Oration* 58.9). His purpose there, however, is to exalt the work done by the *paidagôgos*, who, as he says, works with the student all day long and generally acts *in loco parentis* (58.8–10).

65. Mandilaras 2003, 214. Whether Zosimus' opinion on this point is correct is doubtful; it is not clear what evidence it is based on.

66. Cribiore 2007a, 154.

67. The literal meaning of *orthos* is "straight, correct."

68. The text of the *Panathenaicus*—272 sections—occupies more than one hundred Loeb pages and more than sixty pages in Mandilaras 2003; delivery probably would take upward of two hundred minutes.

69. Johnson 1959; Papillon 1995.

70. As Cribiore 2001 puts it, "It is likely that some of the rhetorical treatises transmitted by the papyri not only served the needs of instructors but also circulated among students" (144).

71. One is tempted to translate *sermonem* as "lecture" (as does the Loeb translation), but the root meaning of *sermo* is "conversation," which seems closer, in the case of a rhetoric teacher, to a notion of instructional "discussion."

72. This sort of compiling was not confined to sophistic schools, of course. As Brad McAdon recently has argued, the text we know as Aristotle's *Rhetoric* may be a compilation not only of Aristotle's teaching notes (or students' notes from his lectures) but also of notes added by his students and successors, especially Theophrastus; and it certainly was an "in-house" document for use within the Peripatetic school. See McAdon 2006b; see also McAdon 2003, 2004, and 2006a. For contrasting perspectives, see Brandes 1989; Kennedy 1991, 299–305; Kennedy 2007, 306–11; and Barnes 1997.

73. Mandilaras 2003, 215.

74. On this point, see Too 1995, 184–94; and J. Poulakos 2004.

75. T. Poulakos 1997, 4 agrees with (and argues for) the Dionysian assessment.

76. I am thinking of Gorgias' *On Nonbeing, or On Nature* and Antiphon's attempt to "square the circle" as well as his *On Truth*. On Isocrates' turn from metaphysics to a "pragmatist" concern with practical deliberation in civil communities, see Schiappa 1995; T. Poulakos 1997; Gagarin 2002; Haskins 2004a; and many of the essays collected in T. Poulakos and Depew 2004.

77. The list of titles that Diogenes Laertius attributes to Protagoras omits the *Correct Diction* and includes a treatise on disputation (eristics) and a set of "antilogies" titled *Lawsuit over a Fee* (*Dikê huper Misthou*); but there is nothing approaching a comprehensive rhetorical *technê*. See *Lives of the Philosophers* 9.55.

78. Gagarin 2002, chap. 5–6 and passim.

79. See Erikson 1998; and Kennedy 2007, 298.

80. See Plutarch, *Demosthenes* 5.6–7; Dionysius of Halicarnassus, *Isaeus* 1; and Pseudo-Plutarch, *Life of Isaeus* 839d–f.

81. Bollansée 1999, 82–90.

82. Hermippus is a probable source, as well, for Dionysius' detailed arguments about the biographies of Demosthenes and Aristotle in his *First Letter to Ammaeus*. See Bollansée 1999, 93.

83. Bollansée 1999, 55. As Bollansée points out, this penchant for colorful anecdotes leads Hermippus to collect stories both favorable and unfavorable, as long as they are "good stories." Like most historians, Bollansée assumes that this anecdotalism is meant to entertain the reader, but it is more likely that the anecdotes are chreiai: factual or not, they embody a morally instructive maxim of some sort associated with the character of the biography's subject (like the story of George Washington and the cherry tree).

84. There is also the improbable-seeming report from Diogenes Laertius that Speusippus "brought forth" (*exênenken*) Isocrates' "secret" doctrines (*aporrêta; Lives of the Philosophers* 4.1.2–3).

Chapter 3: On the *Technê* of Isocrates (II)

1. Chiron (ed. and trans.) 2002, cxlvi–cxlvii. See also Chiron 2000, 2007; and Barwick 1966–67.

2. Chiron 2002 and 2007, 102–3.

3. For a sampling of recent work, see Cahn 1989; Gaines 1990; Masarrachia 1995; Papillon 1995; Schiappa 1995; Too 1995; Halliwell 1997; T. Poulakos 1997; Vitanza 1997, chap. 3–4; Livingstone 2001; Sullivan 2001; Haskins 2004a, 2004b; Konstan 2004; Morgan 2004; J. Poulakos 2004; T. Poulakos and Depew 2004; Atwill 2005; Walzer 2005.

4. There is some doubt that *To Demonicus* was written by Isocrates, chiefly on the grounds of its lack of originality. Too (1995, 58n53) reviews the scholarship on this point and judges it unpersuasive.

5. Hesiod, *Works and Days* line 397; Mandilaras 2003, 213.

6. Sullivan 2001; see also Bons 1997 and Livingstone 2001, 1–28.

7. Isocrates does not mention Gorgias by name, but his criticisms make it fairly clear that he is discussing Gorgias' *Encomium of Helen.*

8. Zosimus in Mandilaras 2003, 212–13; Photius in *Bibliotheca* 159.

9. On Isocrates' notion of prose genres, see Wilcox 1943.

10. See Norlin and Van Hook 1928–45, 2:213; and Mirhady, Too, and Papillon 2000–4, 1:214.

11. Quintilian 3.4.9–11 attributes this same two-part division to Anaximenes.

12. Sullivan 2007.

13. See Norlin and Van Hook 1928–45, 2:207, and Mirhady, Too, and Papillon 2000–4, 1:212.

14. Cahn 1989; Too 1995.

15. In Mirhady, Too, and Papillon 2000–4, 1:66n16. See also Papillon 2007.

16. Again, see Chiron 2002, cxlvii: "Il est très probable que l'auteur de la *Rh. Al.* a suivi l'enseignement d'Isocrate ou qu'en tous cas il avait lu ses oeuvres." ("It is very probable that the author of the *Rhet. Alex.* has followed the teaching of Isocrates, or that in any case he has read his works.")

17. Kennedy 1994, 49–50; and Chiron 2007, 101–3. See also Grenfell and Hunt 1906, 114–38.

18. Aelius Theon echoes Isocrates in saying that the *gumnasmata* are the "foundations (*themelia*) of all the *ideai* of discourse": Spengel 1853–56, 2: 2.70; Patillon and Bolognesi 1997, 2.15; Kennedy 2003, 2.13.

19. Kennedy 2003, x–xii, 1–2.

20. In Spengel 1853–56, vol. 2: chap. 5 in Theon (96–106); in Patillon and Bolognesi 1997, chap. 3 (18–30); and in Kennedy 2003, chap. 3 (15–23). Spengel's text is based on a manuscript tradition that has rearranged Theon to resemble the later handbooks; Theon's original order is restored in the edition of Patillon and Bolognesi 1997 and reflected in Kennedy 2003's translation.

21. Mandilaras 2003, 212–13.

22. On the question whether *To Demonicus* is an authentic Isocratean text, again see Too 1995, 58n53. Even if it is not, it would have had the same pedagogical functions as the other parainetics.

23. For a thoughtful discussion of the political philosophy unfolded in these parainetics (and especially *To Nicocles* and *Nicocles*), see T. Poulakos 1997, chap. 2.

24. The text of *To Demonicus*, for example, runs about fifteen Loeb pages and about ten pages in the translation of Mirhady, Too, and Papillon 2000–4.

25. Spengel 1853–56, 2: 101; Patillon and Bolognesi 1997, 24; Kennedy 2003, 19.

26. Spengel 1853–56, 2: 101; Patillon and Bolognesi 1997, 24–25; Kennedy 2003, 19–20.

27. Spengel 1853–56, 2: 103; Patillon and Bolognesi 1997, 27; Kennedy 2003, 21.

28. See preceding note.

29. Spengel 1853–56, 2: 28; Kennedy 2003, 101.

30. This idea, by the way, explains why the supposed lack of "originality" in *To Demonicus* is not an argument against its authenticity. (See note 4.)

31. This "lengthening" activity bears a certain resemblance to the "generative rhetoric of the paragraph" popularized in the 1960s and 1970s for basic (college first year) writing instruction by Francis Christensen and still reflected in a number of contemporary textbooks. One starts from a "kernel sentence" and expands. See Christensen 1967, 1976; and Morenberg et al. 2002.

32. Sullivan 2001, 90–91.

33. Isocrates does occasionally use the word *topos* to mean the "topic, subject, theme" of a discourse, as well as the subtopics contained within a particular theme (for example, *Encomium of Helen* 4, 38; *To Philip* 109; and *Panathenaicus* 111). These usages approach the notion of "inventional topic" and perhaps reflect the influence of Plato and Aristotle; however, Isocrates generally uses the word *topos* in its usual, nontechnical sense of "place."

34. See Sloane 1991 and 1997, 56–79.

35. George Kennedy's translation of Theon reflects this interpretation with a parenthetical gloss: "and in addition (at a later stage in study) we refute and confirm." See Kennedy 2003, 19.

36. Spengel 1853–56, 2: 64–65; Patillon and Bolognesi 1997, 8; Kennedy 2003, 8.

37. For Theon's discussion, see Spengel 1853–56, 2: 72–96; Patillon and Bolognesi 1997, 30–61; Kennedy 2003, 23–42.

38. Almost identical language is cited by Sopater (in the fourth century). Both Syrianus and Sopater, of course, are likely not quoting Isocrates directly but from an intermediary source, possibly the third-century sophist Apsines of Gadara (whom Syrianus later invokes with a slightly modified version of this quotation, in connection with the "preliminary statement" of the narrative; *Commentary* 170–71). A simpler version shows up in later sources, such as John Siceliotes (eleventh century) and Maximus Planudes (thirteenth–fourteenth centuries): "You should narrate the first thing and the second, and what follows, and not go on to something else before completing the first and then go back again to the first; these are Isocrates' precepts concerning purity, and also

precepts of the art [generally]." See the fragments collected in Mandilaras 2003, 3:239–41 (frs. 3, 8, 13, 17, 18); and Brémond and Mathieu 1960–63, 4:229–32 and 234–39 (frs. 6, 10).

39. It turns up, for example, in the *Rhet. Alex.* (30), the *Rhetorica ad Herennium* (1.14), Cicero's *De inventione* (1.28), and the *Anonymous Seguerianus* (63; see Dilts and Kennedy 1997).

40. The chapter on *ap' arches achri telous* actually appears in book 3, on "confirmation," as a topic for the development of epicheiremes (3.10); however, as Kennedy (2005, 107) notes, this and several following chapters appear to have been moved to this place from somewhere else in the treatise, and the discussion of development "from beginning to end" clearly has narrative material in mind.

41. Spengel 1853–56, 2: 119; Patillon and Bolognesi 1997, 68–69; Kennedy 2003, 46–47.

42. For Theon's discussion, see Spengel 1853–56, 2: 104–6; Patillon and Bolognesi 1997, 28–30; and Kennedy 2003, 22–23.

43. For Theon's discussion, see Spengel 1853–56, 2: 118–20; Patillon and Bolognesi 1997, 66–69; and Kennedy 2003, 45–47.

44. For Theon's discussion, see Spengel 1853–56, 2: 112–15; Patillon and Bolognesi 1997, 78–82; and Kennedy 2003, 52–55.

45. Spengel 1853–56, 2: 122; Patillon and Bolognesi 1997, 85; Kennedy 2003, 57.

46. Spengel 1853–56, 2: 42; Kennedy 2003, 113–14. *Kala* signifies the physically and/ or morally beautiful, whereas *chrêsta* signifies the good and/or the useful (a person who is *chrêstos* is reliable); in contrast with things that are *chrêsta, ponêros* signifies the bad in the sense of "worthless, knavish."

47. See Kennedy (2007, 174), who labels these "Topic 4" and "Topic 4a."

48. Conley 1984; Walker 2000a, 168–84. These examples are from Alcidamas' *Messenian Discourse,* Lysias' *On the Killing of Eratosthenes,* and Aristotle's *Rhetoric* (2.23.5, 1397b). It is likely that all of these examples would have been familiar to Isocrates.

49. For Theon's discussion, see Spengel 1853–56, 2: 115–18; Patillon and Bolognesi 1997, 70–73; and Kennedy 2003, 47–52.

50. Winterbottom 1982 makes a similar point regarding declamation exercises in later antiquity.

51. For Theon's discussion, see Spengel 1853–56, 2: 106–9; Patillon and Bolognesi 1997, 62–66; and Kennedy 2003, 42–45. For a modern version of this *idea,* see Perelman and Olbrechts-Tyteca 1969, 115–20; and Perelman 1982, chap. 3–4.

52. For Aphthonius' treatment of these exercises, see Kennedy 2003, 97–101, 105–8, 120–24 (for English translation) and Spengel 1853–56, 2: 23–27, 32–35, 49–53 (for the Greek text).

53. For Theon's and Aphthonius' treatments of the thesis exercise, see Kennedy 2003, 55–61, 120–24 (for English translation) and Spengel 1853–56, 2: 120–28, 49–53 (for the Greek text).

54. Theon does not actually call these "final headings" but "main headings" (*ta anô-tatô kephalaia,* literally the "topmost" or "ultimate" headings). He then goes on to list twenty-five other headings for the thesis exercise, which he introduces with *eisi de kai hoi topoi hoide,* "there are also the following topics."

55. Again, see Kennedy 2003, xi–xii.

56. See Russell and Wilson 1981, xi–xxxi; on Menander Rhetor, see also Heath 2004.

57. Rabe 1913, 204–11; translation available in Kennedy 2005, 187–96.

58. See Hansen 1991.

59. See Cribiore 2001, 143–47.

60. Gaines 1990.

61. Russell 2001, 2:49n3, notes in his translation of Quintilian that Aeschines' use of *stasis* has no technical meaning but refers to the "stance" or "position" of a boxer. This is true, but (as Russell also notes) Aeschines is using the boxer's *stasis* as a metaphor for argumentational *stasis,* meaning the issue in question; this usage of *stasis* exactly prefigures its later use as a technical term in rhetorical handbooks.

62. See Cicero, *De inventione* 1.9.12; Kennedy 1983; Kennedy 1994, 97–101; Walker 2000a, 59–62; and Heath 1995, 2004.

63. See, for example, Aristotle's *Categories* (2.7) and *Rhetoric* (1.13.9–10, 3.15, 3.17.1–2). See also Liu 1991; Kennedy 1994, 97–98; and Kennedy 2007, 236.

64. Gagarin 2002, chap. 5.

65. For "refutation," Isocrates appears to use the word *dialuein,* "unravel, dissolve, destroy, break up, put an end to [some difficulty]"; see *Archidamus* 33.

66. Mirhady, Too, and Papillon 2000–4, 1:96–97.

67. *Tous logous* here must mean "the arguments," as the *Rhet. Alex.* is speaking of using the copious things-to-say generated by the topics of invention and methods of development reviewed in the preceding paragraph; it cannot mean "speeches" as in Rackham's Loeb translation (Rackham 1957, 375).

68. See Syrianus' *Commentary on Hermogenes' On Types of Style* (25, 28, 170–71), cited in Mandilaras 2003, 3:240 (items 3, 13, 17, 18); and Quintilian 4.2.31–32.

69. Mirhady, Too, and Papillon 2000–4, 2:109–10.

70. See Hibeh Papyrus 15, in Grenfell and Hunt 1906, 55–61. I discuss this declamation in chapter 4.

71. This episode is represented in Xenophon's *Hellenica* (7.4.7–10).

72. Archidamus had in fact commanded Spartan armies; see Xenophon, *Hellenica* 6.4.18, 7.1.28.

73. *Tas nun ousas merizontas dêloun,* more literally "make clear the currently existing divisions" (of things), that is, the groupings and arrangements of the facts.

74. See the annotations on Archidamus' narrative provided by Mirhady, Too, and Papillon 2000–4, 2:113–17. The chief classical authority for the mythology is Apollodorus.

75. Walzer 2005.

76. *Dia chrêmatôn euporian,* literally "because of a good supply of *chrêmata*"; *chrêmata* basically means "useful, needful things" and can also mean "money." In the context of sources of success in war, the "needful things" would be material resources in the sense of both war *materiel* (weapons, supplies, and so forth) and money. Rackham's Loeb translation renders this as "financial resources," which is correct but seems inadequate; see Rackham 1957, 299.

77. This passage has a certain resonance with the maxim given in *To Nicocles* 9: "I think all would agree that it is a king's duty to put an end to his city's misfortunes, to guard it when it is prospering, and to enlarge it when it is small."

78. I discuss the rhetoric of Pindar's odes in Walker 2000a, chap. 7; see also Kurke 1991.

79. I am borrowing the term "inside view" from Booth 1961–83, chap. 6: that is, an extended presentation of Spartan political ideology from a Spartan point of view, so that, on its own terms, it seems reasonable.

80. Not wishing to see Sparta humbled, and (more pragmatically) needing it as a counterweight to Theban hegemony, the Athenians and several smaller states allied with Sparta against Thebes at the battle of Mantinea in 362 B.C.E..

81. Mandilaras 2003, 3:239–41. My list is a digest of items 4, 5, 6, 7, 9, 10, 11, 12, 14, 15, and 16, several of which repeat each other.

82. In John Siceliotes' eleventh-century commentary on Hermogenes' *On Types of Style* (6.39, in Rabe 1913), this remark, attributed to Isocrates, is followed by "people call these things repetitions and interjections and likewise interjecting, or stopping and continuing the expression." Mandilaras 2003 prints this line as a fragment from Isocrates' *technê*, but it is more likely a remark by Siceliotes. (He may be thinking of figures like *epenthesis*, which involve the insertion of a syllable, or a doubled or lengthened syllable at the beginning, middle, or end of a word.)

83. *Tauta men toiauta, ekeina mentoi heterôs:* cf. *men* and *mentoi,* roughly meaning "while . . . yet . . ."

84. These are coordinating particles (or "conjunctions"): *men . . . de . . .* , "on one hand . . . on the other . . ."; *hôs . . . houtôs . . .* , "as . . . so . . ."

85. I am deriving this description mainly from Dionysius of Halicarnassus; see the discussion of *On Composition* in chapter 5. *Sunthesis* may be thought of as including both syntactic (grammatical) and rhythmic (rhetorical) concerns; but for Isocrates, and even Aristotle, rhythm seems to be the dominant concern; grammatical analysis was at a very primitive stage of development in the fourth century. By "rhythmic construction" I mean not only the micro-rhythms of long and short syllables (or poetic "feet") but also the macro-rhythms of phrase and clause cadences (*anapausis*).

86. Perhaps the best example of the sequence in later sophistic teaching is the Hermogenic corpus: *Progymnasmata, On Stases, On Invention* (the parts of the oration), *On Types of Style,* and *On the Method of the Forceful Style. On Invention,* moreover, ends with a discussion of figures.

87. This passage cannot mean, as Rackham 1957 renders it, that one should "adapt the character of your speech to that of the public"; the writer is thinking of verisimilitude in character representation, that is, ethopoiea.

88. The vowel/consonant combinations discussed are VV, CC, and CV. *Taxis* of words includes keeping similar-sounding words together or apart, using repetition of the "same words" for emphasis or varying the words to avoid nonemphatic repetition, using one word or many (for conciseness or amplification and probably for reasons of rhythm), and using words "in order" or transposed (that is, using "normal" word order for speaking plainly, or hyperbaton for effect).

89. For example, where *eipousa alogikôs*, "she spoke illogically," could be mistaken for *eipousa logikôs*, "she spoke logically."

90. In its discussion of vituperative discourse, the *Rhet. Alex.* does counsel avoiding the use of "shameful words" (*aischrois onomasi*) in the description of shameful things and using indirect forms of expression instead.

91. *P.Oxy.* 18.2190; see translation and discussion in Cribiore 2001, 57–58.

92. Tobin 2000 gives an instructive modern example of a "creative process" pedagogy being converted to a rigid set of obligatory steps by an obtuse teacher. See also the *Anonymous Seguerianus*' refutation of the argument of the "Apollodoreans" that a speech must always have a *prooimion* (26–39; in Dilts and Kennedy 1997, 11–15.)

Chapter 4: In the Garden of Talking Birds

1. Walz 1832-36 7.1 49 (ll. 6-8). *Askêsis* implies a disciplining (and transforming) of the self through a regimen of exercise; cf. "ascetic." See Hawhee 2004, chap.4; and Foucault 1988.

2. See Behr 1968; Walker 2005; and Pernot 2005, 194–96.

3. On Psellos, see Kaldellis 1999 and 2006, 3–10; and Walker 2004. For the Greek text and an Italian translation of this encomium, see Criscuolo 1989. For English translations, see Walker tr. 2005 and Kaldellis 2006 29-109.

4. *Kitta,* technically "jay," is a name applicable to both the Eurasian jay and the Eurasian magpie, which resemble each other in appearance and behavior. The modern Greek form of the name, *kissa,* is conventionally translated as "magpie." Psellos' point seems clearly to be that these dream birds with "musical and human" voices are creatures of imitation—unless, perhaps, the parrot signifies the imitative aspect of grammatical studies and the jay/magpie signifies not only mimicry but also the more aggressive "squawking" of rhetoric and "philosophy."

5. Downey 1957, 865, 894; Browning 1962, 177. Holy Apostles was a very large church, nearly as large as the still-standing Hagia Sophia (which has lost its forecourt). Three-dimensional graphic reconstructions of Holy Apostles and Hagia Sophia in the twelfth century, which provide a good sense of what the forecourt at Holy Apostles would have been like, can be seen online at http://www.Byzantium1200.com/.

6. Downey 1957, 860; as Downey points out, the *Description* was written before the Fourth Crusade's capture and sack of Constantinople in 1204 and thus probably between 1198 and 1203. As a speech of "welcome" to the recently installed patriarch, the *Description* may also be a version of the speech to an arriving governor or other dignitary (the *epibatêrios logos*) discussed in Menander Rhetor's treatise on epideictic speeches; see Russell and Wilson 1981. On Menander Rhetor, see also Heath 2004.

7. *Deinotês,* literally "awesomeness" (in the sense of inspiring awe/terror) but usually translated as "forcefulness," in Byzantine contexts often takes on the meaning of supreme skillfulness, frequently in the sense of elaborately layered meaning or subtle indirection; thus *deinotês* can mean a figured, pregnant obscurity, and as such is the opposite of *saphêneia,* "clarity." See Kustas 1973.

8. Mesarites' references to "problem and question" (*problêma te kai zêtêma*) and "dialectical manner" at 42.1 suggest the preliminary analysis of declamation problems

into the "question" in dispute and then the determination of the precise stasis and its division into a sequence of heads through a quasi-dialectical process, as described by Hermogenes. However, it may also indicate exercises in dialectic. Mesarites' description (as it goes on) does not sharply differentiate rhetorical and dialectical disputation, though it might differentiate them by types of subject matter, that is, hypotheses and theses. See Heath 1995.

9. This point is well discussed in Cribiore 2007a, chap. 6–7.

10. On Herodes' wealth, see Philostratus, *Lives of the Sophists* 2.1 (546–66); on Aristides, see Philostratus, *Lives of the Sophists* 2.9 (581–85) and Behr 1968.

11. Cribiore 2001, 65.

12. Cribiore 2007a, 30–37; for a translation of the speech, see Norman 2000, 66–83. The "assistants" in Libanius' school were experienced professional teachers, with salaries from the municipality; Libanius, as head of the school, held the title *sophistês,* while the assistants held the title *rhêtôr.*

13. Translated in Norman 2000, 96, 98. These problems were hardly new in Libanius' day—even Isocrates complains about the drinking and carousing of the average student (*Antidosis* 286–87).

14. On the anonymous schoolmaster, see Browning 1954, 1997. Regarding Tzetzes and his letters, see Wilson 1983, 190–96; and Leone 1972 (in particular letters 18 and 55).

15. Rebhorn 1995, 115–20 and passim.

16. Gregory's writings are mostly unavailable in modern print editions, and my account here is based on Kazhdan's overview in Kazhdan and Franklin 1984, 196–223.

17. Kazhdan and Franklin 1984, 199, 201.

18. Each took a turn in the position of *maistôr tôn rhêtorôn* ("master of the rhetors," head rhetorician), the "sophistic" chair, in the so-called Patriarchal university (of which the school at Holy Apostles probably was a part); Kazhdan and Franklin 1984, 200–201.

19. Kazhdan and Franklin 1984, 201, 202, 203, 205. The complaint about low pay in imperial employ is a recurrent theme in twelfth-century Byzantine literature; see Beaton 1987.

20. Kazhdan and Franklin 1984, 201.

21. On the conditions in late antiquity, see Brown 1992; Heath 2004, chap. 9; and Cribiore 2007a.

22. Xenophon, *Memorabilia* 2.1.21–34.

23. This notion is fairly pervasive in Burke, but the focal statement appears at Burke 1966 53: As Burke maintains, the idea that persons act, things move (or are moved) is pragmatically necessary assumption for ethical-political thought and for human relations generally, whatever its metaphysical or ontological truth may be.

24. That such agency could indeed be (and was) exercised by sophists and rhetors in the Second Sophistic, and even in late antiquity, has been argued persuasively by Millar 1992; Brown 1992; and Heath 2004, chap. 9.

25. On Lucian as a Cynic (or as influenced by Cynicism) and a "Menippean" satirist, see Branham 1989.

26. Triptolemus, the ancient Greek Johnny Appleseed, traversed the earth in a winged chariot, sowing seed, teaching the arts of agriculture to all humanity, and spreading the cult of Demeter.

27. *Rhêtorôn Didaskalos,* translated in the Loeb series as "A Professor of Public Speaking."

28. Cribiore 2007a, 174–83. As Cribiore notes, Lucian's *Teacher of Orators* is "a satirical acknowledgment that two different educational tracks may have already existed in the second century C.E., and that people who followed the shorter route succeeded equally well." I would differ from this only in suggesting that the shorter route probably existed even in Isocrates' day and is reflected in his critique (in *Against the Sophists*) of those who make "easy promises" and teach a simplistic, superficial *tetagmenê technê.* See also Heath's (2007) critique of Cribiore's reading of Lucian and Cribiore's (2007b) expanded treatment of the issue.

29. Cribiore 2007a, 205–13.

30. See, for example, Kennedy 1980, 16–17, and chaps. 2–4; and Kennedy 1994, 18–19, and chap. 3. Gonzalez 2008 provides a good discussion of the development of rhetorical studies in the philosophic schools as discussed in Cicero's *Academica.*

31. On this point see also the detailed discussion of Heath 2004, chap. 8.

32. As Isocrates puts it: *Against the Sophists* 17.

33. *Akroasis* is often translated as "lecture" but literally means a "hearing" or thing-listened-to, and here would include what the teacher said in explicating readings, guiding students through exercises, and providing corrective or "coaching" commentary on their performances.

34. Dilts and Kennedy 1997, x–xiii.

35. While the *Anonymous Seguerianus* looks like it was composed originally as someone's personal collection of notes, the fact that it was preserved, even if only in one surviving manuscript (Parisinus graecus 1874, twelfth century), suggests that it was copied and circulated, and thus was used by at least a few people, over a period of nearly one thousand years. On the manuscript, see Dilts and Kennedy 1997, xxi–xxii.

36. As noted by Dilts and Kennedy 1997, Apollodorus of Pergamon was a "teacher of the emperor Augustus and founder of an influential school of rhetorical theory" (11n31). Apollodorus seems to have taught an especially rigid doctrine concerning the parts of an oration, for example, that a speech must always have a proemium; as the *Anonymous Seguerianus* observes (26–37), Alexander the son of Noumenius thoroughly refuted that proposition. On Apollodorus and his chief contemporary rival, Theodorus of Gaza, see Quintilian, *Institutio oratoria* 3.1.17–18; see also 2.11.2, 2.15.12, 3.1.1, 3.5.17–18, 3.6.35–37, 3.11.3–4, 4.1.50, 4.2.31, 5.17.59–60, 7.2.20, 9.1.12.

37. Rabe 1913, 34–35; see also Heath 1995, 31–32.

38. See Wooten 1987.

39. In Dilts and Kennedy 1995. Heath 2004 considers it a later, perhaps fifth-century compilation. I have no preference on this issue (since it makes no difference to my point here) but have retained the currently received date and identification for simplicity of exposition.

40. Heath 2004, 267–70.

41. Cribiore 2001, 138–47; 2007, 151–52. Cribiore notes that Libanius describes his students coming to school "in the company of slaves who carried their books, which were bulky and quite heavy" (2001, 144; Libanius, *Oration* 25.50, 54.31; see also Norman 1960).

42. Heath 2004, 3–23 ff.

43. Heath 2004, 8.

44. Heath 2004, 9–10; see also Heath 1994. The date of the *Lesser Declamations* is uncertain; Shackleton Bailey 2006, 1, suggests the second century C.E. Heath's analysis of the "breakdown" (or "collapse") of Hermagorean theory focuses largely on the slippage across different authorities of the terms *stasis, krinomenon* (the matter to be judged), *aition* (cause or reason for a claim), *sunechon* (main point), and so forth.

45. Heath 2004, 10, 16.

46. See Heath 1995.

47. According to Cicero, *De inventione* 1.16 and Quintilian, *Institutio oratoria* 3.6.60.

48. For Alcuin, see Howell 1965.

49. For example, if someone charged with a crime enters a procedural objection, that is a "type of action," but as yet there is no determinate *issue* or stasis. If the accused says, "You do not have the legal right to bring this action against me" and the accuser replies, "Yes I do," there is a *question* (a dispute) but as yet no specific point to be judged—no *krinomenon*—and thus no issue or stasis *until* the accused asserts *why* the accuser has no such right and the accuser denies that reason. If the accused asserts that the accuser is banned from bringing legal actions in the courts because his citizenship rights have been curtailed as a result of having previously been convicted of some crime—he is under "stigma" (*ignominia*)—the accuser may rebut the claim in several ways. He may deny that he is under stigma (issue of fact); he may deny that his exclusion from "legal action" under the stigma law includes criminal prosecutions (issue of definition); he may argue that the accused man's crime is too serious to exclude from prosecution on a mere legal technicality (issue of quality). Likewise, if the dispute ultimately centers on legal questions—whether the stigma law is ambiguous, conflicts with other laws, is applicable to cases of this type, or should be interpreted according to letter or intent—the reasons given and the counterarguments to those reasons ultimately will resolve, according to Cicero and Quintilian, into issues of fact, definition, or quality.

50. Heath 2004, 295–96 suggests that Theon's text is probably a late-antique production, but the fact that it mentions no authority later than Dionysius of Halicarnassus inclines me to accept Kennedy's view that the author is probably the first-century Aelius Theon mentioned by Quintilian and the *Suda*.

51. Rabe 1926, 17; see also Kennedy 2003, 105–6.

52. Oddly, Theon's list looks like a set of three lists that have been simply added to each other, rather like Apsines' "anothers." The three lists feature repetitions of (some) *topoi*, shifts in terminology, and differences in syntactic patterning, and seem to have been drawn from different sources. Nevertheless, Theon says they are to be used in order, from the first to the last. See Spengel 1853–56, 2:121–23; Patillon and Bolognesi 1997, 84–86; and Kennedy 2003, 56–57.

53. Rabe 1913, 43–54. For a fuller treatment (translation, commentary, and illustration), see Heath 1995, 36–40, 80–91, 156–75, which is the basis for my discussion here.

54. *Elenchos* here appears to mean what it means in the *Rhetoric to Alexander:* not a "refutation" or "cross-examination" but an irrefutable proof. With Hermogenes it seems particularly to mean evidence given in eyewitness statements, as in "I saw him commit the murder."

55. In Heath's (1995) analysis this two-phase kind of sequence runs through nearly all of the stases.

56. Heath 1995, 80.

57. Heath 1995, 156–75.

58. Cribiore 2007a, 82, 146, 179.

59. Cribiore 2007a, 143–47. Libanius' renditions of the progymnasmata can be found in Foerster 1903–27, vol. 8 and (in translation) Gibson 2008. See also Malcolm Heath's "makeshift translations" of Libanius' renditions of the chreia and encomium exercises, at http://www.leeds.ac.uk/classics/resources/rhetoric/prog-lib.htm/ (accessed May 2009).

60. Rabe 1913, 29–31; see Heath 1995, 28–30.

61. Even an abstract type, such as "the glutton" or "the tyrant," has the sort of background story that is included in the topics of the "commonplace" exercise in the progymnasmata—for example, the "digression" on the character's "past life" prescribed by Aphthonius. This prescription in essence requires invoking a stereotyped image of the life story of a glutton, tyrant, and so on. These stereotyped stories (and character qualities) are thus available for use in declamation exercises, at least for students who have passed through the full course of the progymnasmata.

62. Rabe 1913, 30.

63. This is bought out very clearly in the twelfth-century *Ars Versificatoria* of Matthew of Vendôme, a treatise on elementary verse composition in Latin. Matthew devotes much attention to the topics to be used to amplify the description of stock character types and scenes, which again are nouns more than actual persons or places. These amplified descriptions function as set-pieces to be inserted in a narrative. For English translation, see Parr 1981.

64. Rabe 1913, 30–31.

65. Rabe 1913, 31–33; see Heath 1995, 30–31.

66. Rabe 1913, 32–34.

67. See Psellos, *Synopsis of Rhetoric,* in Westerink 2001 (*Poema* 7). For Tzetzes, see *Epitome of Rhetoric* in Walz 1832–36, 3:670–689; and *Chiliades* 6.748–821, 11.109–365, and 11.696–718, in Kiessling 1826.

68. Russell 1983, 21–39; see likewise Swain 1998, 91–92 (or 89–100 more generally). While Russell's argument (and Swain's) is confined to the Greek tradition, something similar is likely true for Latin declamation also, since most of it was based on Greek models. One major difference, however, may be the relative paucity of deliberative declamation problems in the Latin manuals: The Elder Seneca, for example, treats just 7 deliberative cases (*suasoriae*) compared to more than 60 judicial cases (*controversiae*); and all 311 of the *Minor Declamations* attributed to Quintilian are judicial.

69. On rhetorical education as "civic theater," see Axer 2006 and Walker 2003, both originally delivered at the 2003 Alliance of Rhetoric Societies meeting. Concerning declamation as "game," see Lanham 1976, chap. 1; and Sloane 1997.

70. Usener-Radermacher 1965, vol. 2, *Ars Rhetorica* 10, 359–74. See Heath 2003 and 2004, 236–37. On "dramatism" and the dramatistic notion of "scene" and its relation to "act" and "agent," see Burke 1969a, 3–20; and Burke 1968b.

71. Heath 2003 connects this notion of mixture to what was called "figured speech" —concerning which see Pseudo-Hermogenes *On Invention*, 4.13 (English translation in Kennedy 2005).

72. Heath 2003, 94. Heath sees two concepts of *êthos* at work: (1) the general "philosophical" character of the discourse—"the moral tendency of the text when one abstracts from the individuals involved . . . when, for example, one passes from the individual story of Paris in Homer to the general implications of the contempt which someone of such bad character evokes and the terrible consequences of his misbehavior"—and (2) the particular characters of the speaker and other "persons" of the declamation. Philosophical character ensures the proper treatment, in due proportion, of the particular characters. On the notion of the authorial presence in the text as a "philosophical" ethos that pervades and underlies the whole, see Booth 1961–83 and 1988.

73. *Diatribê* is polyvalent here; it can mean a serious employment, activity, exercise, or study or, pejoratively, a pastime, amusement, or waste of time.

74. Grenfell-Hunt 1906, 1.15 55–61. The site of ancient Hibeh is located on the east bank of the Nile, south of present-day Bani Suwayf, between the towns of Fashn and Fant (on the opposite bank), roughly 75 miles south of modern Cairo.

75. Grenfell-Hunt 1906, 1.15 55.

76. Grenfell-Hunt 1906, 1.15 55. Among other errors, the writer repeatedly renders *humin* (the second-person plural dative pronoun) as *humein*—a hypercorrection, a bit like spelling "yours" as "your's." Other notable mistakes include *mimesthai* as *meimesthai,* and *antilabesthe* as *antilêpesthe.*

77. Grenfell-Hunt 1906, 1.15 56. In all the *i* / *ei* mistakes, the superfluous *e* has been crossed out; in *antilêpesthe* the *lêp* has been crossed out and *lab* has been written above it; and so on. At lines 73–76 the repetition of *parakalô* ("summon") has been crossed out: "but now I foresee the future, and summon you to action and the destiny which." This is a stylistic rather than a spelling change.

78. This translation is based on Grenfell and Hunt's transcription of the papyrus and on their own translation.

79. That is, the death of Alexander.

80. The *eu a-* is not shown in Grenfell and Hunt's transcription but is plainly visible in their photograph of (part of) the papyrus (Plate II in the appendix).

81. See Bartholomae 1985.

82. Grenfell-Hunt 1906, 1.15 55.

83. For Libanius, see Russell 1996; for Aristides, Behr 1981–86; for Polemo, Reader and Chvala-Smith 1996. Another comparison: The extant text of Lysias's *On the Killing of Eratosthenes,* a relatively short judicial speech, takes about twenty minutes to deliver, which suggests about ten modern pages (typed, 12-point font, double-spaced) or, in ancient papyrus, thirty-two columns, eight hundred lines.

84. Ptolemy II was a descendant of one of Alexander's generals, Ptolemy I, who was given authority over Egypt in the dividing-up of Alexander's empire. While Ptolemy I established the Library of Alexandria and in other ways was a patron of the arts and sciences, Ptolemy II presided over a court of Versailles-like splendor.

85. See Bowersock 1969; Anderson 1993.

86. That is, Greek dominance everywhere from the Mediterranean to what is now Afghanistan, the unification of what had once been independent city-states under centralized governments, economic expansion, cultural flourishing, and so on. See Walbank 1981.

87. One might argue that the student's Leosthenes engages in what Kenneth Burke has called "ingenuous and cunning identifications"—self-deluding, ideologically driven rationalizations that can be both "self-protective" and "suicidal." See Burke 1969b, 35–37.

88. Clark 1957, chap. 7 is a good example of the state of thought inherited by contemporary rhetorical studies, that is, from 1970 to now; Clark still was a standard authority when I was a graduate student in the early 1980s. Clark asserts that declamation became "increasingly remote from reality" due to the "evil influences" of (1) the "perverseness and ostentation" of teachers' public performances, and (2) oppressive political conditions that made debating current events ("live issues") too dangerous; modern American schools are "blessed" by comparison because students can debate "actual issues" (215–6, 227). Clark also notes, however, that students "do not usually have enough knowledge or experience to give actual counsel" or deliberate effectively on "real" contemporary issues (219), and toward the end of his chapter he concedes that the fictitiousness of declamation themes may have had some advantages (230–33, 250–51). The modern teacher might, for example, ask students to advise George Washington on whether to cross the Delaware or to retry famous cases (for example, the trial of Socrates), as in the moot courts of modern law schools. But for the most part the chapter echoes the negative judgment of "unreality" that Clark has inherited from his nineteenth- and early- to mid-twentieth-century sources. See also Bonner 1949.

89. Again, see Clark 1957, chap. 7. A notable departure is Bizzell and Herzberg 1995, which presents the student with six "case studies" of cultural conflict in American history. However, this ambitious if unwieldy textbook (of nearly a thousand pages) did not catch on, and in any case it seems designed more for the student to analyze and comment on the conflicts rather than to recreate and reargue particular debates at specific historical moments.

90. Walker 2000a, 96–98. So, too, as I note below, Winterbottom 1982; Sussman 1987, iv–vi; and Bonner 1949, 83.

91. Clark 1957 notes that the *Rhetoric to Herennius* mentions deliberative declamation problems based on "real" current issues. However, the *Rhet. Herr.* mentions three that derive from the Carthaginian wars in the late third century B.C.E. (3.2, 4)—that is, more than a century before—and one that derives from the "Social War" of 91–88, about a decade before (if the *Rhet. Herr.* was composed c. 80). The Social War case, however, is mentioned apart from the others as an *example* of "extraneous motives" for debate, and it may not be a declamation problem. Debating the issues of the Social War (a civil war between Rome and its allies [*socii*]) during the 80s may have been a little like debating the issues of the Vietnam War during the "culture wars" of the 1980s, but doing so in the Roman political climate of that time (that is, the bloody power struggle between Marius and Sulla, mass proscriptions and executions, and the convulsions that

eventually brought the republic to an end) would have been extremely dangerous and daunting for boys to undertake. Clark also forgets the fanciful declamations of the fifth- and fourth-century sophists, such as Gorgias' *Defense of Palamedes* and Alcidamas' *Accusation of Palamedes,* or mythological deliberations such as Prodicus' *Choice of Hercules.* And we have seen the anonymous student's "Leosthenes Addresses the Athenians," from the third century, recreating events and rearguing issues from nearly a century before. Antiphon's *Tetralogies,* likewise, are set in "unreal," archaic contexts that seem to derive from poetry.

92. Translated in Winterbottom 1974 (with slight modifications).

93. These two cases, Vosberg and Palsgraf, were taken from Epstein (2000, 4, 501) but can be found in nearly any torts textbook. I have rewritten the summaries roughly in the form of a declamation problem.

94. Winterbottom 1982; see also Sussman 1987, iv–vi.

95. Again, see Clark 1957, 219.

96. Lynch, George, and Cooper 1997 discusses this problem (and some possible solutions) very thoughtfully.

97. Gleason 1995; Gunderson 2003; Swain 1998.

98. I am thinking here particularly of the Marxian notions of "hailing" and "interpellation" operating through the mundane transactions of everyday life as well as literature and official state propaganda; see Althusser 1971. Perhaps best is Kenneth Burke's more flexible (or usefully vague) notion of "identification" and identity formation, which he proposes in *A Rhetoric of Motives* as a framework for expanding the traditional concept of persuasion: "Often we must think . . . not in terms of some one particular address, but . . . a general *body of identifications* that owe their convincingness much more to trivial repetition and dull daily reinforcement than to exceptional rhetorical skill"; Burke 1969b, 26.

99. See also the account of enculturation by "Protagoras" in the "Great Speech" in Plato's *Protagoras.*

100. This is even more true for Byzantine rhetoric and literature, with its rendition of "Attic" Greek (highly artificial and so far removed from vernacular Greek as to be nearly unintelligible) and its echoes and allusions to the ancient classics. As I have argued elsewhere, "Byzantine rhetoric transpires in a deeply, profoundly resonant echo-chamber, a quasi-sacred space where speaker, audience, and all the canonic voices of the past are joined in one community, and one that is, in ideological terms, co-present and consubstantial, eternal and unchanging (despite actual and considerable historical change)." Walker 2004; see also Magdalino 1993, 352–54.

101. Pagán 2004, for example, in a review of Gunderson 2003, refers to declamation as "that dull, monotonous, tedious practice," though it clearly was not regarded that way in antiquity.

102. On the competitive aspects of declamation in these kinds of private settings, see Sinclair 1995; on the motives of game, play, and competition in rhetorical culture in general, see Lanham 1976, chap. 1.

103. Philostratus calls the Odeion of Agrippa a *theatron* and refers to it as the Agrippeion. On this building, see Camp 1990, 118–23. It survives today only in traces.

104. Camp 1990, 118–23.

105. On Herodes' Marathon estate, which seems to have belonged to his wife Regilla, see Camp 2001, 218–22. The few surviving remains include traces of what was an enclosure wall measuring perhaps 60 x 120 meters, at the northern end of the enclosure a small "podium" temple of the Egyptian gods with a platform measuring 10 x 10 meters and an adjacent structure consisting of several rooms (the largest being 10 x 5 meters), and just outside the enclosure wall on the southeast side a lavish three–sided bath complex measuring roughly 40 x 30 x 30 meters (with an oval pool 10 meters long; various smaller rooms for hot, warm, and cold baths; and changing rooms). The "theater" seating in the Odeion of Agrippa filled a room measuring approximately 30 x 30 meters, and the whole building measured approximately 40 x 50 meters (around its perimeter); Camp 1986, 183–85; Camp 2001, 188–90. On the Omega House, see Camp 1990, 155–59. This house features what appears to be a lecture hall measuring 10 x 5 meters.

106. By *idiôtai,* literally "private individuals"—as opposed, perhaps, to members of the curial elite, the educated *beltistoi* ("the best") who held the civic offices—Lucian seems to mean those capable of appreciating the beauty of the building and the eloquence of the speaker, but not of speaking about it in a sophisticated critical way or performing on stage (*On the Hall* 1–3). It is highly possible that Lucian is describing the Odeion of Agrippa, since he makes references to other sights in Athens and seems to be speaking there. The best available English translation of this text still is Fowler 1905, 4:12–23; I have relied on the Loeb text for the Greek.

107. The Elder Seneca mentions that the declaimer Porcius Latro would, "while seated" (that is, before starting the performance proper), "set forth the issues (*quaestiones*) of the case (*controversia*) he was to declaim on" (*Controversiae* 1.pr.21), that is, he provided a stasis analysis so that the audience could see more clearly how he handled the problem.

108. As edited by Keil 1898 and Lenz-Behr 1976 and translated by Behr 1986. For an analysis of the Sicilian Orations, see Pernot 1981.

109. This is Aristides' interpretation in *Oration* 6.21. Thucydides (6.24.1–3) actually makes this point about Nicias' effort to derail the original decision: After the Athenians had voted to invade Sicily and had put him in command (despite his unwillingness), he estimated the necessary troops, materiel, and costs so high that (as he hoped) the Athenians would be appalled and would reconsider. Instead they granted him everything that he had asked for.

110. Pernot 1981, 21–22.

111. *Blue Guide Turkey* 1995, 216 gives a figure of fourteen hundred for the *ôdeion-bouleutêrion* of Ephesus; I have personally inspected this structure. Few visible traces remain of ancient Smyrna (modern Izmir). Its *ôdeion-bouleutêrion* probably was near the agora, a few remnants of which can be seen today. Traces of a "Roman theater" can still be seen near the Basmane railway station, about eight hundred meters northeast of the agora.

112. See Pernot 1981, 22n69 for discussion of this passage. *Gnorimos,* as an adjective, meant "well-known, notable, distinguished," and as a noun, "acquaintance, associate, student."

113. Behr 1986, 1:483n1; Pernot 1981, 76.

114. For text, translation, and commentary, see Howell 1965.

115. Note that "four persons" here refers to the *types of persons* involved in a trial, not the actual number of people present (since, after all, there are multiple witnesses and possibly multiple jurors).

116. Howell 1965, 92–97.

117. No such thing exists, that is, in Charlemagne's world; courts and other institutions of Roman civil society continued to function in the Byzantine Empire (which was a continuation of the eastern Roman Empire, which survived the collapse of the West). When Western scholars in the Middle Ages imagined "Rome," they could do so with the knowledge that "Rome" still existed somewhere, if not in their own immediate reality. I am indebted for this example from Alcuin to Jeannette Richardson, many years ago, at the University of California, Berkeley.

Chapter 5: Dionysius of Halicarnassus and the Notion of Rhetorical Scholarship

1. De Jonge 2008, 1:25–29; Dionysius *Roman Antiquities,* 1.7.2–3. The latest attested date is 8/7 B.C. At *Rom. Ant.* 1.7.2 Dionysius says he arrived at Rome in the year Augustus ended the civil wars (30/29) and has remained in Rome "twenty-two years from that time," which dates this statement to 8/7. However, as de Jonge points out, at *Rom. Ant.* 7.70.2 he refers to book 1 as already published, so he must have continued to live and work beyond 8/7. Since Dionysius is generally thought to have been born around 60 B.C.E. or shortly thereafter, he seems to have been active at Rome roughly from age thirty to fifty-two and probably longer.

2. In what follows, for the Greek text of Dionysius' critical/rhetorical writings I am using Usener-Radermacher 1965. The most widely available, though incomplete, translation in English is the two-volume Loeb text of Usher 1974–85. A complete translation, in French, is the six-volume Budé text of Aujac 1978–92. For the *Roman Antiquities* I am using the seven-volume Loeb text of Cary 1937–50. The misattributed writings are all collected in Usener-Radermacher 1965. The "Dionysius Rhetoric" on epideictic is available in translation in Russell-Wilson 1981 (as an appendix). On the lecture concerning the evaluation of texts, see Heath 2004, 236–37.

3. Roberts 1901, 43–49; see also Roberts's 1910 edition, translation, and commentary on the *Peri Syntheseôs Onomatôn.*

4. Egger 1902, 15.

5. Carey 1937–50, 1:xv.

6. Usher 1974–85, 1:xi, xv, xx.

7. Bonner 1969, 99.

8. Bonner 1969 23, 53. Bonner's 1939 argument is more or less repeated in G. M. A. Grube's chapter on Dionysius in *The Greek and Roman Critics* (Grube 1965, 207–30). Bonner and Grube are the chief, and indeed the only, authorities cited in Usher's 1975 introduction to his translation. Aside from some scattered articles, there has been no full-length and sympathetic study of Dionysius' critical and historical writings until quite

recently. Dionysius receives two sentences in Brian Vickers's *In Defence of Rhetoric* (Vickers 1988, 51). He is mostly ignored in George Kennedy's *Classical Rhetoric and Its Christian and Secular Tradition from Ancient to Modern Times* (Kennedy 1980 and 1999) but is given fuller treatment in *The Art of Rhetoric in the Roman World* (Kennedy 1972, 342–63), which more or less reflects the Bonner/Grube account; see also Kennedy's *New History of Classical Rhetoric* (Kennedy 1994, 161–66.) A rare "reappraisal" is offered by Thompson 1979, and Laurent Pernot's *Rhetoric in Antiquity* devotes two and a half generally sympathetic pages to Dionysius' critical essays (Pernot 2005, 136–38).

9. Bender and Wellbery 1990; Gaonkar 1993.

10. Bonner 1969, 40.

11. *Rhetorikē esti dunamis technikē pithanou logou en pragmati politikōi telos echousa to eu legein . . . kata to endechomenon. Peri Mimēseōs* fr. 1, Usener-Radermacher, 2:197, 198–200.

12. *Rhetoric* 1.2.1: "Let rhetoric be a faculty *(dunamis)* of observing in each case the possibly persuasive *(to endechomenon pithanon)*."

13. According to Sextus Empiricus, "Hermagoras said that the task of the complete rhetor is to settle the proposed political question as persuasively as possible" *(kata to endechomenon; Against the Schoolmasters* 62); according to Maximus Planudes, "The Hermagoreans [define rhetoric] thus: a faculty *(dunamis)* concerned with speech, having the goal of persuading as much as it can" *(hoson eph' heautēi;* Walz 1832–36, 5:216); both in Matthes 1962, 6, 7 (frs. 4, 5b).

14. Roberts 1901, 40–42; Kennedy 1972, 347–48; de Jonge 2008.

15. Burke 1973, 23.

16. The seven are Theodectes, Philiscus, Isaeus, Cephisodorus, Hyperides, Lycurgus, and Aeschines. See Usher 1974, 2:311n1.

17. See chapter 1.

18. Behr 1968; Walker 2005.

19. Sullivan 2009.

20. Sullivan 2009.

21. Isocrates does, however, elsewhere favor democracy as the best form of government, when properly constituted (for example, *Areopagiticus* 60–70); and Dionysius likewise favors at least a *dēmotikos* (popular) element in government, as becomes apparent in his *Roman Antiquities.*

22. Isocrates' *Against the Sophists* 19–21 and *Antidosis* 46–51, 256; see also Isocrates' *Panathenaicus* 10–14. This view persists among such leading second-sophistic figures as Aelius Aristides and Hermogenes of Tarsus. See, for example, Aristides, *Against Plato on Behalf of Rhetoric;* and Hermogenes, *On Types of Style (Peri Ideōn),* especially 2.10–12.

23. In Kominis 1960, 128.

24. See Woodman and West 1984.

25. See de Jonge 2008.

26. Cribiore 2001 discusses this small-to-larger-units progression in detail.

27. As de Jonge 2008 shows, Dionysius' "linguistic" theory absorbs and reconfigures a complex array of sources from the Hellenistic grammatical and rhetorical traditions. Undoubtedly the same can be said for his more specifically rhetorical teaching.

28. See Isocrates' *Against the Sophists* 21 and *Antidosis* 46–50, 180–91, 253–57, 274–75.

29. *Peri Mimêseôs* fr. 2, Usener-Radermacher 1965, 2: 200.

30. *Chronôi polloi kai makrai tribêi kai alogôi pathei tên alogon sunaskein aisthêsin;* Usener-Radermacher 1965, 1:19. Usher 1974 translates this rather dramatically as "banish reason from the senses and train them by patient study over a long period to feel without thinking"; this seems a bit too romantic for what Dionysius has in mind.

31. Usener-Radermacher 1965, 1:176–77.

32. This is the list (and the order) of authors discussed in the surviving epitome of *Peri Mimêseôs,* which appears as fr. 6 in Usener-Radermacher 1965, 2:202–14. See also Aujac 1978–92, 5:31–40.

33. *Nuni de peri tôn hexês dialexomai, tis ho pragmatikos esti Lusiou charaktêr, epeidê ton huper tês lexeôs logon apodedôka.* As before I have translated this fairly literally.

34. That is, *pathos* in the sense of a "suffering" or something that befalls one and is involuntarily experienced (from *paschô,* "suffer").

35. *Deinos* signifies what is terrifying or awe inspiring, and by extension comes to mean "awesome" speech in the sense of supremely skillful, clever, impressive, overwhelming, or "forceful." Compare *deinotês* in Hermogenes' *On Types of Style* (trans. Wooten 1987) and the Pseudo-Hermogenic *On the Method of Deinotês* (trans. Kennedy 2005).

36. Theon in Spengel 1853–56, 2:65; Patillon 1997, 8; Kennedy 2003, 8.

37. De Jonge 2008.

38. I am quoting from the latter of these two passages; see Usener-Radermacher 1965, 1:26.

39. See, for example, the declamation problems in chapter 4.

40. According to Bowersock (1965, 132), this Metilius Rufus would later be proconsul (the provincial governor) of Achaea (Greece) under Augustus; so his father, Dionysius' "most valued friend," was a person of some significance. See also de Jonge 2008, 27–28, 382.

41. In rough outline, the Lydian king Candaules boasted about his wife's beauty to Gyges, one of his bodyguards, and insisted that Gyges view her naked. Gyges resisted, objecting that it would be improper, but the king insisted and promised that he would arrange for Gyges to view her without her knowing it (as she undressed for bed). In the end Gyges relented, really having no choice, and the thing was arranged. The queen, however, discovered what had been done and conspired with Gyges to assassinate Candaules, so that Gyges became king. Dionysius repeats only the part of the story in which Candaules persuades Gyges to view the queen.

42. De Jonge 2008, 368; for the full discussion, see 367–90.

43. De Jonge recognizes this point but seems to regard instruction as an incidental use of *metathesis,* whereas in my view it is fundamental, that is, as a form of *exercise.*

44. As noted in chapter 3, this sort of dabbling with effects may be what Plato satirizes in Isocratean pedagogy, treating its elementary exercises as if they were the whole or essence of the art.

45. This rubric of subtraction, addition, and alteration is essentially that adopted by Groupe *Mu* (1981) for their theory of figures in their "general rhetoric," and by Quinn's (1993) brief manual on figures of speech.

46. Elsewhere in this text my transliterations do not represent the pitch accents of Greek (which in Greek are represented by diacritics). Here the acute [´] and grave [`] represent rising and falling pitch respectively (as in Greek); likewise the circumflex on *ô* represents the Greek circumflex accent (rising and falling pitch). The same applies, below, to *síga síga leukón* (pitch accents are represented).

47. The avoidance of such awkward syllabic repetitions is a principle attributed in ancient sources to the *technê* of Isocrates. See Mandilaras 2003, 3:239–41, items 4, 8, 10.

48. This is an element commonly ascribed to the *technê* of Isocrates—making long things short and short things long, as well as making old things new and new things old, and so on—as noted in previous chapters. See Mandilaras 2003, 3:239–41, item 2.

49. Usher 1974–85 translates *to kalon* as "beauty," which is correct but seems misleading in this context, especially in view of Dionysius' list of the subsidiary qualities contributing to *to kalon,* which suggest a kind of *gravitas* or moral excellence combined with maturity.

50. "Euphony" here, *eustomia,* literally means "good mouth" and suggests a style that "rolls off the tongue" well or is well pronounced.

51. See Wooten 1987.

52. Marrou 1956, 2.6; Cribiore 2001.

53. That is, in a sort of copy book, consisting probably of papyrus scraps or wax tablets.

54. In classical Greek such "pyrrhic" words would still have *pitch accent,* as opposed to *stress accent* in modern English; Dionysius is referring not to accentual patterns but strictly to patterns of syllable length, or what is called "quantitative" rhythm. Since this distinction is not part of the sound system of stress-accent languages like modern English, it is difficult to illustrate. However, one might say that a line like "Hit it, hit it!" contains stress accents (in a "trochaic" pattern) but in terms of syllable length is *quantitatively* an all-short "pyrrhic" rhythm. Compare "slowly drawn up water," in which the "long" lead syllables create a "trochaic" quantitative pattern (while the stress-accent pattern is "trochaic" too). In contrast, "We'll put these in" may perhaps be analyzed as quantitatively "trochaic" but accentually "iambic," and so on.

55. Usher 1974, 2:141n2 describes Hegesias' faults as "jerky, monotonous rhythms and affected word-order." Ironically, the chief surviving fragments of Hegesias are the passages quoted by Dionysius.

56. This precept is, of course, the source of Alexander Pope's oft-quoted, self-illustrating dictum, "When Ajax strives some rock's vast weight to throw, / The line too labours, and the words move slow" ("An Essay on Criticism" 370–71).

57. Usener-Radermacher 1965, 2: 10.19 374.

58. De Jonge 2008, 27.

59. Such as, perhaps, an equestrian secretary; see Millar 1993.

60. Further, if *askein* can be read as "to work" or "work on," and if *poioumenous* can be read as "making," the line can be read as "I recommend that everyone *work on* this part *when making exercises* in the Lysianic examples" (*en tois Lusiou paradeigmasi,* more literally "in the examples from Lysias"). Note too that *poioumenous* is in the middle voice and may suggest "having [exercises] made" or "having [exercises] done," or in other words *assigning* exercises.

61. We might, perhaps, think of *On the Ancient Orators* as something like a PBS documentary, for example (hypothetically), "The Great Speakers."

62. My rough estimate here is based on the page lengths of the two texts in Usener-Radermacher 1965 (fifteen and thirteen respectively) and a per-page word count of approximately two hundred. At that rate, each page takes about 1.3 minutes to deliver—hence 30 and 26 minutes for the two lectures, or an average of 28 minutes each.

63. Heath 2004, 236.

64. Smith 1995.

65. As cited in the *Suda*; see Adler 1928–38, K 1165.

66. Smith 1995, 79.

67. Cameron 1995, 78.

68. *Hupomnêma* sometimes signifies a brief version or "digest" of a longer text to be used as a "reminder" of its main points and general content.

69. Carey 1937–50, 1:25n2.

70. The notion of *êthos* as "mild" feelings amenable to morality and reason—as opposed to the wild, turbulent passions of *pathos*—appears as early as Aristotle's *Rhetoric*, and later in Quintilian, and seems to be what Dionysius has in mind here. See Wisse 1989.

71. Reid 1996.

72. One might compare this approach to Roland Barthes's *Writing Degree Zero* (Barthes 1953), in which a notion of "style" as something "added" to language is replaced with a notion of "*écriture*" as the embodiment of what Dionysius would call *charaktêr* through a particular configuration (composition, *sunthêsis*) of linguistic resources.

73. Usher 1974, 1:237.

74. Usher 1974, 1:523n2. See Cicero, *On the Orator* 3.52; *Brutus* 261; *Partitiones Oratoriae* 31.

75. Demetrius of Magnesia was a contemporary of Cicero; Callimachus was active (as a scholar and poet) at the Library of Alexandria in the mid-third century B.C.E.. The "grammarians of Pergamon" were literary scholars (philologists, editors, librarians) at the almost equally famous Library of Pergamon in Asia Minor (today's Bergama, on the western coast of Turkey).

76. There is, of course, virtually no mention of Demosthenes in Aristotle's *Rhetoric* —a curious omission. Demetrius of Phaleron says that Aristotle thought Demosthenes too vulgar; see Wehrli 1968, vol. 4, frs. 161–67.

77. Usher 1974, 2:402.

78. There also are fragments from an epitome of the whole work, collected in Usener-Radermacher 1965, 2:197–217.

79. Usher 1974, 2:352–53n1.

80. Flower 1994, 42–62. See also Fox 1993.

81. As Flower declares in his conclusion, he has "removed" Theopompus "from under the shadow of Isocrates" (211).

82. Usher 1969, 240–41.

83. Gabba 1991, 5–9.

84. Gabba 1991, 6.

85. Gabba 1991, 9.

86. Bowersock 1969.

87. The *Atthides* were annalistic accounts of events in Attica written (mainly) in the fourth and third centuries B.C.E..

88. As reported in Diogenes Laertius, *Lives of the Philosophers* 11.2.

89. See Burke 1984, 272.

90. Foucault 1978.

91. The centuries allotted to each wealth class were:

    1. 98 (80 infantry + 18 cavalry)

    2. 22

    3. 20

    4. 22

    5. 30

    6. 1

92. See, for example, 3.21, 5.10.2 (where it is connected specifically to tyrannical ambitions), 6.35–36, 6.43.3.

93. The *tribuni plebei* were "officers" charged to protect the plebeians against patrician injustices. (There were other types of tribunes also.) The *aediles* were magistrates charged with the supervision of public works (such as grain markets and price controls, street repairs, and public safety) and had police powers.

94. On the problems of consensus and its potentially "tragic" consequences for rhetoric, deliberation, and political judgment (set in the particular case of proslavery rhetoric in the antebellum South), see Roberts-Miller 2009.

95. See, for example, Lyotard 1984; Jameson 1991.

96. *Phrontistêrion,* though it appears in Aristophanes' *Clouds* as the name of Socrates' school (and is usually translated as "Thinkery" or the like) is a thoroughly modern term. Athens today is dotted with *phrontistêria* where one can take lessons in foreign languages, typing, secretarial skills, and so on.

97. Since Dionysius came to Rome shortly after the end of the civil war and Augustus' assumption of absolute power (c. 30 B.C.E.), it is possible that he was *brought* there and had a salaried position on someone's staff or even in the imperial chancery, for example, as a secretary for Greek administrative correspondence. That might explain his connections to people like Ammaeus, Metilius Rufus's father, Aelius Tubero, or Gnaeus Pompeius and their circles, as well as his learning of Latin.

98. See, for example, Roberts-Miller 2004.

99. Wichelns 1925.

100. See Mailloux 1989, 1998; and Jost 2004.

101. On rhetoric as an "interdiscipline," see Mailloux 2006.

102. See Anderson 1984; Schmelling 1996; and Grammanidis 2007.

Epilogue

1. See "Lexicon Rhetoricae" in Burke 1968a.

2. Bender and Wellbery 1990.

3. Mailloux 2006.

4. Regarding "lore" as a mode of disciplinary knowledge, see North 1987.

5. For example, the Epicurean treatises on rhetoric and poetics by Philodemus of Gadara and Stoic theories of rhetoric and poetics. Perhaps (to judge from Lucian) there was a Cynic account of rhetoric as well. When the scrolls of Philodemus' *On Rhetoric* found at Pompeii have definitively been reconstructed and edited by the now-ongoing Philodemus Project, we will know much more about the philosophical discussion of rhetoric in the Hellenistic age. Philodemus' *On Poetry* has already been partially published, with a discussion of the papyrus and the methods of reconstruction; see Janko 2000.

6. See, for example, Kennedy 1980. The tripartite division of traditions disappears, however, in Kennedy 1999 (the second edition).

7. Webb 2001.

8. On contemporary rhetoric/composition as a "teaching" discipline, see Harris 1996. For other (and more extended) versions of the story, see Connors 1997 and Crowley 1998.

9. Burke 1984, 37–49.

10. Borradori 2003.

11. See, for example, Roberts-Miller 2004, 2009.

12. Howells 1993, 216.

13. See, for example, Prose's (2007) account of her experience in graduate school.

14. See Derrida's "Plato's Pharmacy," collected in Derrida 1981 (originally published in *Tel Quel* 32–33 [1968]); and Mailloux 1989.

15. One of the few to have remarked on this resemblance is Marjorie Curry Woods. See the "Looking Ahead" section of Woods's (2010) "Afterword."

16. See, for some recent leading examples, Prose 2007; Morley 2008; and Bernays and Painter 2010.

17. See, for example, Mayers 2005, 2009; and Ritter and Vanderslice 2009.

18. See Connors 1997.

19. See, for example, Hagaman 1986; Fleming 1998, 1999, and 2003; Church and Sigrell 2005; and Desmet 2006.

20. D'Angelo 1999; Church and Sigrell 2005. See also the classicizing textbooks of Corbett 1998 (or earlier editions); and Crowley and Hawhee 2008.

21. Selby 2008.

22. On the ludic dimension of rhetoric, see Lanham 1976 and Sloane 1997.

23. As, for example, Cribiore (2001, 2007a) sometimes suggests.

24. See Brown 1992.

WORKS CITED

Adler, Ada. 1928–38. *Suidae Lexicon (Suda)*. 5 vols. Leipzig: Teubner. (Also available at *Suda On Line,* http://www.stoa.org/sol/. Accessed June 2008.)

Althusser, Louis. 1971. "Ideology and Ideological State Apparatuses." In *Lenin and Philosophy, and Other Essays,* trans. Ben Brewster. New York: Monthly Review Press. 127–193.

Anderson, Graham. 1984. *Ancient Fiction: The Novel in the Graeco-Roman World.* London: Croom Helm.

———. 1993. *The Second Sophistic: A Cultural Phenomenon in the Roman Empire.* London: Routledge.

Atwill, Janet. 2005. "Rhetoric and Civic Virtue." In Graff, Walzer, and Atwill 2005, 75–92.

Aujac, Germaine, ed. and trans. 1978–92. *Denys d'Halicarnasse: Opuscules Rhétoriques.* 6 vols. Paris: Société d'Édition "Les Belles Lettres."

Axer, Jerzy. 2006. "Tradition: A Voice from the Peripheries." *Advances in the History of Rhetoric* 9:257–266.

Barnes, Jonathan. 1995a. "Life and Work." In *The Cambridge Companion to Aristotle,* ed. Jonathan Barnes. Cambridge: Cambridge University Press. 1–26.

———. 1995b. "Rhetoric and Poetics." In *The Cambridge Companion to Aristotle,* ed. Jonathan Barnes. Cambridge: Cambridge University Press. 259–285.

———. 1997. "Roman Aristotle." In *Philosophia Togata II: Plato and Aristotle at Rome,* ed. Jonathan Barnes and Miriam T. Griffin. Oxford: Oxford University Press. 1–69.

Barthes, Roland. 1953. *Le Degré Zéro de L'Écriture.* Paris: Éditions du Seuil.

Bartholomae, David. 1985. "Inventing the University." In *When A Writer Can't Write: Studies in Writer's Block and Other Composing Process Problems,* ed. Mike Rose. New York: Guilford. 134–165.

Barwick, Karl. 1963. "Das Problem der isokrateischen Techne." *Philologus* 107:43–60.

———. 1966–67. "Die 'Rhetorik ad Alexandrum' und Anaximenes, Alkidamas, Isokrates, Aristoteles und die Theodecteia." *Philologus* 110 (1966): 212–245; 111 (1967): 47–55.

Beaton, Roderick. 1987. "The Rhetoric of Poverty: The Lives and Opinions of Theodore Prodromos." *Byzantine and Modern Greek Studies* 11:1–28.

Behr, Charles A. 1968. *Aelius Aristides and the Sacred Tales.* Amsterdam: Hakkert.

———, trans. 1981–86. 2 vols. *P. Aelius Aristides: The Complete Works.* Leiden: Brill.

Bekker, Immanuel, ed. 1831–70. *Aristoteles Opera.* 5 vols. Berlin: Reimerum.

Bender, John, and David Wellbery. 1990. "Rhetoricality: On the Modernist Return of Rhetoric." In *The Ends of Rhetoric: History, Theory, Practice,* ed. John Bender and David Wellbery. Stanford: Stanford University Press. 3–39.

Benson, Thomas, ed. 1993. *Landmark Essays in Rhetorical Criticism*. Davis, Calif.: Hermagoras Press.

Bernays, Anne, and Pamela Painter. 2010. *What If? Writing Exercises for Fiction Writers*. 3rd ed. New York: Longman.

Billig, Michael. 1987. *Arguing and Thinking: A Rhetorical Approach to Social Psychology*. Cambridge: Cambridge University Press.

Bizzell, Patricia, and Bruce Herzberg. 1995. *Negotiating Difference: Cultural Case Studies for Composition*. New York: Bedford/St. Martin's.

Blue Guide Turkey. 1995. New York: Norton.

Bollansée, Jan. 1999. *Hermippos of Smyrna and His Biographical Writings: A Reappraisal*. Leuven: Peeters.

Bonner, S. F. 1949. *Roman Declamation in the Late Republic and Early Empire*. Liverpool: University Press of Liverpool.

———. 1969. *The Literary Treatises of Dionysius of Halicarnassus: A Study in the Development of Critical Method*. 1939. Reprint, Amsterdam: Hakkert.

———. 1977. *Education in Ancient Rome: from the Elder Cato to the Younger Pliny*. London: Methuen.

Bons, J. A. E. 1997. *Poietikon Pragma: Isocrates' Theory of Rhetorical Composition*. Amsterdam: Gieben.

Booth, Wayne C. 1961–83. *The Rhetoric of Fiction*. 1st and 2nd eds. Chicago: University of Chicago Press.

———. 1974. *Modern Dogma and the Rhetoric of Assent*. Chicago: University of Chicago Press.

Bornecque, H. 1902. *Les Déclamations et les Déclamateurs d'après Sènéque le Père*. Lille: University of Lille.

Borradori, Giovanna. 2003. *Philosophy in a Time of Terror: Dialogues with Jürgen Habermas and Jacques Derrida*. Chicago: University of Chicago Press.

Bowersock, G. W. 1965. *Augustus and the Greek World*. Oxford: Oxford University Press.

———. 1969. *Greek Sophists in the Roman Empire*. London: Oxford University Press.

Brandes, Paul D. 1989. *A History of Aristotle's "Rhetoric."* Metuchen, N.J.: Scarecrow.

Branham, R. Bracht. 1989. *Unruly Eloquence: Lucian and the Comedy of Traditions*. Cambridge: Harvard University Press.

Brémond, Émile, and Georges Mathieu. 1960–63. *Isocrate: Discours*. 4 vols. Paris: Belles Lettres.

Brereton, John C., ed. 1995. *The Origins of Composition Studies in the American College 1875–1925: A Documentary History*. Pittsburgh: University of Pittsburgh Press.

Brittain, Charles. 2001. *Philo of Larissa: The Last of the Academic Skeptics*. Oxford: Oxford University Press.

Brown, Peter. 1992. *Power and Persuasion in Late Antiquity: Towards A Christian Empire*. Madison: University of Wisconsin Press.

Browning, Robert. 1954. "The Correspondence of a Tenth-Century Byzantine Scholar." *Byzantion* 25:397–452. Reprinted in Browning 1977.

———. 1962–63. "The Patriarchal School at Constantinople in the Twelfth Century." *Byzantion* 32:167–201 and *Byzantion* 33:11–40. Reprinted in Browning 1977.

————. 1977. *Studies on Byzantine History, Literature and Education.* London: Variorum.

————. 1997. "Teachers." In *The Byzantines,* ed. Guglielmo Cavallo. Chicago: University of Chicago Press. 95–116.

Burgchardt, Carl, ed. 1995. *Readings in Rhetorical Criticism.* State College, Pa.: Strata.

Burke, Kenneth. 1966. *Language as Symbolic Action.* Berkeley and Los Angeles: University of California Press.

————. 1968a. *Counter-Statement.* 1931. Reprint, Berkeley and Los Angeles: University of California Press.

————. 1968b. "Dramatism." In *International Encyclopedia of the Social Sciences,* ed. David Sills. New York: Macmillan. 7:445–452.

————. 1969a. *A Grammar of Motives.* 1945. Reprint, Berkeley and Los Angeles: University of California Press.

————. 1969b. *A Rhetoric of Motives.* 1950. Reprint, Berkeley and Los Angeles: University of California Press.

————. 1973. *The Philosophy of Literary Form.* 1941. Reprint, Berkeley and Los Angeles: University of California Press.

————. 1984. *Permanence and Change: An Anatomy of Purpose.* 1935. 3rd ed. reprint, Berkeley and Los Angeles: U California P.

Byzantium 1200. 2008. http://www.byzantium1200.com/. Accessed June 2008.

Cahn, Michael. 1989. "Reading Rhetoric Rhetorically: Isocrates and the Marketing of Insight." *Rhetorica* 7(2): 121–144.

Camargo, Martin. 2009. "Grammar School Rhetoric: The Compendia of John Longe and John Miller." *New Medieval Literatures* 11:91–112.

Cameron, Alan. 1995. *Callimachus and His Critics.* Princeton: Princeton University Press.

Camp, John M. 1986. *The Athenian Agora.* London: Thames and Hudson.

————. 1990. *The Athenian Agora: A Guide to the Excavation and Museum.* Rev. 4th ed. Athens: American School of Classical Studies.

————. 2001. *The Archaeology of Athens.* New Haven: Yale University Press.

Carey, Earnest, ed. and trans. 1937–50. *Dionysius of Halicarnassus: The Roman Antiquities.* 7 vols. Cambridge: Harvard University Press.

Celentano, Maria Silvana, ed. 2003. *Il Manuale Tecnico nella Civiltà Greca e Romana.* Chieti: Edizione dell' Orso.

Chiron, Pierre. 2000. "La Tradition Manuscrite de la Rhétorique à Alexandre: Prolégomènes à une Nouvelle Édition Critique." *Revue de l'Histoire des Textes* 30:17–69.

————. 2002. "La Lettre Dédicatoire Apocryphe Mise en Tête de la Rhétorique à Alexandre: Un Faux si Impudent?" In *Apocryphité: Histoire d'un Concept Transversal aux Religions du Livre,* ed. S. C. Mimouni. Turnhout: Brepols.

————, ed. and trans. 2002. *Pseudo-Aristote: Rhétorique à Alexandre.* Paris: Belles Lettres.

Chomsky, Noam, and Morris Halle. 1968. *The Sound Pattern of English.* New York: Harper and Row.

————. 2007. "The *Rhetoric to Alexander.*" In Worthington 2007, 90–106.

Christensen, Francis. 1967. *Notes Toward a New Rhetoric: 6 Essays for Teachers.* New York: Harper & Row.

————. 1976. *A New Rhetoric.* New York: Harper & Row.

Church, A. P., and Anders Sigrell. 2005. "*Cum Poterit*—Rhetorical Exercises for Transitional and Developmental Students." *Scandinavian Journal of Educational Research* 49(5): 543–556.

Clark, Donald L. 1957. *Rhetoric in Greco-Roman Education*. New York: Columbia University Press.

Clarke, M. L. 1951. "The Thesis in the Roman Rhetorical Schools of the Republic." *Classical Quarterly* 45:159–166.

Cole, Robert. 1991. *The Origins of Rhetoric in Classical Greece*. Baltimore: Johns Hopkins University Press.

Conley, Thomas. 1984. "The Enthymeme in Perspective." *Quarterly Journal of Speech* 70(2): 168–187.

Connors, Robert J. 1997. *Composition-Rhetoric: Backgrounds, Theory, Pedagogy*. Pittsburgh: University of Pittsburgh Press.

Connors, Robert J., Lisa Ede, and Andrea Lunsford, eds. 1984. *Essays on Classical Rhetoric and Modern Discourse*. Carbondale: Southern Illinois University Press.

Cooper, John M., ed. 1997. *Plato: Complete Works*. Indianapolis: Hackett.

Corbett, Edward P. J. 1998. *Classical Rhetoric for the Modern Student*. 1965. 4th ed. reprint, New York: Oxford University Press.

Cribiore, Raffaella. 2001. *Gymnastics of the Mind: Greek Education in Hellenistic and Roman Egypt*. Princeton: Princeton University Press.

———. 2007a. *The School of Libanius in Late Antique Antioch*. Princeton: Princeton University Press.

———. 2007b. "Lucian, Libanius, and the Short Road to Rhetoric." *Greek, Roman, and Byzantine Studies* 47:71–86.

Criscuolo, Ugo, ed. and trans. 1989. *Michele Psello: Autobiografia: Encomio per la Madre*. Naples: M. D'Auria.

Crowley, Sharon. 1998. *Composition in the University: Historical and Polemical Essays*. Pittsburgh: University of Pittsburgh Press.

Crowley, Sharon, and Debra Hawhee. 2008. *Ancient Rhetorics for Contemporary Students*. 1994. Reprint, New York: Longman.

D'Angelo, Frank. 1996. "Rhetorical Criticism." In *Encyclopedia of Rhetoric and Composition*. New York: Garland. 604–608.

———. 1999. *Composition in the Classical Tradition*. New York: Longman.

de Jonge, Casper C. 2008. *Between Grammar and Rhetoric: Dionysius of Halicarnassus on Language, Linguistics, and Literature*. Leiden: Brill.

Derrida, Jacques. 1981. *Dissemination*. Trans. Barbara Johnson. Chicago: University of Chicago Press.

Desmet, Christy. 2006. "Progymnasmata, Then and Now." In *Rhetorical Agendas: Political, Ethical, Spiritual,* ed. P. Bizzell. Mahwah, N.J.: Erlbaum. 185–191.

Diels, Hermann. 1901. *Poetarum Philosophorum Fragmenta*. Berlin: Weidmann.

Diels, Hermann, and Walther Kranz, eds. 1951–54. *Die Fragmente der Vorsokratiker*. 3 vols. Berlin: Weidmann.

Dilts, Mervin R., and George Kennedy, eds. 1997. *Two Greek Rhetorical Treatises from the Roman Empire: Introduction. Text, and Translation of the Arts of Rhetoric Attributed to Anonymous Seguerianus and Apsines of Gadara*. New York: Brill.

Di Marco, Massimo. 1989. *Timone di Fliunte: Silli.* Rome: Edizione dell' Ateneo.

Dindorf, Wilhelm (Gulielmus), ed. 1852. *Scholia Graeca in Aeschinem et Isocratem, ex Codibus Aucta et Emendata.* Oxford: Oxford University Press.

Downey, Glanville, ed. and trans. 1957. *Nikolaos Mesarites: Description of the Church of Holy Apostles at Constantinople. Transactions of the American Philosophical Society* 47:6.

Egger, Maximilian. 1902. *Denys d'Halicarnasse: Essai sur la Critique Littéraire et la Rhétorique chez les Grecs au Siécle d'Auguste.* Paris: Picard.

Enos, Richard Leo. 1988. *The Literate Mode of Cicero's Legal Rhetoric.* Carbondale: Southern Illinois University Press.

Enos, Richard Leo, and Lois Agnew, eds. 1998. *Landmark Essays in Aristotelian Rhetoric.* Mahwah, N.J.: Earlbaum.

Epstein, Richard A. 2000. *Cases and Materials on Torts.* 7th ed. New York: Aspen Publishers.

Erikson, Keith V. 1998. "The Lost Rhetorics of Aristotle." In Enos and Agnew 1998, 3–14. Originally published in *Speech Monographs* 42 (1976): 229–237.

Fantham, Elaine. 2004. *The Roman World of Cicero's De Oratore.* Oxford: Oxford University Press.

Finkel, Raphael, et al., eds. 2001. *Suda On Line.* Stoa Consortium. http://www.stoa.org/sol/. Accessed March 18, 2010).

Fleming, David. 1998. "Rhetoric as a Course of Study." *College English* 61(2): 169–191.

———. 1999. "David Fleming Responds." *College English* 62(2): 275–277.

———. 2003. "The Very Idea of a Progymnasmata." *Rhetoric Review* 22(2): 105–120.

Flower, Michael Attyah. 1997. *Theompompus of Chios: History and Rhetoric in the Fourth Century BC.* Oxford: Oxford University Press.

Foerster, Richard, ed. 1903–27. *Libanius: Opera.* 12 vols. Leipzig: Tuebner.

Fortenbaugh, William W. 2003. *Theophrastian Studies.* Stuttgart: Steiner.

———. 2005. "Cicero as a Reporter of Aristotelian and Theophrastian Rhetorical Doctrine." *Rhetorica* 23: 37–64.

Fortenbaugh, William W., and P. Steinmetz, eds. 1989. *Cicero's Knowledge of the Peripatos.* Rutgers University Studies in Classics and Humanities 4. New Brunswick: Rutgers University Press.

Foucault, Michel. 1978. *The Archaeology of Knowledge, & The Discourse on Language.* Trans. A. M. Sheridan Smith. New York: Pantheon.

———. 1988. *The Care of the Self: The History of Sexuality.* Vol. 3. Trans. Robert Hurley. New York: Vintage.

Fowler, F. W., and H. G., trans. 1905. *The Works of Lucian of Samosata.* 4 vols. Oxford: Clarendon Press.

Fox, Matthew. 1993. "History and Rhetoric in Dionysius of Halicarnassus." *Journal of Roman Studies* 83:31–47.

Freese, J. H., ed. and trans. 1926. *Aristotle: The "Art" of Rhetoric.* Cambridge: Harvard University Press.

Gabba, Emilio. 1991. *Dionysius and the History of Archaic Rome.* Berkeley and Los Angeles: University of California Press.

Gagarin, Michael. 2002. *Antiphon the Athenian: Oratory, Law, and Justice in the Age of the Sophists.* Austin: University of Texas Press.

Gaines, Robert. 1990. "Isocrates, Ep.6.8." *Hermes* 118(2): 165–170.

———. 2002. "Cicero's *Partitiones Oratoriae* and *Topica:* Rhetorical Philosophy and Philosophical Rhetoric." In May 2002. 445–479.

Gaonkar, Dilip. 1993. "The Idea of Rhetoric in the Rhetoric of Science." *Southern Communication Journal* 58(4): 258–295.

Gibson, Craig, trans. 2008. *Libanius's Progymnasmata: Model Exercises in Greek Prose Composition and Rhetoric.* Atlanta: Society of Biblical Literature.

Gleason, Maud W. 1995. *Making Men: Sophists and Self-Presentation in Ancient Rome.* Princeton: Princeton University Press.

Gonzales, Catalina. 2008. "Ciceronian Fallibilism in Kant's *Critique of Pure Reason:* A Rhetorical Theory of Justification of Belief in the Modern Critique of Metaphysics." Ph.D. diss., Emory University.

Graff, Richard, and Michael Leff. 2005. "Revisionist Historiography and Rhetorical Tradition(s)." In Graff, Walzer, and Atwill 2005.

Graff, Richard, Arthur Walzer, and Janet Atwill, eds. 2005. *The Viability of the Rhetorical Tradition.* Albany: State University of New York Press.

Grammanidis, Evangelos. 2003. *Rhetoric in the Ancient Greek Novel: Chariton, Achilles Tatios, and Heliodorus.* London: University of London Press.

Green, Lawrence. 1990. "Aristotelian Rhetoric, Dialectic, and the Traditions of *Antistrophos.*" *Rhetorica* 8(1): 5–27.

Grenfell, Bernard P., and Arthur S. Hunt, eds. 1906. *The Hibeh Papyri, Part I.* London: Egypt Exploration Society.

Grenfell, Bernard P., and Arthur S. Hunt, et al., eds. 1898– . *The Oxyrhynchus Papyri.* 71 vols. London: Egypt Exploration Society. (Also partially available via *POxy: Oxyrhynchus Online:* http://www.papyrology.ox.ac.uk/POxy/.)

Gross, Alan. and Arthur Walzer, eds. 2000. *Rereading Aristotle's Rhetoric.* Carbondale: Southern Illinois University Press.

Groupe m [mu]. 1981. *A General Rhetoric.* Trans. P. B. Burrell and E. M. Slotkin. Baltimore: Johns Hopkins University Press.

Grube, G. M. A. 1965. *The Greek and Roman Critics.* Toronto: Toronto University Press.

Gunderson, Erik. 2003. *Declamation, Paternity, and Roman Identity: Authority and the Rhetorical Self.* Cambridge: Cambridge University Press.

Hackforth, Reginald. 1952. *Plato's Phaedrus.* Indianapolis: Bobbs-Merrill.

Hagaman, John. 1986. "Modern Use of the *Progymnasmata* in Teaching Rhetorical Invention." *Rhetoric Review* 5(1): 22–29.

Halliwell, Stephen. 1997. "Philosophical Rhetoric or Rhetorical Philosophy? The Strange Case of Isocrates." In *The Rhetoric Canon,* ed. Brenda Dean Schildgren. Detroit: Wayne State University Press. 107–25.

Hamilton, Walter, and Chris Emlyn-Jones, trans. 2004. *Plato: Gorgias.* New York: Penguin.

Hansen, Mogens Herman. 1991. *The Athenian Democracy in the Age of Demosthenes: Structure, Principles, and Ideology.* Oxford: Blackwell.

Harris, Joseph D. 1997. *A Teaching Subject: Composition since 1966.* Saddle River, N.J.: Prentice-Hall.

Hartwell, Patrick. 1985. "Grammar, Grammars, and the Teaching of Grammar." *College English* 47.2, 105–127.

Haskins, Ekaterina. 2004a. *Logos and Power in Isocrates and Aristotle.* Columbia: University of South Carolina Press.

———. 2004b. "*Logos* and Power in Sophistical and Isocratean Rhetoric." In Poulakos and Depew 2004, 84–103.

Hawhee, Debra. 2004. *Bodily Arts: Rhetoric and Athletics in Ancient Greece.* Austin: University of Texas Press.

Heath, Malcolm. 1994. "The Substructure of Stasis Theory from Hermagoras to Hermogenes." *Classical Quarterly* 44(1): 114–129.

———. 1995. *Hermogenes: On Issues.* Oxford: Oxford University Press.

———. 1999. "Longinus *On Sublimity.*" *Proceedings of the Cambridge Philological Society* 45:43–74.

———. 2003. "Pseudo-Dionysius *Art of Rhetoric* 8–11: Figured Speech, Declamation, and Criticism." *American Journal of Philology* 124:81–105.

———. 2004. *Menander: A Rhetor in Context.* Oxford: Oxford University Press.

———. 2007. "Raffaella Cribiore: *The School of Libanius in Late Antique Antioch.*" Review. *Rhetorical Review* 5(3): 4–8.

Henry, René, ed. 1959–79. *Photius Bibliothèque.* 9 vols. Paris: Société d' édition "Les Belles Lettres."

Horner, Winifred Bryan, and Michael Leff, eds. 1995. *Rhetoric and Pedagogy: Its History, Philosophy, and Practice. Essays in Honor of James J. Murphy.* Mahwah, N.J.: Erlbaum.

Howell, Wilbur S., trans. 1965. *The Rhetoric of Alcuin & Charlemagne.* New York: Russell & Russell.

Howells, William Dean. 1993. "Novel-Writing and Novel-Reading." In *W. D. Howells: Selected Literary Criticism, vol. 3, 1898–1920.* Bloomington: Indiana University Press.

Howland, Jacob. 1991. "Re-Reading Plato: The Problem of Platonic Chronology." *Phoenix* 45(3): 189–214.

Howland, R. L. 1937. "The Attack on Isocrates in Plato's *Phaedrus.*" *Classical Quarterly* 31(3/4): 151–159.

Hubbell, Harry M. 1913. "The Influence of Isocrates on Cicero, Dionysius and Aristides." Ph.D. diss., Yale University Press.

———, ed. and trans. 1949. *Cicero II: De Inventione, De Optimo Genere Oratorum, Topica.* Cambridge: Harvard University Press.

Irvine, Martin. 1994. *The Making of Textual Culture: 'Grammatica' and Literary Theory, 350–1100.* Cambridge: Cambridge University Press.

Jackson, Brooks, and Kathleen Hall Jamieson. 2007. *unSpun: Finding Facts in a World of Disinformation.* New York: Random House.

Jameson, Fredric. 1991. *Postmodernism: The Cultural Logic of Late Capitalism.* Durham: Duke University Press.

Janko, Richard, ed. 2000. *Philodemus on Poems, Book One.* Oxford: Oxford University Press.

Johnson, R. 1957. "A Note on the Number of Isocrates' Pupils." *American Journal of Philology* 78(3): 297–300.

————. 1959. "Isocrates' Methods of Teaching." *American Journal of Philology* 80(1): 25–36.

Jost, Walter. 2004. *Rhetorical Investigations: Studies in Ordinary Language Criticism.* Charlottesville: University of Virginia Press.

Kaldellis, Anthony. 1999. *The Argument of Psellos' Chronographia.* Leiden: Brill.

————, trans. 2006. *Mothers and Sons, Fathers and Daughters: The Byzantine Family of Michael Psellos.* Notre Dame: University of Notre Dame Press.

Kaster, Robert, ed. and trans. 1995. *C. Suetonius Tranquillus: De Grammaticis et Rhetoribus.* Oxford: Oxford University Press.

Kazhdan, Alexander, and Simon Franklin. 1984. *Studies on Byzantine Literature of the Eleventh and Twelfth Centuries.* Cambridge: Cambridge University Press.

Keaney, John J., and Robert Lamberton, eds. and trans. 1996. *[Plutarch]: Essay on the Life and Poetry of Homer.* Atlanta: Scholars Press.

Keil, B., ed. 1898. *P. Aelii Aristidis Smyrnaei quae Supersunt Omnia.* Vol. 2. Berlin. Reprint, Hildesheim: G. Olms, 2000.

Kennedy, George A. 1959. "The Earliest Rhetorical Handbooks." *American Journal of Philology* 80(2): 169–178.

————. 1963. *The Art of Persuasion in Greece.* Princeton: Princeton University Press.

————. 1969. *Quintilian.* New York: Twayne.

————. 1972. *The Art of Rhetoric in the Roman World.* Princeton: Princeton University Press.

————. 1980. *Classical Rhetoric, and Its Christian and Secular Tradition from Ancient to Modern Times.* 1st ed. Chapel Hill: University of North Carolina Press.

————. 1983. *Greek Rhetoric under Christian Emperors.* Princeton: Princeton University Press.

————, trans. 1991. *Aristotle on Rhetoric: A Theory of Civic Discourse.* 1st ed. New York: Oxford University Press.

————. 1994. *A New History of Classical Rhetoric.* Princeton: Princeton University Press.

————. 1999. *Classical Rhetoric, and Its Christian and Secular Tradition from Ancient to Modern Times.* 2nd, rev. ed. Chapel Hill: University of North Carolina Press.

————, trans. 2003. *Progymnasmata: Greek Textbooks of Prose Composition and Rhetoric.* Atlanta: Society of Biblical Literature.

————, trans. 2005. *Invention and Method: Two Rhetorical Treatises from the Hermogenic Corpus.* Atlanta: Society of Biblical Literature.

————, trans. 2007. *Aristotle on Rhetoric: A Theory of Civic Discourse.* 2nd, rev. ed. New York: Oxford University Press.

Kiessling, T., ed. 1826. *Ioannes Tzetzae Historium Variarum Chiliades.* Leipzig. Facsimile reprint, Hildesheim: Georg Olms, 1963.

Kominis, Atanasio, ed. 1960. *Gregorio Pardos, Metropolita di Corinto e la sua opera.* Rome: Istituto di Studi Bizantini e Neoellenici.

Konstan, David. 2004. "Isocrates' 'Republic.'" In Poulakos and Depew 2004, 107–124.

Kraus, Manfred. 2009. "Grammatical and Rhetorical Exercises in the Medieval Classroom." *New Medieval Literatures* 11:63–89.

Kremer, E. 1907. *Über das rhetorische System des Dionys von Halikarnass.* Ph.D. diss., Strasbourg.

Kumaniecki, Kazimierz F., ed. 1969. *Cicero: De Oratore.* Leipzig: Teubner.

Kurke, Leslie. 1991. *The Traffic in Praise: Pindar and the Poetics of Social Economy*. Ithaca: Cornell University Press.

Kustas, George. 1973. *Studies in Byzantine Rhetoric*. Thessalonike: Patriarchal Institute for Patristic Studies.

Lamberton, Robert. 1986. *Homer the Theologian: Neoplatonist Allegorical Reading and the Growth of the Epic Tradition*. Berkeley and Los Angeles: University of California Press.

——. 1992a. Introduction to Lamberton and Keaney 1992.

——. 1992b. "The Neoplatonists and the Spiritualization of Homer." In Lamberton and Keaney 1992.

Lamberton, Robert, and John J. Keaney, eds. 1992. *Homer's Ancient Readers: The Hermeneutics of Greek Epic's Earliest Exegetes*. Princeton: Princeton University Press.

Lanham, Richard. 1976. *The Motives of Eloquence: Literary Rhetoric in the Renaissance*. New Haven: Yale University Press.

Leff, Michael. 1993. "The Uses of Aristotle's *Rhetoric* in Contemporary American Scholarship." *Argumentation* 7:313–327.

Lenz, F. W., and C. A. Behr, eds. 1976. *P. Aelii Aristidis Opera quae Exstant Omnia*. Vol. 1. Leiden: Brill.

Leone, P. A. M. 1972. *Ioannes Tzetzes: Epistulae*. Leipzig: Teubner.

Liu, Yameng. 1991. "Aristotle and the Stasis Theory: A Reexamination." *Rhetoric Society Quarterly* 21(1): 53–59.

Livingstone, Niall. 2001. *A Commentary on Isocrates' Busiris*. Leiden: Brill.

Long, A. A. 1992. "Stoic Readings of Homer." In Lamberton and Keaney 1992.

Lynch, Dennis A., Diana George, and Marilyn Cooper. 1997. "Moments of Argument: Agonistic Inquiry and Confrontational Cooperation." *College Composition and Communication* 48(1): 61–85.

Lyotard, Jean-François. 1984. *The Postmodern Condition: A Report on Knowledge*. Trans. Geoff Bennington and Brian Massumi. Minneapolis: University of Minnesota Press. Originally published as *La Conditione Postmoderne: Rapport sur le Savoir* (Paris: Les Éditions de Minuit, 1979.)

Magdalino, Paul. 1993. *The Empire of Manuel Komnenos, 1143–1180*. Cambridge: Cambridge University Press.

Mailloux, Steven. 1989. *Rhetorical Power*. Ithaca: Cornell University Press.

——, ed. 1995a. *Rhetoric, Sophistry, Pragmatism*. Cambridge: Cambridge University Press.

——. 1995b. "Sophistry and Rhetorical Pragmatism." In Mailloux 1995a, 1–32.

——. 1998. *Reception Histories: Rhetoric, Pragmatism, and American Cultural Politics*. Ithaca: Cornell University Press.

——. 2006. *Disciplinary Identities: Rhetorical Paths of English, Speech, and Composition*. New York: MLA.

Mandilaras, Basilius, ed. 2003. *Isocrates Opera Omnia*. 3 vols. Leipzig: Teubner.

Marrou, Henri-Irénée. 1956. *A History of Education in Antiquity*. Trans. George Lamb. 1948. Reprint, New York: Sheed and Ward.

Martin, Jean, and Paul Petit, eds. and trans. 1979–. *Libanios: Discours*. 4 vols. Paris: Belles Lettres.

Masarrachia, Agostino. 1995. *Isocrate: Retorica e Politica*. Rome: Gruppo Editoriale Internazionale.

Matthes, Dieter, ed. 1962. *Hermagorae Temnitae Testimonia et Fragmenta*. Leipzig: Teubner.

May, James M., ed. 2002. *Brill's Companion to Cicero: Oratory and Rhetoric*. Leiden: Brill.

May, James M., and Jakob Wisse, trans. 2001. *Cicero: On the Ideal Orator [De oratore]*. New York: Oxford University Press.

Mayers, Tim. 2005. *(Re)Writing Craft: Composition, Creative Writing, and the Future of English Studies*. Pittsburgh: University of Pittsburgh Press.

———. 2009. "One Simple Word: From Creative Writing to Creative Writing Studies." In Ritter and Vanderslice 2009.

McAdon, Brad. 2003. "Probabilities, Signs, Necessary Signs, Idia, and Topoi: The Confusing Discussions of Materials for Enthymemes in the *Rhetoric*." *Philosophy and Rhetoric* 36(3): 223–247.

———. 2004. "Two Irreconcilable Conceptions of Rhetorical Proofs in Aristotle's *Rhetoric*." *Rhetorica* 22(4): 307–325.

———. 2006a. "The 'Special Topics' in the *Rhetoric*: A Reconsideration." *Rhetoric Society Quarterly* 36(4): 399–424.

———. 2006b. "Strabo, Plutarch, Porphyry and the Transmission and Composition of Aristotle's Rhetoric—a Hunch." *Rhetoric Society Quarterly* 36(1): 77–105.

McCloskey, Deirdre N. 1985/1998. *The Rhetoric of Economics*. 1st and 2nd eds. Madison: University of Wisconsin Press.

Millar, Fergus. 1992. *The Emperor in the Roman World (31 BC–AD 337)*. Ithaca: Cornell University Press.

Mirhady, David, Yun Lee Too, and Terry Papillon, trans. 2000–4. *Isocrates*. 2 vols. (Vol. 1, Mirhady and Too; vol. 2, Papillon.) Austin: University of Texas Press.

Montefusco, Lucia Calboli. 2002. "Between Logic and Rhetoric: Aristotle's Concept of the ἐνδεχόμενον πιθανόν" *Euphrosyne* 30:193–199.

Morenberg, Max, Jeffrey Sommers, Donald Daiker, and Andrew Kerek. 2002. *The Writer's Options: Lessons in Style and Arrangement*. 7th ed. New York: Longman.

Morgan, Kathryn. 2004. "The Education of Athens: Politics and Rhetoric in Isocrates and Plato." In Poulakos and Depew 2004, 125–154.

Morgan, Teresa. 1998. *Literate Education in the Hellenistic and Roman Worlds*. Cambridge: Cambridge University Press.

———. 2007. "Rhetoric and Education." In Worthington 2007, 303–319.

Morley, David. 2008. *The Cambridge Introduction to Creative Writing*. Cambridge: Cambridge University Press.

Murphy, James, ed. 1990. *A Short History of Writing Instruction*. Davis, Calif.: Hermagoras Press.

Nails, Debra. 2002. *The People of Plato: A Prosopography of Plato and Other Socratics*. Indianapolis: Hackett.

Natoli, Anthony F. 2004. *The Letter of Speusippus to Philip II: Introduction, Text, Translation and Commentary*. Stuttgart: Steiner.

Neel, Jasper. 1994. *Aristotle's Voice: Rhetoric, Theory, and Writing in America*. Carbondale: Southern Illinois University Press.

Nehamas, Alexander, and Paul Woodruff, trans. 1995. *Plato: Phaedrus*. Indianapolis: Hackett.

Norden, Eduard. 1915. *Die antike Kunstprosa vom VI. Jahrhundert v. Chr. bis in die Zeit der Renaissance.* 2 vols. Leipzig: Teubner.

Norlin, George, and Larue Van Hook, trans. 1928–45. *Isocrates.* 3 vols. (Vols. 1 and 2, Norlin; vol. 3, Van Hook.) Cambridge: Harvard University Press.

Norman, Albert F. 1960. "The Book Trade in Fourth-Century Antioch." *Journal of Hellenic Studies* 80:122–126.

———, trans. 2000. *Antioch as a Centre of Hellenic Culture as Observed by Libanius.* Liverpool: Liverpool University Press.

North, Stephen. 1987. *The Making of Knowledge in Composition: Portrait of an Emerging Field.* Upper Montclair, N.J.: Boynton Cook.

Pagán, Victoria. 2004. Review of Gunderson 2003. *Bryn Mawr Classical Review,* 29 February 2004. http://bmcr.brynmawr.edu/2004/2004–02–29.html/. Accessed June 2009.

Panagiotou, Spiro. 1975. "Lysias and the Date of Plato's Phaedrus." *Mnemosyne* 28 (1975): 388–398.

Papillon, Terry. 1995. "Isocrates' *Technê* and Rhetorical Pedagogy." *Rhetoric Society Quarterly* 25:149–163.

———. 2007. "Isocrates." In Worthington 2007, 58–74.

Parr, Roger, trans. 1981. *Matthew of Vendôme: Ars Versificatoria: The Art of the Versemaker.* Milwaukee: Marquette University Press.

Patillon, Michel, trans. 1997. *Hermogène: L'Art Rhétorique.* Paris: L'Age d'Homme.

Patillon, Michel, and Giancarlo Bolognesi, eds. and trans. 1997. *Aelius Théon: Progymnasmata.* Édition Budé. Paris: Belles Lettres.

Penella, Robert, ed. 2009. *Rhetorical Exercises from Late Antiquity: A Translation of Choricius of Gaza's Preliminary Talks and Declamations.* Cambridge: Cambridge University Press.

Perelman, Chaim. 1982. *The Realm of Rhetoric.* Trans. W. Kluback. Notre Dame: Notre Dame University Press.

Perelman, Chaim, and Lucie Olbrechts-Tyteca. 1969. *The New Rhetoric: A Treatise on Argumentation.* Trans. J. Wilkinson and P. Weaver. Notre Dame: Notre Dame University Press.

Pernot, Laurent. 1981. *Les Discours Siciliens d'Aelius Aristide (Or. 5–6): Étude Littéraire et Paléographique.* New York: Arno Press.

———. 2005. *Rhetoric in Antiquity.* Trans. W. E. Higgins. Washington, D.C.: Catholic University of America Press. Originally published as *La Rhétorique dans l'Antiquité,* (Paris: Librarie Générale Française, 2000).

Petraglia, Joseph, and Deepika Bahri, eds. 2003. *The Realms of Rhetoric: The Prospects for Rhetoric Education.* Albany: State University of New York Press.

Poster, Carol. 1997. "Aristotle's *Rhetoric* against Rhetoric: Unitarian Reading and Esoteric Hermeneutics." *American Journal of Philology* 118:219–249.

Poster, Carol, and Linda Mitchell, eds. 2007. *Letter-Writing Manuals and Instruction from Antiquity to the Present: Historical and Bibliographic Studies.* Columbia: University of South Carolina Press.

Poulakos, John. 2004. "Rhetoric and Civic Education: From the Sophists to Isocrates." In Poulakos and Depew 2004, 69–83.

Poulakos, Takis. 1997. *Speaking for the Polis: Isocrates' Rhetorical Education.* Columbia: University of South Carolina Press.

Poulakos, Takis, and David Depew, eds. 2004. *Isocrates and Civic Education.* Austin: University of Texas Press.

Pritchett, Kendrick W., trans. 1975. *Dionysius of Halicarnassus: On Thucydides.* Berkeley and Los Angeles: University of California Press.

Prose, Francine. 2007. *Reading Like a Writer: A Guide for People Who Love Books and for Those Who Want to Write Them.* New York: Harper.

Purser, L. C., ed. 1964. *Cicero: Epistulae ad familiares.* In *Epistulae,* vol. 1. Oxford: Oxford University Press.

Quinn, Arthur. 1993. *Figures of Speech: 60 Ways to Turn a Phrase.* Davis, Calif.: Hermagoras Press.

Rabe, Hugo, ed. 1913. *Hermogenes: Opera.* Leipzig: Teubner.

———, ed. 1926. *Aphthonii Progymnasmata.* Leipzig: Tuebner.

Rackham, Harris, trans. 1957. *[Aristotle]: Rhetorica ad Alexandrum.* Loeb Classical Library Series. Cambridge: Harvard University Press.

Radermacher, Ludwig. 1951. *Artium Scriptores: Reste der voraristotelischen Rhetorik.* Vienna: Rohrer.

Reader, William W., and Anthony J. Chvala-Smith. 1996. *The Severed Hand and the Upright Corpse: The Declamations of Marcus Antonius Polemo.* Atlanta: Scholars Press.

Rebhorn, Wayne. 1995. *The Emperor of Men's Minds: Literature and the Renaissance Discourse of Rhetoric.* Ithaca: Cornell University Press.

Reid, Robert S. 1996. "Dionysius of Halicarnassus's Theory of Compositional Style and the Theory of Literate Consciousness." *Rhetoric Review* 15(1): 46–64.

Reinhardt, Tobias, and Michael Winterbottom. 2006. *Quintilian Institutio Oratoria Book 2: Introduction, Text, Commentary.* Oxford: Oxford University Press.

Richards, I. A. 1936. *The Philosophy of Rhetoric.* Oxford: Oxford University Press.

Ritter, Kelly, and Stephanie Vanderslice, guest eds. 2009. "Special Topic: Creative Writing in the Twenty-First Century." *College English* 71.3. Special issue.

Roberts, W. Rhys, ed. and trans. 1901. *Dionysius of Halicarnassus: The Three Literary Letters.* Cambridge: Cambridge University Press.

———, ed. and trans. 1910. *On Literary Composition: Being the Greek Text of the De Compositione Verborum of Dionysius of Halicarnassus.* London: Macmillan.

Roberts-Miller, Patricia. 2004. *Deliberate Conflict: Argument, Political Theory, and Composition Classes.* Carbondale: Southern Illinois University Press.

———. 2009. *Fanatical Schemes: Proslavery Rhetoric and the Tragedy of Consensus.* Tuscaloosa: University of Alabama Press.

Roochnik, David. 1996. *Of Art and Wisdom: Plato's Understanding of Techne.* University Park: Pennsylvania State University Press.

Rorty, Amélie Oksenberg. 1996. *Essays on Aristotle's Rhetoric.* Berkeley and Los Angeles: University of California Press.

Russell, D. A. 1983. *Greek Declamation.* Cambridge: Cambridge University Press.

————, trans. 1996. *Libanius: Imaginary Speeches: A Selection of Declamations.* London: Duckworth.

————, ed. and trans. 2001. *Quintilian: The Orator's Education.* 5 vols. Cambridge: Harvard University Press.

Russell, D. A., and N. G. Wilson, eds. and trans. 1981. *Menander Rhetor.* Oxford: Oxford University Press.

Schenkeveld, Dirk M. 1992. "Prose Usages of *Akouein,* 'To Read.'" *Classical Quarterly* 42(1): 129–141.

Schiappa, Edward. 1991. *Protagoras and Logos: A Study in Greek Philosophy and Rhetoric.* Columbia: University of South Carolina Press.

————. 1995. "Isocrates' *Philosophia* and Contemporary Pragmatism." In Mailloux 1995a, 33–60.

Schmelling, Gareth, ed. 1996. *The Novel in the Ancient World.* Leiden: Brill.

Schuckburgh, Evelyn S., trans. 1899–1912. *The Letters of Cicero.* 4 vols. London: Bell and Sons.

Schwartz, Eduard. 1905. "Dionysios von Halikarnassos." In *Paulys Real-Encyclopädie der classichen Altertumswissenschaft.* Stuttgart: Metzler. 5:934–961.

Selby, Jim. 2008. "The Vertical Integration of Aphthonius' Progymnasmata." Paper presented at Rhetoric Society of America conference, Seattle. Available online at http://www.classicalcomposition.com/index.html/. Accessed September 2010.

Shackleton Bailey, D. R., ed. and trans. 2006. *[Quintilian]: The Lesser Declamations.* 2 vols. Cambridge: Harvard University Press.

Sloane, Thomas O. 1991. "Schoolbooks and Rhetoric: Erasmus' *Copia.*" *Rhetorica* 9(2): 113–129.

————. 1997. *On the Contrary: The Protocol of Traditional Rhetoric.* Washington, D.C.: Catholic University of America Press.

Smith, R. M. 1995. "A New Look at the Canon of the Ten Attic Orators." *Mnemosyne* 48(1): 66–79.

Spengel, Leonard. 1828. *[Sunagôgê Technôn]: Sive Artium Scriptores ab Initiis usque ad Editos Aristotele de Rhetorica Libros.* Stuttgart: J. G. Cotta.

————. 1853–56. *Rhetores Graeci.* 3 vols. Leipzig: Teubner.

Sprague, Rosamond Kent, ed. 1972. *The Older Sophists.* Columbia: University of South Carolina Press.

Staikos, Konstantinos. 2004. *The History of the Library in Western Civilization.* 3 vols. New Castle, Del.: Oak Knoll Press.

Struever, Nancy S. 2009. *Rhetoric, Modality, Modernity.* Chicago: University of Chicago Press.

Sullivan, Robert G. 2001. "*Eidos/Idea* in Isocrates." *Philosophy and Rhetoric* 34(1): 79–92.

————. 2007. "Classical Epistolary Theory and the Letters of Isocrates." In Poster and Mitchell 2007, 7–20.

————. 2009. "Isocrates and the Problem of Autocratic Rhetoric." Paper delivered at the 17th Biennial Conference of the International Society for the History of Rhetoric, Montreal.

Sussman, Lewis A., trans. 1987. *The Major Declamations Ascribed to Quintilian: A Translation.* Frankfurt: P. Lang.

Sutton, E. W., and H. Rackham, eds. and trans. 1942. *Cicero: De Oratore.* Cambridge: Harvard University Press.

Swain, Simon. 1998. *Hellenism and Empire: Language, Classicism, and Power in the Greek World, AD 50–250.* Oxford: Oxford University Press.

Tate, Gary, Amy Rupiper, and Kurt Schick, eds. 2000. *A Guide to Composition Pedagogies.* New York: Oxford University Press.

Thompson, Wayne A. 1979. "Dionysius of Halicarnassus: A Reappraisal." *Quarterly Journal of Speech* 65:303–310.

Tobin, Lad. 2000. "Process Pedagogy." In Tate, Rupiper, and Schick 2000, 1–18.

Too, Yun Lee. 1995. *The Rhetoric of Identity in Isocrates: Text, Power, Pedagogy.* New York: Cambridge University Press.

———, ed. 2001. *Education in Greek and Roman Antiquity.* Leiden: Brill, 2001.

———. 2008. *A Commentary on Isocrates' Antidosis.* New York: Oxford University Press.

Too, Yun Lee, and Niall Livingstone, eds. 1998. *Pedagogy and Power: Rhetorics of Classical Learning.* New York: Cambridge University Press.

Trevett, J. C. 1996. "Aristotle's Knowledge of Athenian Oratory." *Classical Quarterly* 46(2): 371–379.

Usener, H., and L. Radermacher, eds. 1965. *Dionysii Halicarnasei Opuscula.* 2 vols. (Vols. 5–6 of *Dionysii Halicarnasei quae Exstant;* originally published 1899–1933.) Stuttgart: Teubner.

Usher, Stephen. 1969. *The Historians of Greece and Rome.* New York: Taplinger.

———, trans. 1974–85. *Dionysius of Halicarnassus: Critical Essays.* 2 vols. Cambridge: Harvard University Press.

Vallozza, Maddalena. 2003. "Isocrate, Il *Poiêtikon Pragma* e la *Technê* Impossibile." In Celentano 2003, 17–29.

Van Eemeren, Frans H., and Rob Grootendorst. 1992. *Argumentation, Communication, and Fallacies: A Pragma-Dialectical Perspective.* Hillsdale, N.J.: Earlbaum.

———. 2004. *A Systematic Theory of Argumentation: The Pragma-Dialectical Approach.* New York: Cambridge University Press.

Vickers, Brian. 1988. *In Defence of Rhetoric.* Oxford: Oxford University Press.

Vitanza, Victor. 1997. *Negation, Subjectivity, and the History of Rhetoric.* Albany: State University of New York Press.

Walbank, F. W. 1981. *The Hellenistic World.* Atlantic Highlands, N.J.: Humanities Press.

Walker, Jeffrey. 1998. "Dionysio de Halicarnaso y la Idea de Crítica de la Retórica." *Anuario Filosófico* 31(2): 581–601.

———. 2000a. *Rhetoric and Poetics in Antiquity.* New York: Oxford University Press.

———. 2000b. "*Pathos* and *Katharsis* in 'Aristotelian' Rhetoric: Some Implications." In *Rereading Aristotle's Rhetoric,* ed. Gross and Walzer, 2000.

———. 2003. "On Rhetorical Traditions: A Reply to Jerzy Axer." Paper delivered at the Alliance of Rhetoric Societies meeting, Evanston. Archived at http://www.rhetoricsociety.org/. Accessed May 2009.

————. 2004."These Things I Have Not Betrayed: Michael Psellos' Encomium of His Mother as a Defense of Rhetoric." *Rhetorica* 22(1): 49–101.

————. 2005."Aelius Aristides." In *Classical Rhetorics and Rhetoricians,* ed. Michelle Balliff and Mike Moran. New York: Praeger. 42–50.

————, trans. 2005."Michael Psellos: *The Encomium of His Mother.*" *Advances in the History of Rhetoric* 8:239–313.

————. 2006a. "What Difference a Definition Makes, Or, William Dean Howells and the Sophist's Shoes." *Rhetoric Society Quarterly* 36(2): 143–153.

————. 2006b. "The Place of 'Theory' in Ancient Rhetoric." *Papers on Rhetoric VII,* ed. Lucia Calboli Montefusco. Rome: Herder. 247–265.

Walz, Christian, ed. 1832–36. *Rhetores Graeci.* 9 vols. Stuttgart: Cottae. Facsimile reprint, Osnaburck: Zeller, 1968.

Walzer, Arthur. 2005. "Teaching 'Political Wisdom': Isocrates and the Tradition of *Dissoi Logoi.*" In Graff, Walzer, and Atwill 2005, 113–124.

Webb, Ruth. 2001. "The *Progymnasmata* as Practice." In Too 2001, 289–316.

Wehrli, Fritz. 1968. *Die Schule Des Aristoteles.* Vol. 4, *Demetrios von Phaleron.* Basel: Schwabe, 1968.

Westerink, L. G., ed. 1992. *Michaelis Pselli Poemata.* Stuttgart: Teubner.

Wichelns, Herbert A. 1925. "The Literary Criticism of Oratory." In *Studies in Rhetoric and Public Speaking in Honor of James Albert Winans,* ed. A. M. Drummond. New York: Century. Reprinted in Benson 1993 and Burgchardt 1995.

Wilamowitz-Moellendorff, Ulrich von. 1900. "Asianismus und Atticismus." *Hermes* 35:1–52.

Wilcox, Stanley. 1943. "Isocrates' Genera of Prose." *American Journal of Philology* 64(4): 427–431.

Wilkins, A. S., ed. 1892. *M. Tulli Ciceronis De oratore libri tres.* Oxford: Oxford University Press.

————, ed. 1902–3. *M. Tulli Ciceronis Rhetorica.* 2 vols. Oxford: Oxford University Press.

Wilson, N. G. 1983. *Scholars of Byzantium.* London: Duckworth.

————. 1994. *Photius: The Bibliotheca: A Selection, Translated with Notes.* London: Duckworth.

Winterbottom, Michael. 1964. "Quintilian and the *Vir Bonus.*" *Journal of Roman Studies* 54(1–2): 90–97.

————, ed. and trans. 1974. *The Elder Seneca: Controversiae and Suasoriae.* 2 vols. Cambridge: Harvard University Press.

————. 1982. "Schoolroom and Courtroom." In *Rhetoric Revalued: Papers from the International Society for the History of Rhetoric,* ed. Brian Vickers. Binghamtom, N.Y.: Center for Medieval and Early Renaissance Studies. 59–70.

Wisse, Jakob. 1989. *Ethos and Pathos from Aristotle to Cicero.* Amsterdam: Hakkert.

————. 2002a. "The Intellectual background of Cicero's Rhetorical Works." In May 2002, 331–374.

————. 2002b. "*De Oratore:* Rhetoric, Philosophy, and the Making of the Ideal Orator." In May 2002, 375–400.

Woodman, Tony, and David West, eds. 1984. *Poetry and Politics in the Age of Augustus.* New York: Cambridge University Press.

Woods, Marjorie Curry. 2010. *Classroom Commentaries: Teaching the Poetria Nova across Medieval and Renaissance Europe.* Columbus: Ohio State University Press.

Wooten, Cecil, trans. 1987. *Hermogenes' On Types of Style.* Chapel Hill: University of North Carolina Press.

Worthington, Ian, ed. 2007. *A Companion to Greek Rhetoric.* Oxford: Blackwell.

INDEX